In The Cause of Liberty

— you are held in
esteem here Bruce

Wm King

In The Cause of Liberty

William Blake, Thomas Paine, Jean-Paul Marat & Revolution in the 18th Century

William S. King

atmosphere press

Contents

Overture

That Liberty is a natural right of humankind burst onto the scene in the most extraordinary way in the late 18th century. We, who now bear the legacy of that principle, find that it is our ever tenuous travail. To re-claim our footing, let's cast a retrospective glance back on three figures, although neglected in the wider narrative, that were each seminal to that behest to posterity.

Little is known of the daily life of William Blake, who lived the life of a London artisan. His poems were unpublished, save by himself in his unusual manner, and were largely unread and unknown in his own time; although not in ours. His ideas and imagery have long inspired music, film and literature, and one or more parts of his work are revered by millions. But he engraved for booksellers, and did not intend to be a poet. The paintings he made were poorly received and disliked but by a few fellow artists. Yet his reputation has come to outshine theirs. No enraptured scribe, as will be shown here, Blake was a practical man who settled down uneasily as witness of his age, refusing to be ground down by the ugliness and inhumanity of common city life. His vision, it seems, he captured directly by peering into the furnaces of the age, industrial and political—the revolutions both in America and in France, as also the struggle for liberty in his own country, Britain, as in far away Saint Domingue, today's Haiti.

Thomas Paine, another of the tradesmen of the age, rose suddenly as in a blaze to become an unrivaled political pamphleteer at the heart of two revolutions. The first, he was a well-known participant in, America—which made our own country; but less well known or appreciated, is that in France.

Shinning a beacon light into the path forward for patriots of both nations in their struggle against empire and monarchy, Paine was embracive of a new and more universalist meaning for "Liberty" and "Equality." Ideals he attempted to enshrine in the foundations of two republics. But when returning from his more than a decade sojourn in France, Paine was largely shunned by his adoptive country, America, and would die in near obscurity.

Notorious for his aggressive and rabble-rousing journalism durning the French Revolution, Jean-Paul Marat is now thought of as having inspired the utmost extremes of violence in the French or of any subsequent revolution. There was no ambiguity about his convictions, nor of his solicitousness for the poor. Seeking neither position nor pension, he avowed his only ambition was to assist in "saving the people"; only to die, an assassin's poniard thrust into his breast.

The banner lofted by these—Blake, Paine, Marat—was sublimely and unequivocally In the Cause of Liberty. Do their lives and legacy mean anything to us today? Do they still speak to our struggles in a way that we can find relevant? Undoubtedly, as is to be presented here, that is the case; as we persevere in realizing our and their ideals. Long the preoccupation of many that have since been sacrificed, well underway into the third century after that concatenation of events in the 18th century, we still ask—whither our freedom?

It has been the aim of this writer to show these three principals of interest as viewed integrally, as they are, as pivotal to that epoch broadly known as the Age of Revolution. From the dust they have become, and that we too shall become—does the redeeming blaze arise? Fire enough to raise a great wind to light up our sky, revealing again what can still be seen through and in their works and writings?

1.

Songs of Innocence

On the title page of *Songs of Innocence*, printed by Blake as he was nearing his thirtieth year, one sees a woman with a book opened on her lap as two children gaze into it. In childhood, one already sees Blake pursuing his solitary course. He was a perambulator too as a boy; his earliest memories are of being among the haymakers on London's outskirts, of wandering through London's networks of alleys and lanes unchanging in hundreds of years.

His first home was at the corner of Broad and Marshall Streets, near Golden Square with its grass plats and gravel sidewalks and statue memorializing King James; and just around the corner was Carnaby Market which included a slaughterhouse, and nearby was St. James Workhouse, a school of industry whose inmates, if boys of age, were sent to sea or apprenticed, or if girls were "placed out in service."

The streets through which he passed jostled with carriages and hackney coaches, of goods being transported in carts, pavements crowded with barrels and casks, baskets and crates. With flocks of foot-travelers hurrying to and fro. A shifting panorama, accompanied by a *Babel* of voices; of sworn oaths and bawdy songs, the cries of milkmaids and orange sellers, fishwives, and piemen, of knife-grinders—with the clatter of wheels and the clog of hooves.

This is where the lineaments of the art and the poetry of William Blake are to be found. He seems to have gotten his first inklings of words and their cadences from a time before he could read; from the Bible and from nursery rhymes, both of which he would have heard read aloud in his household. As he is likely to have developed his later practice of "illuminated printing" from chapbooks peered into as a boy, where he saw words attended by illustrations, engravings or woodcuts; and, as liable, from hearing popular ballads rendered in the streets, vividly launching sound into sight. These, undoubtedly are among his earliest promptings.

Nothing so struck a London visitor as its fetid air, foul with coal and charcoal soot; a miasma of animal and human waste, the offal from butcher's stalls, and garbage of disparate kinds. As on its footpaths, one would have seen countless harlots, and orphaned children and urchins roving in its parks. But London was also a city renewing itself after the great fire in 1666 reduced half the conurbation to ruin. Rebuilt in pink brick, its population was half a million in 1700, as it burgeoned to approximately three-quarters of a million by 1750, raising to roughly one million by 1800. By then it had become the center of a rapidly increasing growth in industry and overseas of empire.

In 1700, the "great and monstrous" city, as Defoe called it, was divided into three: the City (London), the Court (Westminster and St. James), and Southwark (south of the river). By act of Parliament, by 1766, streets were being paved and lighted, and houses numbered, with thoroughfares and pavements regularly cleansed. The city became a market place for the wares of every type of trade, everywhere there was the same mixing of vice and fashion. Environs too starkly divided by classes, where the wealthy few faced the overwhelmingly poor.

In the second half of the 18th century, it became flooded with new arrivals, as London began to bustle with industry and trade of every sort. Mostly these were youths working as apprentices for tradesmen or as domestic servants; Scots drawn after the joining of the parliaments of England and Scotland in 1707, jostling against the Welsh and the Irish. All conveying the distinctive accents and conceits reaching this unusual plebeian's ear, from which he gained his self-awareness, his outlook on life.

Born November 28, 1757—William Blake's father, James, came from a family across the River Thames from London, Rotherhithe, and ran a modest hosiery shop in Soho selling gloves and stockings, while his mother, Catherine was from yeoman stock in the village of Walkeringham in Notting-hamshire. Both belonged to a protestant 'dissenting sect', as they were interred in a 'nonconformist' burial ground when deceased. Whether Anabaptists, Levellers or Diggers, Muggle-tonians, Puritan or Quaker, or Ranters; scholarship often suggests they were Baptists. But whichever, it is clear Blake was imbued with the religious enthusiasm and piety of the evangelical denominations, where he also received encourage-ment in his earliest years toward his visionary experiences.

To Blake, this childhood must have seemed practically a paradise. He was known to have been impetuous and spirited as a boy, as it was also in his youth he had his earliest visions. The images in his poems often suggest these youthful influences, as he assimilated their shape and character in disquietingly transmuted form. As in this simple *A Cradle Song*:

Sweet dreams, form a shade
O'er my lovely infant's head;
Sweet dreams of pleasant streams
By happy, silent, moony beams. (1)

When only eight or ten, he told his mother he'd seen a tree filled with angels, with their wings resplendent in its boughs like stars shinning from heaven. At another time, he saw angelic figures moving among the haymakers. But his first visionary experience occurred when just four, as he told it, when he was "set...ascreaming" as he saw God pressing his forehead against the window-pane as he looked in. These were visions he thought all might see, and it was a facility he continued to experience throughout his life, never doubting his imagination beckoned.

William was the fourth born to the family; there was a sister Catherine and an older brother James who would follow the father as the proprietor of the hosiery shop, and a younger brother Robert, along with another older brother who had died in infancy. Never attending a grammar school, Blake believed it fortunate he had escaped their flogging.

At age ten his clearly forbearing parents sent the precocious boy to drawing school, the preparatory school for the Academy of Painting and Sculpture established by Hogarth, training there as a draughtsman from 1768-72. As a student, he early was studying and collecting reproductions of Raphael and Michelangelo picked out in London's print shops, who remained his masters throughout his life. But it was in the prints of Albrecht Dürer, with their extraordinary strength and subtlety of line, that most actuated his vision. The rudiments of artistic education he acquired from copying engraved prints and antique casts.

By fourteen he began keeping a sketch book and writing verse; his reading in due course including Edmund Spencer,

John Milton, and John Donne. "Already it had been decreed," wrote his mid-Victorian biographer Alexander Gilchrist, "that an inspired Poet should be endowed with barely grammar enough to compose with school boy accuracy." Early on, he said, a spirit spoke to him: "Blake be an Artist & nothing else. In this there is felicity." (2)

His younger brother, Robert, with whom he became preternaturally attached, was born in his fourteenth year. It was also the year he began his seven-year apprenticeship with the engraver James Basire, whose workshop and studio on Great Queen Street became his home. Blake was now on the course he would follow the rest of his life—that of a disciplined and exacting engraver and painter, as he became one of London's artisans, continuously engaged in his relentless task. "Engraving is Drawing on Copper & Nothing Else," he would say, as painting was drawing on canvas or any other backing. He would never suspend his work on copper for a single day, he wrote in 1809, after a labor of forty years. (3)

Two years after beginning his apprenticeship, Blake was sent by his master to make sketches of the Gothic monuments and royal tombs of Edward III, Queen Philippa, Richard II, and other royals, in the Westminster Abby. Basire had a commission to make engravings for Richard Gough's *Sepulchral Monuments in Great Britain*, and there Blake came face to face with many of the images that would later haunt his own art, standing astride the tombs or sitting above to get a view from the top. In these memorials of the dead, framed in alabaster and brass, "he found a treasure, which he knew how to value," Gilchrist again commented. For the remainder of his life, these were the images that visited and possessed his imagination, images from history and art and literature entwining with his own spiritual perception.

From these experiences would grow his entire metaphysic, Blake realizing that he "must create" his own system "or be enslaved by another man's"; as he wrote in his long last poem *Jerusalem*, speaking through the mythic character Los of his invention —"I will not reason and compare: my business is to create." (4)

Once again, Gilchrist related he saw spirits: "The aisles and galleries of the old cathedral suddenly filled with a great procession of monks and priests, choristers and censer-bearers, and his entranced ear heard the chant of plain-song and chorale, while the vaulted roof trembled to the sound of organ music." (5)

Completing his apprentice in 1779, Blake was admitted to the Royal Academy established a few years prior by Sir Joshua Reynolds, obtaining the rudiments of an orthodox classical education, where he proved his proficiency. Already developing a preference for drawing from imagination, life drawing left him cold; "modern Man stripped from his load of cloathing," he later wrote, "is like a dead corpse." For Blake drawing in firm determinate outline was "all in all."

As a commercial or copy-engraver, in his lifetime Blake would complete around 580 plates—hatching and cross-hatching, scratching with his 'iron pen', fashioning his net or web; laboring over metal plates for his bread. Using compass and rule to make the outlines, the images he produced on commission often had a faithful literalness, even naiveté. Hardly the kind of work in which he'd be privately engaged.

Blake began work as a professional engraver at age twenty-three, in August 1780, reaching maturation just as the war against Crown and Parliament in the American colonies was in its fifth year. It was a struggle for independence across the Atlantic Sea for which he would evince complete sympathy. By this time in his life Blake is described as powerfully built; broad at the shoulders, his body thickset, his hands strong and work worn. At five feet five inches in height, his head was a large one, with facial features aptly described as flat; his brow rounded, his hair reddish-yellow; his voice low and musical. As one sees from his portrait, his face bore a pugnacious, yet nervous expression, with large searching brown eyes.

After his apprenticeship and preliminary training, Blake was beginning to feel free enough to develop his own style, and in this year, he conceived a design he'd subsequently execute many times, first titled *Glad Days* at the agency of Gilchrist, later it became *Albion Rose*. It is after the diagrams of the Renaissance showing the ideal male proportions in a full-figured nude youth, standing on a rock balanced on his left leg, his arms outstretched and his hands opened in a gesture of radiance or liberation. Albion, for Blake, became the full personification of all the people of England; but was conceived in this year of his emancipation as a self-portrait, the hair of the figure like his, curling and standing out from his scalp like tongues of flame.

2.

And stood
a naked multitude

Late that spring London was swept up by an extraordinary pageant of incendiarism and riot, that in retrospect would appear to have had a marked bearing on the development of Blake's views, poetical and political. Taking place in June over five days, it would level ten times more property than was destroyed during the entirety of the French Revolution, beginning nine years later, and was itself notable as it became a proto-revolutionary outburst. While the *Gordon Riots* are viewed as little more than a brief moment of calamity for King and Parliament, it managed to open a chasm ominously threatening London and its vaunted political and civil establishments alike. One contemporary wrote ironically, the riots would have been "inconceivable in a city as well-policed as Paris."

Its antecedents are traceable to two years earlier, with Britain in need of conscripts for its military campaigns in the American colonies, a measure had been introduced in the Parliament to relax the anti-Catholic acts begun in 1529 under Henry VIII, to clear the way for Scottish Catholics to serve as conscripts in the American war. A Papists Act of 1778 was duly introduced imposing a loyalty oath to the reigning sovereign, repealing the prosecution of priests, as well as perpetual imprisonment for keeping schools, which passed in Parliament and received royal assent. Then early in 1780, at the behest of the *Protestant Association,* Lord George Gordon, an Anglican Scottish MP and an eccentric personality on the margins of political life, headed a campaign to collect signatures for an "English appeal against the Popery Bill", as press reports disclosed the petition would be presented to the House of Commons on Friday, June 2 at 10 AM.

As a large crowd of what press reports called the "respectable" gathered—as many as forty-thousand all told—the blue cockade rosettes of "Wilkes and Liberty" were distributed so as to distinguish the petitioners as Protestants, and in a short speech before proceeding to the House of Commons, Gordon called for "peaceable deportment and behavior."

Petitioners, who had assembled at St. George's Field, crossed the London Bridge, marching down Cornhill past the Bank of England, onto Poultry and Cheapside; then around St. Paul's Cathedral onto Fleet and the Strand, as the windows along the route thronged with spectators. By that time, too, they had drawn into their ranks a large number, as one report had it, of "ill-conditioned ruffians" drawn obliquely from London's dark courts, blind alleys, and unsavory cellars. This mounting welter was joined at Palace Yard by petitioners who had marched across the Westminster Bridge, and as the two streams merged, they descended on the Houses of Parliament.

Excited by their self-evident numbers, as by their cause, they began stopping and checking every carriage bearing a peer happening by, inquiring whether they were Catholic sympathizers, the air filling with their execrations and hoots. Amid shouts of "No Popery," a peer was hauled from his carriage and pelted with mud. Another had his coach trashed, as another's watch was flinched from his pocket. Then the carriage windows of Chief Justice of the King's Bench, Lord

Mansfield, were smashed, and as the Prime Minister of Great Britain, Lord North's carriage had slowed, his hat was snatched off his head, its remnants shredded and distributed as trophies. A staggering crowd now forced the Archbishop of York toward the river, where he was just able to evade molestation. Other peers, seeking to avert trouble, had their carriages chalked "No Popery".

With the enormous petition wound in a scroll, Lord Gordon stood on the stairs in the lobby to the House chamber, as a portion of the crowd boisterously filed in. Giving a running commentary on the debate within, Gordon soon announced the petition would not be received on that day but would be taken into consideration on the following Tuesday.

The next morning, as troops marched prisoners arrested in the previous day's mêlée to Newgate Prison, they were jeered all along the Strand. That night, in the Irish neighborhood of Moorfields threats were made against "dens of Popery" as three schools were trashed and the home of a prosperous Irish silk merchant, who was able to escape with his stock of silk, was "pulled down". As chapels were torched, and the homes of Sir George Saville and Sir Edmund Burke besieged, troops stood by and did nothing. The following morning handbills were distributed from Fleet Street; one headed "True Protestants No Turncoats", and another "England in Blood". After parading through streets "with colours, music, cutlasses, pole-axes and bludgeons," crowds wearing the blue cockade in their caps were again congregating outside Parliament.

As the First Lord of the Admiralty, Lord Sandwich, was rescued from the mob, an attempted assault on Buckingham Palace was repulsed by nearby guards. With the House of Commons adjourning, the Riot Act was read in Palace Yard, and the order given for the Horse Guards to charge against the multitude. A contemporary report described it: "The crowd were wedged into such firm and compact masses that the cavalry were actually compelled to recede and return at a gallop, to give their career sufficient course to penetrate them." (1) At that moment, a brawny figure mounted on a carthorse unfurled a black flag with a large red cross in the middle. "To Hyde's House, a-hoy!" he shouted. That individual was James Jackson, a watch-wheel cutter, whom Dickens in 1841 would incorporate into the Maypole Hugh character in *Barnaby Rudge*. At his signal, the multitude surged down Parliament Street. (2)

As the House had adjourned and the Riot Act was read, Lord George fled into a nearby inn, where he persuaded its proprietor to lend him his horses and carriage. Caught in his attempted flight, the horses were removed from the carriage and paraded triumphantly down Parliament, then on to Strand and Fleet, then around to Newgate Prison, then to the Mansion House.

An insurrectionary force was now unloosened on the streets of London, and if not yet entirely decoupled from the "No Popery" cause, it was pursuing its actions in parallel and on an alternate course. Justice Hyde's house was "pulled down" and a bonfire made from its splintered shards. With the Whitechapel house likewise besieged, the throng were amused as Enoch Foster, a carnival strongman, hurled floor planks through its windows. Lord Chief Justice Mansfield's house was ransacked, its furniture and his library destroyed, with his manuscripts "containing his lordship's notes on every important law case for near forty years past . . . were by the hands of these Goths committed to the flames." In the course of things, Mansfield's country home out in Hampstead was also wrecked.

With many in the streets now carrying lighted brands, as the hour was close to dusk, Jackson again shouted the course, "A-hoy for Newgate". Not only was Newgate London's most notorious prison, it was the place of detention for most prisoners awaiting trial from the previous day's arrests. It also doubled as a debtors' prison, and it was the holding pen for those awaiting sentence of death at Tyburn—the place of public executions. Scandalously over-crowded, Newgate was as dismal and fetid a confinement as any, so onerous physicians refused to enter it, where, it was said, as many as thirty inmates would die each year.

With a flood of London's denizens approaching the prison on Broad Street, many artisans and apprentices among them, with a teeming following of street urchins, prostitutes, tavern girls, and servants, together with many of the more wretched, William Blake, whose family home was on that street, was swept up into the forefront of their surge as he was perusing unrelated business. Biographer Gilchrist, who noted that Blake "long remembered" the scene, wrote:

> On the third day, Tuesday, 6th of June, 'the Mass-houses' having already been demolished—one, near Blake's neighborhood, Warwick Street, Golden Square—and various private houses also; the rioters, flushed with gin and victory were turning their attention to grander schemes of devastation. That evening, the artist hap-pened to be walking in a route chosen by one of the mobs at large, whose course lay from Justice Hyde's house near Leicester Fields, for the destruction of which less than an hour had sufficed, through Long Acre, past the quite house of Blake's old master, engraver Basire in Great Queen Street, Lincoln's Inn Fields, and down Holborn bound for Newgate. (3)

Fronted by an imposing newly mounted neo-classical stone façade, topped with spikes and points of iron, the noxious prison's exterior walls everywhere over-mastered those seeking to breach it, or for that matter, those desiring to get out. Carrying crowbars, sledgehammers, mattocks and chisels gathered up from blacksmith's benches, and knives pilloried from butcher's shops, their ranks presented, too, a forest of iron bars and wooden clubs, roughly plucked staves of fences, and long ladders for scaling walls.

The besiegers first attempted to batter the prison's main entrance, whose daunting double-leafed iron structure with heavily barred gates they found fast. The keeper's door, which divided the two wings of the complex, became an obvious point for entry. Using mattocks, chisels, and an axe on the door, a second group went to the debtors' door, while a third began work at the felons' door. Working in gangs and at short intervals so as to relieve each other, shortly, the keeper's door was demolished and the contents of the apartment thrown onto the street. Breaking and smashing furniture in a heap reaching halfway across the street, and as high as it would go with men throwing kindling atop ladders; sopped with pitch and tar and turpentine, a fire was soon ignited. As a result, an immense bonfire was blazing against Newgate's main gate.

With tongues of flame brightly rising, twisting like serpents in the night air, the prison's walls began to blacken. And while those in the front fed the inferno, they struggled against those pressing from behind to keep from being pushed into the intensifying blaze. While those standing along the walls and at the rear, instead of doing nothing, tore up the paving stones in the street, or hammered with their bludgeons against the walls. "Not one living creature in the throng," Dickens wrote, "was for an instant still. The whole great mass were mad."

Finally, the heat of the fire liquefied the lead solder holding a hinge at the top of the entrance on one side, as half of the gate swung loose. Working through this gap, as men raked coals and flaming debris to one side, slowly the door began to yield and access to Newgate was gained. Among the multitude in front of Newgate along with William Blake, newspapers reported, were two 'blacks', John Glover and Benjamin Bowsey by name, who later at trial would avoid the gallows by entering His Majesties service along the African coast. Gilchrist concluded:

> This was a peculiar experience for a spiritual poet; not without peril, had a drunken soldier chanced to have identified him during the after weeks of indiscriminate vengeance: those black weeks when strings of boys under fourteen were hung up in a row to vindicate the offended majesty of the Law. (4)

Blake was never implicated as an instigator in the siege; he appears to all commentary as thrust by happenstance among the way-layers of the prison, many of whom significantly had been apprenticed and were journeymen like him. The demonic energy of the throng, both male and female and of diverse ages, and the destructiveness let loose, was to wreck a retribution on the hated prison, as it was a spectacle one might presume, that held Blake, as others, as in the strong grip of a vice. To Blake, it became a prophetic and terrible spectacle, one which he clearly felt sympathy for, along with trepidation. It was to remain with him for his entire life.

It's been noted for example that he became particularly adept at depicting flames, as his presence, along with the impress of the American War, must be taken as harbingers for his coming political radicalism. An inferno flaring so brightly that years afterwards, Dickens reported—"old people who lived in their youth near this part of the city, the church clock of St. Sepulchre's, so often pointing to the hour of death, was legible as in broad day, and the vane upon its steeple-top shone like burnished gold, dotting the longest distance in the fiery vista with their specks of brightness—when wall and tower, and roof and chimney-stack, seemed drunk, and in the flickering glare appeared to reel and stagger—when scores of objects, never seen before, burst out upon the view, and things most familiar put on some new aspect...."

The liquefying of the leaden cruxes on Newgate's iron gate and its down-rendering had worked as the dissolution of the fasteners on Blake's "soul", David Erdman the Blake scholar was to write. (5) This is revealed notably in a poem written in the next decade and included in *Songs of Experience,* one of the bard's most well-known productions, *London*, and has the following stanza in its second part that sounds like a reprise hovering over that hellish scene:

> How the Chimney-sweeper's cry
> Every black'ning Church appalls;
> And the hapless Soldier's sigh
> Runs in blood down Palace walls. (6)

Horace Walpole, Whig politician, letterist, novelist, and 4th Earl of Orford, wrote on 15 June 1780 to his friend The Reverend Mr. Cole:

> You may like to know one is alive, dear Sir, after a massacre, and the conflagration of a capital. I was in it, both on the Friday and on the Black Wednesday; the most horrible sight I ever beheld, and which, for six hours together, I expected to end in half the town being reduced to ashes. I can give you little account of the origin of this shocking affair; negligence was certainly its nurse, and religion its god mother.

Fifty resolute men, it was said, could have turned the multitude let loose on London's streets at any moment, scattering them to the wind. But there was to be no interposition of authority to restrain them, and they had been able to march along their destructive path "as little heeded," wrote Dickens, "as if they were pursuing their lawful occupations with the utmost sobriety and good conduct."

The poet George Crabbe, a newcomer to London and destitute like many of those besiegers of the prison, near Blake's own age (being then 26), probably stood very near his contemporary without either knowing the other. He wrote in his journal of that night:

> The prison...was a remarkably strong building; but, determined to force it, they broke the gates with crows and other instruments, and climbed up the outside part of the cell part, which joins the two great wings of the building, where the felons were confined; and I stood where I plainly saw their operations. They broke the roof, tore away the rafters, and having got ladders they descended. Not Orpheus himself had more courage or better luck. Flames all around them, and a body of soldiers expected, they defied and laughed at all opposition. The prisoners escaped. I stood and saw about twelve women and eight men ascend from their confinement to the open air, and they were conducted through the street in their chains. Three of these were to be hanged on Friday. (7)

With 300 prisoners freed, and all parts of the structure in flames, those wearing manacles were conveyed to neighboring smiths where the bang and clatter of metal sounded through the night. After the assault, George Crabbe lingered at Newgate, reporting he saw Lord Gordon as he passed that night in his carriage, giving the scene his approving glance. In the subsequent enquiry to that which bears his name, Gordon would, however, be held blameless for the violence, and his fleeting presence, attested to by Crabbe, may only signify that the "Anti-Popery" outrages against Catholics were still on-going, however ancillary to the scourge unleashed. The poet hastened to include the following, in a letter to a friend:

> I must not omit what struck me most. About ten or twelve of the mob, getting to the top of debtors' prison, whilst it was burning, to halloo, they appeared rolled in black smoke mixed with sudden bursts of fire—like Milton's infernals who were as familiar with flames as with each other. (8)

After gutting Newgate, more symbols of authority were to be attacked and burned, with the worst retribution happening on the next day, designated *Black Wednesday*. In the streets men and women had vowed there should not be one prison left standing in London, as the city as seen to burn from all points on the compass, with another seven prisons and houses of correction destroyed. But those caught-up in the throes of the tumult were by no means indiscriminate in their violence. No one had been killed outside those in their own ranks, about 450 persons all totaled, and they were seen allowing fire-engines to fight flames in buildings and homes adjacent to those that had been their intended targets. Evidence of concerted leadership was quickly manifest, something perhaps that is always lying dormant but ready to form in the right circumstances in large metropolitan concentrations. Sub-groups with a degree of cohesion were seen to be operating, directed against targets drawn from lists carried by their leaders. Each successive tumult took its form from the circumstances of the moment, and new leaders sprang up as they were wanted, disappearing when the necessity was over, and reappearing at the next urgency. There were also reports of "better dressed" and "respectable" sorts watching approvingly on the periphery of these scenes, and while many were "blue cockade" men, others too might be conjectured given the corruption and intrigue endemic to monarchic society.

On "Black Wednesday," in addition to attacking Fleet Prison and freeing 1600 prisoners, and destroying the nearby home of the chief barrister Lord Mansfield, the Bank of England and the tollhouses on Blackfriars Bridge became the especial targets. Before being repelled with heavy causalities among those assaulting, the attack on the bank was carried three times successively. Doubtless, it became a target because as a symbol it subsumed into a single edifice all that was standing atop those in revolt; but also, without peradventure, for the treasures held within. The defending troops were commanded by Alderman John Wilkes, the radical and influential politician and former MP, with however, a chequered history. The "Gordon Riots" would mark the end of a long career. Before this, he had notably been in opposition to the war in the American colonies, was a promoter of religious tolerance, and had long been touted "a champion of liberty", supporting freedom of the press and advocating for the poor, particularly for weavers and coal-heavers. He was also a notable rake.

In the skirmishing at the bank another of those thrown-up from below was seen coxswaining the second assault. Again, riding a carthorse, he is described as a "brewery drayman," be-decked in chains gathered from Newgate's prisoners and waving handcuffs over his head.

That night, the Lanesdale Gin Distillery, of Catholic proprietorship, was also inundated and demolished, leaving an epitaph as a macabre tableau of that spirit's wretched victims, even more so than Hogarth's worthy *Gin Lane* executed decades earlier—with its central figure, a dissolute woman with bared breasts letting her child fall to its death, as she absently converses with a cadaverous ballad-seller on some forlorn outdoor steps; a caustic depiction of London's denizens caught in the throes of anarchy and despair.

As the Lanesdale Distillery burned, fire hoses had been thrust into its cellars to draw the gin out from the vats, as casks were wheeled into the streets. With men and women imbibing licentiously from cupped hands, from hats, from pails and buckets, even from shoes, many became inebriated. But the liquid pouring from the hoses was unrectified alcohol and poisonous, and they began writhing and dying wretchedly on the street, their corpses mangled by the wheels of fire engines. Inadvertently, too, the gin pouring from the hoses had been directed as a retardant on the flames, and sent a hissing, maddened plumb licking skyward—and as many a wretch had become splashed with the fluid, some became a-light from head to foot—a glare seen, some said, from thirty-miles away.

Dickens also remarks (and his research can be relied on as more than a novelist's fancy), that the faces of inmates at Newgate seen fleeing through the neighborhood were remembered by those who had been infants at the time. Those doomed faces met but an instant, had been an image with force enough "to dim the whole concourse; to find itself an all-absorbing place, and hold it ever after."

As another indelible sign of his mounting radicalism, Blake would commemorate two demonstrations against the American War happening that year in the next decade in his *America, A Prophesy* (1793), occurring in Bristol and London, as indeed, it reflected back on the so-called Gordon Riots:

Across the limbs of Albion's Guardian; the spotted
plague smote Bristol's
And the Leprosy London's Spirit, sickening all their
bands: The millions sent up a howl of anguish and threw
off
their hammer'd mail,
And cast their swords & spears to earth, & stood, a naked
multitude. (9)

As that poem ends:

Stiff shudderings shook the heav'nly thrones! France
Spain & Italy
In terror view'd the bands of Albion, and the ancient
Guardians
Fainting upon the elements, smitten with their own
plagues
They slow advance to shut the five gates of their law-built
heaven
Filled with blasting fancies and with mildews of despair
With fierce disease and lust, unable to stem the fires of
Orc:
But the five gates were consum'd, & their bolts and
hinges melted;
And the fierce flames burnt round the heavens & round
the abodes of men. (10)

3.

For Empire is no more

Two contributions were to leave an enduring imprint, both on the contemporaneous scene and on causes yet to come; as both achieved fame and have received their measure from posterity. Published months apart in 1776; the first was broadcast from the American colonies, from the city of Philadelphia, one of the principal cities in the rebellion roiling colonial rule from Britain. An overnight sensation of undisputed consequence, it was a pamphlet authored by an Englishman new to the colonies, Thomas Paine, and was titled *Common Sense*. The other, appearing after *Common Sense* in March, although not having its celerity, was a book to be equally far-reaching in import. It bore the title *An Inquiry into the Nature and Causes of the Wealth of Nations*, although it is usually simply referenced *The Wealth of Nations*. It was by Adam Smith, a former professor and noted moral philosopher of the Scottish Enlightenment, or the literati, as they styled themselves.

The literati were a gathering of intellectuals that socialized together, meeting in social clubs, often in pubs, and reading, critiquing, and debating one another's work, as they discussed politics and philosophy. They were influenced by the methodology of Isaac Newton, the 17th century English physicist, or "natural philosopher" and mathematician, whose *Philoso-phiae Naturalis Principia Mathematica* was published in 1687 laying the foundations of classical mechanics. Newton saw that nature was ruled by discoverable principles, and so they likewise held it was with human activities. Among this company, and closest to Smith, was David Hume, a noted formulator of this advanced thinking, with whom Smith shared a commitment to empiricism—that knowledge is acquired through the senses rather than through innate ideas.

In moral behavior, Hume asserted, human beings are motivated by their capacity for sympathy; and, however inclined to use their intellects, individuals were more likely to be agents of sentiment. Smith's tome, the writing and study for which was a labor of more than a decade, in effect constituted an attack upon the whole commercial system then prevailing in Great Britain. Reflecting the spontaneously arisen manufacturing order taking hold in the north of England and in Scotland at the time, Smith was among the first theorists to posit that a nation's wealth lay not in metals, which was the mercantilist standard—in gold and silver or in things—but in labor. Thus, Smith's enquiry asked readers to consider the meaning of wealth; what was the real measure of exchangeable values in all commodities. *Wealth of Nations* advocated that a "division of labor" was paramount to the modern commercial system, upholding the novel thesis that that was what made the extraordinary accumulation of capital and goods possible. The more investment there was in this improved mode of production, Smith noted, the more wealth would be created; and those who prospered would be those who grew and managed and protected their capital.

Smith's ideas fell fast on receptive minds; as he had also started a debate about the nature of markets, and had invented the idea of market analysis. While each operator within the commercial system was intent only on promoting their own ends, yet in this each was "led by an invisible hand to promote an end which was no part of his intention." The movement of goods and services would maximize wealth, as both wages and profits accrued.

Smith was a moral thinker above all, who sought fairness and a level playing field for all; and instead of "capitalism" he used the phrase "commercial society", as instead of "economics" he would designate his enquiry "political economy." Smith's prospectus was tailor-made for the Atlantic coastal colonies of the British Empire, as he not only was concerned with the mechanisms of exchange, but more so with the optimal form of government to promote an all-sided commercial advancement. Smith's was an insight for the age of machines and of steam power, and of the new factories just beginning their burgeoning career. And he persuasively advocated a "natural liberty" where markets would be largely self-governed, with free trade and unfettered competition between participants.

Thomas Paine was born in 1737 in Thetford on England's southeastern channel coast in the region known as East Anglia, to a Quaker father and Anglican mother. The town, then of two thousand residents, is situated on the Little Ouse River, in the midst of a large heath and the seat of the dukes of Grafton whose estates' immensity dwarfed the borough. Forty miles in circumference, Defoe reported, the Grafton estate, Euston Hall—"lies in the open country towards the side of Norfolk not far from Thetford; a place capable of all that is pleasant and delightful in nature, and improv'd by art to every extreme that Nature is able to produce." Thetford was one of the "rotten boroughs", so-called because they were controlled by wealthy patrons, where only the mayor, aldermen, and the members of the common council could vote to elect its allotted members of Parliament, and where votes were bought and sold for huge sums. These boroughs had become the basis for George III's grip on both houses of parliament.

Paine's father was a stay-maker by trade, and as it was a shipbuilding region, these, not-withstanding what others might insist, may have been the thick rope stays used in ships for supporting the mast. That Paine later was called a "corset-maker" is attributable to those who found it politic to caricature him for his commitment to democratic government antithetical to their views, and for the anti-theocratic viewpoint he would espouse in *The Age of Reason*, the last of the great treatises he would write, which lost for him by the second decade of the American Republic, all of the esteem he had garnered during its war for independence he was so instrumental in bringing to its completion. The trade in which he made a fitful start, rather than fitting corsets, was properly the manufacture of whalebone stays used in making corsets, a process requiring considerable strength and dexterity. But whatever the specifics Paine was not long at the trade, quitting it by age twenty-five.

More significantly for the young boy, the family cottage was in sight of the execution ground, a small windswept hill known locally as the Wilderness. The scaffold was assembled on a chalk ridge with sentences carried out in the month of March before an amassed crowd, and where the executants were left hanging for an hour. There were scores of offences as the 18th century wore on exacting capital punishment, and many of these were for crimes against property, as even children were sent to the gallows for petty thefts prompted by hunger. Voltaire, in exile, visiting the area a few years before Paine's birth, remarked the English were a people who murdered by law.

After a rudimentary schooling, at age thirteen the son began an apprentice with his father; while his biographer's hold at an early age he tried to enlist on a *privateer*. Retrieved by his father before it embarked, as it turned out on an ill-fated voyage, a few years later, at age 20 he succeeded on a second try, remaining at sea till returning after two voyages raiding French shipping in the Channel, and remunerated for his effort, he set himself up in the trade. In his schooling Paine had already become proficient in mathematics, but his early devotions had been "poetical authors", John Milton, John Bunyan, and William Shakespeare. That he became a master of political prose, was "in no small measure," notes a 20th century biographer, "because of the schooling he received." (1) Thus, he became a mechanic in an increasingly innovative era, imbibing the anti-authoritarian and individualist ethos of his Quaker ancestry, as he did the scientific methodology and empiricism that was the bequest of the enlightenment thinkers.

The decade before his emigration to America in 1774, when he was 37 years of age, were years too where he had married. However, he soon was bereaved of this wife, and so it seems to his life-long detriment, was cut off from intimacy with woman, she dying in child-birth. The trade not being remunerative, he is now reported working for the excise office, following his father-in-law into that post. This involved executing the Excise Acts, or as it was, often collecting taxes from smugglers—a job involving considerable risk. When accused of reporting on goods not inspected, as was the common practice so as not to be too stringent on merchants, he was dismissed, and returned to stay-making in Norfolk.

Most commentaries on Paine's early life are apt to point out he had an apparent lack of success in employment, but they might not themselves be cognizant of the shocks and contingencies tradesmen were liable to. In any case, he could not have been much different in this regard from many of his compatriots, as there was a marked degree of destitution in England. By the time he was again reported an exciseman in Lewes in Sussex, he was already distinguishing himself for his developing persuasive and argumentative abilities. He had joined a debating club, called the *Headstrong Club*, and was selected from among his fellows as spokesman to draft an appeal to the parliament petitioning for higher salaries for excise-office tax collectors. The first product of his to be prolific quill, titled *The Case of the Officers of Excise*, was a seventeen-page brief said to be "as clear and complete as any lawyer could make it"; its presentation necessitating Paine travel to London, where he would remain almost two years.

Once in London Paine began to frequent the scientific lectures and demonstrations on Newtonian astronomy given by Benjamin Martin and James Ferguson, and could be found in coffee-houses and taverns, meeting and becoming conversant with such eminences as Oliver Goldsmith, the well-regarded and congenial but impetuous Irish writer, where Paine's ability in laying out a reasoned argument underwent quick tutelage. Although the exciseman's appeal would be rejected by Parliament, this sojourn was to bring him into an education and acculturation, as he became the center of a circle of attentive auditors and debaters, indispensable in readying him for the political storms he was to encounter, as he would become a key participant in the ferment that set him near the center of two revolutions: first in America and subsequently in France.

Absent his duties, Paine was again dismissed, but had the fortune within his associations of meeting a preeminent exponent of the ideas of the Enlightenment, to become a bit later an iconoclastic figure-of-the-frontier for Europeans, Benjamin Franklin. Franklin was in London to represent the colonies, on a mission, then, still of reconciling disputes between 'America'—a pejorative meaning provincial—and the Crown's government. Impressed by the character and fitness of the man, Paine's biographer Moncure Conway, here being principally followed, was to write: "The discharged and insulted postmaster could sympathize with the dismissed and starving exciseman. Franklin recognized Paine's ability, and believed he would be useful and successful in America." (2)

Whether Franklin induced him to consider emigration to the American colonies, may not be determinable—but Franklin did write Paine an important letter of introduction. Having sold all his assets to avoid debtors prison, penniless and newly divorced from a second wife, with whom, however, he maintained separate residences by the end of their brief marriage, as they ran a grocery and tobacco shop, Paine arrived in Philadelphia November 30, 1774. Able to disembark only on stretcher, the farer would require six weeks convalescence, recovering from typhoid fever and dysentery contracted from drinking tainted water. Six passengers had died on the voyage.

One of thousands of British immigrants to arrive in America seeking new opportunities and a better life in the years prior to its struggle for independence; on recovering, Paine, who had resolved to pursue employment as a school-teacher, was soon introduced to the printer and bookseller Robert Aitkin, whose bookstore was a prime meeting place for denizens among which he was quickly to form strong alliances. In a letter dated March 4, 1775, from Philadelphia, he wrote to Franklin acknowledging his assistance: "Your countenancing me has obtained for me many friends and much reputation, for which please accept my sincere thanks." Aitkin had just begun publication of *The Pennsylvania Magazine*, and Paine was hired as a journalist, and soon would be writing many of its articles, as he did the editing himself.

The first article under Paine's hand in America had been published in the *Pennsylvania Journal, and the Weekly Advertiser* and was an early manifesto of abolitionism, denouncing the slavery of Africans in the American Colonies. In that plea, published March 8, 1775, Paine concluded: "Primitive Christians labored always to spread their divine religion; and this is equally our duty while there is a heathen nation. But what singular obligations are we under to these injured people!"

The first issue of the new magazine appeared in January 1775, before Paine's advent in February, and was fifty-two pages stitched between blue covers, its title page adorned with a logo with a rising sun, behind which was an olive-twined shield together with a globe, a book, a flower, a lyre, and an anchor, with a motto in Latin that translated "Happy it is to live in the woods." It was showcasing essays and commentary, fiction and poetry, with articles on the scientific and the topical, and on political subjects. In the August issue of the new magazine, while Paine was its editor, a number titled "An Occasional Letter on the Female Sex" would be featured. Paine had inserted an article, if not by him, was written in a feminine voice:

> If we have an equal right with you to virtue, why should we not have an equal right with you to praise? The public esteem ought to wait upon merit.... Nature assails us with sorrow, law and custom press us with constraint. Sometimes also the name of citizen demands from us the tribute of fortitude. When you offer your blood to the state, think that it is ours.

Thus, straight away were flung from the hand of this reformer seeds that were to sprout in the furrows of 18th century civilization with universal validity; as he also published six timely pages that summer on events at Lexington and Concord, and featured recent inventions of England not yet in use in America: the threshing and the spinning machine.

Reading Paine's disputation on African slavery, Dr. Benjamin Rush, a leader of the American Enlightenment and a prominent proponent of many reforms, particularly in medicine and education, and himself a seminal abolitionist in America and preeminent among Philadelphia's political radicals, was later to write:

> ...I read a short essay with which I was much pleased... against the slavery of Africans in our country, and which I was informed was written by Mr. Paine. This excited my desire to be better acquainted with him. We met soon afterwards in Mr. Atkins bookstore...He told me the essay to which I alluded was the first thing he had ever published in his life. (3)

Directing the affairs at the magazine for 18 months, its subscriptions would rise from 800 to 1500, and as it had grown in popularity it began to attract the attention of members of the *Philosophical Society* founded by Franklin in 1743, and Paine was introduced into wider contacts.

With the contest entered over the governance of the colonies by the British government and parliament, and over taxation ostensibly levied to pay for the cost of defense and to pay the debt incurred in the Seven Years War fought against France, the first Continental Congress had convened in Philadelphia where they had summoned a Continental Army into being, commanded by a Virginia planter and slaveholder, a man of modest military achievement in "the French and Indian War", but with an authoritative comportment, George Washington. In April, blood had been shed at Lexington and Concord by the "Sons of Liberty", as by "redcoats" alike, as eight men lay dead; Boston was occupied by British troops, and Falmouth and Norfolk burned. Paine was urged to write something about "English-American relations" by Dr. Rush, with some remarks for the justifications for independence. (4)

"Independence was a doctrine scarce and rare even towards the conclusion of the year 1775," remarked Benjamin Franklin. (5) Scarcely, too, had it been heard in public forums, particularly in the Continental Congress where delegates had been instructed by their respective colonial governments, that it was not a topic for debate. Once the document was completed in November and December of that year, on review, Dr. Rush suggested its title be changed from Paine's "Plain Truth" to "Common Sense". (6) Published in early January 1776, timed to coincide with the King's address to the Parliament which would be arriving from across the Atlantic, its author was unknown in the broader colonies, and the publisher, Robert Bell, located on Philadelphia's 3rd Street, credited the pamphlets originator on the title page only as an "Englishman".

Soon after the pamphlet reached him, and he'd read it in his headquarters near Boston, General Washington wrote: "A few more of such flaming arguments as were exhibited at Falmouth and Norfolk, added to the sound doctrine and unanswerable reasoning contained in the pamphlet 'Common Sense,' will not leave numbers at a loss to decide upon the propriety of separation." (7) Among the pamphlets many readers were the delegates of the Second Continental

Congress, given minority leadership by proponents of "independence" like the lawyer from Braintree, Massachusetts, to become one of the founding "statesman" of the new country, John Adams. Years later, Adams, who without attribution had been supposed initially to have been the author because he too was an early supporter of independence, remarked that Paine's pen bid-fair Washington's sword could effectively be raised in the first place. Becoming Paine's often inveterate opponent, and disparaging his "democratical" ideas, he admitted the author's style was much too "manly" to allow attribution from his hand.

Without the high-sounding Latin phraseology and rhetoric common in treatises of its kind, Paine's tract above all was meant to be heard, written for people who would stand and listen. His was an unadorned prose, and it was read aloud in roadside taverns and in town meetings, on street corners and in private homes. With the author foregoing copyright and without remuneration, in its first three months the forty-seven-page pamphlet was flourishing up and down the eastern seaboard, as 100,000 copies were sold. Within six months it would be translated and published in German for the Pennsylvania "Dutch", with copies circulating throughout parts of Britain, with many of these making it to the continent, to France, Poland, and even to Russia. 500,000 copies of *Common Sense* were sold in the first year, marking its author overnight celebrated as a political philosopher of undoubted talent and significance.

Repudiating the idea then prevailing of a continuing, but fairer compact with Britain, the pamphlet crystalized the latent sentiment for independence, as it argued for republican government; moving from merely resisting British misrule, to encouraging accelerated recruitment for the Continental Army. Sub-divided into three sections, it attacked and ridiculed monarchy as it denounced the decaying despotisms of Europe; pillorying hereditary monarchy as an absurdity, it issued a clarion call to resist the corrupt British courts. Paine had demonstrated the inevitability of American independence, as his *Common Sense* proclaimed the world significance of an American Revolution.

"Common Sense", as its author became known, had succeeded too in exhibiting a distinctly American political identity, as the pamphlet would become the most incendiary and popular of the revolutionary era. By virtue of this tract alone, Paine was to rise to a stature in the Revolution in the minds of patriot's equal to that of Washington in military affairs, and of Benjamin Franklin in diplomatic affairs. But he could not have known its issue, then as now as much an historic as a literary document, would ignite such a wildfire. He was to write his benefactor Benjamin Franklin, by then in Paris, a lengthy letter dated from York, Pennsylvania, May 16, 1778, where he remarked—"For my own part, I thought it very hard to have the Country set on fire about my Ears almost the moment I got into it...."

A selection from an introduction added a month after the pamphlet's publication serves to indicate how its message fell on those it stirred:

> In the following sheets, the author hath studiously avoided every thing which is personal among ourselves.... The wise, and the worthy, need not the triumph of a pamphlet; and those whose sentiments are injudicious or unfriendly, will cease of themselves unless too much pains are bestowed upon their conversion. The cause of America is in a great measure the cause of all mankind. Many circumstances hath, and will arise, which are not local, but universal.... The laying a Country desolate with Fire and Sword, declaring War against the natural rights of all Mankind, and extirpating the Defenders thereof

from the Face of the Earth, is the Concern of every Man to whom Nature hath given the power of feeling....

Carried on the floodtide following *Common Sense*, the *Declaration of Independence* was broadcast 4 July 1776, authored in committee, which included John Adams, by Thomas Jefferson, another of the Virginia planters, and hence slaveholder, a lawyer and scholar and future statesman of the first rank in the American concordance.

Shouldering a musket as a private, Paine went to war and soon was enlisted with the army commanded by General Nathanael Green, from Rhode Island of a Quaker family, as his aide-du-camp. Writing and reading the general's orders, his main contribution however, and again it was a crucial one, was to be sixteen *American Crisis* pamphlets, published between 1776 and 1783. The first of these, where—*camp fires*, *winter storms*, and *the waves of the Delaware* are suffused with *ink*—was dated December 23. Read by Washington to his troops before the battle of Trenton, its celebrated opening paragraph resounded to almost Shakespearian conceits:

> These are the times that try men's souls: the summer soldier and the sunshine patriot will, in this crisis, shrink from the service of his country; but he that stands NOW, deserves the love and thanks of man and woman. Tyranny, like hell, is not easily conquered; yet we have this consolation with us, that the harder the conflict, the more glorious the triumph.

The Hessian mercenary troops engaged at Trenton were

defeated, giving the American's their first victory in the central seat of the war; and one that made a slumbering world momentarily look-up in astonishment. To "Tom Paine"—a rendering of his name employed by those who disparaged him—went the laurels of sustaining patriot moral through months when its prospects seemed to be ebbing.

But his conduct and services during the next seven years were a record of some controversy; particularly with "the Silas Deane affair", were Deane had been appointed as a secret envoy to France, and was involved in negotiations that would form an alliance between the two nations. Begun in 1778, after the consummation of the American victory at Saratoga, concluded in October 1777; Deane was Connecticut born and the same age as Paine, and like him was a prominent supporter of independence. Twice married into wealth, he had crucially been involved in the procurement of weapons and supplies for the Green Mountain Boys led by Ethan Allen in the territory between New York and New Hampshire, known by 1777 as the Republic of Vermont, who had captured, together with the militia commanded by Connecticut Colonel Benedict Arnold, the crucially strategic fortification on Lake Champlain called Fort Ticonderoga in May 1775. Congress had been so impressed by Deane's success that he was approached in regard to procuring weapons and supplies, so vitally needed, from France.

Commissioned by Congress to join Arthur Lee, of the famous Lee family from Virginia then living in London, and Benjamin Franklin, Deane would prove successful in obtaining arms and supplies gratis or at nominal prices for an army of 25 thousand men from French arsenals—cannon, muskets, military clothing, along with cash from the French treasury, a gift bestowed at the direction of Louis XVI. But so as not to overtly antagonize the British government, these were given in secret and laundered through a company set up by Deane for that purpose.

Deane had also been commissioned to procure European goods to be distributed to Native Americans in negotiations with Congress; and lastly, to assist Franklin and Lee in negotiating the treaty of commerce and alliance between Congress and France. For these services, Deane was offered his travel and living expenses and a 5 percent commission on all purchases for the American war effort.

Deane had a reputation as a flamboyant schemer, and moreover, had grown accustomed to dapper living; and when he presented his invoice to Congress it was far in excess of what the fledgling government could afford. As Lee exposed his evident double-dealing, Deane was recalled by Congress. Robert Morris, a prominent Philadelphia merchant and until recently a delegate in Congress, and a personal friend of Silas Deane, had remarked before his departure, "If we have but luck in getting the goods safe to America the profits will be sufficient to content us all." (8)

Morris, as chairman of a committee purchasing military supplies, had directed contracts to his own company, and it was this largess he had proffered to his friend Silas Deane. Earlier that year too, Thomas Mifflin, quartermaster general of the army, had misused his position by employing government wagons to transport goods for sale on the open market. Then, Dr. William Shippen, head of the medical department, had seen to the sale of medical supplies to private entities and pocketed the proceeds himself.

Returning to Philadelphia, Deane appeared as summoned before Congress, albeit without bringing any of the accounting ledgers or receipts that would have validated his charges. Congress was now rent by supporters of Deane on one side, and on the other his critics. Soon after Deane's return, Washington had caustically given his views to the Congress:

"Speculation, peculation, and an insatiable thirst for riches seem to have got the better of every other consideration and almost of every order of men." (9)

Regarding themselves as among the leaders and founders of the independence movement, Samuel Adams and Richard Henry Lee bewailed the decline in public spiritedness these transactions portended. Referred to as the Eastern party, they found themselves opposed by the merchant faction, led in Congress by two representatives of New York, both men of wealth, John Jay and Gouverneur Morris. As Deane published a lengthy defense and diatribe in December 1778, the fractures became evident. His critics, he charged, were working illicitly against the treaty with France and for reconciliation with Britain, and were therefore counter-revolutionaries. Henry Laurens of South Carolina, a man accruing a large wealth both from his plantation and from the slave-trade, then presiding as president in the Congress, resigned, protesting Deane's "highly derogatory" maledictions against members of Congress, and "the honour and interests of these United States." (10) John Jay was immediately elected in his stead to the presidency.

In 1777 Thomas Paine had been appointed secretary of the Committee of Foreign Affairs in Congress, and was privy of the inside story on these dealings through the classified documents that were passing over his desk. Excoriating Deane for his patent self-enrichment in a letter published in the *Pennsylvania Packet*, Paine declared Deane unfit for public service, saying he was guilty of "embezzlement", chargeable to his "mercantile connections", especially implicating Robert Morris.

Paine himself was then castigated by Deane's prominent supporters for disparaging the reputation of a patriot. In an open letter, Morris reacted sharply: "If Mr. Deane had any commerce that was inconsistent with his public station, he must answer for it, as I did not, by becoming a Delegate for the State of Pennsylvania, relinquish my right of forming mercantile connections. I was unquestionably at liberty to form such with Mr. Deane." (11) Business was business, said Morris; as Thomas Mifflin joining the fray, charged, "Paine, like the enthusiastic madmen of the East, was determined to run the *muck*."

Relishing a good engagement, Paine struck back, again in the *Packet*, reiterating his imputations of corruption and embezzlement, he invited anyone with an interest to stop by and read the congressional report disclosing Deane's dealings; a contract that had been consummated, evidently, even before he arrived in France.

His enemies now saw they had a plank over which they could drive Paine, that he himself had laid. For evidently, he had offered to disclose classified information and therefore had violated his oath of secrecy.

The new French envoy to America, who had arrived with Silas Deane, Conrad Alexandre Gerard, now added to the impression that an Eastern party was working to embarrass the French government. Writing Congress of his misgivings, Gerard insisted that Paine publicly retract his allegations against Deane. Paine would have none of it, writing the French envoy that his suspicions were unfounded, and drawing a distinction between the French granting of material and Deane's misuse of his authority. Paine wrote: "My design was and is to place the merit of these supplies where I think the merit is most due, that is in the disposition of the French nation to help us."

In a subsequent edition of the *Packet*, as Paine renewed his attack on corruption, Gerard lodged a written protest with Congress, urging that measures be taken to ameliorate Paine's "indiscrete assertions." At this, faced with the unacceptable option of being silenced, Paine offered his resignation as secretary of the Committee of Foreign Affairs. Congress responded by summoning both Paine and his publisher to appear before it at eleven o'clock in the morning, Wednesday, January 7, 1779.

When the proceedings began, Paine's publisher, John Dunlap, was asked if he had published the articles by Paine offensive to Gerard. As this was acknowledged, he was asked to leave the chamber. Now Paine was called. John Jay, with calculated iciness, picked up a copy of the *Pennsylvania Packet*, saying—"Here is Mr. Dunlap's paper of December 29. In it is a piece entitled 'Common Sense to the Public on Mr. Deane's affairs'; I am directed by Congress to ask you if you are the author." Paine replying, "Yes, sir, I am the author of that piece"; Jay put the same question about the two other articles on the subject of Deane, and received the same reply. Paine was directed, "You may withdraw," as Jay ruled nothing further need be elicited for the discussion.

As he was ushered out the door, John Penn of North Carolina moved that "Thomas Paine be discharged from the office of secretary of the Committee of Foreign Affairs." This was seconded by Gouverneur Morris. The hall immediately erupted into strident debate where the motion was narrowly defeated.

That same day Paine submitted a memorandum to Congress that challenged the maxim that a little sincerity was dangerous, and a great deal of it fatal. Paine wrote:

> I cannot in duty to my character as a freeman submit to be censured unheard. I have evidence which I presume will justify me. And I entreat this House to consider how great their reproach will be should it be told that they passed a sentence upon me without hearing me, and that a copy of the charge against me was refused to me; and

likewise how much that reproach will be aggravated should I afterwards prove the censure of this House to be a libel, grounded upon a mistake which they refused fully to inquire into. (12)

In effect, Paine was saying Congress was acting despotically, as arbitrarily as a monarchy. Would he become the first person ever to be impeached by an American government? For ten days the congressional delegates wrangled over the issues, but Paine's enemies were intent that he walk-the-plank. In the debate, Gouverneur Morris emphasized Paine's "threatening letter". Here was a contemptible individual suffused with "mad assertions," he charged; he was naught but a rough-cut commoner, a "mere adventurer *from England*, without fortune, without family or connections, ignorant even of grammar." Congress had every right to censure one of its loose-tongued employees. (13)

As Morris braced himself before the derision of his colleagues, he shouted over their heads: "What! Are we reduced to such a situation, that our servants shall beard us with insolent menaces, and we shall fear to discuss them without granting a trial forsooth?" Paine had been crafty, said Morris, in fabricating the impression that he wrote on behalf of Congress, and so had usurped his duties, and now must be sacked from his post. "And what are we?" he concluded; "[t]he sovereign power, who appointed, and who when he no longer pleases us, may remove him. Nothing more is desired. We do not wish to punish him." Paine was but a state employee, Morris contended, and the Congress was within its jurisdiction to discipline its employee unheard.

To throw a stay before his personal humiliation, the next day, at the opening of business Paine hand-delivered his resignation to Independence Hall. It was his right, he wrote, as a freeman to "yield up to no power whatever;" asserting—

"I have betrayed no trust because I have constantly employed that trust to the public good. I have revealed no secrets because I have told nothing that was, or I conceive ought to have been a secret. I have convicted Mr. Deane of error, and in so doing I have done my duty."

During the clash Paine was twice assaulted by supporters of Deane on the streets of Philadelphia, hirelings of merchants who it seems might have had had double-dealing of their own to protect. But in the cause to which he was devoted, Paine bore its hardships and sacrifices as well as others, and with "American ideals" emblazoned in his writings, gave readers timely reflection on crucial events.

By the sixth year of war, nearly destitute of financial means, and with the will to continue the war waning, the effectiveness of Congress was constrained by the majority of its members who would not increase taxation. Working as clerk of the Pennsylvania Assembly after his dismissal, with his salary of L500 per annum, Paine took the entire proceeds to start a subscription for a bank, quickly joined by other subscriptions, to eventually be incorporated as *The Bank of North America* under the agency of Robert Morris. But even this would not be enough. "It was plain," wrote Moncure Conway "that the money could not be got in the country."

Paine now "drew up a letter to Vergennes" (Charles Gravier, Count of Vergennes, Foreign Minister of Louis XVI)—

>...informing him that a paper dollar was worth only a
>cent, that it seemed almost impossible to continue the
>war, and asking that France should supply America with
>a million sterling per annum, as subsidy or loan. This

letter was shown to M. Marbois, Secretary of the French Legation, who spoke discouragingly. But the Hon. Ralph Izard showed the letter to some members of Congress, whose consultation led to the appointment of Col. John Laurens, one of Washington's aids, who would be able to explain the military situation. He was reluctant, but agreed to go if Paine would accompany him. (14)

John Laurens was the well-educated son of Henry Laurens, having attended a private school at Geneva, where he became fluent in French; and had taken his legal training at Middle Temple in London. Laurens had joined General Washington's inner circle, comprised at that time by Lafayette and Alexander Hamilton. He had imbibed principles at odds with his aristocratic southern station, arguing: "I think we Americans, at least in the Southern Colonies, cannot contend with a good Grace for Liberty until we have enfranchised our Slaves. How can we reconcile our spirited Assertions of the Rights of Mankind with the galling abject Slavery of our Negroes?" (15) That Thomas Paine flourished in friendships among such young men as represented by Laurens and Lafayette, and well as others, as he embraced his own plebeian origins, is as remarkable as it is characteristic.

Sailing from Boston February 1781, the duo would return on a French frigate June 1, reaching Boston August 25. With another ship in convoy laden with clothing and military stores, they would carry with them two and a half million livres in silver from King Louis XVI of France. This relief, coming when it did, was seen to be of an importance of the first order, and was brought largely at the agency of Thomas Paine. (16)

Sixteen teams of oxen were now harnessed to carry the clothing and stores to Washington's camp on the Hudson, where he would receive them to outfit his destitute troops, as some of the money would be disbursed into the pockets of soldiers. As yet unaffected by this material relief, in conjunction with the Marquis de Lafayette (recruited by Deane in 1778, along with Pulaski and other Europeans) and by French troops arriving in convoy, the American's would now confront, and, as it happened, defeat the British Lieutenant General Charles Cornwallis and his army in Virginia, at Yorktown.

With Washington moving south commanding the American Continental Army and the French Army arriving led by the Comte de Rochambeau, the surrender and capture of Cornwallis and his army would prompt the British government to negotiate an end to the conflict, finally resulting in the Treaty of Paris in 1783.

With the fighting concluded, Paine was how a recognized and an honored figure throughout America as well as in Europe, but was himself nearly destitute. The fight for Liberty in American had been successfully waged, but the country had not afforded him any pecuniary security, as he had conducted his important literary/political career entirely foregoing remuneration or copyright protection. In his last *Crisis* pamphlet, issued just as Washington announced the cessation of hostilities, Paine wrote his "farewell address" to the patriotic citizens of the prospective republic:

> It was the cause of America that made me an author. The force with which it struck my mind, and the dangerous conditions in which the country was in, by courting an impossible and an unnatural reconciliation with those who were determined to reduce her, instead of striking out into the only line that could save her, a Declaration of Independence, made it impossible for me, feeling as I did, to be silent; and if, in the course of more than seven years, I have rendered her any service, I have likewise added something to the reputation of literature, by freely

and disinterestedly employing it in the great cause of mankind....

In the following decade, Paine's reputation would cross the Atlantic to Albion's shore and the eager attention of the London engraver, judged "one of the subtlest and most far-reaching figures in the intellectual liberation of Europe that took place at the end of the eighteenth century." (17) *America, A Prophecy*, was published by William Blake a year after the British Parliament would enact its seditious writings act in May 1792 directed largely against Thomas Paine, in which Blake notably included his own name as author, the place of origin of the work, and the date on the title page— *Lambeth/Printed by William Blake, in the year 1793*. There could be no mistaking that the author understood the bold significance of his stance vis-à-vis the government and the crown. Had it come to their attention and had they understood it, as he himself wrote in his notebook—"I say I shan't live five years. And if I live one it will be a wonder. June 1793." (18)

The events Blake depicts a decade after the American War in his "continental prophecy" are narrated in compressed episodes and without regard to the historical chronology, where the hostilities across the Atlantic in the thirteen colonies are seen as the harbinger of universal revolution, whose fires would soon ignite Albion's combustible shore, as indeed Revolution was then raging in France. The King of England, George III, is not mentioned by name—that would have been directly seditious—and although the King was 37 years of age at the time, he trembles with "aged limbs" as representative of decrepit monarchy, as he sees Blake's mythical figure Orc, the spirit of revolt and freedom, arising for the first time in Blake's poetry from the rebelling American colonies.

Freedom is not yet conquered in the poem; this is only the record of the process of attaining it. *America, A Prophecy* in this way is linked with Blake's other writing at the time—a year earlier, *Visions of the Daughters of Albion,* and a year afterwards, *Europe, A Prophecy,* followed in 1795 by the *Song of Los,* where Africa and Asia are cited—all depictions of geographical entities, not individuals, struggling to attain freedom across a continental breadth, all united by similar historical and social themes in Blake's treatment.

The political expressions in *America* include lauding of the leading patriots, among them Thomas Paine with whom he would become personally acquainted in the year before the poem was completed. Gilchrist, commenting on the work, the fourth of Blake's Illuminated Books, remarked—"[t]hat over the leaves it is sometimes like an increase of light on the retina, so fair and open is the effect of particular pages." Blake wrote:

> In the flames stood and view'd the armies drawn out in
>   the sky,
> Washington, Franklin, Paine, and Warren, Allen, Gates
>   and Lee,
> And heard the voice of Albion's Angel give the thunderous
>   command....
> And the red flames of Orc, that folded roaring, fierce,
>   around
> The angry shores; and the fierce, rushing of th'
>   inhabitants together!
> The citizens of New York close their books and lock
>   their chests;
> The mariners of Boston drop their anchors and unlade;
> The scribe of Pennsylvania casts his pen upon the earth;
> The builder of Virginia throws his hammer down in fear.

Engraved in eighteen plates, the work was several years in maturation suggesting an obvious congruity with Blake's writing on the French Revolution, as indeed with the tumult taking place at the same time in Saint Domingue, (19) as the bard wrote:

> Let the inchained soul, shut up in darkness and in
>   signing,
> Whose face has never seen a smile in thirty weary
>   years,
> Rise and look out; his chains are loose...."
> For Empire is no more.... (20)

4.
Albion's Mills

With the union of William Blake, journeyman engraver, and Catherine Boucher, a market gardener's daughter, one discovers again a child-likeness, both in husband and wife. Married in 1782, she was six years younger than he, and illiterate, as were most girls of her class. Hearing him recount the story of his jilted love of another, when Blake asked, "Do you pity me?", she replied affirmatively; whereupon he said, "Then I love you." The two would share a belief in his visions, and in his astonishing intuitions and insights, and he would teach her to read and to write as she participated in the production of his Illuminated Books as if these were their own children to be defended and protected once he'd invented the process for producing them. Catherine Boucher, or Kate, as her husband called her, to his Will, was the one person who never doubted him. His youngest brother, Robert, also adopted his older brother's artistic preoccupations; the elder teaching the younger to be a draughtsman, and he was good enough to enroll in the Royal Academy School after his brother, and became a familiar presence in their household after their wedding at St. Mary's Church, Battersea.

In 1784 Blake brought a heavy, wooden, five-star handle rolling press, together with James Parker, his senior by seven years, who also had apprenticed with Basire, and they established an engraving and print selling shop. Parker was exceptional at mezzotint, Blake a master of line engraving, with the two sharing an interest in British Gothic and antiquity. The partners and Catherine divided the first-floor apartment above the shop, until the Blake's rented their own flat just around the corner. With the war in America ended and peace with France, prosperity was on the ascendency in Britain. Print selling was then a lucrative trade, with new shops opening throughout London, and all commentary agrees, the main pre-occupation of the business was sales from an of inventory of prints. Shop hours were between six in the morning until nine in the evening, and William or Catherine could be found behind the counter at "Parker and Blake". The time he could devote to his creative work as it became his ongoing concern, therefore, would have to been late in the night.

The partnership with Parker was not long-lasting, however, and when they amiably parted, Blake kept the rolling press and Parker the inventory of prints and the shop. The press standing at five feet and weighing seven hundred pounds, was cumbersome, and whenever it need be moved had to be disassembled, but still would require the assistance of three other men besides Blake to move it.

Robert Blake, a consumptive, died in the first days of February 1787, at age nineteen. His brother sat at his bedside nursing him through the illness, and when he died, slept three days and nights as if it had been his rite of passage. This perhaps was the first of numerous death-bed scenes that would figure over the years in Blake's illuminated prints, he telling of observing his brother's spirit at the moment of death, ascending through the ceiling "clapping his hands for joy." (1) Blake would converse daily with his brother's spirit; he writing, "I See him in my remembrance in the regions of my Imagination", adding, "I hear his advise & even now write from his Dictate."

In these years Blake and his wife came under the influence

of the theological doctrines espoused by Emanuel Swedenborg; a Swede who had been a distinguished scientist and engineer, gaining an international reputation for his work in metallurgy, on the smelting of iron and copper. In his middle-age, Swedenborg experienced an intense bout of dreaming, while having a vision of Jesus who revealed to him that the last judgement had taken place in 1757, incidentally the year of Blake's birth, and that it was his dispensation to establish a *New Jerusalem Church* to replace the existing Christian churches. Publishing his experiences and views prolifically, among his most significant works were *Arcana Coelestia* and *Heaven and Hell*, he attracting a following with his writings. Blake and his wife attended a five-day conference under the auspices of the Swedenborgian church in April 1789, passing under an inscription at the entrance to the building, 'NOW IT IS ALLOWABLE'; words the mystic had seen in a vision.

Swedenborg believed angels and devils had an actual physical presence on the earth, and like Blake, that the spirit of the deceased rose from the body to reassume physical form in another world, and had himself died in London in 1772. But like all influences, Blake would grapple with, ultimately, he would use Swedenborg's theological fancies for his own ends, demonstrating a preoccupation rather with elucidating ideas into philosophical maxims. Although not a philosopher, Blake expressed himself with a precision many might envy, the key to which for him was 'Poetic Genius'. In one of the first of the prints made with an innovative development in printing to include both text and illustrative designs as a single process, Blake expressed this conception. Titled *All Religions are One*, it was—

> The Poetic Genius is the true Man, and...the body or outward form of Man is derived from the Poetic Genius.... As all men are alike in outward form, so (and

with the same infinite variety) all are alike in the Poetic
Genius.... The Religions of all Nations are derived from
each Nation's different reception of the Poetic Genius....
As all men are alike (tho' infinitely various), So all
Religions &, as all similars, have one source. The true
Man is the source, he being the Poetic Genius. (2)

Blake's radicalism was always strikingly imbued with
spiritual and millenarian impulses such as those Swedenborg
professed, and soon afterward he began reading Jacob
Boehme, the 17th century German philosopher and mystic, but
this was the closest he would ever come to joining an
organized group, if indeed he and Catherine were not
members at the time.

Boehme, spelled Behmen in England, was perhaps among
the most significant intellectual influences on the development
of Blake's views. He had apprenticed and worked as a
shoemaker, writing his manuscripts by hand which were
copied by friends and circulated, the first being *Aurora* or *The
Rising Dawn* after experiencing a vision. In this way, perhaps
instructively for Blake, Boehme began to pierce the edges of
his obscurity. Considered a heretic by the orthodox Lutheran
theologians, he was threatened with exile if he persisted in his
"blasphemies" "smell[ing] of shoemaker's pitch and filthy
blacking." A deportment very much in consonance with Blake.

After Robert's death, his older brother became preoccupied with developing a method that could employ the three
distinct areas of his art—poetry, engraving, and water-
coloring; a process, moreover, that would be economical,
where on a single plate he could include the drawings of his
own hand together with his poetic works, and thus he would
have under his control every aspect of their publication. The
first of these coming to fruition was a series called *Songs of
Innocence* printed and illuminated in 1789. Reflecting the state

of childhood innocence disporting as wisdom, it contains titles like *Infant Joy* and *The Lamb*, as well as the first of Blake's chimney sweeper poems, and another, *The Little Black Boy* displaying Blake's acute sensibility against racial stereotyping and exploitation, making its debut in Britain that year as the anti-slave trade agitation. Blake wrote in his introduction of his expected audience:

> And I made a rural pen,
> And I stain'd the water clear,
> And I wrote my happy songs
> Every child may joy to hear.

Illuminated printing, the process settled upon by Blake, was a technique of relief etching, though not in itself new, he gave a distinctive application, that was unknown in England at the time. The result of intense deliberation and experimentation, it was obviously inspired by the illuminated books of the Medieval monks, but Blake would credit his brother Robert with the revelation in a dream of how he was to proceed.

Cutting a plate to receive his designs and writings out of a large copper plate, he then made it ready to be given to the work with hammer and chisel, filing the plates edges, and rounding its corners to prevent the edges from cutting into the paper once printed. Rather than etched into the plate, letters and images must be engraved, raising them from the surrounding metal. So, rough sketches were made with chalk, the script painted in mirror-image with a brush with acid-resistant inks and varnishes (something he had practiced from his earliest years as an apprentice). Blake referred to the nitric acid he would use to remove the metal as an "infernal

corrosive," it "...melting apparent surfaces away, and displaying the infinite which was hid." Words and images were made
to stand out now to a depth of approximately a thirty-second
of an inch. Various etching tools would then be applied to
impart detail, resolved under a lamp and magnifying glass.
The plate was now cleaned with vinegar to degrease the metal,
polished to a mirror finish, and finally lightly blackened with
a printer's ball, leaving deposits of ink in fine layers, until it
was built up sufficiently for printing, often using also blue,
brown or yellow.

The inked plates were then placed face down on the rolling
bed over a paper (Blake used paper hand-made from cotton or
rags) that was to receive the imprint. A dampened piece of
paper was placed on top over which was placed a thin layer of
cloth; the upper wooden roller then lowered to apply a
moderate pressure on the assemblage, the bed moving
smoothly between the rollers, where the star wheel which the
printer turns is connected to the upper-roller and is joined by
cog-wheels to the lower. Considerable strength was needed to
turn the wheel, and it must be grasped with both hands, the
operator gaining leverage by pushing hard against the floor or
the base of the machine.

With the plates lightly printed, the paper afterwards
received a wash of glue and water, and the figures and
illustrations given detail with ink, before being hand-painted
with color pigments mixed with carpenter's glue. Once
colored and detailed, and dried by hanging on a line strung
over the work area, the paper was punched and stitched and
bound within paper covers; every page unique, each a
spontaneous composition, the opposite of the trend prevalent
in the industry of Blake's day. Working his books up from
copper plates became the ideal for Blake in realizing his art,
wherein the unity of human vision was proclaimed, combing
the artist's conception with its technical execution.

In 1790, if not in the year following, Blake and his wife moved to 13 Hercules Road in Lambeth on the south side of the River Thames, on an access road to the Westminster Bridge, where they occupied a terraced cottage large enough to accommodate a studio and printing press on the ground floor, as well as affording them a garden with a fig tree and a vine, replete with marigold: the postal address, "Mr. William Blake, Engraver, Hercules Building, Westminster Bridge." They would reside there almost ten years, or till 1800.

Lambeth was still largely rural, but there was an almshouse and an asylum for orphaned girls, workshops of the Philanthropic Society, with some factories and a pottery works, with adjacent over-crowded housing. The famous (or infamous) Albion Mills, regarded as the finest steam-powered mill in the world and a model for the future, was nearby; and then, of course, so was Lambeth Palace, the official residence for the Archbishop of Canterbury.

In Lambeth, Blake would produce all of his striking Illuminated Books as well as composing his most enduring poetry, completing *The Marriage of Heaven and Hell, Visions of the Daughters of Albion, Songs of Experience, America, Europe,* and *The Book of Urizen.* He also fulfilling commissions, and work that is still known today; illustrations for Mary Wollstonecraft's *Original Stories,* and etchings for John Gabriel Stedman's *Narrative of a five years Expedition against the Revolted Negroes of Surinam, both* published by the bookseller Joseph Johnson. Blake's commercial work included engravings for such disparate subjects stylistically as the exotic flora for Erasmus Darwin's *The Botanic Garden,* and four urinary tract stones for James Earle's *Practical Observations on the Operation of the Stone.* The work on the illustrations for Stedman and Darwin are said to have supplied Blake with themes for his own work, as well as influencing motifs later used in his imagery and poetry, while the work for Earle's *Observations* was strictly utilitarian.

Albion Mills had been established on Blackfriars Road on the southeast corner of Blackfriars Bridge, with the mill facing out onto the river. With construction completed in 1786, it was the largest mill in the world in its time, designed by the architect Samuel Wyatt and executed by the Soho Manufactory run by Boulton, Watt & Co. of Birmingham, with some components coming from the manufactory of John Wilkinson. It employed two 50 horse power double acting steam-engines with rotary shafts to turn mill-stones—twenty pairs of them— each capable of processing 9 bushels of 'corn' (wheat or barley) per hour, and projected to produce 6000 bushels of flour each week. The engines also supplied power for sifting and fanning the corn, freeing it of impurities, while powering the machinery for dressing the meal and lowering it into barges. It was the most efficient mill yet achieved, capable of suppling the bakers and brewers of London with enough raw material to feed the entirety of the city's growing population, then getting their staple from bread and beer. The mill had a monopoly on flour production in London, and thus, its owners had control of the price of bread, as, coincidentally they ran the numerous wind-driven mills in Lambeth out of business.

Built at five stories, it loomed large over rooftops in the surrounding neighborhood, with its façade finished in neo-classical style with large Venetian windows having the elegance of a country manor. During its construction, the massive wheels and shafts, gears and pinions, and engines (all made of iron, cast iron or wrought iron, with an occasional gear still fashioned from hardwood, and the bearings of brass), were an impressive sight as they were winched up from barges and rigged into place by millwrights, attracting flocks of sightseers and crowds of dignitaries. Erasmus Darwin, one of the more discerning of these, called the assemblage "the most powerful machine in the world."

On the night of March 2, 1791, as a harbinger of the calamitous industrial career being embarked upon, a fire ignited in the interior of the building, and within an hour and a half had consumed it in entirety. Arson was first suspected, but in fact, it was determined that the owners, in order to realize their profit, were compelled to drive the machinery at such a pace that a bearing in one unit overheated, sparking the fire. The result, sublime as it was awful, was to remain scored in the memory of Londoners for years to come.

For its time Albion Mills exemplified the apex of a process begun decades before when an ironmonger from Dartmouth, Thomas Newcomen, invented a self-acting atmospheric engine to draw water up from coal mines in 1708. Driven on a huge timber mounted on a pivot to swing vertically through the arc of a circle, the end of the beam was attached to a piston, moving up and down as steam was injected, then condensed in a cylinder. This movement was transmitted from the beam to rods, drawing water by means of pumps and piping from the mineshaft. By 1765 there were nearly a hundred of these devices in the northern coal fields of England. (3) The consolidating era for these innovations, now called the "Industrial Revolution," was to take place in the span of years between the accession of George III in 1760 and that of his son William IV in 1830. The men who created this great conversion in the techniques of industry and trade in the 18th century, together, whether as associates or rivals gathering in taverns, coffee-houses, or any number of clubs, were mostly men from the artisan class, both Englishmen and Scots, and many were from 'Dissenting' backgrounds. Developments that both of our protagonists, Blake and Paine, were a part of, and without which neither could have had the profile or careers they subsequently did; nor indeed, could have Jean-Paul Marat, with a noted scientific/experimental career in optics and electricity, both in Britain and in France. "The age is running mad after innovations," Samuel Johnson, the lexicographer of English usage would say, "all the business of the world is to be done in a new way; Tyburn itself is not safe from the fury of innovation."

Marat published works on fire and heat, electricity, and light, as he published a well-regarded translation of Newton's *Opticks*. Seeking validation from the French Academy of Sciences for his experiments with fire, where he hypothesized it was not an element, as widely believed, but rather an "igneous fluid". The Academy endorsed his experimental methods, calling them "well-executed" and "appropriately and ingeniously designed," but said nothing about his conclusion.

Drawing the disapproval of Antoine Lavoisier, the Academy would disavow this indorsement, as a few of its members took umbrage at Marat, including Condorcet and Laplace. In his experiments with light, Marat contended that it bends around objects, not as Newton maintained by refraction, but by diffraction. Light shown through an aperture split into its components, or colors, not in the prism, but at the edges of the aperture itself. Marat also demonstrating there were only three primary colors, and not seven as Newton had argued. Again, a commission assigned to judge the validity of Marat's experiments and of his conclusions, wrote in its report "...they do not appear to us to prove what the author believes they establish."

Some have regarded these judgements as slights that would later excite in the ardent researcher an animus toward authority. In his journalism during the revolutionary years beginning in 1789 in France, he was to be noteworthy for his fierceness of tone, and uncompromising stance.

Somewhat before Newcomen's machine, a great innovation in the production of iron came with the substitution of coke for charcoal. The sulfur content in coke had rendered wrought-iron unusable until 1709, when Abraham Darby, a Quaker who owned a brass foundry, decided to substitute iron for brass. Iron-ore was smelted and poured in a molten state into "pigs", then re-melted and poured into castings, making cast-iron, or was passed on to forges, where it was heated and hammered into wrought iron. Darby began producing a superior pig-iron smelted with coke, a success attributable to the low sulfur content of the coal at hand. This eventually led, in suitable coalfields, to the spread of foundries and furnaces, as in turn wrought iron began to be substitutable for cast iron in many uses.

Intermediate between these metals is steel, made by placing pieces of wrought iron covered with charcoal and leaving it at high temperatures for many days. The result was blister steel, to be cut into small gads when cooled, then bundled and re-heated in a furnace. This steel was expensive to manufacture, and its use was confined to edge tools and implements, swords and guns, and the moving parts of clocks and watches.

Cast-iron is a hard, brittle metal and had good domestic uses in pots and pans; whereas wrought iron, because of its lower carbon content, is malleable, and thus, better able to withstand stress, and could be passed on to slitting mills to be drawn out into rods. At first this metal was used predominately in tools and utensils, picks and spades, wire and nails, bolts and horseshoes, chains, and locks. Nail manufactories found a ready market in America where wood houses were commonly being constructed.

By the 1740s, another Quaker, a clockmaker named Benjamin Huntsman, using small crucibles began producing a purer and more uniform steel. As production and specialization continued to proliferate, becoming scattered among various localities, roads for wheeled traffic and organized transport became requisite; spurring the development of commerce and credit, as an extensive coast-wise trade took hold, leading in turn to greater concentration and localization of industry. Many of the waterways in the North were widened and deepened, leading to the rise of new centers in salt and long-staple wool production, and in the metal trades.

With shipping greatly increasing, the importance of ports like Liverpool, with the rise of the slave-trade, displacing Bristol, and the newly risen manufacturing cities like Manchester, soaring in prominence. Most of the trade was still with countries nearest Britain, but fortunes had been made in East India, and in the slave and plantation markets of the West Indies, as that trade became the famous triangular traffic with its basis in black-skins, sugar, molasses and its concomitant product, rum. As the practice of selling shares in joint-stock companies increased, many merchants, manufacturers, and master mariners, mutually took an interest in the coast-wise and foreign trade. Britain became the leading exporter of firearms, textiles and hardware, and an importer of sugar, rum, coffee and tea; of cotton and silk, and the dyestuffs for textile industries. The lynch-pin of this trade was the slave-trade, spanning four centuries in Britain (1564-1808), and was directly attendant to the rise of empire.

Most capital at this nascent stage for "industrialization", as the new modes of production came to be called, was embodied, not in buildings and machinery, but in the stock of materials needed to carry on production and requiring only rudimentary labor processes. An owner was at once master manufacturer and merchant, the material of production transferring easily from trade to industry, from industry to trade.

This meant—as became requisite in a later period—that they had not fully undertaken the function of providing capital and bearing the risks. The laborer still might be the owner of tools, of the loom or the hammer and anvil; which for the laborer often meant the assumption of debt. Miners were engaged not only in extracting and drawing coal, but in delivering it to customers, and hence could only expect their pay when it was sold. In this way, in pin-making production was carried on by outworkers who employed other journey-men; as smiths, following the custom, paid their own hammer men; silk-weavers hired women to wind, and children to fill the quills for their shuttles. This led to a degraded form of apprenticeship, offering little or no training, compounded by overwork and ill-treatment.

In this era, if labor was hired for the long term, it was usually for a year or for the production cycle; but this at least was an assurance the laborer would not be impressed by the Crown's Forces, as they were called; a fate awaiting the more destitute, as there was a marked degree of beggary, of prostitution, of debt-peonage and vagabondage, than in the period after 1760. The system of social gradation of that earlier era—lord, freeholders, copyholders, lease-holders, cottagers (who cultivated a few strips, supplementing their income by hiring out)—was suitable for agricultural communities growing grain for subsistence and raising small numbers of livestock, but could not withstand the parceling out and enclosure of common fields taking place in England since the thirteenth century. The systematic fettering of persons in the feudal period, gradually gave way, under a less encumbered administration of agriculture with an increasing orientation toward markets.

Hedges, stone walls, rows of trees, fencing, was suitable on lands for pasturing; and much of this was tied to the production of wool and an expanding textile industry, and to the leather trades. But with enclosure had come concentration in the hands of landholders who were able to mortgage their estates and use the proceeds to buy new land. This meant, concomitantly, a 'freeing' of labor from the land, and the disappearance of the yeoman.

In this way, change came in increments, with many tributaries and contributing factors. The introduction of ponies into mining, meant boys could be exploited in place of men, reducing the cost of coal. An increased out-put in iron meant iron tubbing would allow shafts to descend to greater depths. In 1777 John Curr introduced iron rails in the pits around Sheffield, allowing loads to be brought direct to the surface without being unloaded at pit bottom. As methods for better ventilation improved, the output of coal rose again.

The basis on which the "infernal metals" industries, as Blake would characterize it, and on whose innovations his own experimental techniques were oriented, had founded their existence was coal. And as these became profligate, so too many other industries flourished. Iron production began reaching into every facet of industry and building, from shipbuilding to cannonry, from hardware to engineering. The demand for improved munitions, again, stimulated the building of iron furnaces, and for all the ancillary works. Now pig-iron was being re-heated and stirred with iron ladles to remove carbon and slag impurities before it was poured and passed through rollers to remove the remaining dross—an innovation pioneered by Henry Cort. In a very short time, production was being concentrated within large integrated facilities located in densely populated areas. Now the offspring of those later to be called the 'proletariat' would grow up amid pit-hills and slag-heaps; or be overworked in the lint bearing air of textile mills, while living in housing little more than jerry-built slums.

It was in 1765 that James Watt, an instrument maker and surveyor in Glasgow, after long pondering the proposition, and discussing it at length with university colleagues with which he was acquainted, resolved upon a solution for improving Newcomen's contrivance for pumping water. The problem lay in preventing the condensation of steam on the piston's upward stroke, while maintaining the temperature of the cylinder, and providing for it to cool on the return stroke; a quandary resulting in an exorbitant loss of potential energy. His solution was to introduce a condenser that would remain continuously cool, while the cylinder remained continuously hot. Within a few weeks, a model was ready which would pass through years of trial and experimentation. Finding a competent works with experienced artisans, Watt's workable steam engine would be the first complex mechanism to apply the methods of systematic scientific experimentation. Parenthetically it may be noted that William Blake was then eight, and would mature as these innovations were beginning to exert their dominance.

For many years the engine remained a single-acting device with a reciprocating stroke; however, with greatly increased efficiency over Newcomen's pump. Employed again in coal mines to remove water; it was also put to work in metal mines, in breweries and distilleries, at water reservoirs and at brine works. In the iron industry, Watt's engine was used to raise water to turn the great wheels to operate bellows, forge hammers, and rolling mills. A problem that remained—now to adopt its action to rotary movement to power machinery?

By 1781 Watt had invented a number of devices allowing for this enhanced latitude, and in the following year, a rotating engine was produced by applying the expansive force of steam to both sides of the piston alternately. Coming at the same time as Cort's innovations in iron making, the first engine in operation would be at the iron foundry of John Wilkinson, to work a hammer. A new form of power was now available to replace the brawn and the hands of men, of brute animals, and of water and wind.

But it was in the manufacture of textiles that the transformation based on the employment of machinery was to be most dramatic. A weaver-carpenter named James Hargreaves introduced an important change with the 'jenny' in the mid-1760's, allowing an operator to spin multiple threads at once, and eventually as many as eighty, thus allowing spinners to keep pace with weavers; an innovation that was rapidly adopted. In 1768 a patent was granted to a barber and wigmaker named Richard Arkwright, who, aided by a clockmaker named John Kay, produced the 'frame' using rollers to draw out the rovings before passing these to a spindle to make yarn suitable for warps. The jennies yarn had only been suitable for the weft, and now with its complement, the basis was set for weaving cheap calicoes. This necessitated large mills, the first of which, powered by water, was in operation by 1771, employing six hundred workers, most of them children. Finding the old methods of carding inadequate for production requirements, in 1775 Arkwright obtained a patent for carding by cylinders. New factories were to follow in Lancashire, Cheshire, Derbyshire, Nottinghamshire, Yorkshire, and North Wales, and by 1788 as many as 20,000 jennies were at work in England.

The next important innovation came in the mid-80's when a weaver, Samuel Crompton, produced a yarn suitable for both the weft and the warp, easily adaptable in making all sorts of textiles. His invention, called the 'mule', combined both the jenny and the frame. Watt's engine would soon be applied to spinning by rollers, and in 1790 it became possible, freed from the necessity of putting factories near water streams, to place them in towns. In the next decades, the growth of urban factories with their superior forms of organization and transportation links, would become standard, resulting in a boom in the number of workers employed, of both sexes and in a range of ages.

By mid-century to lower the costs of transport a system of canals had begun, the first dug in 1757. Requiring extended engineering for trenches, aqueducts, bridges, and tunnels; soon works were undertaken to connect centers of commercial activity to rivers, requiring more capital than could be raised privately. One of these, begun in 1767 and completed in 1777, passed through salt-mining and pottery manufacturing areas in Cheshire and Staffordshire, to connect the Mercy to the Trent, and so with the Humber. This enterprise was called the *Grand Trunk*; an endeavor in its construction resembling a military campaign. Pioneered by the engineer James Brindley, who had received no formal education, apprenticing as a millwright and wheelwright; the dig for the works penetrated the central ridge of England by the Harecastle Tunnel, and the Staffordshire and Worcestershire, the Coventry, the old Birmingham, and the Chesterfield canals; a network that covered 360 miles overall.

Parenthetically it is notable here that Matthew Boulton's Albion Mills was erected with capital raised by City financiers, that included the organ player and composer Joah Bates, who had put up all of his own money, and 10,000 pounds belonging to his wife.

Albion Mills was less than a ten-minute walk from the abode of William Blake, and he passed by it every time he crossed the Blackfriars Bridge. With the conflagration beginning at night and at low tide, making it difficult for the fire-engines to battle it, a large swarm of spectators gathered, drawn to the fiery glow as they were transfixed by the sight of such spectacular flames. With displaced millers celebrating on the bridge, with none lending a hand to contain the blaze as was customary, as they became unruly and fights broke out, the fire brigades were compelled to turn their hoses on the crowd. One of those attracted to the scene, walking among the flock that lined Blackfriars Bridge was a sixteen-year-old Robert Southey, still a student at Westminster School, to become one of the noted members of the "lake poets", together with Wordsworth and Coleridge, to whom he became brother-in-law.

Noting there were groups of displaced millers dancing in jubilation by the light of the flames, Southey's account suggests that ballads celebrating the mill's destruction were already being improvised by the break of day among those loitering on the bridge, as that night during the conflagration a placard had been on display that read, "Success to the mills of Albion, but no Albion Mills." (4) A ballad printed only a week later reiterated the theme:

> And now the folks begin to shout,
> Hear the rumours they did this and that.
> But very few did sorrow show
> That the Albion Mills were burnt so low.

The final throes came when the structure's roof collapsed sending a plume of debris, with cinder and ash, spiraling into the night sky, falling across the river as far away as St. James Park. On the night of the fire, a southwesterly breeze may have carried smoke and ash overhead, as flames may even have been visible through Blake's upper windows, perhaps dancing in his eyes and across his forehead, as against the far wall of the cottage. At any rate, he alluded to it in what has become Britain's unofficial anthem referred to as *Jerusalem,* but is in Blake's poem titled *Milton*:

> And did the Countenance Divine
> Shine forth upon our clouded hills?
> And was Jerusalem builded here,
> Among these dark Satanic Mills?

In the distance were two hills, Highgate and Hampstead, shrouded in London's sooted air.

With the Albion Mills' destruction, five shuttered mills were restored to business; the ruined mill would stand a charred shell until demolished in 1809.

5.

Awake the thunders
of the deep!

Days after the storming of the Bastille in Paris, *The World*, a newspaper issuing in London, commented on the similarity of that extraordinary event to that in their own city against Newgate and the other prisons, where "all the prisoners were set at liberty". With the storming of its prisons, as noted had been remarked at the time, such would have been inconceivable in a city so well policed and lighted as Paris, and the incident led to the establishment of a regular municipal police force throughout the greater city of London. Now prison breaking from the outside by the teeming multitudes had become *a tale of two cities*.

The events ushered in by the fall of the Bastille on July 14th of that year, as is well studied, had been occasioned by a crisis to deal with the over-weening governmental indebtedness—brought on by the expenses incurred in the American War for Independence, as previously with the Seven Year's War (a European war largely fought as a global rivalry between Britain and France from 1756 to 1763), as also by the profligate spending of the court, and finally, by the government's attempt to impose an onerous taxation scheme to restore its financial status. The burden was to fall on the commoners, the *Tiers État* (3rd estate)—or the vast majority of the population (the bourgeoisie, the small shop owners, the artisans and laborers, and the peasantry)—with the 1st estate, the clergy, exempt from taxation, and 2nd, the nobility, mostly exempted. The majority of the populous, particularly the poor, were harried too by the effects of several years when harvests had been deficient on account of drought and unusually cool weather, when privation became widespread due both to a dearth and to a dearness of grain. With turmoil in Paris and other urban centers, there was sustained outcry.

To manage the situation Jacques Necker, a Swiss-born diplomat and financial expert, had been appointed Comptroller-General of Finance in 1786, recommending since the tax system was already extremely regressive, subjecting the lower classes to excessive burden, that some of the tax exemptions for the clergy and nobility be reduced. Dismissed by the King, Necker was retained for the moment as his financial adviser. But as a goodly number of the educated were aware, many of them lawyers among the 3rd estate, they too possessed rights. Led by these, and influenced by writers with *Enlightenment* ideas with its trifecta of Rousseauite themes—liberty and equality, and, to be added somewhat later, fraternity—pamphleteers and publishers had charged the public into an opposition; an opposition that the monarchy in turn tried to suppress.

To allay the growing crisis the King called for the convocation of the *Estates General* in May 1789, recommended by the *Assembly of Notables* in 1787 (nobles, ecclesiastics, and state functionaries summoned by the King to consult on matters of state), something that had not been done since early in the previous century.

On May 5, the Estates-General convened at Versailles, listening to a three-hour speech by Necker. But Necker's creditability was diminished as he was long on financial data, when many had expected him to detail a reform policy. With the conclave quickly devolving into heated wrangling over credentials and over voting procedures, the 3rd estate moved to establish a National Assembly, inviting like-minded members from the 1st and 2nd estates to join them; as, however, they made it clear they were prepared to conduct the nation's business without them. Louis XVI now ordered the closing of the hall where the Estates-General had been meeting. In a heady atmosphere, the designated National Assembly convened at the nearest readily available location, a tennis court, where they swore an oath not to separate until they had given France a constitution, as the majority of the clergy now joined them, along with 47 members of the nobility.

Continuing to meet per their oath, on July 9 the Assembly became the *National Constituent Assembly* and were duly, if ruefully, acknowledged by the King. With the press publishing the Assembly's debates, political meetings had spread throughout Paris, the cafes in the garden of Palais-Royal, the palace of the duc d' Louis-Philippe Orléans, the king's cousin, becoming the preferred site for ongoing gatherings. Then, on the Assembly's authority, the Abbaye prison was opened to release some half dozen grenadiers of the *Gardes Françaises,* (French Guards) imprisoned days before for refusing to fire on crowds. With the flashpoint of insurrection reached, the Assembly stepped back, recommending clemency to the King, as the prisoners were returned to the prison to await a royal pardon.

On July 11, the Assembly was presented with a draft of the "Declaration of the Rights of Man and Citizen" stewarded by Abbé Sieyès and the Marquis de la Fayette, in consultation, among others, with Thomas Jefferson who was in Versailles as the American minister to France, and the comte de Honoré Mirabeau who'd become the fulcrum for the bourgeoisie for his oratory in the deliberations of the assembly. Laureled for assisting the American rebels in their fight for independence against the British government and Crown, and as a member of the 2nd estate, Lafayette had joined the concave, as had the vast majority of the Assembly, as had Mirabeau, a constitutional monarchist, and were to play a prominent role in guiding the initial stages of what is universally designated *The French Revolution*.

The Declaration was a litany of *Enlightenment* precepts, closely paralleling some of the founding documents of the American republic, particularly the *Bill of Rights* published by the Virginia colony and the *Declaration of Independence,* whose experience culminating in independence and a new nation in the earlier part of the decade was seen to have opened the way for France's own transformation. Introduced by a preamble describing fundamental rights as being "natural, unalienable and sacred", consisting of "simple and incontestable principles"; in the second article (there were 26 articles in the draft, reduced to 17 in the completed text), "the natural and imprescriptible rights of man" are defined as "liberty, property, security and resistance to oppression." The Declaration asserted the principle of popular sovereignty, in contradistinction to the divine right of kings, and social equality among citizens. Surely it would be responded to as grounding for *Insurrection* by an absolutist monarch.

On the day the Declaration was published, Necker was dismissed and banished by the King when he refused to attend his speech to the Estates-General, that is, of those who had not joined the National Constituent Assembly. The conservative Baron de Breteuil now stood in Necker's place, as Marshal Broglie was recalled from Alsace to head the Ministry of War. The King then ordered 25,000 troops, half of them dreaded foreign mercenaries, the Swiss and Hessians, to positions in Versailles and in Paris, as troops were dispatched to protect the Royal Treasury, and some of the strategic bridges such as the Sevres and St. Cloud were militarily occupied.

On July 12, with crowds gathering throughout central Paris, more than 10 thousand of the Parisian multitude converged on Palais-Royal in demonstrations displaying the busts of Necker and of Louis Philippe II, Duke of Orléans, who had become a persuasive advocate of constitutional monarchy. Marching from Palais-Royal through the theatre district, then continuing along the boulevards, they were run into and dispersed by a Royal German Cavalry Regiment between the Place Vendome and the Tuileries Palace. Another charge by French cavalry dispersed the remaining protesters.

But some among those gathering earlier at the Palais-Royal had not been a part of the demonstration; no more than a thousand, most of them artisans from the Parisian faubourg's with many women among them, and with some deserting soldiers. In a cafe in the garden of the Palais-Royal frequented by political dissidents, a young journalist and lawyer, Camille Desmoulins, a boyhood friend of the still unknown lawyer Maximillian Robespierre, and an ally and confidant of the lawyer Georges Danton, soon to be a rising politician and patriot, leapt upon a table, exclaiming: "Citizens, there is no time to lose; the dismissal of Necker is the knell of a Saint Bartholemew for patriots! This very night all the Swiss and German battalions will leave the Champ de Mars to massacre us all; one resource is left, to take arms!"

Desmoulins further urged that all present adopt a cockade

by which they might know one another. Because of its association with liberty the color green was chosen, as many pulled leaves from the boughs of the numerous horse-chestnut trees ready to hand. But very soon this was to give way in favor of the colors of Paris—blue and red.

Desmoulins' words quickly spread through the faubourgs of Paris, as the shops of armorers and ordinary stores were broken into and looted for arms, for supplies, and for food. Blamed for the high price of bread and of wine, 40 of 54 customs posts were looted and destroyed, as Royal officials were chased from the city. With plundering continuing through the night, rumor circulated that there was a large horde of grain at Saint-Lazare, a property of the Catholic Church functioning as a convent, hospital, and school. Descended upon by tumultuous crowds, 52 wagon loads of wheat was seized, to be wheeled to a public market for distribution.

On the morning of July 13, the electors of Paris, meeting at the municipal hall, the Hôtel de Ville, agreed to the recruitment of a "Bourgeois militia" of 48,000 to act as police to restore order. This body was to be raised by sending agents to the churches throughout the various sections of Paris, with each to contribute 200 volunteers as the nucleus of a citizen militia. With the defection of two regiments of the French Guard, the popular cause acquired a trained military contingent.

The next morning, learning from these soldiers where a large number of arms had been stored, delegates were sent to negotiate their transfer to arm the new militia. That site was the *Hôtel des Invalides*, a complex of buildings, monuments and museums, some housing military archives, among whose cellars were stockpiled up to 30,000 muskets, together with cannons. The commander at the *Invalides*, meeting with a delegation, declined to negotiate their removal. As he retired, the first determined attack by elements of the Parisian revolutionary multitude struck, marshalling their assault under a blue and red banner, and armed with pikes, scythes, pruning hooks, and swords, with some carrying pistols and muskets.

As the opposition tendered was negligible, arms were seized and distributed to those on hand, as wagons were loaded and five cannons were wheeled out to the street. With a body of foreign troops encamped only 400 yards away, and unwilling or hesitant to initiate a massacre, regiments with local ties remained confined to their barracks. For the moment, it was evident the Royal military leadership had abandoned central Paris.

The arms, however, were of no use without powder and shot, and it was how learned for safe keeping 250 barrels of gunpowder had been removed from the Hôtel des Invalides a few days before, to the Bastille. As this became known the cry was heard, "To the Bastille!"

The Bastille was a fortification built during the 13th century at a time of extended war with the English, and was intended to keep them out of Paris. Already 400 years old, its eighty feet high walls, with eight crenelated towers, loomed like a colossus in the midst of the "working-class" or "sans-culotte" Faubourg Saint-Antoine. Housing only a small garrison comprised of Swiss-mercenary troops with 18 cannons, its primary use had been as a prison, with a small number of political prisoners held at the King's pleasure. Before his death in 1778 at age 83, Voltaire had twice been imprisoned there, and only ten days before the aristocrat known under the nom-de-plum as the Marquis de Sade had been among its inmates, which included four long-time forgers and an Irishman who should have been committed to bedlam. The notorious and profane De Sade himself had been transferred, leaving behind in his cell the manuscript-roll of his masterpiece, he now presumed lost, *One Hundred and Twenty Days of Sodom*.

Brandishing the weapons available to them, and with several cannons in tow, the Parisian multitude arrived outside the fortress about 11 in the morning. Fewer than a thousand persons in all, they consisted mostly of artisans from the neighborhood, with some regular army deserters, with one of the categories among them given numerical weight being wine merchants. There would be 21 on the list later complied of the *vainqueurs de la Bastille* (conquerors of the Bastille), a distinction to which Dickens drew attention in his novel about London and Paris published in 1859: *A Tale of Two Cities*.

Deputations were sent to speak with the commander, the Marquis de Launay, a proud, authoritarian officer, who, those looking on hoped, might acquiesce as had the commander at Hôtel des Invalides. These talks lasted from the time of arrival until early afternoon, when access to the Bastille courtyard was gained through a half-raised drawbridge. At that point, De Launay ordered his troops fire, and a brief engagement with the populace commenced where ninety-eight attackers and one defender were killed. An eye witness to the incidents made indelible on that occasion, Thomas Jefferson, was to offer his vivid rendition to the acting American Secretary of State, John Jay, in a letter scored with the numerals of that famous day in 1789:

> ...the people rushed against the place, and almost in an instant were in possession of a fortification, defended by 100 men, of infinite strength, which in other times had stood several regular sieges and had never been taken. How they got in, has as yet been impossible to discover. Those, who pretend to have been of the party tell so many different stories as to destroy the credit of them all.
>
> They took all the arms, discharged the prisoners and such of the garrison as were not killed in the first

moment of fury, carried the Governor and Lieutenant Governor to the Greve (the place of public execution) cut off their heads, and set them through the city in triumph to the Palais Royal. (1)

The murder and decapitation of De Launay came by a blade brandished by an unemployed baker, the single culprit often cited, whom the elderly man had lashed out at, trying to kick him in the groin. A deed that worked through the night with powerful effect on the whole aristocratic party, and that formed a conviction in the King that he must "seize the principal members of the Estates-General," and "march the whole army down upon Paris and to suppress its tumults by the sword."

"But at night," as Jefferson reported in his letter—"the Duke de Liancourt forced his way into the king's bedchamber, and obliged him to hear a full and animated detail of the disasters of the day in Paris. He went to bed deeply impressed." The stunned monarch, asking if it was a revolt, the reply came, "No sire, it is a revolution."

The next day, July 15, as all could see, nothing stood as it had before. Louis XVI's dismissal of Necker had ushered in a startling train of events, as in the subsequent days, Lafayette was appointed commander-in-chief of the "Bourgeois" militia, to be renamed the *National Guard*. At the same time the municipality, renamed Commune de Paris, was to be headed by a newly selected mayor, Jean Sylvain Bailly, replacing Jacques de Flesselles, assassinated the previous day. Bailly, a famed astronomer and mathematician and member of the *French Academy of Sciences* since 1763, had also been the presiding figure at the *Tennis Court Oath*, now decreed the Bastille be torn down, as its demolition had indeed already begun, and almost immediately construction companies assisted by ordinary people drawn from the unemployed and soldiers were strenuously engaged in the gargantuan task.

In another letter dated 16 July, Jefferson offered this striking vignette to his superior:

> The king came to Paris, leaving the queen in consternation for his return.... The king's carriage was in the center, on each side of it the States general, in two ranks, afoot, at their head the Marquis de la Fayette as commander in chief, on horseback, and Bourgeois guards before and behind.
>
> About 60,000 citizens of all forms and colours, armed with the muskets of the Bastille and Invalids as far as they would go, the rest with pistols, swords, pikes, pruning hooks, scythes &c. lined all the streets thro' which the procession passed, and, with the crowds of people in the streets, doors and windows, saluted them everywhere with cries 'vive la nation.' But not a single 'vive le roi' was heard. The king landed at the Hôtel de Ville. There, Monsieur Bailly presented and put into his hat the popular cockade, and addressed him. The king being unprepared and unable to answer, Bailly went to him, gathered from him some scraps of sentences, and made out an answer, which he delivered to the Audience as from the king. (2)

At the suggestion of Lafayette, the cockade given the King had changed: it now became the tri-color, with the addition of royal white between the Parisian colors blue and red. The French nation had gained its symbol.

As news of the successful revolution rapidly spread, in accord with its principle of "popular sovereignty", parallel structures for the governance of municipalities and for the new militia were established in cities and towns across France. Two days after the fall of the Bastille the court of St. James' ambassador to France, John Frederick Sackville, 3rd Duke of

Dorset, was able to report emphatically to Secretary of State for Foreign Affairs Francis Osborne, 5th Duke of Leeds:

> Thus, my Lord, the greatest revolution that we know anything of has been effected with comparatively speaking—if the magnitude of the event is considered— the loss of very few lives. From this moment we may consider France as a free country, the King a very limited monarch, and the nobility as reduced to a level with the rest of the nation. (3)

Having its antecedent in the poor harvest of the previous year, starting that day and lasting into early August, a wave of incendiarism fueled by mass anxiety spread across the French countryside. Called *la Grande Peur* (the Great Fear); with grain shortages endemic, rumors that bandits were burning grain, or alternately that a foreign army was destroying crops in the fields, caused peasants to congregate and to begin arming themselves. Given impetus by these rumors, along with long-standing grievances, peasants began directing their protests at the basis of the feudal system, in many cases attacking manor houses, and burning deeds of title.

The alarm came first in the Franche-Comté, spreading along the Rhône Valley south to Provence, traveling east to the Alps, and then counter-wise to the west, into central France. Almost simultaneously, revolts had been sparked in desperate far-flung places and were including in its ranks those classes that had risen against the feudal regime in the cities. As the target became the seigneurs, there was little doubt as to the source of the contagion: there had been a rise in defaults on leases, as demands were made for the reclaiming of tithes and of grain; for the cancellation of harvest payments, and for the restoration of grazing rights.

Responding with alacrity and in an atmosphere verging on hysteria, on August 4 the National Constituent Assembly announced that the feudal system was abolished "in its entirety", adopting 18 decrees concerning the feudal estate between the night of the 4th and the 11th; as the tithes gathered by the clergy, and the seigneurial rights of the nobility, were abolished. Mirabeau, whose venality would soon leave his reputation in tatters, described the night of August 4 as an "orgy" wherein the liberal nobles in the Assembly, as was he, had surrendered the legal rights of their class "with a kind of rapturous enthusiasm, naturally startl[ing] France and the rest of the world." (4) For his part, Mirabeau's stewardship was intended to devolve France along the path of constitutional monarchy as practiced in Britain, but as with most politicians, Mirabeau was a compromised figure, and the events of July/August had a scope and import reaching far beyond his maneuvering.

In the course of two months, the entire edifice of the *ancient régime* had largely been swept asunder, rendering a new basis for personal, social, civil, and national associations: Equality of legal punishment, admission of all to public office, freedom of worship, abolition of venality in office. As game-laws were abolished, as were seigneurial courts, favoritism in taxation, and the purchase and sale of posts in the magistracy.

The decisive groundwork for the parturition of a new society, a bourgeois society, was laid on August 26, as the National Constituent Assembly decreed the *Declaration of the Rights of Man and of the Citizen*. Arrived at after intense and continuous debate shepherded by Honore Mirabeau; it encapsulated in a single document the achievements of the Revolution, enshrining equality before the law rather than the system of privileges; making judicial procedures paramount over the abuses of the King such as *letter de cachet* (summary notice of imprisonment); as it transferred political power from the monarchy and the privileged estates, to the general body of propertied male citizens.

The *Declaration* was an attack on the basis of the entire monarchical regime, as indeed, it was seen to recapitulate the whole philosophic movement called the Enlightenment, as manifest in France in the writings of Montesquieu, Voltaire and Jean-Jacques Rousseau among others, as if these too had collaborated in its creation.

Montesquieu (1689-1755) had extended the methods of classification to the political forms of society, securing the word "despotism" in the political lexicon as he became the theorist of the "separation of powers". Voltaire (1694-1778), prolific as a writer of plays, novels, essays and of scientific works, above all today is noted as an outspoken satirical polemicist. He was an advocate of "freedom of religion" and "freedom of speech", as he promoted "the separation of church and state". Jean-Jacques Rousseau (1712-1778), was a Genevan and a writer and composer and author of seminal works on political philosophy. His *Principes du droit politique* and *Du Contrat Social* formed the foundation in Enlightenment political and social thought during the French Revolution; as his novel *Julie, ou la Nouvelle Héloïse* was of importance in the development of the novel; as *Emilé, ou De L'Education* was his widely read treatise on education; and whose *Confessions* would initiate the literary genre of autobiography.

In the wake of the triumphs of July and August, particularly in Paris, the activities of journalists and pamphleteers proliferated, with leaflets and brochures, often with a friable existence, springing up on every side. In May and June, Camille Desmoulins had written his pamphlet *La France Libre*, which his publisher had refused to print. But after the storming of the Bastille with his crucial instigation, it was issued July 18, and what he espoused was considerably in advance of current opinion. Calling for a republic, he wrote, "...popular and democratic government is the only constitution which suits France, and all those who are worthy of the name of men." Desmoulins' fame as a pamphleteer was again enhanced with the publication in September of *Discours de la lantern aux Parisiens*, which used as an epigraph a quotation from the *Gospel of St. John*, "He who does evil hates the light." This was an allusion to the iron bracket of a lamppost at the corner of the *Place de Greve* used as a rough-and-ready-gallows for aristocrats, anti-revolutionaries, and profiteers. Celebrating political violence, the discourse was written from the perspective of the lamppost, extolling the motives of the multitude by whose hands the executions were carried out. Desmoulins became known as the *Procureur-general de la lantern* (lantern prosecutor).

With a singular brashness of attitude, Jean-Paul Marat launched his *L 'Ami du Peuple* on September 16. Professing independence as he avowed a genuine concern for the "poor and oppressed", he won a broad following among the Parisian *sans-culotte*. The first edition of the paper demanded all nobles be expelled from the Assembly; the second directed its aim against bourgeois bankers and financiers who "build their fortunes atop the ruination of others." He ran furious assaults against Necker, who had been recalled by the King after the perceived disaster on 14 July, and against Bailly, as against Lafayette. Of all the presses that sprang up, Marat's became the most widely read in Paris, as its many hawkers were heard giving its cry in the streets; the "friend of the people" became a synonym for the author and publisher.

The eight octavo pages usually constituting it was made almost completely from critique and comment on current events. It was in fact, more a bi-weekly pamphlet than a newspaper, but there was no dearth of matter being offered, so that it was often expanded to twelve and sometimes sixteen pages. The only part not written by Marat were letters received from victims of "official tyranny", which he edited, presenting the pith of their substance. Marat later remarked:

> I regularly employ six to receive the complaints of the crowd, to read and reply to a multitude of letters, to overlook the publication of a work I have in the press, to take notes of all the interesting events of the Revolution, to receive denunciations, to assure myself of the bonnafides of the denunciators, and finally to bring out my paper. (5)

Marat was of Swiss birth (then a part of Prussia), but French speaking; the family name was Mara indicating a Semitic north African origin, to which he added the letter "t" to give it a French identification. His literary career began in 1772 with a pamphlet written in English while he lived in Britain titled *The Chains of Slavery*. "I am about to retrace the slow and continuous efforts," Marat wrote of his object, "which, bending little by little the head of the people under the yoke, causes them at last to be lost, together with the strength and desire to shake it off." (6) It was to be self-published and distributed by him to various societies throughout the north of England and in Edinburgh, and to be published in France in 1793.

With almost twelve years residence in England, he arrived there in 1765 to establish his medical practice (he became a specialist in the treatment of eye ailments), after pursuing study in France, also taking an active interest in experimental physics, as it was then practiced. He came in contact with Joseph Priestley, the chemist and co-discoverer of oxygen, at the Warrington Academy where Priestley taught and was active. Priestley, as was his French colleague, was an uncompromising freethinker, and a "republican" who'd been educated in philosophy, science, languages, and literature.

Returning to France, early in the decade Marat would gain a high reputation in scientific circles and as a court physician, as well as being a great friend of ladies. (7) Fabre d' Eglantine, a playwright who became active in the Cordeliers and Jacobin clubs, and the private secretary of Danton, described Marat (as entered in Ernst Belford Bax's *Jean-Paul Marat),* as about five feet in height. Without being stout, his figure was firm, his shoulders broad, the lower portion of his frame, lank; his arms strong, his legs short and bowed. When walking Marat was described as having a determined, confident stride, often with his arms firmly crossed over his chest. Withal, he was said to have carried himself with vigor and grace.

Marat's head, for which there is good portraiture, was of pronounced character, which he carried on a short neck, with a large bony face with aquiline nose, its underpart prominent, his forehead large. His lips curled at one corner by constant contraction and were thin; his eyes yellowish-gray, but piercing when animated, at other times appearing soft, even gracious; his hair, brown. In the years of the Revolution, a change would come over his appearance, as he sacrificed his health, his rest, and his means. His complexion became thick and withered, his eyebrows thin, his hair neglected; his voice, sonorous and slightly hoarse. No longer sprucely attired, he was disheveled in dress.

Harassed and subjected to particular scrutiny by Lafayette's police, Marat would buy his own press to relieve his sheets from the inconvenience of relying on printers who could be pressured or bribed to undercut him. As his pen made him the target of enemies, and he periodically became subject to arrest, as in October and November 1789, he was forced into hiding. Making his habitat in the sewers and catacombs of Paris, he contracted the skin disease he suffered from in the last years of his life, as his body reeked from the ailment.

To some extent by September 1789 the political position of the monarchist and conservatives in the Assembly began to improve. With 400 deputies, they began working to transfer the proceedings of the assembly to the distant royalist city of Tours, situated on the lower portion of the Loire River between Orléans and the Atlantic coast. And they had been able to secure veto power for the King regarding any legislative act he might oppose.

On September 18, Louis XVI issued a formal statement giving his approval to some of the measures in the August decrees, with the possibility he might renege on them altogether; as there was growing anticipation, with the increasing presence of royal troops, he might be emboldened to dissolve the assembly.

In late September, the Flanders Regiment was ordered to Versailles, and as these arrived on October 1, they were given what was described as a lavish welcoming banquet in the Opera House by the officers of the royal guard. With the royal couple attending briefly—walking among the tables that had been set up for the occasion, and with the boxes filled with spectators from the Court—inebriated officers offered toasts and oaths of fealty to the sovereign. And as these grew more demonstrative, other officers sought to join in.

In the intervening weeks, to break the growing political deadlock in the Assembly between Royalists and Constitution-alists, as to bring relief to a people verging on starvation, orators at the Palais-Royal had been broaching the notion of a march on Versailles. An idea that was being reiterated by the choir of agitators in the streets. In the next days, as the scene with the Flanders Regiment was reported in *L 'Ami du Peuple* and in other papers, it was with the elaboration that there had been a gluttonous orgy at Versailles in which the tricolor cockade was scornfully desecrated under the boots of those professing allegiance solely to the white cockade of the House of Bourbon.

On the morning of October 5 without any pre-concerted plan, at the edge of the market where *les poissardes* sold their fish in the Faubourg Saint Antoine in the eastern section of Paris where the Bastille had stood, a girl struck a drum. Seemingly spontaneously the market-women began to stream out of their stalls to commiserate with one another, many carrying long knives for gutting and scaling fish in hand. Incensed by the chronic shortage of bread and at its exorbitant price, at a nearby church they demanded the bells be tolled. Compelled by unremitted hunger, and by the number of women continuing to join them, they began marching through the abutting neighborhoods, compelling each church in-turn to sound the tocsin.

Taking up make-shift weapons as they came, and brandishing their knives, with some men dressed in women's clothing joining them, they converged by the thousands on the Hôtel de Ville to demand bread and arms. With revolutionary agitators circulating in their midst, one of whom was an audacious figure popular among the market-women, and already well known as a leading *vainqueurs* of the Bastille, Stanislas-Marie Maillard—they confronted the municipal authorities. A former soldier and bailiff's clerk, Maillard would earn the nickname *Tape Dur* (hit hard) for the leading role he played in the major *journées* of the French Revolution. Faced with a multitude approaching six thousand, the stores of grain and food in the Hôtel de Ville were thrown open to them. Seizing these, along with weapons and powder, the women now threatened the building with incendiarism. At that moment, Maillard prevailed, winning a leadership role among them.

It was now everyone's understanding they would continue with a march to Versailles, till then only inchoate, to bring their plight to the King's attention. Versailles was thirteen miles down the road, so they might expect to arrive that afternoon.

To assure order, by acclamation Maillard deputized dozens of women to act as group leaders, and in driving rain, Maillard and his deputies began leading the marchers out of the city. As these set out, hundreds of National Guardsmen had begun assembling at the Place de Greve, adjacent the Hôtel de Ville, and began insisting that they too should join the marchers to Versailles. Without provoking their mutiny, and to manage them, Lafayette was enjoined by the Parisian municipal authorities to ride before them so as to guide their movements, as their number had grown to several thousands. He was also instructed to request of the king that he return voluntarily to Paris to assuage *his* people.

At four o'clock in the afternoon, as a swift messenger was sent to forewarn the King, fifteen-thousand National Guardsmen, infused by a growing welter of latecomers, set out for Versailles. The Marquis de Lafayette, riding on his white charger occupying the foremost position, aware if he did not acquiesce he might lose his life.

Ostensibly the multitude on the road to Versailles had set out to obtain relief from a condition nearing starvation, and as importantly to redress a perceived insult to the tricolor cockade. But in the women of the market and in the men of the National Guard the idea had taken hold that they could only have assurance of the King's intentions if his royal bodyguard was dismissed and replaced by the new patriotic body. To this idea would be added, at the persistence of revolutionary agitators, that the king, the court, and the assembly must be compelled to come back to Paris and reside among them. Only then could the crisis of food, the presence of foreign troops, and the king's fealty to the nation, be resolved.

Outside of their plight of hunger, these ideas gave the marchers determination and direction; as undoubtedly for many the idea of bringing home *le bon papa* was a sagacious, a reassuring plan. To the revolutionaries the necessity of preserving the decrees and the declaration of rights and the creation of a constitution were paramount. And it was within the sections of Paris, that the best possible environment that the Revolution might succeed could be assured.

After six hours in the autumn rain, with several cannons in tow, the "woman's march" began arriving in Versailles. Along the way they had recruited or impressed into their rank others of the dispossessed, and those expectant of change, and as they surged into the royal retreat many from the surrounding area also came out to join them. Holding session, the Assembly broke-off, with many deputies coming out to greet the weltering crowds. Inviting Maillard into their hall to address them, many of the women, too, came pummeling in, sitting exhausted and damp on the deputies' benches. Maillard told the Assembly, "We have come to Versailles to demand bread, and to request the punishment of the royal bodyguards who have insulted the patriotic cockade."

With deputies declaring their support, many of the women, impatient to hear the great orator Mirabeau, shouted them down. Mirabeau, however, declined the moment, instead stepping down to mingle with the women and exchange embraces, even sitting for a time with a girl upon his knee. Maximilien Robespierre, still relatively obscure, was received appreciatively for his words of support, which lessened somewhat the defiant pose the *poissardes* had assumed on entering the hall. The president of the assembly now selected six women to accompany him to the palace for an audience with the king.

Once in the royal chambers, after a brief meeting, one of the women fainted at the king's feet, and Louis found occasion to display sympathy for their plight, as arrangement was made to disperse some of the royal stores, with more promised to be forthcoming. With some women feeling the goals of the march had been met, and Maillard perhaps having delayed other affairs—in pelting rain, a portion of the marchers began the trek back to Paris. The multitude, however, was far from appeased and remained in the palace square and gardens, ominously exchanging rumor and opinion in their *poissard* slang. Maillard and those that had departed had been duped by the king, they said; in any event his wife, Marie Antoinette, would soon see to it that the king broke his promises. "No more talking," one determined woman shouted. "We'll cut the Queen's pretty throat! We'll tear her skin to bits for ribbons!"

About six that evening, faced with the still volatile situation, and realizing there had not been adequate preparation to defend the palace against insurrection, the king announced he would accept the decrees and the Declaration of the Rights of Man without stipulations. Later that evening Lafayette, spattered in mud, as were the troops of the National Guard, came down the avenue of approach to the palace. Lafayette dismounting, immediately went to see the king, where he announced grandiloquently: "I have come to die at the feet of your Majesty."

That night an alliance was struck between the market-women and the men of the National Guard: Fayette had been too tardy, they said, he had not even wanted to leave Paris in the first place; he was a traitor—as the rowdy *poissard* insistence of the women continued. At six in the morning several women came upon a gate left unguarded. Gaining access to the palace, they hurriedly began a search for the queen's bedchamber. With guards racing to cut them off, one intruder was shot and killed. Shouting for the "Austrian whore," in full fury, the multitude now surged forward, over-powering the guards, as they hoisted two shorn heads at the end of pikes. The Queen, in bare feet, fled desperately to safety in her husband's chamber.

With the tempest subsiding, royal guards and former French Guards and the core of Lafayette's staff—after the general had been roused from his slumber—were able to form a fragile truce, as they cleared the building. In the breach, Lafayette re-gained his tenuous footing; but given the temper and insistence of the multitude, it was doubtful the regular units present, the Flanders Regiment and the Montmorency Dragoons, would be willing to act. To placate the multitude, Lafayette now convinced the King to address them from the balcony. As the two stepped out, to everyone's surprise, amid the chant 'Le Roi a Paris!" cries of "Vive le Roi!" were also heard, and to everyone's relief the king expressed his willingness to return to Paris, acceding "to the love of my good and faithful subjects." As the king was cheered, Lafayette shrewdly pinned a tricolor cockade on the hat of his nearest bodyguard.

As Louis XVI withdrew, the multitude insisted the queen too come out on the balcony. When Lafayette brought her out wearing a dressing-gown of yellow and white strips, her hair disheveled, she was clutching her two children, a son of four and a girl of eleven. The crowd insisted the children be taken away. With many muskets leveled against her, the queen stood alone, her arms folded over her chest.

As the crowd began to acknowledge her for her pluck, again, Lafayette sought to finesse an advantage, cannily stepping forward and bowing chivalrously. Then he took the queen's hand in his, as he kissed it. In the garden below the duc d'Orléans was seen, dressed in a gray frock-coat and round hat, walking "cheerfully" among the multitude, acknowledging some with smiles while engaging others "in a carefree manner." It would be his calculation he was better suited than his cousin to assume the titular head in any forthcoming arrangement for a constitutional monarchy.

It was in the early afternoon that same day that a cannon was fired signaling that the king was leaving Versailles for Paris. A vast procession now set out, headed by the troops of the National Guard, and following these came carts of wheat and flour released from the royal stores to feed the starving of Paris. Then came the Regiments of Flanders and the Swiss Guard followed by the royal carriage with the king and queen and their children, attendants and governesses. Behind them rode Lafayette on his white charger, before the carriages conveying a number of the deputies of the Assembly. Then came the vast cavalcade of market women making their return to Paris; a precession that was somber and dignified in the magnitude of its accomplishment, at times plaintive with the sounds of song lilting in the air, as bread was offered to hungry women on the ends of the bayonets of guardsmen. The women called out that they were bringing back to Paris the baker, the baker's wife, and 'le petit mitron', the baker's boy.

All combined the train had grown to over sixty thousand, and the journey would take nearly nine hours. As gun shots rent the air, some women rode astride the cannons. It was a macabre scene too, the march adorned by severed heads swaying on the ends pikes, and many placards and banners, with many of the women carrying branches decorated with colored ribbons, so that the multitude resembled a "walking forest".

The acute observer in London, William Blake, would remark with scorn on the part assumed by the Marquis de la Fayette, included in the writings in his notebook that had been his brother's, later part of the "Rossetti Manuscripts", containing some early drafts for the poems of *Songs of Experience,* unfinished and not part of that final compilation (1793):

> Fayette, Fayette, thou'rt bought & sold,
> And sold is thy happy morrow;
> Thou gavest the tears of Pity away
> In exchange for the tears of sorrow. (8)

6.

Without Contraries

is no progression

As seen from Britain, the enthusiasm of youth for events across the English Channel in 1789 was made most affectingly by William Wordsworth in *Book Ten* of his autobiographical poem *The Prelude,* where he wrote of that year when he turned nineteen:

> Bliss was it in that dawn to be alive,
> But to be young was very heaven! O times...
> When Reason seemed the most to assert her rights,
> When most intent on making of herself
> A prime Enchantress—to assist the work,
> Which then was going forward in her name!

As he'd become enraptured by the revolutionary movement in France, so notably recalled in later decades, in November 1791 Wordsworth journeyed to that country where he took a French lass, Annette Vallon, as his lover, who in the following year gave birth to their daughter Caroline. Notwithstanding this parturition, and facing financial woes, Wordsworth was back in England by the end of 1792, as France began to approach its *Reign of Terror* and he underwent a change in attitude, abandoning his love.

Two names with which the future poet-laureate became confidentially associated, fellow poets Robert Southey, already noticed within these pages, and Samuel Taylor Coleridge, were youths likewise in the flush of enthusiasm for a revolutionary France, as with the precepts presented by Enlightenment thought. A few years the younger of Wordsworth, as was Coleridge, Southey would be expelled from Westminster School for an essay against flogging he contributed to its school magazine, as his future friend returned from France. Already reading Voltaire, Rousseau, Paine, and Godwin, Southey had no trouble matriculating at the college at Oxford. Coleridge, studying at Cambridge during the years of Revolution, was already noted as an exceptional scholar with a startling fluency with words, as he was at this time, too, in the English sense, a political radical and enthusiast of the French Revolution.

Undoubtedly perplexed, both with the attentions of youth preoccupied with Revolution, and with the sign of unruly miller's celebrating on Blackfriars Bridge with the fateful destruction of the Albion Mills, London's establishment mutually held them in disapproval. Many reformers in Britain, too, had greeted revolution in France with furor, seeing it as an attempt to achieve what England had already done in 1688 in the "Glorious Revolution"—establish a constitutional monarchy on the basis of the recognition of the rights of citizens and for representative government. It would provide, as well, incentive to those who wanted to extend the reforms from that imperfect settlement, and to take hold the opening to regenerate society; as Wordsworth also wrote in his famous overture—

> Not in Utopia, subterraneous Fields,
> Or some secreted Island, heaven knows where!
> But in the very world, which is the world
> Of all of us,—the place where in the end
> We find our happiness, or not at all!

In England, the first literary portrayal extant was provided by William Blake, to be realized however only to the extent of printer's sheets before being withdrawn, whether at the publisher's, Joseph Johnson's trepidation, or by Blake's own dissatisfaction with it. Promising six more books on the theme on the title page, where he wrote at the beginning of the poem *The French Revolution,* "From my window I see the old mountains of France, like aged men, fading away." This was to be the only opportunity in his career for the poet to bring his work before the public, outside of his own efforts with his illuminated books, and this failure would have a marked effect on that prospectus.

In this work Blake's notion of pacifism is contrasted with images of war; and instead of regicide there is a place for the king in the new order, while the text follows the biblical arrangement of Paradise regained, with Paris becoming the new Jerusalem. Conjuring an apocalyptic scene out of the historical reality presented by the first year of revolution, 1788-89, the poem is replete in grotesque flourishes: the archbishop of Paris arises "in the rushing of scales and hissing of flames and rolling of sulphurous smoke...."

"To [Blake], at this date, as to ardent minds everywhere, the French Revolution was the herald of the Millennium...;" (1) and he was to avow himself a "Liberty Boy", and would later jestingly insist in justification, in line with the then popular phrenology, that the shape of his forehead made him such. Revolution, as Blake came to regard it, was the recognition of creative purpose embodied in the upheaval of the multitude, and it became the *event* that would translate his purely intellectual revolt, not only into a political apotheosis, but an aesthetic one as well. As he pondered the contemporary

French experience, as he had the American experience in the previous decade, he was spurred toward the development of his own mythological system.

Joseph Johnson was one of a growing number of publishers in London, or booksellers as they were called. Opening his business in 1761 with a book list dominated by religious tracts by dissenting writers; starting in 1774 he began publishing a series of anti-government pro-American pamphlets, and in 1780 published the collected political works of Benjamin Franklin. But his success in large part was due to his friendship and association with Joseph Priestley, who'd introduced him to other writers and who published dozens of books with him. It was Priestley who was responsible for Johnson leaving his Baptist faith and becoming a Unitarian. Helping to shape an era as he occupied an important place at the center of like-minded individuals, every Tuesday Johnson began hosting a dinner with his author's, together with other notables, becoming known as the "Johnson circle".

Gilchrist offers a glimpse into these gatherings at No. 72, St. Paul's Churchyard, in central London—

> in a little quaintly-shaped upstairs room, with walls not at right angles, where his guests must have been somewhat straitened for space. Hither came Drs. Price and Priestley, and occasionally Blake; hither too Godwin whose *Political Justice* Johnson published in 1793 whom Blake barely got along with. (2)

At table, regularly at various times through the years was Holcraft, "a literary man-of-all work", the painter Henry Fuseli, confidant to Blake, Mary Wollstonecraft, and a bit later Thomas Paine and Joel Barlow, the American patriot, poet, and diplomate, who like Paine became an ardent of the French Revolution, and whose *Advise to the Privileged Orders* Johnson would publish in 1792. Barlow was especially noted for his epic poem on the American Revolution, *Vision of Columbus*, but readers might more readily remember his *The Hasty-Pudding*.

Political literature became the mainstay of Johnson's enterprise in the 1790's, he supplying an increasing number of pamphlets on the French Revolution, done at an affordable price and finding readers among a growing middle-class and self-educated artisans and laborers. He was also a member of the *Society for Constitutional Information* founded in 1780, promoting reform of Parliament. In 1788, he had founded the *Analytical Review*, becoming an important platform for British reformers; offering summaries and analysis of new publications, as it provided a forum for radical political and non-conformist religious views, while promoting scientific and philosophical articles.

Beginning in 1784, and lasting for nearly twenty years, Johnson had a working relationship with William Blake as engraver and illustrator, commissioning around one hundred works from him. It is suggested that, while it offered Blake employment and exposure in a burgeoning market, he found in this association with Johnson's circle an important fount for his developing ideas and for his radicalization, as was undoubtedly the case, although many of them were antithetical to his views. In 1793, Johnson also published Wordsworth's *Descriptive Sketches*, followed by *Evening Walk*.

One of these author's, subsequently seen as of importance, was a woman who had left her employment as governess to a prominent Irish family in 1786, to go to London and become, as she informed one of her sisters (Everina), "the first of a new genus," a woman writer. Johnson was to publish a children's educational book she'd written in 1788, *Original Stories from Real Life*; Johnson also finding a place for her to stay and work so that she could support herself. Soon she was learning French and German so she could do translations for the

Analytical Review, and the growing number of articles it was publishing from authors from those countries. One of the first of these productions was Jacques Necker's *Of the Importance of Religious Opinions*. Describing Johnson in her letters to her sister as a father and a brother she had never had, she signed herself Mary Wollstonecraft.

In England, the travails of the monarchy in France and the storming of the Bastille elicited a strong rejoinder from Tories and conservatives, as Edmund Burke, an Irishman in the House of Commons and a prominent Whig politician, author, and essayists, published his *Reflections on the French Revolution* on November 1, 1790. Written in response to a speech by Richard Price, *A Discourse on the Love of Our Country*; Price was well-known and well connected in radical and republican circles, prominent in that era's many campaigns in the cause of liberty, including for remission of the penalties on nonconformists. A 'dissenting minister' (Unitarian) and a pamphleteer publishing on ethics, politics, and theology, he also advanced probability theory and the use of actuarial tables, and was invited by the American Continental Congress to assist in the financial administration of the States, as he was also a *Fellow of the Royal Society*. His speech and Burke's rejoinder would set off a debate, later called the *Revolution Controversy*, with many contributors, among the better known of whom now are Mary Wollstonecraft and Thomas Paine.

Burke's *Reflections,* begun as a letter to a Frenchman in October of the previous year fast on that summer and fall's signature events, the storming of the Bastille and the October Women's March, were elaborated upon the following January, and when published it sold 13,000 copies within a few weeks almost wholly to the perplexed and anxiety-ridden 'upper-classes'. By September 1791, it had gone through eleven editions.

Before this Burke had been noted for an essay written when he was nineteen on aesthetics, *A Philosophical Enquiry into the Origin of Our Ideas of the Subline and the Beautiful*, attracting the attention of thinkers like Diderot and Kant. Burke's views on aesthetics had been foundational too for the painter Sir Joshua Reynolds whose "Grand Style" of portraiture promoted idealization of his subjects, and therefore anti-thetical to those developing, as will be seen, in the mind and practice of William Blake. Blake later writing—"I read Burke's Treatise when very young.... I felt the Same Contempt & Abhorrence then that I do now." (3)

As a member of Parliament Burke was outspoken in his criticism of British policy and conduct in regard to the American colonists, supporting their right to resist, but not going so far as to tender his support in their bid for independence. He had also been a leader in the impeachment fight against Warren Hastings in 1788, the Governor-General of Bengal, for abuse of office and corruption. Yet his *Reflections* was to put him at the center of controversy that become in after years a foundational text for "conservatism."

Burke wrote:

All circumstances taken together, the French revolution is the most astonishing one that has ever happened. The most amazing things are brought about, many of them by the most absurd and ridiculous means, in the most ridiculous ways, and apparently by the most contemp-tible instruments. Everything seems out of nature in this strange chaos of levity and ferocity....

Burke predicted, because of its abstract footing, the Gallic political upheaval would end badly; while he repudiated belief in "a divinely appointed monarchic", he established his argument on the efficacy and necessity for gradual constitutional reform. Human nature and society were complex, he suggested, and the French partisans risked too much and should look for their forms of governance in the past, and in institutions having their basis in traditional, even feudal forms. Abstract rights such as liberty and the rights of man could easily be abused to justify tyranny. Perhaps thinking of Lafayette, he presciently foresaw continuing disorder might make the army "mutinous and full of faction," when a "popular general" might become "master of your assembly, the master of your whole republic."

No less amazed by the upheaval, but with an equally sophistorific response, the famous professor of philosophy at Konigsberg in Prussia, Immanuel Kant, insisted although he supported representative democracy, that civil rebellion was never justified. Nevertheless, he stipulated, the monarch had made an error, when, facing an intractable debt crisis he had invited all male taxpayers over 25 years of age to elect deputies to a representative assembly which was to deliberate on solutions. The 3rd estate, the commoners, had thus been enabled to assert *their sovereignty*; and once the popular assembly had been set up, the king was reduced to a constitutional monarch. The uprising in summer and fall 1789, therefore, was not a revolution because sovereignty already was with the people. Thus, in Kant's view, further revolution was prohibited.

Edmund Burke's *Reflections* so angered Wollstonecraft she spent the entire month writing a rebuttal as a letter to the eminent statesman, published, initially anonymously, on 29 November by Joseph Johnson, titled *Vindication of the Rights of Men*. So as to enable swift response, Johnson had prepared her pages for printing as they were received from the author but before the text was completed, perhaps daunted by her adversaries' reputation and the nature of her own ambition, she stopped writing, suffering a "loss of nerve". That is how her future husband, William Godwin, put it in the famous *Memoirs* written after her untimely death in 1797 from complications in the birth of their daughter, Mary (this child of Mary Wollstonecraft and William Godwin, as Mary Shelly, would pen the immortal tale, *Frankenstein*). Johnson then cannily sent word to Mary Wollstonecraft that she was not to worry, he would dispose of the text. In this way, he had provided the author the impetus she needed to race on to its completion.

Wollstonecraft's polemic was as much about language and argument as about political theory; she, writing her goal was "to shew you [Burke] to yourself, stripped of your gorgeous drapery in which you have enwrapped your tyrannic principles." Wollstonecraft called the French Revolution a "glorious chance to obtain more virtue and happiness than hitherto blessed our globe"; and, as Burke denigrated the 3rd estate as the "swinish multitude," she wrote that "this obscure throng knew more of the human heart and of legislation than the profligates of rank, emasculated by hereditary effeminacy."

The second edition of *Vindication* brought Wollstonecraft overnight fame as author, as her gender and identity were revealed. That edition was published December 18 of that year, she editing the text this time, sharpening her attack upon Burke, changing the first person to third person, and achieving great rhetorical effect. Burke had written of Marie Antoinette standing on the balcony at Versailles:

> It is now sixteen or seventeen years since I saw the queen
> of France, then the dauphiness, at Versailles; and surely
> never lighted on this orb, which she hardly seemed to

touch, a more delightful vision. I saw her just above the horizon, decorating and cheering the elevated sphere she had just begun to move in... little did I dream that I should have lived to see such disasters fallen upon her, in a nation of gallant men, in a nation of men of honor, and of cavaliers! I thought ten thousand swords must have leaped from their scabbards to avenge even a look that threatened her with insult.—But the age of chivalry is gone.

While Blake's engagement with the events in France in his writings proceeds only allegorically—Book One of *The French Revolution* ends before the storming of the Bastille, where presumably the discontinued Book Two would have re-commenced—his unfinished ballad now designated *Fayette* does touch on its actual chronology as reflected in the career of Lafayette. The ballad, as noted, is included in the notebook with the eighteen poems comprising *The Songs of Experience*, and while it was not incorporated within these, it follows at their end, indicating it was composed in 1793. Showing he was very familiar with Burke's argument, Blake mocks his depiction of Marie Antoinette quoted above:

> The Queen of France just touched this Globe,
> And the Pestilence darted from her robe;
> But our good Queen quite grows to the ground,
> And a great many suckers grow all around.

As if lamenting the fall of the Bastille, Burke too had written in his *Reflections*: "We have rebuilt Newgate and tenanted the mansion; and we have prisons almost as strong as the Bastille for those who dare to libel the Queens of France."

Wollstonecraft's *Vindication of the Rights of Women*, to be published in January 1792, showed its effect too on William Blake, as is noted by scholars of his *Visions of the Daughters of Albion*, written and produced by him that same year in his series of Illuminated Books. Albion is the ancient Welsh name for what came to be called England, and hence the daughters are the present females in an allegory of Britain, Blake's poem a mythic tale of emancipation and sexuality. The poem ends with the voice of the female protagonists, Oothoon, who's been raped and chained to the perpetrator of the crime by her former lover, symbolizing her 'disgrace', when she says using a voice in the third-person, protesting—

> Till she who burns with youth, and knows no fixed lot, is
> bound
> In spells of law to one she loaths? and must she drag the
> chain
> Of life, in weary lust? (4)

William Blake was two years the elder Mary Wollstonecraft, and their paths if not prosperities as contemporaries were entwined, above all, by the influence of the French Revolution. Wollstonecraft wrote reviews of novels for *Analytical Review*, as Johnson also published her *Thoughts on the Education of Daughters*. The second edition of *Original Stories* was issued in 1791 with six simple illustrations produced by Blake, reminiscent of his own *Songs of Innocence* and gauged to appeal to the imagination of children. In his burlesque of 1784, *An Island in the Moon*, not published, of that reputed society of "blue-stocking" individuals hosted by Rev. Henry Mathew and his wife Harriet he was then socially engaged with, and who had encouraged his first publication, *Poetical Sketches*, a complication of the poems of his youth, Blake as "Quid" in his satire, disparaged Johnson as "a book-seller without aesthetic values whose repetitive questions reveal his ignorance", depicted in the character Abstruse Angle, and indicating, as in all these arrangements, tensions between the parties.

Another of the notables in Johnson's circle while in London, and in association with these two, was the famed pamphleteer of the American Revolution, Thomas Paine. Twenty years the senior of Blake, Paine had left his adopted home and country in America for France and England in 1787, a sojourn he'd projected lasting only a year, but was to stay away fifteen. In the years after the cessation of hostilities with Britain, Paine had been involved in a protracted effort to get compensation for his services from the various states during the war, and was, as ever, engaged in the ongoing polemics about the direction and form the new state would take. New York had granted him a 200-acre farm in New Rochelle, and one or two others had belatedly awarded him a stipend, but he'd found it more convenient to continue on in Bordentown, New Jersey, due to its proximity to Princeton, for a time the seat of the government, and to New York and Philadelphia, also serving as capitals for the new nation, and where important associates of his lived.

One of the papers issuing from Paine's pen was *Dissertations on Government, the Affairs of the Bank, and Paper Money*, dated February 18, 1786. The first part of that work is devoted to general principles, where "sovereignty" when applied to the people, Paine points out, has a different meaning from the arbitrariness it signifies in a monarchy. "A republic is a sovereignty of justice," he wrote, "in contradistinction to a sovereignty of will;" a republic "secures the individual from becoming the pry to power, and prevents might from overcoming right." Paine offered this warning against the use of paper money:

> Paper money appears, at first sight, to be a great saving, or rather that it costs nothing; but it is the dearest money

there is. The ease with which it is emitted by an assembly at first, serves as a trap to catch people in at last. It operates as an anticipation of the next year's taxes. If the money depreciates, after it is out, it then, as I have already remarked, has the effect of fluctuating stock, and the people become stock-jobbers to throw the loss on each other. (5)

Pursuing an idea for a new type of bridge, Paine was among the first to advocate their construction using wrought iron. Envisaging the construction of a prototype across the Schuylkill River, his was to be a single arch spanning five hundred feet without the support of piers anchored in the river, as he sought to give expression to the American Revolution carried into mechanics. Its design was to utilize five hundred and twenty tons of iron, not easily procurable at the time, the weight to be distributed through thirteen ribs to commemorate the thirteen United States (Paine had been the coiner of that flourish in phraseology in designating the new country, the *United States of America*). He wrote of his bridge: "The idea and construction of this arch is taken from the figure of a spider's circular web, of which it resembles a section, and from a conviction that when nature empowered this insect to make a web she also instructed her in the strongest mechanical method of constructing it." (6)

Paine was assisted in this work by John Hall, a mechanic and expert in steam engines. He had worked for the firm Boulton and Watt for three years, and afterwards at the iron works of John Wilkinson, and finally had emigrated to America in 1786 with a letter of introduction addressed to Thomas Paine. (7)

Carrying a model with him and the details of his planning, Paine sailed on a French packet, where, arriving in Paris he was received by Thomas Jefferson. His main object in Paris was to secure a verdict on the bridge from its *Academy of Sciences*, the most prestigious scientific academy in the world at that time, where he was received with honors due to his association with Benjamin Franklin, his membership in the *Philosophical Society*, and for an honorary degree conferred by the University of Pennsylvania. A committee appointed to consider the feasibility of an iron bridge reported they concurred with its principles of construction; as Paine came into relation with men having eminence in philosophical and political circles, among them Condorcet and the son of a duke, Achille DuChâtelet, with whom he would form a valuable political liaison.

Paine followed this up with protracted meetings in Britain, where he obtained a patent, and managed to see his plan move toward practical fruition as Walker's Iron Works in Yorkshire undertook the visionary project, with Thomas Paine appointed director of the work; with the foreman, now a Mr. Buel, as mechanic first class. On August 30, 1790, in one of many letters written to Thomas Walker, proprietor of the iron-works, Paine remarked, as the work commenced: "I am always discovering some new faculty in myself—either good or bad—and I find I can look after workmen much better than I thought I could." Paine was a keen observer, as he was a participant, in that other promontory, the "industrial revolution." His friend Joel Barlow, was to suggest that biographers should not forget his "mathematical acquirements and his mechanical genius," he also devising an improved planing machine, a crane, and a smokeless candle. Blake's friend Fuseli reported an anecdote to his own biographer regarding the engraver William Sharp employing Paine's talents, Sharp also a participant in the "Johnson circle". "Paine was an excellent mechanic," said Fuseli—

when Sharp was about to engrave my picture of "The Contest of Satan, Sin and Death" he employed a carpenter to construct a roller to raise or fall it at pleasure; in this, after several ineffectual attempts, he did not succeed to the expectations of Sharp, who mentioned the circumstance in the hearing of Paine; he instantly offered his services, and soon accomplished all, and indeed more than the engraver had anticipated. (8)

His efforts on behalf of his bridge had taken him to the several leading fabricators in England and Scotland. On June 17, 1790, in the midst of his canvas Paine wrote to a friend— "I have been to see the Cotton Mills,—the Potteries—the Steel furnaces—Tin Plate manufacture—White Lead manufacture. All those things might be easily carried on in America." (9) As part of this tour Paine reported, in a letter of September 15 in the previous year—"Mr. Le Couteulx desired me to examine the construction of Albion Steam Mills erected by Bolton and Watt." (10)

Paine's name was now well-known throughout Britain, and he enjoyed cordial relations with such eminences as Edmund Burke, before their controversy. Paine had read notice in one of the London papers that Burke was preparing an address to Parliament that was to become his *Reflections,* and had vowed when it appeared he would publish a rejoinder, as he was then writing a history of France's first year of revolution. Accordingly, he had already begun compiling notes and writing drafts, later to be included in the *Rights of Man.* With the government of William Pitt the Younger, succeeding North at age 24, no longer the adversary of American "revolutionaries", Paine became in effect the senior emissary of his government, in the way Franklin had been in France some years before. (11)

But Thomas Paine was no politician, and, although he had

allies, he always stood apart from political parties. He was however preeminent as a political writer, cobbling out a colloquial style to be seized upon later by the poet Walt Whitman—a democratic writing for democratic ends. Visiting Paine just as he had returned to Philadelphia after his successful mission to Paris with Col. John Laurens in 1781, at a time in which he was particularly hard pressed, the Marquis de Chastellux, in his *Travels in North America*, espied the exceptionality of Paine's situation:

> His existence at Philadelphia is similar to that of those political writers in England, who have obtained nothing, and have neither credit enough in the State, nor sufficient political weight to obtain a part in the affairs of government. Their works are read with more curiosity than confidence. Their projects being regarded as the play of imagination, than as well concerted plans. (12)

Paine's quarters, often only a single room, were untidy it was remarked, collecting dust on all surfaces, his writing table heaped with manuscripts in various stages of completion, the books he was consulting opened to their last reading, and distributed haphazardly.

From November 1789 through March 1790 Thomas Paine was in Paris, and would return in spring 1791 staying till early July, and remain there outlasting the decade beginning in September 1792. On the return trip to Paris, averred to above, he was selected by Lafayette to convey the key to the Bastille to President Washington, together with a drawing of the fortress/prison then being demolished. Carlyle in his *The French Revolution* gives notice to Paine's presence in the previous visit, reported in *Le Moniteur* 7 December 1789, the paper founded by Brissot and Condorcet the prior year:

Her (sic) Paine: rebellious Staymaker; unkempt; who feels that he, a single Needleman, did, by his *Common Sense* Pamphlet, free America;—that he can and will free all this world; perhaps even the other. Price-Stanhope Constitutional Association sends over to congratulate, welcomed by National Assembly, though they are but a London Club; whom Burke and Toryism eye askance. (13)

On May 1, 1790, he wrote to Washington on the progress with his iron bridge: "I have manufactured a Bridge (a single arch) of one hundred and ten feet span, and five feet high from the cord of the arch. It is now on board a vessel coming from Yorkshire to London, where it is to be erected." Of the symbolic memento, he wrote: "Sir,—our good friend the Marquis de la Fayette has entrusted to my care the Key of the Bastille, and a drawing, handsomely framed, representing the demolition of that detestable prison, as a present to your Excellency...." (14)

In a following letter to Washington, May 31, 1790, he wrote: "My Bridge is arrived and I have engaged a place to erect it. A little time will determine its fate, but I yet see no cause to doubt of its success, tho' it is very probable that a war, should it break out, will as in all new things prevent its progress so far as regards profits." He continued in view of that other pertinent matter: "In the partition in the Box, which contains the Key to the Bastille, I have put up half a dozen Razors, manufactured from Cast-steel made at the works where the Bridge was constructed, which I request you to accept as a little token from a very grateful heart."

That the principles that made America a republic had "opened the Bastille," was not something for posterity alone to judge, but something conveyed from Lafayette to Washington via Thomas Paine.

William Blake's *The Marriage of Heaven and Hell*, as he himself dated it—"[a]s a new heaven is begun, and it is now thirty-three years since its advent"—was a production of the year 1790. Regarded as among his most trenchant works, seemingly half dream, half allegory, it imbibes all the facets and purposes thrown into the world at that time, and is the first and most atypical in Blake's series of prophetic Illuminated Books. Its foremost distinction being that it reads like a pamphlet, as such undoubtedly was Blake's intention, as indeed it resembles the chapbooks he would have read as a boy. It is above all a perplexing medley of prose fragments defying description.

This was his first full attempt at presenting his theo/ philosophic view that the human imagination is the principal facet by and in which the divine manifests in the world. The key to Blake's spiritual vision now became the inheritance of Jacob Boehme, who wrote "Heaven is in hell, and hell in heaven...;" as he instructed—"The outward Essence reacheth not the inward in the soul, but only by the imagination." So, Blake has the prophet Isaiah declare—"I saw no God, nor heard any, in a finite organical perception; but my senses discover'd the infinite in everything."

Excepting the opening, 'The Argument', where "Rintrah (Pitt) roars and shakes his fires in the burden'd air", written in verse, and its closing 'A Song of Liberty', "The eternal Female groan'd!" that is verse-like and enumerated for added emphasis; its other parts are constituted by axioms entitled *The Proverbs of Hell*, derived from Lavater's *Aphorisms of Man* published by Johnson, that Blake began reading and annotating the previous year, and a series of short narratives each titled *A Memorable Fancy* with argument interspersed between an Angel and the Devil, along with parody of Swedenborg's theology. The title of the work itself is part parody, part radical exhortation.

At the outset, Blake states his central notion, the principal tenet of his method and vision, that without *contraries* creative movement is not possible. As with *innocence* and *experience,* in thought as in social practice, *contradiction*, Blake sees, is the primary force in historical causality. Only through an oppositional dialectic—Attraction/Repulsion, Reason/Energy, Love/Hate, Heaven/Hell—is new freedom won. On the title page of a later poem, *Milton, Book the Second* (1804-1808), Blake was to specify, "Contraries are Positives. A negation is not a contrary"; and was to write in that text—"The Negation must be destroy'd to redeem the Contraries. The Negation is the Spectre, the Reasoning Power in Man." (15)

Good and Evil, Heaven and Hell, assume for Blake a meaning opposite conventional usage; they are dualisms seen as vision tyrannized by hegemonic power: Passive acceptance is evil, active opposition is good. Angel and Devil exchange places. Blake's vision represented a maximal humanism, both for his time and thenceforward, disclosing a startlingly revolutionary mode of thought. In Blake's view that is the reality of all thought, of all philosophic cognition—and that human-kind lives in a web of abstract estrangement.

Above all, a proper reading of *Marriage* requires one be attuned to the author's wit and humor structured through satire of Swedenborg's doctrines, who now struck Blake only for the conventionality of his vision, while professing to be inspired; and the presentation of his own personal views. Viz.—"Man has no Body distinct from his Soul; for that call'd Body is a portion of Soul discern'd by the five Senses, the chief inlets of Soul in this age." (16) Declaring the distinction must be expunged, he proposes to do this, in a passage quoted earlier, by, "...printing in the infernal method, by corrosives, which in Hell are salutary and medicinal, melting apparent surfaces away, and displaying the infinite which was hid." Adding: "If the doors of perception were cleansed every thing would appear to man as it is, Infinite." (17)

In Plate 15 titled *A Memorable Fancy*, Blake writes: "I was in a Printing house in Hell & saw the method in which knowledge is transmitted from generation to generation." The contrary to this printing house where books were made and organized into libraries, was that of Blake's own production, where the work of engraving was exacting and where the engraver's greatest reserve was in patience, in discipline and precision. Blake's views were deeply imbued with the accoutrements of his trade; and the formidable metaphysical system he began developing cannot be properly understood divorced from these—the words of his poems becoming objects to be burned out of the metal, images built around a foundation with figures in strongly etched outline. The reference to printing suggests the radical pamphleteers both in France and England, as earlier in America; the work of "printer's devils" being routinely denounced from the pulpit.

Untidy with the technical appurtenances of his trade, the room where he worked presented a procession of iron pots for mixing inks, varnishes and pigments; jars containing acid, along with containers of water, oil, and glue; stacks of copper plates and the paper for printing. There was a bench with shelves with racks of needles, and assortments of gravers; a work table with grinding stones for sharpening tools, and pumice for polishing the plates, and another small table where he worked the copper plates with his graver on a leather cushion filled with sand, a lamp and magnifying glass. Along the walls, or under the tables were rags for wiping, and fine linen cloth for straining, and woolen cloth for covering the prints. As there were too, feathers to smooth the varnish across the plates; pans for warming the copper, and pots for boiling oil. A room, no doubt he endeavored to arrange in proper utilitarian fashion, with the rolling press occupying the central location, free to work around on every side. Tables and benches, nonetheless, often soiled with the grim and disorder of the on-going labor, encumbered by all the necessary supplies, such as stocks of tallow candles. Blake also had a large collection of prints, perhaps arranged in crates, and there were his plates, no doubt carefully stacked, each protected from damage by a cloth or paper covering.

Blake used a fine stone and water to polish a plate before it was ready for inking. Then it would be touched with charcoal, and any small strokes or scratches erased with a steel burnisher, after which it would be cleaned with stale bread or chalk. Varnish was then smoothed over the plate, the varnish dried with the flame of a short tallow candle or over a fire without burning the varnish.

The plate was ready now for a final incising with a needle whetted on an oil stone. With the strokes made, it was placed in the 'aqua fortis' and the 'biting in' was completed. The plates then washed and cleaned, polished, and prepared to be inked.

Once sheets were printed and dried they were ready for the final painting with an application of ink and watercolors. At most, two or three sheets could be lightly printed from a single inking before the plates need be cleaned and inked again, and so this stage of the process too was laborious. Blake used his wife Catherine as an invaluable assistant, helping in the work on the final images, and she finally became expert, having, it was said, an "excellent idea of colouring". As she might also be the one turning the press as he inked the plates. Blake too grinding and mixing the colors; deferentially selecting Prussian blue, yellow ocher, Indian red, various blacks, vermilion, rose madder, raw sienna, and alizarin crimson, along with the coloring of Buddhist monks' saffron robes, gamboge, for the French word for Cambodia. (18)

On the title page of this work, the word MARRIAGE is inscribed in swash capital letters, while the words HEAVEN and HELL are rendered in block capitals. Below are a pair of androgynous figures, female nudes, an angel and the devil embracing face to face; while on the left, carried by flames towards the surface of the nether world, borne up by contrasting or antagonistic elements, are single figures and embracing couples, showing that the energy of Hell will impregnate the passivity of Heaven. Above, Blake introduces the principal participants of the drama to be enacted on the earth's surface. Representing 'material existence' is a cluster of leafless trees stretching out from the margins on right and left, as if to entwine with the preposition of Blake's title. Four figures are seen, two of them are walking hand in hand from the left to the right, and the other two, on the right, a man is playing an instrument, perhaps a lute or a harp as the text says, as he kneels before a female nude reclining at the trunk of a tree—the orphic and the erotic. Birds soar in the sky, depicting the words in the text:

> How do you know but ev'ry Bird that cuts the airy way,
> Is an immense world of delight, clos'd by your senses five?

The magnificent effects produced on this and on the 26 other plates comprising the work, were attested to by Gilchrist, who wrote: "The ever-fluctuating colour, the spectral pigmies rolling, flying, leaping among the letters; the ripe bloom of quiet corners, the living light and bursts of flame, the spires and tongues of fire vibrating with the full prism, make the page seem to move and quiver within its boundaries." (19) Later, Samuel Palmer remembered Blake explaining to him that there were passages in it that "would at once exclude the work from every drawing room table in

England." But it also has a playful sense of mystery throughout, as Blake dons his cloak as artist-prophet, and optimistically was expecting a ready audience.

In *Marriage,* there are a welter of voices, seemingly part over-heard conversation, part folk-wisdom, part diatribe and pedantry, part street cry—as contrarian argument intermingles with paradoxical exhortation throughout: "...thinking that as the sayings used in a nation mark its character, so the Proverbs of Hell shew the nature of Infernal wisdom better than any description of buildings or garments." (20)

Blake's *Proverbs of Hell* are an assemblage of seventy gnomic pronouncements that are now among the most heralded of all his creations. Four of which are the following:

- Drive your cart and your plough over the bones of the
    dead.
- The road to excess leads to the palace of wisdom.
- The most sublime act is to set another before you.
- The roaring lions, the howling of wolves, the raging of
    the stormy sea, and the destructive sword, are
    portions of eternity too great for the eye of man.

Blake discloses himself as a man who no authority could impose upon (Blake's Nobodaddy); nor war or the rule of kings, nor priests. It is as though he wrote for everyone—for children, for women, even for babies, and adventitiously, for chimney sweepers. Again, his biographer Alexander Gilchrist to whom all subsequent Blake scholarship is indebted, wrote: "...Blake does not set up as an instructor of youth, or of age either, but rather as one who loves to rouse, perplex, provoke; to shun safe roads and stand on dizzy brinks...." (21) As prophet, which Blake tells us is the meaning in the *Old Testament* of poet, he was, above all, herald of the Millennium.

Another of Blake's paradoxical proverbs expresses a truth germane to his apparent friendship with Thomas Paine. "'[I]t is but lost time to converse with you whose works are only Analytics.' Opposition is true Friendship." (22) The kith and kin of these two has been the object of not entirely fanciful speculation, but its residuum can be found in Blake's annotations of Bishop Watson's take on Paine's *The Age of Reason* (1793-95), with Watson's critique published in 1796 as *An Apology for the Bible*. Blake read the book and several of his observations follow: "Paine is either a Devil or an Inspired man. Men who give themselves to their Energetic Genius in the manner that Paine does are no modest Enquirers." Then, in an allusion to *Common Sense*: "Is it a greater miracle to feed five thousand men with five loaves than to overthrow all the armies of Europe with a small pamphlet." (23)

It was in the beginning third section of *Common Sense*, "Thoughts on the present state of affairs in America", that Paine quotes John Milton from *Paradise Lost*, the great 17th century British republican poet: "never can true reconcile-ment grow where wounds of deadly hate have pierced so deep." These words were cited to buttress the argument for total independence; but in Milton, this is the utterance of Satan directed to other fallen angels, to make plain his contempt for God. The fall from grace had only secured Lucifer's independence from the King of the celestial sphere.

In "Of Monarchy and hereditary succession," with which Paine's treatise opens, he takes up the Hebrew Bible, The Book of Samuel, as the basis for an extended disquisition, where Gideon has helped to defeat the Israelites foes and is beseeched to take the title King, but replies "I will not rule over you, neither shall my son rule over you, the Lord Shall Rule Over

You." John Adams, of whom it could be discerned he was just able to tolerate Paine, in conversation shortly after the publication of the famous pamphlet, said "I told him further that his beginning from the Old Testament was ridiculous, and I could hardly think him sincere. At this time he laughed, and said he had taken this Ideas in that part from Milton...." (24)

That Paine chose the devil to justify the actions of the rebelling colonists, was actually the optimal solution; "there is ten times more to dread from a patched-up connection," he wrote, "than from independence." Literally in urging separation from Britain Paine was playing "devil's advocate." One reads echo of this strategy in Blake's *Marriage* published fifteen years later; and if Blake, being a teenager had not read *Common Sense* at the time he certainly sought it out eagerly in the subsequent years. Paine, in fact, had derived his argument from Milton's *Defence*, where the bard reasoned "to depose a tyrant is clearly a more divine action than to set him up." (25) On Plate 6 of *Marriage* Blake wrote, "The reason Milton wrote in fetters when he wrote of Angels & God, and at liberty when of Devils & Hell, is because he was a true Poet and of the Devils party without knowing it."

"Strange to conceive," wrote Gilchrist, "a somewhile associate of Paine producing these 'Prophetic Volumes!'" (26) Yet both believed that the most important prerequisite for all cognition was free inquiry, as both knew evenly that the reality of symbols and images are made, not given. Beyond this, one might suppose, there were points of mutual contention between them. For one, obviously, they did not agree on the doctrine of materialism, finding rather fundamental concurrence on matters pertaining to dogmatism and the desirability for the emancipation of human energies. Although Paine may have regarded Blake's highly idiosyncratic views with deep curiosity, for all his much vaunted "mysticism" Blake was remarkably plain-spoken. Paine, like all rationalists and mechanics of that age, regarded the physical universe as operating strictly within the Newtonian framework, while Blake saw Newton's was a dead world, saying he had petrified "all Human Imagination into rock & sand." (27)

The concluding part of *The Marriage of Heaven and Hell* added a year or two later—*A Song of Liberty*—forms and restates its central theme. Using images and language of the apocalypse, Blake welcomes the liberation of mankind from the tyranny personified by King George III and Louis XVI, and from the religious dogma foisted by the Anglican Church and the Church in Rome, as he lauds the ascendancy of rebellion over presumption and inflexibility:

2. Albion's coast is sick silent; the American meadows faint!
3. Shadows of Prophecy shiver along by the lakes and the rivers and mutter across the ocean: France, rend down thy dungeon;
4. Golden Spain, burst the barriers of old Rome;
5. Cast thy keys, O Rome, into the deep down falling, even to eternity down falling...
19. Where the son of fire in his eastern cloud, while the morning plumes her golden breast,
20. Spurning the clouds written with curses, stamps the stony law to dust, loosing the eternal horses from the dens of night, crying: Empire is no more!... (28)

It is not known whether Blake as bard of this extraordinary work was known to Paine. He may only have known him as an engraver with radical opinions. Yet it is clear that the acquaintance of these two went beyond being merely incidental. Paine undoubtedly visited the Blake's at their cottage in Lambeth, enjoying dinner and lodging with them. At these meetings, or perhaps it was only singular, Blake might have sung his poetry for his visitor, rather than recited it, as Paine must have seen some of his work in his proliferating print shop. Paine's preferred beverage was either wine or brandy, Blake's drink was port.

In his *Reflections on the French Revolution*, Edmund Burke had declared that society is a contract that must not be altered: "As the ends of such a partnership cannot be obtained in many generations, it becomes a partnership not only between those who are living, but between those who are dead, and those who are to be born." Blake crisply countered this in his proverbs with—"Drive your cart and your plow over the bones of the dead"; while Paine retorted in the *Rights of Man*—"Mr. Burke is contending for the authority of the dead over the rights and freedom of the living.... As government is for the living and not for the dead, it is the living only that has any right in it."

Paine's refutation of Edmund Burke, his "Rights of Man", was published in its first part with a dedication to George Washington, March 13, 1791. The manuscript had been prepared for printing in time for the opening of Parliament in February by Joseph Johnson; however, in a climate threatening the repression of political dissent, he withdrew his commitment, and only a few copies bearing his imprint found their way into private hands. (29) After J.S. Jordon of Fleet Street consented to publish it, Paine took his leave for France, entrusting the work to a committee of three friends—William Godwin, Thomas Holcroft, and Thomas Brand Hollis. (30) Inexpensively printed, the pamphlet was a great success in Britain, the entire hubbub since Burke's *Reflections* eliciting over twenty pamphlets, finding an avid audience among religious dissenters, reformers and radical republicans, as it found readers among the artisans of London, and among skilled factory workers and common laborers all across the industrial north. One of these readers was certainly William Blake; in fact, it has been seen that Paine's writing played a key role in shaping and sharpening Blake's social vision at this time, and with his most well regarded short poem, *London*, Blake discloses himself as a thorough-going Paineite.

It has been noted, for example, Paine wrote in regard to freedom of movement in Britain: "In these chartered monopolies, a man coming from another part of the country is hunted from them as if he were a foreign enemy. An Englishman is not free in his own country: Every one of these places presents a barrier in his way, and tells him he is not a freeman—that he has no rights...." (31) Whereas Blake a little over a year later, as he copied out *London* in his notebook for *The Songs of Experience,* wrote:

> I wander thro' each dirty street,
> Near where the dirty Thames does flow,
> And mark in every face I meet
> Marks of weakness, marks of woe. (1794)

Borrowing words suggested from Paine's tract, "each dirty street" is changed to "each charter'd street" and the following line to "charter'd Thames". As in the earlier version "The german forged links I hear" referring to the Hessian mercenaries of George III, has been transformed to "mind-forged manacles", echoing the Gordon Riots of more than a dozen years before, as Paine wrote: "Every office and department has its despotism, founded upon custom and usage. Every place has its Bastille, and every Bastille its despot." And the "youthful Harlots curse", also added at the end to the later version of the poem, is an argument following Paine's contention in the *Rights of Man* that *chartered* London was "a market where every man has his price, and where corruption is common traffic." To which amendments Blake adds "the hapless soldiers sigh", as Paine wrote—"All the monarchical governments are military. War is their trade, plunder and revenue their objects." Thus, the finished poem reads:

> I wander through each chartered street,
> Near where the chartered Thames does flow,
> And mark in every face I meet
> Marks of weakness, marks of woe.
>
> In every cry of every man,
> In every infant's cry of fear;
> In every voice, in every ban,
> The mind-forged manacles I hear.
>
> How the chimney sweeper's cry
> Every blackening church appalls,
> And the hapless soldier's sigh
> Runs in blood down palace walls.
>
> But most through midnight streets I hear
> How the youthful harlot's curse
> Blasts the newborn infant's tear
> And blights with plagues the marriage hearse.

The question has been asked was Paine himself a sublimated Wordsworth? The "scribe of Pennsylvania", as Blake referred to him in *America*, wrote, "I had some turn, and I believe some talent, for poetry; but this I rather repressed than encouraged." (32) Paine also saying of himself, in a letter to Franklin, he found it necessary to use words to find out what he thought, and remarked, "thoughts are a kind of mental smoke, which require words to illuminate them." His biographer Moncure Conway concluded, "It is your half-repressed poets that kindle revolutions."

Wordsworth confided privately to Crabbe Robinson that *Songs of Innocence and Songs of Experience* was "undoubtedly the production of insane genius." (33) Coleridge would remark, "There is something in the madness of this man, which interests me more than the sanity of Lord Byron and Walter Scott." Blake never commented on Coleridge, but met him at the end of his life. He did however read and comment upon Wordsworth. In Wordsworth's *The Excursion* the laureate declares the mind was "fitted" to the external world, and in the same way "the external world is fitted to the mind." Blake wrote in his annotation for the poem: "You shall not bring me down to believe such fitting and fitted; I know better and please your Lordship." (34)

Rights of Man, Part the First was widely distributed across the Atlantic world, in America as well as being translated and published in France, and went through eight editions in its first year, selling 200,000 copies within two years. Introducing readers to the importance of the French Revolution and to a new conception of government. Moncure Conway observed that "[t]he majority of histories of the French Revolution, Carlyle's especially, are vitiated by reason of their inadequate attention to Paine's narrative...." (35)

Paine's iron-bridge had been erected in preview June 1790 at Leasing-Green, attracting visitors at a shilling each, and receiving many favorable notices as it was viewed by deputations sent from river-side towns, with negotiations tendered to utilize the invention. But Paine's engagement with his bridge project was to await a later time and his return to America, as he would be drawn now toward France. He remarked in a letter to Washington dated July 21, 1791: "After the establishment of the American Revolution, it did not appear to me that any object could arise great enough to engage me a second time...but I now experience that principle is not confined to Time or place, and that the ardour of seventy-six is capable of renewing itself." (36)

7.

A Mighty Spirit Leap'd

One September day in 1789 a ship sailed into Cap-Français on the northern coast of Saint-Domingue, the French colony occupying the western third of the island of Hispaniola. Hurrying ashore, the captain began bawling out his bulletin so that all might hear: On July 14th the Bastille had fallen to the French people; the dread citadel was no more! (1)

By then Saint-Domingue had become the crown jewel of French colonial possessions in the Caribbean. The world's most prolific colony, the value of goods shipped in sugar, coffee, cocoa, and indigo, was nearly equaling the value of goods transported from the entire thirteen colonies in America to Britain. Responsible for 60% of the world's coffee, and 40% of the sugar imported by France and Britain together, by 1789 the commodities imported from Saint-Domingue formed the basis for the livelihood of upwards to one million Frenchmen, and indirectly of several million more. (2) Six hundred ships were engaged in trade from the port of Bordeaux to the colony, as Nantes became its rival, and Marseilles occupied third tier. Around these port cities sugar refineries had begun to proliferate, while a maritime and industrial bourgeoisie burgeoned. After the Treaty of Paris ended the American war in 1783, trade going to and from the colony doubled, with investment from Bordeaux alone accounting for 100 million livres. (3)

Divided geographically and by economic importance into three regions; foremost came the north coast, ahead of the west and south coasts. Beginning in the 1730's French engineers had constructed a complex system of irrigation there, and a decade later, together with the British colony of Jamaica, these became the world's principal suppliers of sugar. In 1787 as a sign of the importance of these possessions to the rival powers, the French transported 20,000 African slaves into Saint-Domingue, while the British shipped about 38,000 slaves into all their Caribbean colonies.

The political economy of a slave plantation in Saint-Domingue—its technical and labor processes, its profitability, as its caste composition—dictated that the produce (whether sugar cane, coffee, cocoa, or indigo), be grown on factory-sized allotments. The lots in cane were to be no smaller than 150 acres nor larger than 600 acres, and utilize a regimented workforce with at least one able-bodied slave for two acres of cane. The slaves lived in quarters the size of villages insulated by the surrounding fields, and hunkered in the shadow of the mills. Within these confines and in easy access of adjoining plantations, slaves labored at assigned tasks, graded according to function, utility, and value.

Classified within a rigid cast system; *les blancs* (the whites), occupied the top strata. These in turn were separated into *grands blancs* comprised of plantation owners and the high royal administrative officials, and *le petit blancs*, a lower class comprised of shopkeepers, plantation overseers and administrators, artisans and laborers, and a deleterious assemblage of sailors, buccaneers and vagabonds. The strata below these were referred to as *mulattoes*, or mixed-race persons and free blacks designated *gens de couleur libre* (free persons of color); these often were educated and literate, and served as overseers on plantations, administrators in the minor posts in the towns, or served in the army, and could even be among the plantation owners. A last stratum, the African slaves, forming the overwhelming multitude, outnumbered all other population groups by a factor of 10 to 1. These were without much gradation except by type of service and their proximity to whites. This mass was Creole-speaking, a *patois* based on the French language, and spoken by everyone who needed to communicate with them. Predominately these were of Yoruba lineage (modern Nigeria), Fon (Benin), and the Kingdom of Kongo (northern Angola and the western Congo). (4) By 1789 in Saint-Domingue *les blancs* numbered 40,000, *mulettoes* and free blacks 28,000, while the Africans were estimated to encompass 452,000 persons. The Africans were forced to adopt the Catholicism of their French masters, and developed a syncretic mixture as their spiritual and ritual practice, a Roman Catholic facade over the West African religion known as *Vodou*.

The most fertile area was Plaine-du-Nord, with the most bountiful sugar plantations, and the largest slave population. Bounded on the north by the ocean, and on the south by a ridge running almost the length of the island known as the *Massif du Nord*, it had been cultivated since the 1670's. This north plain was about fifty miles in length and ten to twenty miles in breadth. Cap-Francais was its center, the chief port, and the fulcrum of the island's economic, social and political life. It had about 12,000 slaves within its precincts, and as the hub of shipping and trade, was the administrative center that served as the capital before Port du Prince was given that distinction. The plantations strung through it were in close proximity, the slave gangs working and living together by the hundreds, were closer, C.L.R. James pointed out, to a modern proletariat than any group of workers in existence at that time. (5)

With the publication of the *Declaration of the Rights of Man* in August 1789, the colony's *grands blancs* saw it as their opportunity to increase their wealth and power in a bid for independence. This objective, however, would be left twisting in the intricacies of a power struggle, with alliances of classes and parties exchanging places in a never-ending pirouette. Julien Raimond and Vincent Oge, both *free people of color*, led an effort before the National Assembly in Paris to gain full civil equality for their station. Oge, returning to Cap-Français demanded the right to vote, which was refused by the colonial governor. After the brief insurgency he led failed, he was "broken on the wheel" before being beheaded. In May 1791 when the French Assembly granted citizenship to the *free people of color* the *grands blancs* refused to recognize it.

In France, these developments began to raise the righteous indignation of individuals like the journalist Jacques Brissot and the playwright Olympe de Gouges, and the enlightenment philosophe Condorcet; as in Britain, the lawyer Granville Sharp and Thomas Clarkson became Britain's leading anti-slavery campaigners, joined by William Wilberforce, a member of parliament; as it had in the American colonies of the likes of Benjamin Franklin, Benjamin Rush and Thomas Paine—beginning a two decades agitation leading up to the abolition of the Trans-Atlantic Slave-Trade.

In Britain, the first meeting of the *Society for Effecting the Abolition of the Slave Trade* had taken place in May 1787, as twelve men met in the London print shop of James Phillips, nine of them Quakers and three Anglicans. Of the latter, the most noted were Thomas Clarkson, a campaigner and author of influential essays against the slave trade, and Granville

Sharp, a lawyer with decades long involvement in cases in support of enslaved Africans, of which there were 20,000 then living in Britain. In Paris in 1788 *Société des amis des Noirs* (Society of the Friends of the Blacks) was founded by Brissot, which would publish translations of British anti-slavery literature, as well as their own; de Gouges contributing *Reflexions sur les hommes negres.* The *Philadelphia Society for the Relief of Free Negroes Unlawfully Held in Bondage* (called the Abolition Society) had been formed in 1784, while Benjamin Rush's engagement began as early as 1766, when on route to study in Edinburgh he'd been stunned as he saw 100 slave ships in Liverpool. His first writing on the subject appeared in 1773, *An Address to the Inhabitants of the British Settlements in America, Upon Slave-Keeping.* In 1787 Benjamin Franklin became the president of the Abolition Society, publishing *Address to the Public* in November 1789, a thorough anti-slavery statement. In 1788 Clarkson would publish *A Summary View of the Slave Trade and of the Probable Consequences of its Abolition,* as the following year there appeared *The Impolicy of the African Slave Trade,* providing William Wilberforce, a conservative MP from Yorkshire and friend of Pitt, who was recruited as the campaigns' spokesman in the House of Commons, with the material for his first speech in Parliament against the trade on 12 May 1789.

Clarkson became a tireless campaigner throughout England and would undertake a lecture tour of port cities, London, Bristol and Liverpool, to gain membership and gather information, and would enlist subscriptions throughout the North, particularly in Manchester. Attacked by sailors in Liverpool hired by ship-owners to silence him, he would eventually interview many thousands of ordinary seamen as well as some ship's officers, learning the circumstances and conditions of the slaves on their voyage from the African coast to the West Indies. This campaign would eventually be supported by a large number of pamphlets and posters, the most dramatic being a diagram of a slave-ship, created from Clarkson's interviews, showing how slaves were chained in the hold of ships for the voyage across the Atlantic, and found its most enduring medallion in that created by the Unitarian pottery-maker Josiah Wedgwood with the emblem **Am I Not A Man And A Brother?** —showing a supplicating and kneeling male slave clothed only in a loin cloth, manacled hands to ankles.

Clarkson wrote in his diary at the time: "My walk is a public one. My business is in the world, and I must mix in the assemblies of men or quit the post which Providence seems to have assigned me." Wilberforce's first bill to abolish the slave trade came in April 1791, defeated 88 votes for to 163 against; a reaction in parliament both against the increasing radicalism in Britain, and of the association of anti-slavery with the French Jacobins. As the slave rebellion in Saint-Domingue later that year would also intensify the reaction against the hearing of anti-slave trade legislation.

In Paris on the evening of 20 June 1791, an unusual dramatist's persona was in preparation at the Tuileries Palace. The king and queen had determined it was a propitious moment they flee to the frontier, dropping all pretense of relinquishing hold on power in favor of a constitutional monarchy. The mastermind of their escape was a Swedish nobleman, Count Axel von Fersen, an officer in the French army and devotee of the monarchy of the Bourbons, who as consort of Marie-Antoinette had conspired at her urging in organizing the plan. The royals were to leave the palace at night by unguarded exits, making their way in two parties to taxi carriages awaiting on nearby streets. These were to carry them undetected through Parisian streets to the city gate in the east, where two swift carriages would be waiting. Once safely in the country-side, they would be joined by a platoon of Hussars as escort.

As swiftly as possible the fugitives were to be conveyed to the French citadel at Montmedy, near the border with Luxemburg, where there was a garrison of 10,000 royal troops, along with four foreign mercenary battalions. From there, a counter-revolution against the events of May 1789-June 1791 would find its center, from which redoubt too it might advance.

The royal family were furnished with false passports and would travel in disguise. In the guise of a Russian baroness under the name Baroness de Koeff was the dauphin's governess, Marquise de Tourzel. Marie-Antoinette appeared in the role of governess, known as Madame Rocher; and Madame Elisabeth, the king's sister, as nurse, was called Rosalie. The king, dressed as a valet-de-chamber was called Durand; his children, a boy and girl, alleged to be the baroness', were alike dressed as daughters, Amelia and Aglae.

Louis XVI would leave behind a *Declaration of the King* in the Tuileries Palace to justify his actions. This declaration ended with the following:

> Frenchmen, and above all Parisians...disabuse yourselves of the suggestions and lies of your false friends; return to your king; he will always be your father, your best friend. What pleasure will he not take in forgetting all his personal injuries, and beholding himself again in your midst, when a constitution freely accepted by him, shall cause our holy religion to be respected....

The expedition to the frontier was a distance of around

200 miles and would involve several stops for fresh horses. But the king was having second thoughts: wouldn't it be better if all of the party traveled together in the same carriage? This would require a larger and more conspicuous and slower-moving coach.

With these preparations on-going, late in the evening the Marquis de la Fayette and Jean-Sylvain Bailly came to the Tuileries Palace for a meeting with the king, staying later than expected. As he was leaving, Lafayette crossed paths with Marie-Antoinette just as she was making for the waiting taxi, after which she was to lose some time in finding it, as it awaited with the other women and her two children. The entire party was 90 minutes behind schedule as they got underway in a great coach, drawn by a team of six horses with three coachmen. With more stops for replenishing the horses and delays for refreshment, slower travel could now be expected. As it happened, in addition, they would be required to stop to repair a wheel along the way; consequently, Sainte-Menehould, thirty miles from their destination, was reached four hours behind schedule.

By that time news of their fight had reached the town and the National Guard alerted. The local postmaster, Jean-Batiste Drouet, had once seen Marie-Antoinette when he was in the army, and he recognized her. Checking the face of the 'valet' against an assignat, the paper bill issued as French currency in September 1790 bearing the King's silhouette, he hurriedly rode to Varennes where the coach carrying the royals would arrive at midnight. As the coach arrived, Drouet alerted the town authorities that the wayfarers were the royals. After some hours, the claim would be confirmed when the elderly mayor who had once lived in Versailles was brought in; as he saw Louis XVI his knee involuntarily crooked in homage. Their true identities now confirmed, Louis had to admit France was without a king!

News of the flight of the royals' spread through France even quicker than had news of the fall of the Bastille. Over the subsequent days, on their return to Paris the royals were escorted by the National Guard and scrutinized with reserve by people at roadside, who did not now bother to curtsy nor to remove their hats. The *flight to Varennes,* as it is now called, was a major *journée* opening a second great schism in the French Revolution, as it would "start a new party into life." (6)

Thus far the revolution had been about forming the basis for a constitutional monarchy, led by the constitution-making Emmanuel Joseph Sieyès, commonly known as the Abbé Sieyès, a Roman Catholic clergyman, and after the publication of his *What is the 3ʳᵈ Estate?* in 1789 one of the chief political theorists of the French Revolution. Sieyès book is now considered to be one of the seminal wellsprings of modern political theory, he stating in his 180-page pamphlet: "The Third Estate embraces ... all that which belongs to the nation; and all that which is not the Third Estate, cannot be regarded as being of the nation. What is the Third Estate? It is the whole."

The king and queen's re-appearance in Paris, where they would be held by a more stringent guard in the Tuileries Palace, was met by crowds along the boulevards drawn in numbing, stony silence. Marie-Antoinette, reviled as the instigator of the contrivance, would bear the epithet "Austrian Bitch." Capturing this new attitude, one of the most trenchant productions of the revolutionary period, whether in France or in Britain, was written by William Blake who mocked the French queen in this refrain of his ballad *Fayette* already quoted:

> "Let the Brothels of Paris be opened
> with many an alluring dance
> to awake the Pestilence thro' the city,"
> said the beautiful Queen of France

Then followed a chorus on the station of the King:

> The King awoke on his couch of gold,
> As soon as he heard these tidings told:
> "Arise & Come, both fife & drum,
> and the Famine shall eat both crust & crumb."

> Then he swore a great & solemn Oath:
> "To kill the people I am loth,
> But If they rebel, they must go to hell:
> They shall have a Priest & a passing bell." (7)

With this ballad—notwithstanding that the bard used the Revolution in France, as he did that in America, for its allegorical aspect as part of a larger impulse towards spiritual rebirth and revelation in his "prophesies" *America* and *Europe*—Blake followed its historical chronology rigorously too. His castigation of the royals was conceived entirely from the point of view of 'plebian' revilers swept up in the cavalcade of popular insurrection, and suggests the breadth of his engagement.

In the early morning hours of June 21, after he'd discovered the king and royal family had fled, Lafayette burst into Thomas Paine's bedroom before he'd gotten out of bed, exclaiming: "The birds are flown!"

"It is well," said Paine; "I hope there will be no attempt to recall them." (8)

As soon as he had dressed and gone out, Paine was stunned by the clamor being raised in the streets; the entire city seemed "disturbed by the folly of one man." This sudden fascination at recovering a king that had not the slightest value to anyone in the street nor to any party in the state, showed the absurdity of monarchical government. (9) Lafayette and his entire coterie in the National Assembly contrived to conceal the royals' flight under the fiction that they had been kidnapped, and later that afternoon they issued a bulletin to that effect. But the people congregating in the streets were having none of it. In that moment Paine and a few of his French conferees united for a purpose.

Etienne Dumont, the Swiss/French political writer, gave an account of a remarkable occurrence happening immediately after the news was abroad of the king's flight, published post-humously in 1832 in his *Recollections of Mirabeau.* Among Paine's first conversions to the idea of republicanism in France had been his friend Achille du Châtelet; it was he and Paine, after the flight of the king, who covered the walls of Paris with a *Proclamation of a Republic.* Uniformly drawing only cursory notice in the histories issued under the designation *The French Revolution;* Dumont wrote:

> DuChâtelet called on me, and after a little preface placed in my hand an English manuscript—a Proclamation to the French people. It was nothing less than an anti-royalist manifesto, and summoned the nation to seize the opportunity and establish a Republic. Paine was its author.
>
> DuChâtelet had adopted and was resolved to sign, placard the walls of Paris with it, and take the consequences. He had come to request me to translate and develop it. I began discussing the strange proposal, and pointed out the danger of raising a republican standard

without concurrence of the National Assembly, and nothing being as yet known of the king's intentions, resources, alliances, and possibilities of support by the army, and in the provinces. I asked if he had consulted any of the influential leaders,— Sieyès, Lafayette, etc. He had not: he and Paine had acted alone. (10)

On July 1, the "Société Republicaine" was inaugurated, as its members, as yet only five in number, began placarding central Paris with its manifesto. Nailed to the door of the National Assembly by the hand of Thomas Paine, it began:

> Brethren and fellow citizens: The serene tranquility, the mutual confidence which prevailed amongst us, during the time of the late King's escape, the indifference with which we beheld him return, are unequivocal proofs that the absence of a King is more desirable than his presence, and that he is not only a political superfluity, but a grievous burden pressing hard on the whole nation. (11)

Regarding it with disdain, some royalist members of the Assembly angrily tore the hand bill from the door, enraged at the 'desecration'. After ascertaining its purveyors' identities, they demanded their prosecution in the National Assembly, and the motion was seconded as there was considerable agitation in the hall. But the majority, in its embarrassment and disquietude, voted the order of the day, letting the issue fall.

The author of the manifesto, as indicated, was Thomas Paine in collaboration with Achille du Châtelet, a young nobleman imbued with republican ideas close to those of Condorcet. The names of the others in the society were unknown for many years, but Moncure Conway identified them as Condorcet, Brissot, and, he remarks, "probably" Paine's especial friend, the journalist and printer Nicolas

Bonneville, along with, it is now evident, Dumont, an intimate of Mirabeau who had died suddenly that April at age 42, a great hero even as his position of accommodation was slipping away. The new Society sought to follow up its sudden celebrity with a journal christened *Le Republicaine*, which however was to have no more than a few issues, or perhaps four at most, all appearing in that month.

Immediately following this, Sieyès, as spokesman for the constitutional monarchists in the National Assembly, launched a spirited debate with Paine in the pages of *Le Moniteur*. France had already adopted an "elective monarchy" and therefore any talk of republicanism was a mere indulgence, he wrote. But it was not from sentimentality that he was a monarchist, it was because, Sieyès added, "there is more liberty for the individual citizen under a monarchy than under a republic." He hoped at some later time to prove to republicans that monarchy was the more desirable system, but his salient point now was that neither a monarchy nor a republic were representative. But the superiority of the former arose from its executive power—all ministers and officials were subject to "an individual of superior rank, representing the stable unity of government." Conceding that hereditary succession was inadmissible in theory, but as elective monarchies seldom proved successful the Assembly could not be held liable for establishing a hereditary monarchy. (12)

Paine responded to Sieyès 8 July 1791:

At the moment of my departure for England, I read, in the Moniteur of Tuesday last, your letter, in which you give the challenge, on the subject of Government, and offer to defend what is called *Monarchical Opinion against the Republican system.*

I accept of your challenge with pleasure... The respect which I bear your moral and literary reputation, will be your security for my candour...but...let me promise, that I consider myself at liberty to ridicule...Monarchical absurdities, whensoever the occasion shall present itself.

This debate, occurring at a crucial moment was of considerable import, as it began to garner new partisans to the republican cause, among them Condorcet who had formerly been working closely with Sieyès, but had since transferred his allegiance. Jacobin and Cordeliers Club members, which had heretofore failed to sanction republicanism, and had scarcely given any thought to its meaning—Robespierre and Marat among them—were perplexed by the announcement of a society more forward-thinking than they. (13) Although the Paine/DuChâtelet document had been greeted with fervor, it would be considered a superfluity and was destined for obscurity, an idea awaiting a further re-appearance. That time, however, was not long-off, as the royalist rage it had elicited would raise the issue to a moment with preeminent consequence. (14)

In the following week Paine was back in London to honor an invitation he'd received from *The Society for Constitutional Information,* to attend the second anniversary celebration of the fall of the Bastille, to be held at the Crown and Anchor. That society, of which Paine was a member, had adopted his "Rights of Man" as their "Magna Charta" as soon as it came out, and its officers directed that all corresponding societies in England, Scotland, and France receive copies.

As he returned to London on the 13th Paine found the press, instigated by the government and its supporters under the banner "Church and King" were in outrage over his Republican manifesto in Paris, and lest the two movements across the channel be connected by his presence, he decided it prudent not to attend the advertised fête. The landlord of the Crown and Anchor nevertheless was prevailed upon to close its doors to the meeting, and it did not take place. Paine, and the "Paineites" as they were now called, were to be viewed with increasing calumny. Only a year later the government and its supporters would force him from the island, while others, among them the Unitarian minister and chemist Joseph Priestley, had their property destroyed, and, as in his case, he emigrated to America in 1794.

The tenor of the campaign against republicanism in Britain was seen in a savage caricature of Priestley and Paine by Isaac Cruikshank, whose work was a fixture in London print shops, dated 15 November 1792 and caustically titled *The Friends of the People*. In a pamphlet advocating reform, Priestley had prescribed "laying gunpowder" under the "old building of error"; this reference, however obliquely to incendiary means, evidently spurring the editorial cartoon. In it, Paine sets at a table opposite Priestley, as the two are surrounded by haphazardly strung weaponry. Ready to hand is a musket, and on the upper edge of the table there is a stack of pistols, while perched atop it is a demonic grinning putto. The Paine figure sits on an over-turned keg of gunpowder, daggers balanced precariously in both hands; Priestley's likeness, uncharacteristically holding a mug of ale, sits with the back of his chair tilted against a stack of books with titles that read "conspiracy," "treason," "plots," "revolutions," etc. Guns and knives abounding, there is a dish labeled phosphorous, and a gun butt inscribed with the words "Royal Electric fluid", in evident reference to Priestley's experiments.

On July 11, 1791, as Paine was returning to London, a Birmingham newspaper had carried a notice announcing that on the second anniversary of the storming of the Bastille a commemorative banquet, like that to be precluded at the

Crown and Anchor in London, would be held at a local hotel, inviting "any Friend of Freedom" to attend. Happening against a background of simmering controversy in a city with a record of riot against Dissenters—Birmingham was a caldron in the eyes of the propertied Anglican and pro-monarchy class, with its numerous brass and iron foundries, factories and work-sites, filled with the potentially recalcitrant. The announce-ment of the gathering of tribute came on the heels of an argument about the inclusion of some of Priestley's books in the local library, and on the same day, the temperature had again been raised as a handbill was distributed of unknown authorship espousing perceived "incendiary" ideas.

As city authorities demanded the identity of the writer, graffiti appeared: "Destruction to the Presbyterians," and "Church and King forever." With these strains abounding, Priestley was dissuaded from attending the celebration. But as the other attendees began to arrive they were harangued by a gathering crowd, which, by the time they adjourned had grown to many hundreds. Recruited from among the many artisans and laborers in Birmingham for a pint of beer, or some other pitiful sum, it would soon be evident the rowdies were purposively being directed from a prepared list of targets.

Beginning with stone throwing, they proceeded to the sacking of entire buildings. Moving quickly on from the hotel where the windows were broken, the first target became a Quaker Meeting house, until someone in the crowd yelled that the Quakers "never trouble themselves with anything, neither one side nor the other." The next target slated was the New Meeting chapel where Priestley presided. Burned to the ground, it was followed by the firing of another "Dissenting" chapel. Then advancing to Priestley's home—the residence was invaded by a large crowd, male and female, just as he and his family escaped. Its contents smashed and thrown from the windows, the building was razed to the ground—Priestley losing in the attack his scientific laboratory, his library, his manuscripts, all consumed by flames! (15) In four days twenty-seven homes and four "Dissenting" chapels were looted and burned. The *Lunar Society*, an informal gathering of scientific-minded individuals with which Priestley was closely associated, whose members included Matthew Boulton, James Watt, Erasmus Darwin, and Josiah Wedgwood, was threatened. Boulton and Watt became so concerned they armed their employees to protect their Soho Manufactory.

In Paris, the next day the National Assembly voted to temporarily suspend the authority of the king until the new constitution was ratified, but declared the king's person inviolable, and that he could not be put on trial. On July 16, when radicals in the Jacobin Club published a pamphlet proposing a petition to remove the king be signed *en mass* the following day at the Champ de Mars, the club's majority and its conservative members split from the main body, forming the Feuillants, or the "Society of the Friends of the Constitution." Robespierre then withdrawn Jacobean support for the pro-offered petition.

On the 17th two leading members of Cordeliers Club or the "Society of Friends of the Rights of Man and Citizen," Danton and Desmoulins, led off the signing of the petition, authored under the pen of Brissot, by delivering fiery speeches. With the signing ongoing, two men found lurking under the wooden altar built in the previous year for the considerable Fête *de la Federation*, the precursor of the Bastille celebration, were seized as suspected spies. Their lifeless bodies were soon seen dangling from lantern posts.

Hearing of this, the mayor of Paris, Jean Sylvain Bailly, declared martial law, ordering Lafayette and the National Guard to disperse the crowd. About 6,000 persons had signed the petition when dispersed, many of them illiterate sans-culottes who had merely inscribed an X. But that afternoon as a crowd began to amass again, this time the gathering was larger and more determined. A pro-republican pamphlet, *Les Revolutions de Paris* (No. 106) reported in its issue of July 17-23, 1791:

> The field of the federation…is a vast plain, at the center of which the altar of the fatherland is located, and where the slopes surrounding the plain are cut at intervals to facilitate entry, and exit. One section of the troops entered at the far side of the military school, another came through the entrance somewhat lower down, and a third by the gate that opens on to the Grande Rue de Chailot, where the red flag [signifying martial law] was placed. The people at the altar, more than fifteen thousand strong, had hardly noticed the flag when shots were heard. "Do not move, they are firing blanks. They must come here to post the law." The troops advanced a second time. The composure of the faces of those who surrounded the altar did not change. But when a third volley mowed many of them down, the crowd fled, leaving only a group of a hundred people at the altar. Alas, they paid dearly for their courage and blind trust in the law.

With fifty killed and a hundred wounded, this was called the *Champ de Mars Massacre*. To all appearance it marked the death knell for "republicanism", as the political clubs and their newspapers were ruthlessly suppressed by Lafayette and the police. Danton, who would later be accused of not having signed the petition he held out to others, fled to London; Marat and Desmoulins went into hiding in Paris. The suppression caused panic within the revolutionaries generally; but the prestige of Lafayette and his National Guard too had been damaged. The fusillade on the *Champ de Mars* would become the genesis of a wholly new Jacobinism, to be driven by the sans-culottes of Paris under the banner of "fraternity".

In the three years and counting beginning from 1789, the bourgeoisie, through their representatives in the National Assembly and in the political clubs and in the press, had set about rationalizing and reforming French society; their program, entirely liberal, had unfolded within the framework of an emerging constitutional monarchy, that had included a significant re-organization of the Catholic religious hierarchy in France. For the first time an alternative avenue had been opened outside the deliberations of the Assembly. Coming to the fore in the revolution now were the Parisian laboring classes and the poor led largely by artisans and small shopkeepers, the "sans-culottes"—those wearing the full trousers or pantaloons, and denigrated as being "without breeches" like those fashionable among the nobility and bourgeoisie; who also wore silk stockings with buckled shoes. In contrast, the sans-culotte laced their shoes and were considered anything but gentlemen.

These were the people that felt the sting of their precarious condition most acutely—economically and socially, as indeed politically—and it was they, during the years of revolution who had fully imbibed the spirit of the Declaration of the Rights of Man and of the enlightenment philosophy, particularly as epitomized by Jean-Jacques Rousseau. As it is they who would push through the abolition of monarchy, and the abolition of the privileges of the nobility and of the Roman Catholic clergy, as they would also favor the establishment of fixed wages and the implementation of price controls on staple commodities so that they and their families might afford a modicum of security. They would be directed into battle by populist revolutionaries such as Marat and Jacques Hébert, also a radical journalist and editor of his own newspaper and member of the Cordeliers Club—the so-called *Enragés,* as the Paris Commune and the Parisian sections became their redoubt.

The seed thrown from the hand of Thomas Paine was beginning to bear a bountiful fruit; (16) henceforward republicanism would become the driving force.

Late that fall (November 2) in a letter to William Short, U.S. Charge d'Affairs in Paris, Paine wrote: "We have distressing accounts here from St. Domingo. It is a natural consequence of Slavery and must be expected everywhere. The Negroes are enraged at the opposition made to their relief and are determined, if not to relieve themselves to punish their enemies." (17)

On the night of August 22, 1791, the "sugar-factories" covering the North Plain had been the first to rise. For weeks before, through the medium of Vodou, leaders had prepared and organized a mass movement where a "huge man", Dutty Boukman, the head man on a plantation, was the chief. His plan was for the blacks to eliminate the whites on a colony-wide scale, and to take the land for themselves. Working and living in groups, each was to proceed on the plantation to which they were attached, slaying their own masters and his family and his overseers.

The night of the uprising had been ravaged by a tropical storm with driving rain. Carrying torches to light the way between intermittent flashes of lightning and rolling thunder, the slave cabal met in an opening in the dense forest covering

Morne Rouge, the mountain overlooking "Le Cap." Boukman gave some instructions and incantations, as all present sucked the blood of a gorged pig. Then Boukman offered a prayer: "Our god who is good to us orders us to revenge our wrongs. He will direct our arms and aid us. Throw away the symbol of the god of the whites who has so often caused us to weep, and listen to the voice of liberty, which speaks in the hearts of us all." (18)

The revolt in the French colony of Saint-Domingue, today's Haiti, was to be the largest rising of slaves since the Spartacus revolt in antiquity against the Romans. But this revolt, unlike its antecedent, in attaining its objectives, became a revolution, ending finally in 1803 with the defeat of the French army at the Battle of Vertières, and in the creation of an independent black republic on January 1, 1804. Regardless of its imperfections as they may be perceived, and although it may be seen rather as a series of episodes, its decisive economic importance as the jewel of French colonial possessions, coming at the time of France's own 'moral tempest', and its impact on the subsequent development of the United States, as may be seen—places Saint-Domingue at the conjunction of events with decided historical ramifications.

In the last week of August and into October 1791, as seen from Le Cap, the North Plain lay in ruins, with the whole of the horizon in flames. During the day, as cane ash swirled over the city and the harbor, and was driven, as the saying goes, like trails of snow through its streets, the sunlight dimmed. C.L.R. James wrote of those who had reaped the whirlwind:

> Like the peasants in the Jacquerie or the Luddite wreckers, they were seeking their salvation in the most obvious way, the destruction of what they knew was the cause of their sufferings; and if they destroyed much it was because they had suffered much. They knew that as

long as these plantations stood their lot would be to labour on them until they dropped. The only thing was to destroy them. (19)

In revolt, the slave camp was an exhibition mostly of unclothed bodies, with some in rags, some with the detritus of finer clothing picked up on the plantations. The weapons were those that had been seized from their master's stock; a musket, a pistol, swords, but most carried plain agricultural implements, things they could lay their hands on—a hoe became a stick with a point of iron. There was a small cavalry mounted on worn horses and old mules. Divided among three bands, each had its own leader. The officers were dressed in what scraps of military uniform that could be found, and referred to themselves as "general" or "marshal", "colonel" or "commander". Among them were brave men, men ready for the most dangerous exploits; but some were fire eaters, always drunk. And some were men with exceptional intelligence.

After a month, into their camp walked a man who had been a steward of livestock on a plantation outside Le Cap. He was a man of practical education, who'd learned to read and was versed in administration and in intercourse with men, with a mind cultivated concerning affairs at home and abroad. He was 45 and was already considered 'old'. From the moment he joined the revolt he rose to the first rank without rivalry, and helped give shape, fitfully, to a world in which he'd been waywardly taught. His name was Toussaint, to which would be added the appellation L'Ouverture. (20)

And didn't the bard of London give an "infernal" reading to *The Declaration of Independence* in his *America, A Prophecy* (1794), as previously cited in this narrative:

Let the slave grinding at the mill run out into the field
Let him look up into the Heavens & laugh in the bright
    air;

Let the inchained soul, shut up in darkness and in
   signing,
Whose face has never seen a smile in thirty weary years,
Rise and look out; his chains are loose, his dungeon doors
   are open.
And let his wife and children return from the oppressor's
   scourge. (21)

William Blake was unusually well informed among Londoners
about the developments in the colonies, both the British and
French, as of the Dutch. It was in this period of unprecedented
revolt in Saint-Domingue that he was engaged in illustrating
John Gabriel Stedman's *Narrative*.

Stedman, who was born in the Austrian Netherlands, but
of a Scot father, was an officer in the Dutch Republic's Scots
Brigade, and he'd completed his book by 1790. With
illustrations from his amateur but capable hand, he had taken
the book to Joseph Johnson for publication. Johnson
distributed eighty of Stedman's drawings to nine engravers,
William Blake and Francesco Bartolozzi among them. Blake
engraved sixteen plates, completing the first batch in
December 1792 and the remainder at the same time the
following year. Since engraving, particularly of this quality
(these are among Blake's most striking published images) was
a protracted process, it was already in the prior year that
Stedman wrote in his journal, 1 December 1791: "I wrote to the
Engraver Blake to thank him twice for his excellent work but
never received any answer." Such tardiness was characteristic
of the engraver, as his biographers have noted; but in any
event, he was engaged in multitudinous and exacting tasks.

Although himself a monarchist, and although he may have
recoiled at the horrors of slavery which he was documenting,

he was not an abolitionist as it was then beginning to be understood, but the book would have an instructive value for many decades as an anti-slavery tract. While Stedman chaffed at what he perceived as Johnson's *Jacobinism*, he found himself at ease with the engraver and his wife in Lambeth while he was in London. He had retired to Devon, and on several occasions, would take bed and hospitality in their cottage.

Blake's engravings, all concerning the condition and punishment of slaves, are of densely cross-hatched figures against a blank background, while most of the other illustrations in the book were of the flora and fauna of Surinam. These are the prints, since the book was a wide success well into the nineteenth century among abolitionist societies, Blake was most known in his time. Among these are *Flagellation of a Female Samboe Slave, The Execution of Breaking on the Rack, A Negro hung alive by the Ribs to a Gallows*. Blake's engravings emphasize the dignity of his subjects in their suffering, giving to each a force of expression as they look directly into a viewer's eyes. Stoical under the overwhelming cruelties of their torturers, defiant of tyranny, they are the spirit of human freedom.

Per Stedman's instruction, the *finis* page is "an emblematical picture" executed by Blake titled *Europe Supported by Africa & America*. It depicts three young nude women, each amply but tenderly rendered, clasping one another with sisterly regard. On the ground, at their feet roses auspiciously blossom, while the European figure takes the center, supported on either side by her sisters wearing their slave bracelets, while their white sister wears a long string of beads. Before them a vine is held forming a bow, entwining the hands and delicate limbs of Africa and America, signalizing that the bond of servitude might be broken.

His book completed and ready for publication, Stedman's

journal entry for June 24, 1795, reads: "On Midsummer Day receive the first volume of my book quite marr'd, oaths and sermons inserted &c. . . . How dreadful London; where a Mr. B—declared openly his lust for infants, his thirst for regicide, and believes in no God whatever...." (22)

8.

And thus her voice arose

Concluding a conference at Pillnitz Castle near Dresden on August 27, 1791, the brother of Maria-Antoinette, Austria's emperor Leopold II, and Prussia's Frederick William II issued a declaration on the revolution in France and the state of affairs with which their kindred monarch was threatened. Although the conference dealt mainly with Austria's on-going war with the Ottoman Empire and with the "question" of Poland's partition; the four-sentence pronouncement, written at the behest of noble émigrés from France, was a warning to French revolutionaries that the prerogatives of the King must be restored. Knowing that Britain's government led by William Pitt would not yet support war, Leopold crafted his words to forestall such commitment. The so-called *Pillnitz Declaration* stated that the participants viewed the situation as "a subject of common interest for all Europe's sovereigns," as it called upon those powers to "use the most efficient means...to place (him) in a position to be totally free to consolidate the basis of a monarchical government."

The *reign of Reason* envisioned and foretold for a century and more before the cataract of events known as the French Revolution, had been the object of a co-fraternity of *philoso-phes* living largely in western Europe, with Great Britain and

France and Holland being the nations where these carried the greatest influence. With obvious connection with the rise of European empires and the exploration and division of the globe induced by their overseas rivalry—one must surely designate its initial phase as the plundering of these 'possessions' carried forward on a continental and oceanic scale. But the proliferation of the ideas of the Enlightenment too were concomitant with the spread of printing technology and the rise of literacy, and with the interconnectedness these fostered within states and nations, as across borders, and across seas. With burgeoning trade and industry, and the new scientific investigation, this facilitated the development of institutes, academies, and societies.

18th-century civilization in Britain and France was especially noted for its salons, with France being uniquely noteworthy for their sway; gatherings that included eminent literary and political figures, scientists, and scholars, with a strong admixture of aristocratic notables and patrons, sponsored and conducted by women who were often endowed with exceptional intelligence and educational attainment, as also with social status, not to say with beauty and graciousness as hostesses.

In a salon of the sort in pre-revolution France in 1788, with the eminent mathematician and secretary of the *Academe Française* the Marquis de Condorcet in attendance, a farseeing individual without hesitation was able to foretell of his rise to preeminence in writing a new constitution after the abolition of the monarchy, and of his subsequent tragic death by poisoning on the flagstones of a prison floor!

And what of the women? it was asked. Won't they be lucky "to go for nothing" in these revolutions you foresee? "T'is not that we don't meddle in them, but it seems we shall not suffer." "You are wrong, Mesdames," said the diviner, *"for this time you will be treated like men."* (1)

Indeed, women were to become a vector for the transformations in France as revolution gripped the nation in the years 1789-95; but it would only be in the decades following its tragic denouement, women began to assess the conquests yet to be made.

On September 3, 1791, the National Assembly finished its work in drafting a governmental structure and the assiduous negotiations attending, adopting a new French Constitution. Curtailing the King's executive authority, it allowed him a suspensive veto whereby he could withhold assent to bills up to five years, after which the Assembly could enact a bill without royal approval. It also amended the king's title from "King of France" to "King of the French," implying he was not a ruler by "divine right"; the King retaining the right to form a cabinet, and to select and appoint ministers. The constitution distinguished between *active* citizens, those having property with the right to vote, and *passive* citizens, those below the threshold for property qualification, the poor without the vote; as the category of active citizenship was also two-tiered, with those who could vote and those in addition, who were eligible to hold public office. The constitution did nothing to acknowledge or affirm the rights of women, nor of slaves to be free, but did acknowledge *free blacks* as citizens. Further, it created a unicameral legislature, which now was designated to succeed the National Assembly on the basis of new elections.

While the King reluctantly acquiesced and signed the constitution on 14 September, it did not appear he had any faith or interest that it might be a workable political arrangement. Yet it was clear his standing had been fatally compromised by the "flight to Varennes", and that he perhaps felt the only way forward for him was to demonstrate its defects by putting it to the test.

The constitution of 1791 had as its preamble the seventeen

articles under the title *The Declaration of the Rights of Man and of the Citizen*; a framing to be contested in the following month by a counter-declaration of *the rights of women*. The author, who was especially prolific during the years 1789 through 1793—the year of her execution by guillotine—was a woman who like Wollstonecraft was wholly focused on "mounting the rostrum" denied her sex. The writer's name was Olympe de Gouges, who as Marie Gouze was born in 1748 in the south of France, a butcher's daughter. Bound in an arranged marriage at 16, her husband died in the following year, and she and her infant son went to live in Paris with her sister, she vowing never to marry again, calling betrothal "the tomb of trust and love." (2)

In the 1780's she became known as a playwright, writing as many as forty plays, some of which were read at the *Comédie-Française,* but not preformed there. In 1789, to ameliorate this, she published a pamphlet, *Le Bonheur primitive de l'homme (The Original Happiness of Man),* where she urged a national theatre for women. Her best-known play was titled *L'Esclavage de Negres (Black Slavery)*, the first play in France to deal directly with the in-humanity of slavery, and to be written from the perspective of the slave. Dramatizing a direct connection between autocratic monarchy and the institution of slavery in the French colonies, after three performances in 1788 it was shut down by the mayor of Paris for being incendiary. The mayor's action had been precipitated by a press campaign of French colonists and slave traders, who encouraged disruptions to wreck the performance.

Fashioning herself in dress and with the accompaniments to allow an easy fit into Parisian 'society', among her merits, she attended the salon of Marie-Louise-Sophie de Grouchy, or Madam de Condorcet, wife of the famed Inspector-General of the French mint, the Marquis de Condorcet. All were members of an important political club launched in October 1790 called

Amis de la Verité (Society of the Friends of Truth), or the so-called *Cercel Social* (Social Club). It had 130 members, but an audience that ranged from five to eight thousand per week. Established by the bookseller, printer, and journalist Nicolas Bonneville and the French bishop Claude Fauchet, with the design to raise the level of discourse. By 1791 the *Social Club* had become wholly republican and was an advocate for 'women's rights', as well as the place for what became known belatedly as the Girondins to present their ideas and promote action. Introduced by Lafayette to the influential couple, Thomas Paine was also an attendee in these years when in Paris of the salon of Sophie de Condorcet, as well as of the meetings of the Social Club. She would translate his work, as she did that of fellow attendee Adam Smith, as the couple entered into a concordat or friendship of the first order with the political pamphleteer.

In the revolutionary years, Olympe de Gouges would author as many as seventy pamphlets and posters disseminated around Paris, signing herself *citoyenne*, as she completed two novels. She was self-taught and often wrote hastily, sometimes dictating the text to a printer as she composed it. To the extent she believed it was the best means to keep the nation from falling into anarchy, she had advocated preserving the monarchy, but by 1791 embraced republican revolution as a beacon of hope.

Disenchanted with the revolutionary process when the constitution was presented, as equality was not extended to women, Olympe de Gouges is known today for her *Declaration of the Rights of Women and of the Female Citizen,* entirely framed in discussions in the *Cercel Social.* Paralleling the 'Rights of Man' article by article, in her pamphlet her wording is succinct and contains some biting satire, while in the preamble she issued a rousing call for action:

Women, wake-up; the tocsin of reason sounds through-out the universe; recognize your rights. The powerful empire of nature is no longer surrounded by prejudice, fanaticism, superstition, and lies. The torch of truth has dispersed all the clouds of folly and usurpation. Enslaved man has multiplied his forces, and needs yours to break his chains.

The following for comparison are two articles of the two declarations, one and ten:

I. Men are born free and equal in rights. Social distinc-tions can be based only on public utility.

I. **Woman is born free and lives equal to man in her rights. Social distinctions can be based only on common utility.**

X. No one should be disturbed on account of his opinions, even religious, provided their manifestation does not upset the public order established by law.

X. **No one is to be disquieted for his very basic opinions; woman has the right to mount the scaffold; she must equally have the right to mount the rostrum, provided that her demonstrations do not disturb the legally established public order.** (3)

This inexorable judgment—"Women has the right to mount the scaffold, so she should have the right to mount the rostrum"—is a sentence said to have first been uttered in debate at the *Cercel Social*, where women's rights were supported, but whose time they merely heralded; one whose author was very much in earnest, paying with her life for her speech.

De Gouges declaration would lie barren of result in the Legislative Assembly, as the National Assembly was now called, but that body did attach two articles later that fall protecting the rights of Protestants and of Jews.

Marie-Jeanne Philpon, the daughter of a Parisian engraver, or Manon as her friends called her, was to become well known as Madame Roland. She was unusually accomplished to say the least, in languages, in philosophy, and in literature. Captivated by Plutarch's *Vitae Parallelae* at nine, at twenty-one she was singularly struck as were many by Jean-Jacques Rousseau's *Julie, La Nouvelle* Héloïse *(1761),* and would re-read it periodically. Marrying Jean-Marie Roland, when he was twenty years her senior—he had been a manufacture in Lyon and author of works with bearing on industry, and an expert in the textile industry—before his election to the municipal government in Lyon, and then to the French National Assembly. In 1791, as the couple moved to Paris, she became famous as the all-conquering wife of the soon to be famous statesman; a success garnered not solely by the powers and eloquence of her voice and pen—theirs, as was the Condorcet's, was a collaboration.

Matching Rousseau's ideal conception of femininity with her own, she became the conduit and soul of an important salon that became the center of the Girondin 'faction'. John Abbott writing in mid-19th century had this description of her in his *Madame Roland*:

At the political evening reunions in the salon of Madame Roland, she was invariably present, not as a prominent actor in the scenes, taking a conspicuous part in the social debates but as a quiet and modest lady, of well known intellectual supremacy, whose active mind took the liveliest interest in the agitations of the hour. The influence she exerted was the polished, refined, attractive

influence of an accomplished woman, who moved in her
own appropriate sphere. (4)

This salon, however, was not really a social gathering, but
rather a political meeting held twice weekly, conducted
between the ending of the session of the assembly and the
beginning of the meetings at the Jacobin Club. She was
invariably the only woman present, where for a time, Danton
was among the attendees; as was a young lawyer, as Abbott
wrote, from the country "with a stupid expression of
countenance, shallow complexion, and ungainly gestures." He
had made himself unpopular, by wearing the assembly with
"the posy speeches" he delivered in the body.

> [T]his young man silent and moody, appeared with
> others in the salon of Madame Roland. . . She was struck
> by his singularity. . . He was captivated by those charms
> of conversation in which Madame Roland was unrivaled.
> Silently—for he had no conversational powers—he lin-
> gered around her chair, treasured up her spontaneous
> tropes and metaphors, and absorbed her sentiments. (5)

This was Maximilien Marie Isidore Robespierre. He was
from Arras in the old province of Artois in north-eastern
France. Receiving a scholarship to study at the College Louis-
le-Grand in 1769, among his fellow pupils were Camille
Desmoulins and Stanislas Fréron. Schooled to the admiration
of an idealized Roman Republic, the young Robespierre
became enamored with the rhetoric of Cicero and Cato, and
other figures in classical history. The philosophe of Jean-
Jacques Rousseau had particular appeal to him, whose *Contrat
Social* would soar to the heights in his spiritual pantheon. In
1781, he was admitted to the bar; in 1789, he'd been elected as
one of 16 deputies for Arras to the Estates-General. In June of

that year, Robespierre, then 31, joined the National Assembly, moving thence to the National Constituent Assembly. He was the coiner of that famous flourish "Liberte, Egalité, fraternite." The historian Jules Michelet would write of the fascination that Robespierre was to exercise over his auditors in the subsequent years of his career as a revolutionary, in his *Histoire de la Revolution français* (1847-53): "The inquisitorial figure of Robespierre, sickly, blinking, hiding his dim eyes behind his glasses, was a strange sphinx of a man, whom one watched ceaselessly despite oneself, and whom one disliked watching."

Also figuring in September 1791 was a 216-page report on public instruction prepared by Charles Maurice de Talleyrand. A member of the 1st Estate as Bishop of Autun, a post he had purchased, he had been the representative of the church to the Bourbon court whose name was to become, as he survived for three decades on the French and European political scene, a by-word for crafty and cynical diplomacy. His report, written in the spirit of the Enlightenment was praised for its principles, but never applied to any reform legislation. He had, however, recommended that females be excluded from the newly founded public education system after mid-level. Mary Wollstonecraft, in the midst of her two-year sojourn in Paris, 1791-1793, read Talleyrand's report and immediately began writing her response.

As ever the commensurate stylist, Wollstonecraft employed emotion and the female voice to appeal for support from her middle-class readers. She wrote: "Liberty is the mother of virtue, and if women be, by their very constitution slaves, and not allowed to breathe the sharp invigorating air of freedom, they must ever languish like exotics, and be reckoned beautiful flaws of nature."

Engaging at length in her essay in dispute with Jean-Jacques Rousseau, she assailed that author's *Émile, ou De l'Éducation* (1762) where he advocated females should be educated differently from males to ensure they were submissive and compliant to men's needs. Rousseau wrote of females:

> They must be subject all their lives, to the most constant and severe restraint, which is that of decorum: it is, therefore, necessary to accustom them early to such confinement, that it may not afterwards cost them too dear; and to suppression of their caprices, that they may the more readily submit to the will of others.

Wollstonecraft wrote: "Contending for the rights of woman, my main argument is built on this simple principle, that if she not be prepared by education to become the companion of man, she will stop the progress of knowledge and virtue; for truth must be common to all." In *Vindication of the Rights of Women* she advocated, if not yet for women's suffrage, then for a place in government nonetheless: "I really think that women ought to have representatives, instead of being arbitrarily governed without having any direct share allowed them in the deliberations of government."

Wollstonecraft's new treatise was written in three months and published in January 1792 by Johnson in London, with a second edition appearing that same year. It was during this time that the publisher Joseph Johnson was engaged both in work on Stedman's *Narrative of a five-year Expedition*, and in issuing Mary Wollstonecraft's *Vindication*, which would bring her before a wide public as a 'woman writer'. The especial relation of the engraver William Blake to these authors has received due commentary, as clearly, he and Stedman were confidentially conversant. But the importance of Stedman's book to Blake as bard of *Visions of the Daughters of Albion*, completed in his illuminated series in 1793, also deserves notice. That was in regard to the Scotch officer's unusual relation to Joanna, his lover and domestic servant while in Surinam.

Stedman had purchased Joanna in 1773 from her mother when she was fifteen years old. Describing her as "rather more than middle size—She was perfectly streight with the most elegant Shapes that can be view'd in nature moving her well-formed Limbs as when a Goddess walk'd—Her eyes as black as Ebony were large and full of expression, bespeaking the Goodness of her heart." Stedman returned to the Dutch Republic in 1777, taking with him a son born of their union, Joanna remaining in Surinam still a slave. Stedman explained why she refused to go with them: "She said, that if I soon returned to Europe, she must either be parted from me forever, or accompany me to a land where the inferiority of her condition must prove a great disadvantage to her benefactor and to herself; and in either of these cases, she should be most miserable." (6)

Although Stedman and Blake were in opposition in many of their views, there was an evident friendship, perhaps due to a melding of temperaments that allowed for an influence and accord that did not exist between that author and his publisher. It has been surmised that Joanna was among the promptings enabling Blake to realize his startling conception of female sexual freedom with Oothoon in *Visions*. It's been suggested also that Theotormon in that poem is a mythicized version of John Stedman. Oothoon, who Blake calls the "soft soul of America", is in love with Theotormon (from the Greek *Theos* and the Latin *tormatum*) representing the chaste man filled with a false sense of righteousness, but suddenly she is brutally raped by Bromion, a slaveholder, symbolizing the passionate man full of lustful fires:

Bromion rent her with his thunders. On his stormy bed
Lay the faint maid, and soon her woes appaled his
    thunders hoarse.

Bromion spoke: "Behold this harlot here on Bromion's
　　bed,
And let the jealous dolphins sport around the lovely
　　maid;
Thy soft American plains are mine, and mine thy north
　　& south:
Stampt with my signet are the swarthy children of the
　　sun
They are obedient, they resist not, they obey the scourge;
Their daughters worship terrors and obey the violent.
Now thou maist marry Bromion's harlot, and protect the
　　child
Of Bromion's rage, that Oothoon shall put forth in nine
　　moons' time."

In the poem Blake condemns woman's sexual slavery, abetted
by marriage and religion:

At entrance Theotormon sits, wearing the threshold hard
With secret tears; beneath him sound like waves on the
　　desart shore
The voice of slaves beneath the sun, and children bought
　　with money,
That shiver in religious caves beneath the burning fires
Of lust, that belch incessant from the summits of the
　　earth. (7)

Wollstonecraft's *Vindication* was published one year
before Blake produced *Visions*, Blake suggesting an analogy
between the daughters of African slaves in America, and the
daughters of Albion, or English women. Wollstonecraft had
written: "When I call women slaves, I mean in a political and
civil sense." Blake carried that critique into psychic and sexual
repression; the daughters of Albion share in Oothoon's
infuriation and agony—"The Daughters of Albion hear her
woes, and echo back her sighs."

On Thomas Paine's return to London in summer 1791, he had followed his republican manifesto in Paris, with a second manifesto titled *Address and Declaration of the Friends of Universal Peace and Liberty*. This document was taken up and considered at a meeting August 20 at the Thatched-House Tavern, signed by John Horne Tooke, as chairman. Paine wrote:

> We congratulate the French nation for having laid the axe to the root of tyranny, and for erecting government on the sacred hereditary rights of man; rights which appertain to all, and, not to one more than another.

> We know of no human authority superior to that of a whole nation; and we profess and claim it as our principle that every nation has at all times an inherent and indefeasible right to constitute and establish such government for itself as best accords with its disposition, interest, and happiness. (9)

Paine was at the forefront of a growing and energized group of radicals, literary men and women, and nonconformist preachers, convening in taverns or at arranged meeting places. The *London Corresponding Society* was formed March 1792, Thomas Hardy, the shoemaker, chairman. Attracting tradesmen, shopkeepers, mechanics, it grew from a handful of dues paying members to over two thousand in short order. Its central tenet was that every adult man, of sound mind and without criminal record, should have the right to vote for a member of Parliament. "At this juncture," his biographer Moncure Conway wrote, "Paine held a supremacy in the constitutional clubs of England and Ireland equal to that of

Robespierre over the Jacobins of Paris;" and his "'The Rights of Man' was the first exposition of the republicanism of Jefferson, Madison, and Edmund Randolph that ever appeared." (10) In a private communication—when published reflecting on his capacity as Secretary of State for the United States—Thomas Jefferson had endorsed Paine's pamphlet, giving it increased celebrity.

Staying at the home of the bookseller Thomas Clio Richman, publisher of political pamphlets and a friend from the days before he left for America and later his biographer, Paine began writing another book—his great projection toward the future, its working title *Kingship*, but was to be appended to the *Rights of Man, as Part the Second.*

Frequently lounging at the White Bear Tavern or in coffeehouses, he kept company with another engraver interested in reform, William Sharp, the historical painter George Romney, Horne Tooke, an organizer of London reform societies and former Wilkes aide, Dr. Priestley, and Joseph Johnson, and with Joel Barlow, or was in meetings with eminences like the French or American ambassadors, or with his close friend, Lord Edward FitzGerald, a Whig member of parliament and supporter of Irish independence, as he continued an acquaintance with William Blake.

To conform to the new age, many people began going without powdered wigs and were wearing simplified clothing, as men were cutting their hair short in the manner of the Jacobins. Still, Rickman was to write this portrayal of Paine in the old guise:

> ...in his person [he] was about five feet ten inches high, and rather athletic; he was broad shouldered, and lately stooped a little. His eye, of which the painter could not convey their exquisite meaning was full, brilliant, and singularly piercing; it had in it the 'muse of fire.' In his

dress and person he was generally very cleanly, and wore his hair cued, with side curls, and powered, so that he looked altogether like a gentleman of the old French school. His manners were easy and gracious.... (10)

Behind the scenes, as previously mentioned, the government began efforts to isolate Paine, beginning with pressuring the landlords of the Crown and Anchor and the Thatched-House to refuse their rooms to the "Paineites." (11) The alarm of the aristocracy and conservatives with the constitution clubs grew as they began to manifest support for the French Revolution, culminating that July with the attacks on Priestley and other non-conformists in Birmingham, they reacting, one writer remarked, as though they need contain and quarantine an invasion of "political cholera."

Of his growing influence and the attentions of the government, Paine wrote the mechanic John Hall November 25, 1791: "I have so far got the ear of John Bull that he will read what I write—which is more than was done before to the same extent." In the letter previously cited to U.S. Charge d'Affaires at Paris William Short, Paine elaborated further on the situation in England and on his concurrent writing:

I am again in the press but shall not be out till about Christmas, when the town will begin to fill. By what I can find, the Government Gentry begin to threaten. They have already tried all their under-plots of abuse and scurrility without effect; and have managed those in general so badly as to make the work and the author more famous; several answers also have been written against it which did not excite reading enough to pay the expense of printing. I have but one way to be secure in my next work which is, to go further than in my first. I see that *great rogues* escape by the excess of their crimes, and, perhaps, it may be the same in honest cases.

However, I shall make a pretty large division in the public opinion, probably too much so to encourage the Government to put it to issue.... (12)

In *part the first* of *Rights of Man,* written in view of the survival of royalty in the French Constitution are Paine's general principles, as well as his exposition of the scene in France through October 1789. In *part the second,* as the situation in France shot beyond securing a safe harbor for the continuance of monarchal forms, he fully elaborated his political philosophy; and as it was hailed by the public, he was emboldened. The republican form of government had for its object the well-being of the whole of a nation he contended; monarchy was government in the interest of the individual over those of the people; aristocracy, the interest of class. A hereditary monarchy, meanwhile, had its foundation in war and conquest, in plunder.

Paine's was an argument to put civil society in a condition, as he believed might be the case with the American constitutional system but for its lamentable and inexcusable inclusion of slavery, whereby it could proceed on the basis of reform, eliminating the necessity for revolution by abolishing hereditary government and its institutions. Delivering a systematic augment on the origins of government, Paine advanced a strong case for economic equality, proposing a progressive taxation that would prohibit a new aristocracy from arising, even suggesting salary limitations on governmental representatives. The social order exists and has existed without government, Paine reasoned; government is only necessitated to secure those natural rights which, as individuals, we cannot secure alone. All in society, therefore, must acquiesce to these controls in exchange for the benefit of those rights.

The second part of *Rights of Man* became Paine's

argument for a program of social legislation to ameliorate the deplorable conditions perpetuated everywhere for the poor:

> When countries that are called civilized, we see age going to the workhouse and youth to the gallows, something must be wrong in the system of government. It would seem, by the exterior of appearances of such countries, that all was happiness; but there lies hidden from the eye of common observation, a mass of wretchedness that has scarcely any other chance, than to expire in poverty or infamy....

Paine's 'social' treatise was published in April in France, which he dedicated to M. De La Fayette. But this was to be omitted in the French edition, where he wrote:

> The only point upon which I could ever discover that we differed was not as to principles of Government, but as to time... That which you suppose accomplishable in fourteen or fifteen years I may believe practicable in a much shorter period. Mankind, as it appears to me, are always ripe enough to understand their true interest, provided it be presented clearly to their understanding, and that in a manner not to create suspicion by anything like self-design, nor offend by assuming too much. Where we would wish to reform we must not reproach.

With Paine's new book soon to be in the hands of Cornish tin-miners, journeyman potters, and Sheffield cutlers (13), as it spread too across Ireland and Scotland, and was read in France, that time had bypassed Lafayette.

9.

Deluge o'er the earth-born man

In the years immediately following the storming of the Bastille the indigent in France were hard-pressed even for the means to meet subsistence levels, as the price of bread, the main staple in their diet, spelled ruination as it reached onerous levels. In Paris, a laborer with two children and a wife to support, or with elderly parents and relatives to care for, required at least two four-pound loaves per day to feed four.

With sugar and coffee and cocoa widely available, what were formerly luxury items now became necessities. Many of the working poor became habituated to consuming strong drinks with sugar in the morning to tide them over till the late afternoon, when they were accustomed to having their largest meal. That the vast majority of French citizens paid scant attention to the plight of the slaves in the colonies can be granted; indeed, even in the Legislative Assembly the rights conferred upon *free blacks* were conflated with that of the slaves. But by the winter of 1791-92 the revolt in Saint-Domingue was heard echoing across the Atlantic waters ominously in the Parisian markets, as it reverberated throughout the country in the form of shortages in sugar and coffee. With the colony in turmoil, and the commodities on which the economic prosperity of France depended threatened by rising prices, speculators began hoarding scarce colonial products.

On January 23 food riots erupted in Paris, and would recur sporadically over the next two months in the capital city and across France. In one town where the mayor refused to act by freezing prices against speculation, he was seized and killed. In February, although under military escort, cart loads of sugar were seized. There were arrests and trials, as the Assembly was spurred in debate about the plight of the poor. Known as the "sugar riots," although there were shortages in coffee, bread, and soap, many shops were looted, as goods were seized from warehouses to be sold at market, or directly from the proprietorship, at "just prices" that people were calling "taxation populaire". With the products sold, the owners would be given the proceeds. Women became the most energetic accomplices in this activity, "they were the real furies," one chronicler wrote.

The popular female militants, or "patriotic women" were known to police informants as *tricoteuses* (knitters), for the propensity some would display in the galleries of the Assembly for carrying their needlework with them, or a bit later when encouraged by Robespierre, to bringing their knitting to executions by guillotine. Two of these who would rise into prominence and just as suddenly fall into obscurity, although undoubtedly not knitters, were the theatrical performer Claire Lacombe, and Pauline Leon, from a family of chocolate makers, as she was herself of that trade. They both began to frequent the Cordeliers Club which admitted women, as both would form a liaison with Theophile Leclerc, a soldier and political radical and one of *les Enragés;* he first with Lacombe, but he would subsequently marry Leon. Lacombe and Leon are recognized today for the *Société des républicaines révolutionnaires* (Society of Revolutionary Republican Women), founded in May 1793 with 170 members, whose meetings were held in the library at the Jacobin Club, Leon becoming the president. Charles Dickens, whose *A Tale of Two Cities* was based on a close and near exhaustive reading of Thomas Carlyle's *The French Revolution*, patterned his Madame Defarge, also a knitter, after these women. In his chapter "The Knitting Done", he wrote:

> There were many women at that time, upon whom the time laid a dreadfully disfiguring hand; but, there was not one among them more to be dreaded than this ruthless woman, now taking her way along the streets. Of a strong and fearless character, of shrewd sense and readiness, of great determination, of that kind of beauty which not only seems to impart to its possessor firmness and animosity, but to strike into others an instinctive recognition of those qualities; the troubled time would have heaved her up, under any circumstances. (1)

Another of the women revolutionaries coming to notice even more to Dickens' leitmotif was Théroigne de Mericourt from the Austrian Netherlands, or todays Belgium, called "la belle liegeoise" for having resided in Liege. To her, more than any other women during the Revolution, goes the provenance of *Liberty leading at the barricades*, memorialized in a painting circa 1830 by Eugene Delacroix, as she became an advocate for arming women to fight along-side men in defending *la patre*. A trained singer, previously she had had a musical career and became an effective orator, as she had also been a courtesan in pre-revolutionary France. Projecting a smart martial air, dressed in an English riding-habit, often in flamboyant colors, her accruement including a felt cap with feathered plume; while for arms, in her belt she carried a brace of pistols, with a sword strapped to her side. She was in appearance a veritable "amazon." Often seen in the gallery of the Assembly, she had returned to her home in 1790, and subsequently was imprisoned in Austria. Before she was released, her incarceration included an interview with the Austrian Kaiser. It was around this time, early in 1792, that she was again in Paris and was acclaimed as she gave an account of her travails before a rapt Legislative Assembly.

As a voucher for her martial activity on behalf of the nation, on September 3, 1792, *Le Moniteur* announced that the federates would bestow upon Mlles Théroigne and on Lacombe a civic crown for distinguishing themselves by their courage on August 10, along with another woman named Reine Audu. Lacombe had received a wound in the arm as she was encouraging the assault on the Tuileries Palace during the dethronement of Louis XVI. (2)

After its formation, it soon became apparent the Legislative Assembly was comprised of four broad political groupings. To the right of the presidential chair sat the deputies called the Feuillants, the royalists and the constitutional monarchists, with 165 members. To the left sat the members of the Jacobin and the Cordeliers "clubs" (a word chosen for its English derivation), who themselves were divided between radicals led by Danton and Marat, and by Robespierre, and a grouping that later came to be called the Girondins, led preeminently by Jacques Pierre Brissot. This 'faction', as indicated still part of the Jacobin Club, was largely from the department of Gironde around Bordeaux, and represented liberal bourgeois and mercantile interests, and the *petite noblesse* of France, who combined had 330 members. The remaining deputies occupying the middle were referred to as the "Plain" or the "Marshes", and had 250 members. This designation, associating seating ranging from 'right' to 'left' to define the political spectrum, they would bequeath to posterity.

At their peak, the Girondins were comprised of about 200 members, many representing the apex in their professions and educational attainment; and as they became increasingly influential, their inner policy-making clique were dubbed the "inner sixty". Among their most persuasive and popular orators were Jacques-Pierre Brissot, Francois Buzot, and Pierre-Victurnie Vergniaud.

As a leading political figure in the Revolution, Brissot was unrivalled in the Legislative Assembly. Twice imprisoned in the Bastille, the Girondins at first were referred to as *Brissotins*. He was a tireless pamphleteer and edited his own influential newspaper *La Patriote françois*. He was also the most cosmopolitan of the deputies, the one with the more extensive international political contacts, as he, in addition, was the founder of the *Society of the Friends of the Blacks* and was communicant with the anti-slavery movement beginning in Britain, where he had lived, and in the United States where he traveled in 1788, meeting with abolitionists and with members of the *Constitutional Convention*. But in his jousting with his opponents, he often appeared eager and impetuous, and in the increasingly intricate political terrain lacked the ruthlessness of his antagonists.

Buzot was a lawyer, and in the Legislative Assembly was a leader among those demanding the nationalization of the holdings of the Catholic Church, as he was a proponent of the right of citizens to bear arms. He came to prominence among the Girondins under the influence of Madame Roland, with whom he formed a liaison, if not of a romantic nature, it was in any event transcendental and all consuming.

Vergniaud, although quiet and studious, was the orator most noted for the brilliance of his pronouncements, coming as they often did at crucial moments, and having a decisive effect in articulating the course of action. Another of the important figures in this political grouping was Jean-Marie Roland, who abetted by his exceptional wife had risen to the attention of politicians in Paris on the basis of articles written by her, but under his name. Thus, a loosely affiliated political alignment in the Legislative Assembly would begin to assume a definitive contour against the intransigence of their opponents. By early 1792 this Girondins faction had fully consolidated and was ready in a bid to lead the Revolution, but would have in their way Maximilien Robespierre. Robespierre loathed Brissot and the "statesmen" of the Gironde, as he derisively called them.

Up to this point in its political comportment the French nation had experienced the most far-ranging and fundamental changes of any modern nation till that era, not excepting America, nor indeed England in the 'Glorious Revolution' or during the reign of Oliver Cromwell. At each step, the Bourdon monarchy sought to rectify its situation to assure the continuance of its rule. But the growing radicalization, bringing to the forefront the hitherto marginal and the poor, together with the middle-classes and the laboring population, and the declassee elements, would be wrought by the very pervasiveness of this reaction itself, and by a deteriorating economy. Counter-revolution, in short, was turning a potential mass-rising into an actual rising. (3)

The most sensational result of this mobilization had been the storming of the Bastille, followed by the *Grande Peur,* and then the march to Versailles by the market women, all in 1789. That first year of the Revolution had won the bourgeoisie its manifesto: *The Declaration of the Rights of Man and of the Citizen.* A more radical and epoch-making phase, most historiography agrees, dates from the return of the Royals after their "flight to Varennes" in 1791. But on balance in the early part of 1792, the tumult had merely been momentary and contingent, like the "sugar riots."

In the deliberations in the Legislative Assembly an item of importance to the prevailing enlightenment credo was a new 'humane' way to provide for executions, while 'equalizing' them for every citizen. The new method decreed on March 20, 1791, had been advanced and studied in committee by the National Assembly in October 1789, where one of the committee members was the physician Joseph-Ignace Guillotine. He had counselled capital punishment be performed by decapitation on everyone convicted of a capital crime regardless of station "by means of a simple mechanism." Louis XVI, sensing execution by *breaking on the wheel* only increased dissension, had already banned that horrific practice. Decapitation, previously reserved for royalty, would now simply be the means for ending life, rather than a means of inflicting pain.

A beheading machine was first used in Place de Greve in Paris on April 25, and consisted of two upright grooved beams surmounted by a horizontal beam, with a diagonally-edged, heavily weighted blade guided between the grooves, that forcefully fell on the back of the neck of the executant. The victim was restrained face-down on a plank in the prone position, and readied for decapitation by being secured by wooden chocks just above the shoulders. The head of the victim would simply drop forward into an open basket.

The machine would soon carry the popular name *Madame Guillotine*, the *National razor*, or simply the *guillotine*, but was first called *louisette*, or *louison*, after its inventor, Antoine Louis; a contrivance he based on earlier prototypes he'd studied. Dr. Guillotine in recommending the device, remarked "the mechanism falls like thunder."

There were perhaps a dozen names for the contrivance in usage. One of these, besides simply "la machine" was *La*

Monte-a- regret (The Regretful Climb). William Blake's *Songs of Experience* completed in 1794 in their illuminated form are poems that may carry an enduring intimation of this device as intuitively captured by an observer in London.

Although commentators have been wont to cite the author as having "no interest in history," saying he sought rather symbols for his expression, and are usually disposed to emphasize the poems psycho-sexual associations, *The Sick Rose* can be regarded as exhibiting convincing suggestion of the French killing-machine about to embark on its macabre career; words forming an almost secret, if beguiling invocation:

> O rose, thou art sick!
> The invisible worm
> That flies at night,
> In the howling storm,
>
> Has found out thy bed
> Of crimson joy
> And his dark secret love
> Does thy life destroy. (4)

At the bottom of Blake's plate depicting this scene, a worm has inched its way along the main stem onto a rose, encountering and ravishing a girl with outstretched arms embedded within its petals, then continuing on its course into the opened blossom. On first thought it is the human female who the poet sees is destroyed, as the worm passes on to kill the rose. The flower and the girl are white, her face and gesture registering hopelessness. Such reading, of the worm's flight "at night in the howling storm," indeed as the guillotine, would be a rendition of these elegiac words in their infernal or diabolical sense, where the most direct attention to the historical context restores to the words their allusions and their effect. The poem evokes the brevity, the swiftness, and the finality of death by decapitation—as indeed it disgorges its "crimson joy".

Apropos Blake's *Songs of Experience,* another of the poems, again improvised in the notebook he kept at the time, enjoins the breadth of emancipation still slumbering in the world for which Blake frequently strikes the dominant chord. Repeated in fragment, as it carries the same language as *London,* Blake pays heed to the deluge about to begin, and of the concurrent persecution of the Paineites:

> Why should I care for the men of thames,
> Or the cheating waves of charter'd streams,
> Or shrink at the little blasts of fear
> That the hireling blows into my ear?

As Blake sees himself as one with the humanity about to be liberated....

> Tho' born on the cheating banks of Thames,
> Tho' his waters bathed my infant limbs,
> The Ohio shall wash his stains from me:
> I was born a slave, but I go to be free. (5)

The Girondins, active from 1791 to 1793 in the Legislative Assembly and in its successor, the National Convention, had initially been subsumed into the Jacobin Club. What would begin to distinguish them as a faction against the members called the *Montagnards* (the Mountaineers), again, a pejorative, a term that was applied to them for their designated seating in the upper benches of the *Salle du Manège* (the "riding hall" of the Royal Equestrian Academy where the assembly convened its sessions)—was war with Austria, and soon after with Prussia.

Austria and Prussia had signed a military convention in Berlin on February 1 to invade France to defend the monarchy. In response, on February 9 the assembly decreed confiscation of the property of noble émigrés for the benefit of the nation, an issue broached in a speech by Vergniaud. Then, unexpectedly on March 1, 1792, the brother of Marie-Antoinette, Leopold II of Austria died, leaving the throne to his more venturesome 24-year-old son. To the enemies of the Revolution—the large number of French émigrés that had sought refuge with the cities of Europe, in London, Vienna, Hamburg, Aix-la-Chapelle and in Coblenz (where there were as many as 20,000 of these Émigrés)—and the signers of the Pillnitz Declaration, not only was war and the rescue of a brother sovereign an act of solidarity, it would be retribution against the appalling ideas being propagated from France.

The Girondins were themselves a bellicose force; in their view, the liberation of France was merely the precursor for the universal liberation of Europe, as there was genuine passion among them for the spread of freedom. Had not, asked Brissot, the leading advocate for war, the Americans consecrated and shored up their revolution with fire and sword? In the strongest terms, the voice of Madame Roland too was advocating for war: "Peace will set us back... We can be regenerated through blood alone." War, it was also seen, could be useful in alleviating domestic problems, and uncertain economic prospects, such as the devaluation in the currency. Britain, after all, had assured its economic supremacy by systematic aggressiveness. (6)

The Feiullants too wanted war, as did the King—it would serve to increase his popularity, and he might even benefit by exploiting a defeat. In any event he would emerge in a stronger position.

Those who opposed war were in a weaker position in the Legislative Assembly. Robespierre thought there was little chance France could win, and in any event, it would only serve to strengthen the King at the expense of the Revolution, as it would incur the enmity of the common people in Austria and elsewhere. "It is during war," he warned in a speech at the Jacobin Club on December 18, 1791—

> that a habit of passive obedience, and an all too natural enthusiasm for successful military leaders, transforms the soldiers of the nation into the soldiers of the King or of his generals. [Thus] the leaders of the armies become the arbiters of the fate of their country, and swing the balance of power in favor of the faction that they have decided to support. If they are Caesars or Cromwells, they seize power themselves.

With Jean-Marie Roland at the Ministry of Interior and effectively head of the government, on April 20, 1792, under a Girondin ministry, war was declared against Austria. War began in the north on the 28th, as the Austrian Netherlands was invaded (Luxemburg and Belgium), under the lead of the nobleman Jean-Baptiste Rochambeau, who had commanded French troops at Yorktown, aiding the thirteen British Atlantic colonies in their war for Independence from the mother country. French planners projected the Austrian enemy in the Netherlands would have no more than 30,000 troops at their disposal, arranged in a cordon from the sea to Lorraine. Three armies, with a total of 50,000 troops, would assault this line at three different points, and a plan with that overview was set in motion April 29.

April 30 Roland's government issued three hundred

million assignats to finance the war. This currency was backed by the value of properties formerly held by the Catholic Church which were confiscated in November 1789 on motion of Mirabeau. Originally meant as bonds, the assignats had been re-defined in April 1790 as legal tender to address the liquidity crisis. Credit had been secured in land rather than in precious metal, while the properties backing the assignats were designated *bien nationaux* (national goods) to be auctioned by district-level authorities.

The first clash in the war was a slight success for the French. The next day, however, Theobald Dillion, the general leading a second column ordered retreat at the first sight of the enemy. Deemed a traitor by his troops, he was set upon and murdered that night, as Lafayette, at the head of the third column, surreptitiously proposed to the Austrians that fighting be suspended. He then intended to turn his army against Paris, disperse the Jacobins and establish another, and stronger regime. Direction of the war had proved unmanageable under the Girondins ministry, and the generals advised the King make an immediate peace. Rochambeau, commanding the Armée *du Nord*, resigned.

In the assembly, Girondins tried to salvage their position by ordering Dillon's murderers be prosecuted, along with the journalist/agitator Jean-Paul Marat, who was deemed an accomplice because he'd exhorted soldiers to get rid of their generals. (7)

On May 5, the Assembly ordered the raising of thirty-one new battalions for the army. On May 6 and 12 respectively, the Royal-Allellemand regiment (German mercenaries) deserted to join Austrian-Prussia, with Hussar regiments following.

Thomas Paine meanwhile was in Bromley, in Kent, where Joseph Johnson had convinced him to go into seclusion near the home of a mutual friend, the engraver William Sharp. When he learned a summons had been issued to his publisher, Jordan, he hastened back to London. Intending to defend Jordan at his own expense, he now learned the publisher had privately agreed to plead guilty, and had surrendered his notes relating to Paine, receiving "a verdict to the author's prejudice—that being really the end of the government's business with the publisher." (8) A summons to appear at the Court of King's Bench on June 8, was left at Paine's lodging (Rickman's house) on May 21; that same day a *Royal Proclamation Against Seditious Writings and Publications* was issued, the information against Paine covering forty-one pages:

> Thomas Paine, late of London, gentleman, being a wicked, malicious, seditious, and ill-disposed person, and being greatly disaffected to our said Sovereign Lord the now King, and to the happy constitution and government of this kingdom...did write and publish, and caused to be written and published, a certain false, scandalous, malicious, and seditious libel...intitled, 'Rights of Man, Part the Second, combining Principle and Practice'.... In one part thereof, according to the tenor and effect following, that is to say, 'All hereditary government is in its nature tyranny'.... (9)

Eager to defend himself, when he appeared at court Paine would be disappointed to learn that the court had postponed trial till December. At the issuance of the proclamation, which was to be enforced at the level of local magistrates, corporations and boroughs had responded with loyal addresses to government and Crown. With all deliberation, Paine would respond on July the 4th from his old hometown of Lewes, with a publication entitled *Letter Addressed to the Addressers on the Late Proclamation*, where he began:

> Could I have commanded circumstances with a wish, I know not of any that would have more generally promoted the progress of knowledge, than the late Proclamation, and the numerous rotten Borough and Corporation Addresses thereon. They have not only served as advertisements, but they have excited a spirit of enquiry into principles of government, and a desire to read the RIGHTS OF MAN, in places, where that spirit and that work were before unknown.... It seldom happens, that the mind rests satisfied with the simple detection of error or imposition.—Once put in motion, *that* motion soon becomes accelerated: where it had intended to stop, it discovers new reasons to proceed, and renews and continues the pursuit far beyond the limits it first prescribed to itself.

In the Legislative Assembly in France during the intervening time, the radical Jacobin deputies had three objects of antipathy: the royal family, the noble émigrés, and the non-jurant clergy. As mentioned, on February 9 that body had decreed the confiscation of the property of all noble émigrés; there were 140,000 of these. Non-juring clergy were those who refused to swear an oath under the *Civil Constitution of the Clergy* enacted in July 1790. That law was mandated to complete the destruction of the monastic orders—and hence the names of those orders, Jacobin and Feuillants, had come into usage for the political clubs occupying their former premises, or in the case of the Cordeliers, for the street in which they were domiciled—as the law had regulated the dioceses to align with the administrative districts just created, forbidding commitment to any authority outside of France, and stipulating bishops and priests be elected.

May 27 the Assembly passed a decree against priests who had refused the oath to the civil constitution, providing if twenty "active" citizens "demanded that a nonjuring priest leave the realm," the director of the department must order his deportation, or if he does not agree, it shall be determined through committee. If opinion then supported the petitioners, "the deportation shall be ordered."

There soon followed another measure in the Assembly directed at the King's bodyguard. Enacted on the 29th, the King's guard was dissolved, and its commander arrested. Another decree now passed, urged by Madame Roland, providing for a camp of 20,000 *fédérés* (federates) or volunteer national guardsman to be assembled near Paris on June 14.

Militarily French forces were in a diminished state. Some of its most potent and combat ready regiments had defected or were about to; half of its officer corps, formerly comprised entirely of noblemen, had either left service, defected or become émigrés. Munitions and stores were depleted, as the condition of France's fortifications were deplorable.

Another critical issue was the French currency; ravaged by inflation, payment for procurements and the pay of soldiers was in disorder, making the new volunteer regiments, with limited call to service, more attractive than the under-manned regular units. The decree in regard to 20,000 federates was made with all these contingencies in view, and because of the persistence of threats against the Legislative Assembly. Documents showing a plot to dissolve that body were found, and for that reason, it had decreed its sessions should be continuous; that the guard in Paris be doubled; and that the mayor should report daily on the condition of the capital.

On June 16, the King issued vetoes for the decrees for penalties against émigrés and refractory clergymen, and indicated it was his intention to veto the measure for twenty-thousand federates for the protection of Paris. Madame Roland now sent a letter to the King denouncing the vetoes and the queen's role in them, warning of an "Austrian Committee" that would deliver the country into the hands of the Hapsburg's.

After receipt of the letter, Louis XVI dissolved the Girondins ministry, forming a new government comprised of Feuillants. With Austria too weak in the Netherlands to take the offensive against France, it now called on its ally, Prussia, to join the fight.

With the Parisian sans-culottes and agitators showing their enmity for the royal couple by referring to them jointly in the streets as "Monsieur Veto" and "Madame Veto," a demonstration was proposed for the anniversary of the *Tennis-Court Oath*, June 20. On the 18th Lafayette appeared before the Assembly to warn that such demonstration must not be allowed to proceed, that the clamor for democracy it represented be curtailed. "[The] Constitution of France," he declared, "[is] threatened by seditious groups within the country as well as by its enemies abroad."

The demonstration on June 20 began assembling at 5 in the morning at the Place de la Bastille in the Faubourg Saint-Antoine, and when its numbers had grown to many thousands it began an orderly procession through the narrow streets of central Paris toward the hall of the Legislative Assembly at the Place Vendome. Carrying banners and singing songs of solidarity, the march was driven by sans-culotte dissatisfaction with Louis XVI's vetoes and their resolve to display unity of force associated with the ideas of liberty, equality and fraternity, as it was the demonstrator's intention to plant a

"Liberty Tree" in the gardens of the Tuileries Palace. While they are noted for their forbearance and orderly deportment, every participant was mindful of the massacre at the Champ de Mars in the previous year. Their ranks bristled with every weapon available to hand—they were a moving forest of pikes, as many carried muskets, and there were women with sabers and even children with long knives. Almost any instrument was seen to suffice: halberds, cudgels, and clubs of every kind, scythes, spits, hatchets, pitchforks. Although this display had not been approved—there would be no attempt at dis-arming. The military and the National Guard and the Assembly stood aside for this *manifestation politique* of the Parisian san-culottes.

There had been wide-spread agitation in the Parisian faubourgs in the days prior, and the event had been publicized with posters and in meetings in the various political clubs. Jointly organized by trade and neighborhood sub-groupings, observers remarked the demonstration included carpenters and fabric cutters, woodcutters, sawyers, and wood- carriers, stay and carriage-makers, brewers, and furniture-makers; each division holding pride of place as well as loyalty to their greater community and neighborhood.

The day before the Assembly had received a deputation asking permission to plant the *Liberty tree*, and requesting they be permitted to march through the hall itself. The night before, Antoine-Joseph Santerre and other organizers held a five-hour meeting where they adopted a petition to be read to the Assembly. The success of the demonstration depended on being formerly received by the deputies.

The conservatives and Feuillants were adamant in opposing entry, but by then the demonstration had grown to 10,000. With a furious debate ongoing, Santerre sent a note saying it was the protestor's desire to commemorate the Tennis-Court Oath and to "present their homage to the

National Assembly." The demonstrators "intentions had been misunderstood," he wrote in a mollifying tone, and asked they be given a chance "to prove that they are the friends of liberty and the Men of 14 July."

The 'left' applauded the note as it was read, while the 'right' remonstrated. After negotiations, and after a voice vote the Assembly agreed to hear the petition. Arms in the assembly were illegal; but then the number of marchers bid this be overlooked. After all, Article 2 of the *Declaration of the Rights of Man* had been invoked which called for "resistance to oppression." Assured of these "patriotic sentiments," on a second voice vote the deputies allowed for the demonstration to continue through the hall.

That procession, in an unbroken line, took from 1:30 to 3:15 in the afternoon. The anthem *Ca ira* was sung. First heard in May 1790, "it'll be fine" became emblematic of the revolutionary era, a phrase inspired by Benjamin Franklin. Representing the Continental Congress to the French Court, whenever asked how the American war was faring, he reputedly replied, "Ca ira, ca ira."

> Ah! It'll be fine, it'll be fine, it'll be fine
> The people on this day repeat over and over
> Ah! It'll be fine, it'll be fine, it'll be fine
> In spite of the mutineers everything shall succeed.

The songs second refrain began:

> Our enemies, confounded, stay petrified
> And we shall sing Alleluia
> Ah! It'll be fine, etc.

This, and the slogans "Long live our representatives!...Long live the law!...Down with the veto!" were applauded by like-minded deputies, while a calf's heart atop a pike with a sign that read "Heart of an Aristocrat," caused consternation among others. The benches broke into applause again when a man called out—"Legislators, this isn't two thousand men, but twenty million who present themselves before you, an entire nation that must arm itself to fight tyrants, their enemies and yours." (10)

Leaving the Assembly, the demonstration passed on to the Place du Carrousel in front of Tuileries Palace. The approach to the palace was blocked by National Guard troops with cannon, and by cavalry reinforced by other battalions stationed nearby. It's not known whether any among the multitude intended to try to gain entry to the palace; however the case, that was completely unprecedented. But the National Guard, many of whom commiserated with the demonstrators and were as dissatisfied as they with the current political stalemate, by some kind of symbiosis, stood aside to the mere jostling and crush of the crowd as the Tuileries Palace was entered by the protestors. This was the ultimate rebuke against the King and Queen, and to their conservative supporters.

With the palace suddenly overwhelmed, at the King's command the outer doors were opened as protestors ascended to the royal apartments. As they rushed in, the King was placed on a chair in the embrasure of a window with the National Guard surrounding him as a barrier. Entrapped in his own apartment, but displaying dignified calm and remarkable courage for the brazenness of the demonstrators, Louis was imported to approve the decrees he'd rejected. The King responded: "This is neither the method nor the moment to obtain it of me." When a *bonnet rouge* was extended at the end of a pike toward him, he obligingly placed it on his head. Then a man carrying a flask of wine, who himself had been imbibing, bid the King drink from a glass he offered.

Whereupon, applauded all around, the King drank to the health of the nation.

But the King had promised nothing; the demonstrators had achieved none of what they had hoped. The next day the Legislative Assembly banned gatherings of armed citizens within the city limits.

Those who wished to see monarchy flourish in France saw that their king had been insulted and treated as a prisoner, and significant counter-demonstrations took place over the next days. Department administrators, physicians, and lawyers, throughout France protested against this affront to the dignity and majesty of the King. Lafayette, leaving his post, appeared before the Legislative Assembly on the 28th demanding action be taken, and that "a sect capable of infringing the national sovereignty" be destroyed, i.e., the Jacobins.

As the *journée* on the 20 June had deployed, it had shown a determination never seen in a political demonstration before, and those who trod in its ranks knew they had opened a road to a more thorough-going transformation. There was no place for Lafayette under a republican emblem now. As he left Paris he was denounced by Robespierre in the Assembly and burned in effigy at the Palais-Royal.

A thought now grew in minds that had not accommodated its presence before; the occurrence of an idea expressed by Blake in *The Chimney Sweeper*:

> A little black thing among the snow,
> Crying "weep! weep!" in notes of woe!
> "Where are thy father & mother? Say?"
> "they are both gone up to the church to pray.

Because I was happy upon the heath,
And smil'd among the winter's snow,
They clothed me in the clothes of death,
And taught me to sing the notes of woe.

And because I am happy & dance & sing,
They think they have done me no injury,
And are gone to praise God & his Priest & King,
Who make up a heaven of our misery." (11)

Within fifty days Louis XVI would be hurled down, effectively issuing a challenge that this "heaven of...misery" be brought down across the whole of Europe.

10.
When the stars threw down their spears

The dethronement of Louis XVI with the storming of the Tuileries Palace on 10 August 1792, has arisen in historical retrospection as a veritable lightning bolt, cascading down a path searing in its course. Accordingly, it is accruable only within the maelstrom in which it fell; with many contributors and effects, none by themselves fully determinant on balance of the outcome.

To circumvent the king's veto of the federates camp outside of Paris, on 2 July the Assembly decreed the National Guard was authorized to come to Paris for the annual Federation Ceremony on the 14th. Then on the third, the Girondins lead orator, Pierre Vergniaud, gave a sharper focus to the debate in the Assembly by pronouncing for the first-time grave insinuations against the King. Signaling, when set against the machinations, the inefficacy and the incompetence of the monarchy, that even for constitutionalists a republic was now preferable, he said:

> It is in the name *of the King* that the French princes have endeavoured to raise all Europe; it was to avenge the *dignity of the King* that the treaty of Pillnitz was concluded; it is to come *to the aid of the King* that the sovereign of Bohemia and Hungry [have] declared war

with us, and that Prussia is marching towards our frontiers. And, I read in the constitution, that if the king puts himself at the head of an army, and directs its force against the nation, or if he does not oppose, by a formal act, such an enterprise, executed in his name, he shall be considered as having abdicated the throne. (1)

In the first weeks of July, as Austrian and Prussian armies began to muster on the Rhine before commencing their advance toward Paris, they did so without any substantial opposition, raising alarm throughout France and in particular in the capital city. Then on the 5th the Assembly decreed that in event of danger all able-bodied men could be called into service and the necessary arms requisitioned, as it also decreed that all sessions of administrative bodies were to be open to the public. In addition, earlier that month the Marseille Club, having just put down a Royalist rebellion, responding to Charles Barbaroux, deputy in the Legislative Assembly from Marseille, declared—"Here and at Toulon we have debated the possibility of forming a column of 100,000 men to sweep away our enemies.... Paris may have need of help. Call on us."

From the Assembly on the 11th came the decree *la patrie en danger,* as banner-size exhortations appeared in Parisian public squares and on bridges: "Would you allow foreign hordes to spread like a destroying torrent over your countryside! That they ravage our harvest! That they devastate our fatherland through fire and murder! In a word, that they overcome you with chains with the blood of those you hold most dear...."

With this pronouncement, all local authorities, the councils of the communes, those of the districts and departments, and the Assembly itself, were to be considered as permanent and to hold their sittings without interruption.

The day after the Federation ceremony on the Champs de Mars, regular army units supporting Lafayette were sent far outside the city, as that same day, the Cordeliers Club, led by Georges Danton, demanded the convocation of a National Convention to replace the Legislative Assembly.

On the 17th, when Jerome Pétion, the mayor of Paris and a confidant of Brissot (suspended from office after the *journée* of June 20 as he was held responsible for the conduct of the demonstrators), was reinstated, he promptly established "a central bureau of correspondence" between the sections of Paris. Duly elected commissioners were to bring acts passed each day, and carry away the corresponding acts of the remaining forty-seven sections, as they were to hold their meetings in the Hôtel de Ville across the corridor where the municipal body convened, appoint a president and secretary, and provide an official report of their proceedings. To assure direct contact with the sections, the federates too set up a central committee, that included some of the Parisian political leaders; as a coordinating committee had been established consisting of one member from each of the 83 departments. To assure expeditious action, five of these, all of them unknown and unheralded men, were conjointly designated a secret committee. This committee, with the support of two officials of the Commune, Manuel and Danton, designated themselves the *Insurrectional Committee*. In a bid to gain control of the popular discontent, Robespierre began to meet with this committee in the home where he domiciled.

The radical republican faction now had its deliberative assemblies, its executive power, its central seat of govern-ment, and in the Parisian sans-culotte and the federates, an enlarged, tried, and ready force. "Scarcely does the viper leave its nest before it begins to hiss," remarked Hippolyte Taine, the celebrated French proponent of sociological positivism and practitioner of historicist criticism in the 19th century. (2)

Now the sections commissioned Pétion to propose the dethronement of Louis XVI in their name. Cautioning against any descent into illegality, Pétion said:

> This important measure once passed, the confidence of the nation in the actual dynasty being very doubtful, we demand that a body of ministers, jointly responsible appointed by the National Assembly, but, as the constitutional law provides, outside of itself, elected by the open vote of freemen, be provisionally entrusted with the executive power. (3)

Responsible for maintaining public tranquility, Pétion by the nature of his position felt it judicious to appear Janus-faced; he was "bound," Carlyle wrote, "under pain of death, one may say, to smile dexterously with one side of his face, and weep with the other."

On the 26th the cautiousness of the Girondins before the challenges posed by the gathering storm was conveyed by Brissot, who said: "If there are men who aim to establish a Republic on the ruins of the Constitution of 1789, the sword of the law should strike at them as at the counter-revolutionaries of Coblenz." (4) Brissot's volte-face was offered in the calculated expectation that with a forced resignation of the Feuillant Ministers, the Girondins could return to power, where he envisioned the Dauphin might be installed in the abdicating King's place. Unable to restrain the rising tide, on the morning of August 3 the Assembly was entreated to take the petition for dethronement of the King under immediate consideration, where his removal was demanded by August 9.

Previously dethronement had been discussed by the clubs, and by the federates, and by the Commune; now it assumed the always fresh attribute of an unprecedented event as the section of Manconseil declared they would no longer acknowledge Louis XVI as king of the French nation, and invited every part of the "empire" (no longer using the word kingdom) to follow their example. This act met with incredulity in the Assembly, as it duly annulled the decree. Vergniaud harshly criticizing it as a "usurpation of the sovereignty of the people," while however, seeming to object, not on principle but on the impropriety of the language.

Adding further perspicacity to the ultimatum, another of the sections, *Theatre-Français,* among the most radical in Paris, had abolished the distinction between "active" and "passive" citizens, establishing the right to vote for all males twenty-five and over. In the coming days, this section would allow passive citizens to serve in the National Guard, extending the notion of *Egalité* more broadly to the sans-culotte.

Without settling these issues, after intense deliberation the sections consented to restrain their combatants until 11 o'clock on the evening of the 9th. Effecting this calculation, the preceding day by a two-thirds majority the Assembly had refused to indict Lafayette, the great enemy of the insurrectionists, while many of the deputies who dared to defend him were roughly accosted in the street.

When, on the 25th, the Duke of Brunswick, commanding the invading armies of monarchical Europe, at the behest of French noble émigrés, issued a manifesto drafted by Count Fersen to the people of Paris, it was done without becoming well known to the public till August 1. That declaration warranted that if Louis XVI and his family were harmed, then it's forces would "wreak an exemplary and forever memorable vengeance, by giving up the city of Paris to military execution, and total destruction, and the rebels guilty of assassinations, to execution that they have merited." (5)

That same day the Assembly authorized the Parisian sections to meet in permanent session, many sections being under control of Jacobin and Cordeliers Club members. As that day, too, 300 radical republican federates from Brest had arrived, encamping in the Parisian faubourgs under the auspicious of the clubs. When on August 1ˢᵗ 515 more of these federates arrived from Marseille, they brought with them a stirring anthem, *les Marseillaise*, newly composed with the melody (among others commonly cited) of Mozart's Allegro maestoso of Piano Concerto No. 25:

> Arise, children of the Fatherland,
> The day of glory has arrived!
> Against us, tyranny's
> Bloody standard is raised, (repeat)
>
> Do you hear, in the countryside,
> The roar of those ferocious soldiers?
> They're coming right into your arms
> To cut the throats of your sons, your women!

On the evening of the deadline set for the dethronement of the King, the "correspondence bureau", becoming the "Insurrectionary Commune," in a resolution, informed the municipal body it was suspended. That resolution stated—"When the People puts itself into a state of insurrection, it withdraws all powers and takes it into itself." The insurrectionary Commune retained three officials however from the suspended government—the mayor Pétion, the procureur-general (executive) Louis Manuel, and the deputy-procureur Georges Danton.

Till now known only as a leading orator at the Cordeliers Club, in subsequent days Danton would be thrust into prominence. Although exercising general influence, Danton possessed no absolute hegemony in the insurrectionary Commune. The most he could do was to rally it in a moment of hesitancy or vacillation, and by an audaciousness of impulse "give the final direction to their plans"; Carlyle calling him the "cloudy invisible Atlas of the whole."

Acknowledged as a capable lawyer with a good classical education, he is described as a "colossal" figure with an "athletic" physique. As a boy, his face had been disfigured when he was ravaged by wild dogs, and then by the scourge of smallpox. Usually depicted as a man prey to his passions, but also, one who threw himself into political agitation with fiery zeal. "His countenance," remarked one historian, "alternately expressed all the animal passions, as well as gaiety, and even benevolence." (6) He was likewise seen as self-dealing; in this instance, he took money the King proffered to prevent "riot", and used that money to urge it on.

The group leaders of the Parisian sections included, foremost, Antoine Joseph Santerre, leading the eastern units of the sans-culotte of the Faubourg Saint-Antoine; a brewer and owner of the largest of Paris's seventeen breweries, the Hortensia brewery. At five feet four inches tall, he was always well powered and arranged, and became inordinately popular with the poor of Saint-Antoine, one of Paris's most industrial districts. By his own account, during one famine he spent three hundred thousand francs distributing bread, and in the severe winter of 1792 brought rice and flocks of sheep, turning his brewery coppers into stewpots. Not adept at martial arts, he was reputed to have been, however, one of the best horsemen in all of France and an expert trainer of horses, second only to Louis-Philippe, Duc d'Orléans. His brewery, where he excelled in English ales and beers, which flowed freely to the National Guard, was among the first to install a steam engine for its operation.

The meetings to plan the insurrection would take place in

Santerre's house, with his co-leader, a captain of the National Guard and member of the Templar order, Frederic Rouille. He was a cobbler's son, and a reveler in the slaughter of enemies. It was Rouille who would be delegated to search the King's office for documents during the assault, in particular any letters exchanged with Mirabeau.

Another of the leaders of the sans-culottes, and the National Guard and Federates, was Francois Joseph Westermann, confidant of Danton, who commanded the central column in the assault on Tuileries Palace; the only professional soldier in the leadership of the insurrection, he would later achieve distinction in the revolutionary wars of the republic, but end his life under the guillotine during the terror. Another, was the journalist and pamphleteer of high repute Jean Louis Carra; he held a seat in the secrete directory of the Federates, and was responsible for drawing up the plan of insurrection. Another, and one of the most indefatigable of the insurrectionary leaders, was Claud Fournier, always designated *la Americain*. He was the son of a poor weaver and once had been a distiller of *tajio*, a low-grade rum, in Martinique. Losing everything in a fire, he returned to France.

Taine tailored the leaders of the sections in accord with an evaluation in line with that of Edmund Burke:

> Santerre is a brewer of the faubourg St. Antione, commander of the battalion of "Enfants trouves,...stout and ostentatious, with stentorian lungs.... Legendre is an excitable butcher.... There are three or four foreign adventurers, adapted to all slaying operations.... Rotonde, the first one, is an Italian, a teacher of English and professional rioter.... The second, Lazowski, is a Pole, a former dandy, a conceited fop, who, with Sclave facility, becomes the barest of naked sans-culottes.... His drawing-room temperament, however, is not rigorous

enough for the part he plays on the streets, and at the end of the year he is to die, consumed by a fever and by brandy.... The third...Fournier, known as the American, a former planter who has brought with him from St. Domingo a contempt for human life; "with his livid and sinister countenance, his moustache, his triple belt of pistols, his course language, his oaths, he looks like a pirate".... By their side one encounters a little hump-backed lawyer named Cuirette-Verrieres, an everlasting talker, who, on the 6th of October, 1789, paraded the city on a large white horse and afterwards pleaded for Marat, which two qualifications with his Punch figure, fully establish him in the popular imagination; this boisterous crew, moreover, who hold nocturnal meetings at Santerre's, needed a penman and he probably furnished them with their style.... They have discovered the cries best calculated to set the popular animal in a tremor, what gives him umbrage, what charm attracts him, what road it is necessary he should follow, he will march blindly on, borne along by his involuntary inspiration and crushing with his mass all that he encounters on his path. (7)

In a letter sent from Paris on August 7, Madame Jullien, an eminence of bourgeois society, wrote, "A terrible storm is coming up on the horizon.... At this moment the horizon is heavy with vapours which must produce a terrible explosion." (8) The federates of Marseilles were "men of action" and quick to strike; "[m]en who do such good work, and so expeditiously," remarked Taine, "must be well posted near the Tuileries."

Accordingly, on the night of the 8th without informing the commanding officer of the National Guard, Mandat, Mayor Pétion ordered them to leave their barracks on the outskirts of Paris and take up quarters, with their arms and cannons, in barracks belonging to the Cordeliers. That same night Fournier and Lazowski hastened to Faubourg Saint-Marceau; Santerre and Westermann were active in Faubourg Saint-Antoine; as Danton, Desmoulins, and Cara remained domiciled at the Cordeliers Club with the battalion from Marseilles. Occupying the tribune, Danton thundered out his condemnation to the ill-fated monarch:

> The people can only now have recourse to themselves, for the constitution is not able to help them, and the assembly has acquitted Lafayette; it remains only, therefore, for you to save yourselves. Hasten, then, this very night to accomplish your deliverance, for the satellites of the palace will doubtless sally forth on the people to butcher them, before their departure for Coblentz. Hasten then! Save yourselves! Save yourselves! To arms! To arms! (9)

Against this background, if only for the trice, illumination may be gained by directing the narrative to a single figure in the crowd. "Demoiselle Théroigne," as Carlyle was wont to call her, to be sure, presented a striking figure: Passionate, fearless, eloquent; she was an unrivalled apostle in the cause of liberty, only to be thrown into the shadows, at last, as her spirit soared in the coming vortex of blood and terror. Lamartine called her—"The impure Joan of Arc of the public streets." (10)

One of the devices used by those striving to defuse the looming revolt, in this instance by the Directory of the department of Paris, was to send out squads entrusted with the mission of verifying the state of things and report back to the general prosecutor. Dressed in National Guard uniform, and under the leadership of the royalist pamphleteer Francois-Louis Suleau, one contingent (Carlyle cites them as 17) were in front of the Tuileries on the evening of the 9th.

In the previous weeks, Suleau had been assiduously working for the court, distributing bribes to insure a constitutional monarchy, which he also advocated in his journalism. In the previous days, he'd sought interviews with Danton and Robespierre in an effort to sway them to his cause; as indeed, Danton was then accepting the pay of the King, while Robespierre, to be sure "Incorruptible," undoubtedly had been circumspect.

In the evening of the 9th these sham guards crossed a patrol of actual guards, and their subsequent exposure before the Assembly led to their arrest. On the night of July 30, a brawl had taken place in the gardens of the Champs-Elysees between the Marseillais battalion of the federates and royalist members of the battalion of the Filles Saint Thomas, and a Marseilles patriot had been critically wounded and a royalist killed. With the spirit of revenge abroad—Suleau, a tall figure with distinctive features, was seen by the crowd for what he was, a royalist. Then, while being conveyed through a crowd to a guardhouse near the cour de Feuillants, a general commotion ensued.

With a mêlée supervening, the commander of the guard sent for reinforcements, which duly arrived. With two hundred guardsmen ready to clear the courtyard, it was necessary that the gates be closed. At that point, the officer of the reinforcing detachment declared without orders he could not send his men outside of their section—which it would have been necessary to do.

The commander at the guardhouse was a young man subsequently to have a long military career, begun as he had enlisted in the Parisian National Guard after the storming of the Bastille. This was Paul Thiébault, later a lieutenant-general under Napoleon, whose career would extend into the Bourbon Restoration, as he would publish as well, highly regarded histories and a memoir. His *Memoirs de Baron Thiébault* was printed in 1895, although he had died, aged 76, in 1846.

With the throng threatening the prisoners, and having no other recourse, Thiébault rushed into their midst. Mounting one of two cannons that stood in the courtyard, he shouted, "Are you Frenchmen? So are we no less. Are you patriots? So are we no less. But you will cease to be worthy, of one or the other title if you cannot get beyond the detestable idea of replacing justice by assassination. You will indeed be rebels, for the assembly has put the prisoners under our guardian-ship. What have you then to demand? It can be only one thing, namely, that the prisoners—against nearly all of whom, by the way, there is no charge—should not escape. Well, I answer for them on my honour, and, if that is not guarantee enough, I will add to their guard any three of you whom you like to choose." With the crowd refusing to give way, so as to gain time, Thiébault appealed to them again, just as Théroigne de Mericourt entered the courtyard. Pressing her way forward, embellished with black felt hat with a black plume, with her usual accoutrement of arms; Thiébault takes up the scene in his *Memoirs*:

> She was a dark girl of about twenty, and, with a sort of shudder I say it, very pretty, made still more beautiful by her excitement. Proceeded and followed by a number of maniacs, she cleft her way through the crowd, crying 'Make room! Make room!' went straight to the other gun and leapt upon it.... Having heard what was going on, she had hurried up from Robespierre's house, and confident of her influence with the populace, she had come to restore all its ferocity to the mob. As long as I live that creature will be present before my eyes; the sound of her

voice will ring in my ears as she uttered the first sentence of her discourse. 'How long,' she shrieked, 'will you let yourselves be misled by empty phrases?' I tried to answer, but I could no longer make myself heard. A thousand voices greeted with applause every word she uttered.

Thiébault had no alternative but to dismount the gun on which he remained and retreat with his prisoners to the guardroom. As its doors were shut and barred, those outside hurled themselves against it, shattering the glass, showering those inside; but found their way further checked by loaded muskets and fixed bayonets. The Baron continued:

> They found it more dignified to put me on my trial, their beautiful fury, Mlle de Mericourt presiding, and to condemn me, unanimously, and by acclamation, to death. I never saw her again after that day, but, though I am as susceptible as most men to the influences of women, I certainly never met another woman who, in half an hour, could have left on my mind a recollection of her which a thousand years would not weaken. (11)

Seeing he was a danger to the other prisoners, Suleau cried: "Comrades, I believe that the people mean to shed blood to-day, but perhaps one victim will satisfy them. Let me go to them. I will pay for all." Attempting to leap out a window, he was restrained by the National Guard. At that moment, the crowd burst the door, seizing a man described as "a harmless dramatic author of the name of Bouyon," who they dragged into the courtyard and "rent limb from limb." Suleau was then seized and "despoiled of his uniform and arms." He pointedly had ridiculed Théroigne in an article of his in the previous days, calling her "the mistress of the populace," with a "hideous" and "old" face. Seizing him by the throat, her aroused felinity pulled the journalist into the thick of the throng, where, fighting valiantly, twenty pair of outstretched arms subdued him. His body pierced by a dozen swords, the corpse, along with eight or nine others was flung out into the Place Vendome. (12)

"Thus," wrote another eyewitness to the scene, the royalist Peltier, "perished the amiable Suleau, whose gaiety, candour, and friendship endured him to me."

With the tolling of church bells in the faubourgs, the tocsin sounding on the night of August 9 and into the morning of 10th is memorialized now in *tableau* of the sans-culottes seizing their assortment of weapons and forming into line of battle: Against the kingdom of the Feulillants! Against the Legislative Assembly! Against the King's mercenary soldiers; against the armies of foreigners threatening *la patrie*! And if need be, against the majority of Paris! Theirs' now: to bring a *coup* against Louis XVI and kingcraft.

Marshaling under a *red banner,* the "emblem of a new power" held before each of the columns now as symbol of the martial law of the people, and not the pennant signifying martial law unfurled on the Champ de Mars the previous year. (13) To royalists and bourgeois, it was a hideous faced populace they beheld, on which they traced the disfiguring marks of poverty, the marks of misconduct. Ragged men without coats, wearing shirt sleeves, and standing in full legged trousers, each wearing that frightful *bonnet rouge*! But in fact, predominate in their numbers were the better off in the strata called sans-culottes—small shop keepers and artisans, and scattered among them, journalists and revolutionary agitators, and even some men from the professional ranks.

Providing the defense of Tuileries Palace were 950 Swiss mercenaries of the *Gardes Swisse*, backed by two thousand National Guard, and 930 *gendarmes*, and 2 to 3 hundred royalist volunteers—the *Chevaliers de Saint Louis*, or as they were called by the popular masses, *chevaliers du poignard*. In all, almost five thousand armed men if suitably deployed that could have made the palace a formidable redoubt for royalism. In addition, Antoine Jean Galiot Mandat, Lafayette's replacement as commander of the National Guard, and a Feulillant like him, to prevent conjunction between insurgents on opposite banks of the river, had stationed troops with supporting cannon on the *Pont Neuf*, and mounted squadrons near the Hôtel de Ville, ready to charge out on maundering crowds coming out of the Faubourg Saint-Antoine.

During the early pre-dawn hours, before being recalled by the Insurrectionary Commune, the legal body of the municipality had summoned Mandat to answer for the disposition of his troops. Reporting without escort, before he could return to his post at the Tuileries he was arrested on the steps of the Hôtel de Ville as the insurgents asserted control, and it was ordered that he be consigned to the Abbaye "for his own safety". These were the significant words spoken by Danton, before "he was murdered at the door by Rossignol, one of Danton's acolytes, with a pistol shot at arm's length." (14) "[A]las," wrote Carlyle, "more blood will flow: for it is as the Tiger in that; he has only to begin."

This divesting the National Guard of its commander had a decisive effect, as it disorganized the defenses at the Tuileries Palace. Another disruption of its defenses occurred between three and four in the morning, when Louis Manuel, the procureur-general of the Commune, appeared on the Pont Neuf and gave orders that the battery emplacement and troops be withdrawn. Nothing now was to prevent the sans-culotte of Saint-Antoine from linking up with the federates and sans-culotte of Saint-Marceau.

At dawn, the assembly of sections converged on the Hôtel de Ville, substituting itself for the legal commune, thereby buttressing the insurrection with the support of an organized public tribunal. On the right bank of the Seine, the battalions of the Faubourg Saint-Antoine, on the left, those of the Faubourg Saint-Marcel, the Bretons, and the Marseillais units were "marching forth," observed Taine, "as freely as if going to parade." At that hour, an advance guard of women, children, with some men, armed with shoe-knives, cudgels, and pikes, spread over the abandoned Place du Carrousel.

Later, writing on the springing of the battalions in the early morning of 10 August, hear it again from Carlyle: "— immeasurable, born of the Night! They march there, the grim host; Saint-Antoine on this side of the River; Saint-Marceau on that, the blackbrowed Marseillese in the van." In William Blake's best-known lyric, *The Tyger*, readers have long been habituated to interpreting the limerick-like description of a grotesque yet wondrous beast, with its mystical contrast between "Tyger! Tyger! burning bright", twice repeated, and the twice repeated refrain "forests of the night"—as an attempt to reach the sublime.

But the first two lines of that fifth stanza are no mere compressing of "astronomical observation and mythological lore" (15), as a standard explanation maintains. Rather they should be heard as words demarking an epoch. That Blake followed this with a rhetorical question, the answer to which he may have been indifferent, indicates the poet's purpose merely is in drawing a bridge between the contraries of

Innocence and *Experience,* and to provide the obligatory unity of vision that he sought. Blake asks:

> When the stars threw down their spears
> And water'd heaven with their tears,
> Did he smile his work to see?
> Did he who made the Lamb make thee?

Many maintain these images evoke associations in Blake's own experience; the tigers in an exhibition he may have seen in the Tower of London, or in illustrations from natural history, as likewise, in biblical literature—all suppositions commonly ventured. A biographer tells us, at this time as he was working on Stedman's *Narrative* with its graphic depiction of slave life and punishment, where he would have read the "tiger cat... with its eyes emitting flashes like lightning", the "red tiger...its eyes prominent and sparkling like stars." (16) But the haunting imagery and the destructive fury of the tiger, doubtless had as much to do with what was happening in France, which Blake followed closely and with great sympathy at this time. The audacity of Danton and the Parisian sans-culotte and the furnace from which they issued as from the "forests of the night" on 10 August is as apposite an analogy. Blake's vision was that encompassing! as well as being the more stringent, than those engaged in a more puerile interpretation have supposed. The poem "reminds one of Blake's contrived enigmas," Erdman wrote, "—a contrivance forced upon him by the truth, one feels." (17)

Leaving no doubt as to his revolutionary sympathies, Blake wrote mockingly of the expiring monarchal authority in his ballad "Fayette", as 'nobody's daddy':

> Then old Nobodaddy aloft
> Farted & belch'd & cough'd,

And said, "I love hanging & drawing & quartering
Every bit as well as war & slaughtering.
Damn praying & singing,
Unless they will bring in
The blood of ten thousand by fighting or swinging.

This last line is a reference again to Edmund Burke's *Reflections*, where he wrote of the perceived insult to Marie-Antoinette, "I thought ten thousand swords must have leaped from their scabbards...," which Blake uses here as a satiric refrain.

Meanwhile early that morning, after the death of the ill-fated Mandat, Pierre Louis Roederer, the chief prosecutor of the Paris department, convinced the King that his only recourse was to seek sanctuary with his family with the Legislative Assembly. Surrounded by his ministers, and between two lines of Swiss Guards, the King and Queen, their children, and a few ladies in waiting, crossed the leaf-littered Tuileries gardens through glowering crowds—the King remarking that the leaves were falling early that year (the trees were parched, and the weather, sweltering). Entering the hall of the riding academy, the King said, "Gentlemen, I come here to prevent a great crime. I shall always believe myself and my family safe amid the representatives of the nation."

The column marching out of the Faubourg Saint-Marceau crossed the Pont Neuf without hindrance, reaching Place du Carrousel around six o'clock. Santerre's forces were divided into three columns: one proceeding along the river, another along the boulevards, with the mass marching straight down rues Saint-Antoine and Saint-Honore. Toward 8 o'clock, the advance column, commanded by Westermann, debouched in front of the palace.

As they arrived, the federates from Marseilles and sans-culotte of Saint-Marceau began fraternizing with National Guard gunners positioned in the courtyard of the Tuileries. Responding by removing the ammunition in their guns, the guard pivoted the weapons so as to face the palace. With the gendarmes dispersed in such a way as to be useless, resistance from the palace, particularly with the withdrawal of the King, became problematic.

The defense of the palace now fell to the Swiss Guards, the noblemen, and a few dozen grenadiers of the National Guard. With the courtyard invested by the insurgents, soon the main entrance to the palace was breached, the two sides confronting each other on the main staircase, the Swiss Guard and noblemen holding the first floor.

"Surrender to the nation!" Westermann shouted in Alsatian German.

"We should think ourselves dishonored!" replied a sergeant—"We are Swiss, the Swiss do not part with their arms but with their lives. We think that we do not merit such an insult. If the regiment is no longer wanted, let it be legally discharged. But we will not leave our post, nor will we let our arms be taken from us." (18)

Entreaties were made, the insurgents promising they'd consider their foe as brothers if they came over to the side of the nation. Many Swiss responded to these advances by throwing cartridges to show that they were only powder. This tenuous stand-off continued for about forty-five minutes, when, as a cannon discharged by the insurgents harmlessly sailed over the roof of the Carrousel, a pistol was let off among the royalists, and a general mélange in competing fuselages began.

Firing down the staircase, the Swiss quickly recovered the ground that had been relinquished, reaching the guns of the National Guard outside. These were promptly turned on the insurgents. Driven out of the courtyard and across the Place du Carrousel, which was now on fire, the insurgents rallied behind the buildings there. Presiding at that moment in a tumultuous assembly at the Hôtel de Ville, and observing the retreat along the quays, Danton cried, "Our brethren require our assistance; let us go out and give it them." This immediately was done, and "[Danton's] presence brought them back to the scene of battle, and decided the victory," one commentary remarked. (19)

With the battalions of Saint-Antoine still arriving, the beleaguered insurgents held their ground, and as casualties mounted, the Swiss were driven back inside the palace. Around 11 o'clock, a note sent by the King was introduced, saying that the Swiss must "lay down their arms at once", and "retire to their barracks."

The main body of the Swiss now fell back through the salons of the palace, retreating through the gardens at the rear of the building. Brought to a halt near the central Round Pond, they were broken into smaller groupings and without hesitation slaughtered like bevies.

Perceiving that they'd been betrayed by the Swiss when fired upon as they sought to parley, the sans-culotte showed no mercy, women too joining the killing and the wanton mutilation. Heads and limbs were hacked from bodies, the bodies stripped of their uniforms, gentiles sliced off with scythes, as a group of about sixty Swiss Guards, seeking refuge with the Assembly, were surrounded and summarily marched to the Hôtel de Ville to be executed. Only about a hundred of the Swiss Guard would survive the slaughter, a killing that spread to the male courtiers and servants found throughout the palace. As several of the women of the court knelt beseeching for their lives, as swords were raised against them, a voice interposed: "Spare the women. Do not disgrace the nation!"

Nearly a thousand insurgents had been killed or

wounded—the sans-culottes and the federates combatants—
while the carnage among the besieged was even greater. Once
the fight was decided, the president of the Insurrectionary
Commune, a man named Huguenin, who on the previous day
had been a customs clerk, addressed the Legislative Assembly
in words that clearly implied that it too had come to its end:

> It is the new magistrates of the people who present
> themselves at your bar.... The people have charged us
> with declaring to you that they invest you anew with
> their trust, but it has charged us at the same time with
> declaring to you that they can only recognize, as sole
> judge of the extraordinary measures to which necessity
> and resistance to oppression have brought them, the
> French people, your sovereign and ours, gathered
> together in their primary assemblies. (20)

Emerging from the hiding place in which he'd been
concealed by Danton for his protection before the battle in the
event of failure, Marat "now promenaded in the streets of
Paris, brandishing his sabre, in front of a battalion of
Marseillais...." (21) In *L'Ami du peupl* on August 13, Marat
unequivocally supported the Commune against the Assembly:

> You, worthy compatriots of the Sections of Paris, true
> representatives of the people, beware of the snares that
> these perfidious deputies lay for you; beware of their
> honeyed expressions; it is to your enlightened and
> courageous citizenship that the capital owes in part the
> success of her inhabitants and the country will owe her
> triumph. (22)

11.
What the hand, dare seize the fire?

Asserting they were delegated by parties avowing themselves *the popular sovereignty of the people,* chroniclers have reported that by dauntless operation and under cover of night, roughly a hundred unknown men had installed themselves in the Hôtel de Ville. Locally, they had overthrown the administrative and the military power of the State, intimidated and entrapped its legal executive, and by favor of eight to ten thousand sans-culotte adherents to their cause, held sway in a capital of 700,000 people.

By the evening on the day of their historic conquest more than half of the national representatives had abandoned their seats, leaving only 284 deputies. In this setting, the Girondins ministry dismissed by the King would be reinstated with Roland again in the ministry of interior, but in recognition of the real power of the moment—the *Commune de Paris*—with thirty-two-year-old Georges Danton, as Minister of justice, and de-facto head of government. The office of "king of the French people", as recognized in the previous year's constitution, was temporarily suspended, and the King and the royal family placed under strong guard. The assembly wanted to assign the royals to the Luxemburg Palace, but, at the insistence of the Commune, the Temple Prison was chosen, centrally located and easier to secure.

The next day Robespierre was elected by his section, Place du Vendôme, to the Commune, where he became its most forceful and demanding representative; as Jean-Paul Marat, becoming an advisor to the Commune, was invited to take over the royal printing operation and began publishing *Journal de la republique française*. Indicating the tenor of that guidance in the prospectus for the new periodical, Marat cautioned: "No one in the world is more revolted than I by the establishment of an arbitrary authority.... In any event, it was in a spirit of civic obligation...that I believed I had to advise this severe measure...[i.e.] bringing down 500 heads...in order to save 500,000 innocent ones." (1)

With the *journées* of 20 June and 10 August, for those ostensibly acting on their behest the Parisian sans-culottes had become a talismanic legitimating constituency, and it was to these Marat had the greatest appeal as he became the embodiment of the Revolution carried to its logical conclusion. (2) A Jacobin member of the Assembly, Rene Levasseur, described the first impressions made on him by the figure of Marat:

> This demoniac fanatic inspired in us a sort of repugnance and stupor. When they showed him to me for the first time...I considered him with that anxious curiosity which one feels in contemplating certain hideous insects. His clothes in disorder, his livid face, his haggard eyes had something repellant and frightful which saddened the soul. (3)

With the King and his family prisoners in the Temple, it was resolved that all decrees vetoed by the King would immediately become law, and of particular importance was that pertaining to the deportation of non-jurant priests. The following day, each section of Paris had in place an elected committee of vigilance ready to respond to and ferret out all "counter-revolutionary" activity. These committees were authorized to make *visites domiciliaiares*, allowing them to force their way into homes without warrant, and to disarm and to arrest suspects. Under their aegis, the category of suspects too was to be expanded drastically, first to include clergy and aristocrats and the relatives of émigrés, and finally to anyone who could be accused of being suspect at all. After only a few days there would be some 3,000 suspects imprisoned in Paris, as 20,000 of these *comites de surveillance* would spread across France. On the next day, the Commune ordered that all printers and authors of "anti-civic" materials be arrested, and Feuillant and royalist newspapers shut down, with their facilities and materials turned over to "revolution-ary" usage.

On 14 August Danton issued a warrant for the arrest of Lafayette, dismissing him from the National Guard; but the Assembly took no action until it was learned on the 19th, seeking asylum behind the Austrian lines, he had crossed the Belgian frontier. Unwilling to submit to the 'scourge' he'd been instrumental in bringing to France, Lafayette would spend the next six years in various prisons custodian of the European royal powers.

On the 15th Robespierre came before the Assembly to demand the punishment of those who had defended the Tuileries on 10 August, a punishment he characterized as *la juste vengeance du peuple*. It had settled in the minds of the Parisian sans-culottes that their rising and the stand-off on the main staircase at the Tuileries Palace had been a pre-planned ambush by the Swiss Guard and the general staffs of the gendarmerie and National Guard, and was an act of betrayal. The next day, in response to petitions coming in from peasants concerning persecutions based on former seigniorial rights, the Assembly decreed "that all feudal and seigniorial rights of all kinds are suppressed without indemnity, unless they were the price of the original granting of the tenement." (4)

On the 17th the Assembly established an extraordinary tribunal composed of judges and juries elected by the sections of Paris. This "tribunal" was to hear cases arising out of the eventful day of the monarch's overthrow; and the popular sentiment was for vengeance.

The first of those to be tried and found guilty by the tribunal was Arnaud de La Porte former minister of the King's Household and disperser of the king's secret funds. He stepped up to the guillotine on August 23, 1792. In the first weeks of its existence, the Tribunal condemned three of the accused and acquitted three; through October, fifty-nine cases were heard with twenty-two suspects condemned to death by guillotine.

Revolutionary France however had no effective authority constituting a national government. The main political institutions residing in Paris, the Legislative Assembly, the Council of Ministers and the Commune, together competed in an inter-layered system of quasi-government. On August 10, the Legislative Assembly delegated twelve representatives to go to the armies in the field, three to each army—"with the power to suspend, provisionally, both the generals and all other officers and public officials, civil or military, and even to arrest them if circumstances require, as well as to provide for their provisional replacement." Eighteen representatives would also be dispatched by the Assembly to the *departements* to facilitate national cohesion; while the Council of Ministers sent twelve representatives; as the Commune sent its own representatives to assert control in the *departements* around Paris, that would be answerable to the Commune alone. (5)

In accord with Danton's demand prior to the insurrection, and with a large consensus, a new National Convention was mandated to replace the Legislative Assembly by direct election, and was announced the day after Louis XVI's dethronement. The selection of the word "convention" was in tribute to the Constitutional Convention held in the city of Philadelphia in the United States five years previously, as its purpose likewise was in framing a constitution. With this, it was evident a leap in the Revolution had been realized; a succeeding phase had been ushered-in that would soon establish a republic with universal male suffrage as its basis, ending the property qualification for voting and with it the distinction between "active" and "passive" citizens.

The first round of voting—for the electors' proper—would take place on August 26 and 27. The second round—the election of deputies, to the exclusion of those who previously held any privileged post—would be carried out in the first three weeks of September. The retiring Legislative Assembly was to hold its last session on September 20, and the incoming National Convention open its first session the next day.

On 20 August, the fortress at Longwy in northern France came under siege by the combined Austro-Prussian invasion and was surrendered on the 23rd. This news reached Paris two days later, along with the report that its commander had deserted. Was it cowardice, or treason? The Assembly decreed the death penalty for anyone thereafter who even spoke of the surrender of any military installation while under attack. With the city rife with rumors of counter-revolutionary plots, and with the advance of the Duke of Brunswick and the Prussian army across the frontier, the feeling of the Parisian sans-culotte and of the political leadership in the new Commune was that they were "encamped over a mine." (6) On August

26, refractory clergy were given two weeks to leave France; after which deadline they faced deportation to Guyana.

On the 28th, Danton spoke before the Legislative Assembly:

> The anxieties that are being spread with regard to our situation are much exaggerated, for we still have armies ready to pursue the enemy and fall on him if he advances inward.... It was only through a great upheaval that we shall be able to repel the despots.... Up to now you have seen only the simulated war of Lafayette; today we must wage a far more frightful war, the war of the Nation against the despots. It is time to tell the people that, that the people en masse must hurl themselves against their foes. (7)

In this speech Danton proposed the Assembly authorize a search of houses to find weapons that "indolent or ill-disposed citizens may be hiding," and that commissioners be appointed to encourage the *levee en masse* he proposed for the defense of the nation.

On 1 September news arrived that the last fortification between the enemy and Paris, Verdun, was under attack. Almost with this came reports that royalists in the Vendée had risen. The largest city in that region, Bressuire, had been besieged and the republicans had lost more than 200 men in repelling them.

The Girondins ministers were apoplectic and over-taken by panic. Roland, a fastidious man with a Quaker appearance, often wearing a round hat (he had visited Philadelphia), declared the government should leave Paris for Tours or Blois, and take with them the treasury and the king as a ransom. But Danton stood fast. On September 2, he called for the ringing of the tocsin throughout France. Said he: "This is not a signal of alarm, but a signal to charge against the enemies of the *patrie*. In order to conquer, gentlemen, we need audacity, and yet more audacity, and always audacity." The delegates of the Commune came to the bar and read a proclamation: "Citizens, march out forthwith under your flags; let us gather on the Champ-de-Mars; let an army of 60,000 men be formed this instant. Let us expire under the blows of the enemy, or exterminate him under our own." (8)

Many hearing the declaration recalled the Duke of Brunswick had threatened to lay waste to the city and bring a scourge to its inhabitants. With the Commune's summons, with so many counter-revolutionary plots rumored, many facing conscription were reluctant to leave Paris and their families. Even now Paris's prisons held several hundred Swiss Guards, and were brimming with aristocrats, with plotters and supporters of the king, and with anti-revolutionaries of every sort. If any of these escaped or were released by the enemy during a siege, might they not themselves participate in the scourge Brunswick promised?

Before any citizen called up by the levee left with the troops, the Quinze-Vingt section demanded that the families of émigrés be imprisoned, and that punishment be meted out to all conspirators responsible for the deaths on August 10. Faubourg-Poissoniere demanded that all priests and im-prisoned suspects be put to death; as this also won approval by the sections of Luxembourg, Louvre, and Fontaine-Montmorency. (9)

With the tocsin sounding and the firing of guns on the morning of September 2, that afternoon refractory priests carried in six coaches under escort by guards to the Abbaye prison were fallen upon with the sword and massacred by federates from Marseille and Brittany after one of the senior prelates trashed a man across his skull as he'd been verbally accosted. Then refractory priests held in the Carmelite convent were seized and killed. By night fall, before an improvised tribunal under judgement of Stanislas Maillard, lighted by torches and candles, condemned priests and Swiss and royal guards were "tried", and then killed in a savage manner.

The bloodletting continued through two days, September 2nd and 3rd, leading to the death of as many as 1400 inmates, almost half of them, modern commentary maintains, common criminals. Taine enumerates these—"...171 murders at the Abbaye, 169 at LaForce, 223 at the Châtelet, 328 at the Conciergerie, 73 at the Tour-Saint-Bernard, 120 at the Carmelites, 79 at Saint Firmin, 170 at Bicetre, 35 at Salpetriere...." Heaps of corpses were drawn off in carts to the Montrouge quarries for disposal. Marie-Victorie Monnard, a sans-culotte girl wrote of seeing the bodies hauled away:

> The carts were full of men and women who had just been slaughtered and whose limbs were still flexible because they had not had time to grow cold, so that legs and arms and heads nodded and dangled on either side of the carts.... I can still remember those drunken men and remember in particular one very skinny one, very pale with a sharp pointed nose. The monster went to speak to another man and said, "Do you see that rotten old priest on the pile there?" He then went and hauled the priest to his feet, but the body, still warm, could not stand up straight. The drunken man held it up, hitting it across the face and shouting, "I had enough trouble killing the old brute." (10)

Women at the scene helped load the carts, and occasionally broke off from their work to dance the Carmagnole, laughing as they slipped on the gore-wetted paving stones. After the

August insurrection, the song and dance *La Carmagnole* had become the rallying cry and entertainment for san-culottes revolutionaries:

> Madame Veto had promised.
> Madame Veto had promised.
> To cut everyone's throat in Paris.
> But she failed to do this,
> Thanks to our gunners.

Then this refrain:

> Let us dance the Carmagnole
> Long live the sound
> Long live the sound
> Let us dance the Carmagnole
> Long live the sound of the cannons.

To great consternation, incidents of the killings were reported across the Channel in London, as throughout Britain. September 10, 1792, the *London Times* editorialized:

> Cardinal de la Rochefaucoult, the Archbishop of Arles, M. Botin, Vicar St. Ferrol, &c. have been since particularly marked as trophies of *victory* and *justice*!!! Their trunkless heads and mangled bodies were made the mockery of the mob.
>
> Are these "The Rights of Man"? Is this the LIBERTY of Human Nature? The most savage four footed tyrants that range the unexplored desarts of Africa, in point of tenderness, rise superior to the two legged Parisian animals....

Later Carlyle in his volumes wrote of the *September Massacre*:

That a shriek of inarticulate horror rose over this thing not only from French aristocrats and moderates, but from all Europe, and has prolonged itself to the present day, was most natural and right. The thing lay done, irrevocable; a thing to be counted beside some other things, which lie very black in our Earth's Annals, yet which will not erase there from. (11)

Almost a century later, as he denounced this *Saturnalia of Hell*, Taine was still livid: "All the unfettered instincts that live in the lowest depths of the human heart start from the human abyss at once, not alone the heinous instincts with their fangs...." (12) The novelist of the erotic Restif de la Bretonne witnessed some of the atrocities, recording them in *Les Nuets de Paris*. There were only a hundred men self-delegated or otherwise to carry out this vengeance and reprisal, he wrote. Others have estimated perhaps at the core of the slaughter there were 160 men, and these had divided into units of twenty to carry out the work, attracting numerous hangers-on. Later those involved were to be known as *Septembriseurs*, and were awarded twenty-four *livres* as agents of the Commune.

The most unspeakable retribution was meted out to one of thirty women to be killed, Marie Therese, or Princess de Lamballe, a former lady-in-waiting to Marie Antoinette. On September 3' she was taken from her cell in a prison in eastern Paris, received a perfunctory trial by tribunal, and was given over to the ferocity of would be executioners. Her biographer later described the scene:

> ...as she was dragged into the centre of the courtyard, a man struck at her with his pike, thrusting it through that crowning glory of her beauty, her fair and abundant hair. Down fell the rippling masses of it, and with them a letter in the Queen's writing, which she had concealed there:

the ruman's hand, too, unsteady with drink, wounded her on the forehead, and blood trickled from her ear. At the sight of it, like wild beasts mad for slaughter, all rushed and flung themselves upon her.... (13)

Her breasts hacked-off, her genitals cut from her body, her head severed—a head, it has been suggested, that was cleaned and dressed, to be garishly paraded at the end of a pike outside the Queen's window at the Temple prison. The head of the Comte de Montmorin, the King's former Foreign Minister, was likewise impaled and carried off in the direction of the Assembly.

As with all of London, surely too William Blake was informed of the details of the massacre in the days after it occurred, but he must have purchased this, however regretfully, with the attending circumstances for the Revolution. The middle stanzas of the six-stanza poem "The Tyger" may attest to this:

> And what shoulder, & what art,
> Could twist the sinews of thy heart?
> And when thy heart began to beat,
> What dread hand? & what dread feet?

A song that combines the rhythms of nursery rhyme with lyrical incantation, as it has too been considered a hymn. Blake pounds out a hypnotic cadence:

> What the hammer? What the chain?
> In what furnace was thy brain?
> What the anvil? What dread grasp
> Dare its deadly terrors clasp? (14)

But all commentary by-and-large fails to see the world that Blake saw, as the poem's composition was contemporaneous with the carnage in France. Blake's lamb and tiger are depicted in two separate collections of poems; *Songs of Innocence* published in 1789, and *Songs of Experience*, published in 1794. Thereafter Blake would publish both together as *Songs of Innocence and of Experience - Shewing the two Contrary States of the Human Soul*. Both lamb and tiger are integral to Blake's vision.

> Little lamb, who made thee?
> Does thou know who made thee

Blake wonders too about the creator of the fearsome creature, the tiger; a creature molded in fire at the forge of a blacksmith who is hammering it into being. But students and teachers through generations have queried—how could God who is all-loving make both lamb and tiger, the gentle and the meek, the destructive and the ferocious? The question reveals naught about Blake, but of the naiveté of the question. It were specious to answer. The two contraries co-exist, each necessary to the other as expressions of the human soul. This clarifies Blake's "fearful symmetry": While *innocence* is wont to see the world differently, *experience* speaks in the poem in a dialogue of contraries by which the imagination of the reader is catechized.

The poet was an exacting reviser. At the bottom, right hand margin of a page in his notebook is an earlier fragment of the poem, that suggests the horrid, sanguinary scene in Paris:

> Could fetch it from the furnace deep
> And in thy horrid ribs dare steep
> In the well of sanguine woe

In what clay in what mould
Were thy eyes of fury rolled. (15)

The Tyger, one commentator has averred, doesn't answer the question it poses. (16)

12.

Divide the heavens
of Europe

On August 26, the out-going Legislative Assembly conferred the title of French citizen on "Priestly, Payne, Wilberforce, Clarkson...Anacharsis Clootz...Washington, Hamilton, Maddison, Kosciusko...," among others, inscribing an international dimension for their revolution. Wilberforce, having brought another bill for the abolition of the slave trade before the Parliament that April, was embarrassed by this association with Jacobinism. In the following week, as the balloting for the National Convention began, Paine and Priestley were both elected to that body, Paine by four different Departments, and Priestley by two. (1) With Priestley declining the honor in favor of emigration to America, selected in the balloting by the department of Calais on September 6, a week later a municipal official, Achille Audibert, arrived in London with a certificate of election to entreat Paine's acceptance.

Eager to elicit a fresh decision from the court in favor of freedom of speech and of the press in his defense against charges of "sedition", Paine was hesitant. But as he had thrown himself headlong into the battle to defend the French Revolution, his friends urged his acceptance.

Paine was not noted as a loquacious public speaker, but at a gathering identified as the "Friends of Liberty", an organization formed to disseminate his "Rights of Man, Part the Second" after its publication, on the evening of September 12 he is said to have poured forth in exceptional articulacy. Blake's biographer Alexander Gilchrist in his book reported on it in this way:

> ...Paine was giving at Johnson's an idea of the inflammatory eloquence he had poured forth at a public meeting of the previous night. Blake, who was present, silently inferred from the tenor of his report that those in power, now eager to lay hold of noxious persons would certainly not let slip such an opportunity. On Paine's rising to leave, Blake laid his hands on the orator's shoulder, saying, "You must not go home, or you are a dead man!" and hurried him off on his way to France, whither he was now, in any case bound, to take his seat as French legislator. By the time Paine was at Dover, the officers were in his house...and some twenty minutes after the Custom House officials at Dover had turned over his slender baggage with, as he thought, extra malice, and he had set sail for Calais, an order was received from the Home Office to detain him. England never saw Tom Paine again. (2)

A few paragraphs after this Gilchrist adds: "Those were hanging days! Blake on the occasion showed greater sagacity than Paine, whom, indeed, Fuseli affirmed to be more ignorant than himself even. Spite of unworldliness and visionary faculty, Blake never wanted for prudence and sagacity in ordinary matters."

There is an earlier analogous story concerning a premonition of the young William Blake when he and his father approached the engraver William Ryland to enquire about an apprenticeship, before the son was to find a place with James Basire. In any event, Ryland was too expensive for the father's purse, but on leaving the studio the boy remarked to his father, "'I do not like that man's face: *it looks as if he will live to be hanged.*' And so it was: twelve years later the celebrated engraver was hanged at Tyburn for forgery, and thus became the last man slain at that place of execution." (3)

With his discerning intuition on the occasion related, Blake was able to forewarn his friend of that prospective fate, which had of course been affected by the report that government spies or "hirelings" were following him in the streets, and by newspapers like the London *Times* which had indeed written July 12, 1792: "It is earnestly recommended to Mad Tom that he should embark for France, and there be naturalized into the regular confusion of democracy."

Accompanied by the official from Calais, and by John Frost (a trusted confidant and lawyer and secretary of the *London Corresponding Society)*, and traveling a circuitous route to avoid the vigilance of government agents by way of Rochester, Sandwich, and Deal—the trio reached the coast and Dover to observe the royal proclamation had raised general apprehension. Reporting on the search of the correspondence he carried in his luggage, Paine wrote September 15 in a letter of protest addressed to "Mr. Secretary Dundas" (Henry Dundas, Scottish Tory MP, and Pitt's Secretary of War):

> Among the letters which he [the customs agent] took out of my trunk were two sealed letters, given into my charge by the American minister in London, one of which was addressed to the American minister in Paris, the other to a private gentleman; a letter from the President of the United States, and a letter from the Secretary of State in America, both directed to me, and which I had received from the American minister, now in London, and were private letters of friendship; a letter from the electoral body of the department of Calais, containing the notification of my being elected to the National Convention; and a letter from the president of the National Assembly

informing me of my being also elected for the department of Oise.... (4)

After removing the items and taking up President Washington's letter, as the official began to read Paine remonstrated it was rather extraordinary that General Washington could not write a private letter to a friend without it being read by a custom-house officer. Frost then laid a hand over the letter, saying he should not read it. Casting his eyes on the concluding portion, Frost said, "I will read this part to you." This is its transcript:

And as no one can feel greater interest in the happiness of mankind than I do, it is the first wish of my heart that the enlightened policy of the present age may diffuse to all men those blessings to which they are entitled and lay the foundation of happiness for future generations. (5)

Washington's letter, dated May 6, 1792, was in reply to Paine's having dedicated *Rights of Man* to him in the previous year, as he sent a letter to the president telling of his activities, where he'd written "the adour of Seventy-six is capable of renewing itself", quoted earlier in this narrative. This letter together with fifty copies of his pamphlet as a gift to Washington, presumably to be handed out to other patriots. Washington let a year pass before responding, and notwithstanding the pressing issues of his office and the protracted nature of such communications, this would indicate Washington's view of Paine's political writings had cooled since the days of *Common Sense*. And, as will be seen, it was embarrassing his governments' attempt to secure better commercial relations with Britain. Washington's dour response to the activities of his erstwhile comrade-in-arms was perhaps unregistered, except in this tardiness of response.

At shore, as those gathering began muttering that the author of "seditious" writings deserved a light-coat of tar and feathers, Paine boarded the vessel on which he was to depart Britain for the last time. With a general clamor being raised, including stone throwing, Paine safely embarked, just in advance of the arriving government agents.

As the vessel reached Calais, Paine was to be feted by a salute from the battery, with cheering along the shoreline. Stepping aground, the representatives of the municipality were there to greet him, while opening the way to the official delegation was a parted line of National Guard with a young girl advancing "requesting the honor of setting a cockade in his hat." On the way to an official reception shouts of "Vive Thomas Paine" were heard. When meetings and celebration continued the next day, Paine was ushered to a theatre box with the banner "For the Author of 'the Rights of Man," where he took his seat under a bust of Comte de Mirabeau draped with the American, British and French flags.

The honors accorded Paine were being extended to other elected deputies of the National Convention as well, which had included Paine's American friend, Joel Barlow; but this representative of America, and now of France, it was being reported, "had been hunted by British oppressors down to the very edge of the coast." (6) The story got related across France, and, although it was known he'd devoted his life and study to the events now at hand, this enhanced his stature in the esteem of the public. Paine's biographer Moncure Conway wrote: "From the ashes of Rousseau's "Contrat Social," burnt in Paris, rose "The Rights of Man," no phoenix, but an eagle of the new world, with eyes not blinded by any royal sun." (7)

The two "grand prerequisites" for republican government spelled out the previous year by Thomas Paine had been assumed in France: the hereditary representative had been supplanted and a national convention summoned.

Paine reached Paris September 19. The next day there was a gathering of *Conventionnels,* and on the 21st there was a procession to the Tuileries for verification of credentials by the expiring national body. For its first act, carried by a round of applause and cheering, the National Convention decreed: "Royalty is from this day abolished in France." Year One of the Republic had begun, to become retroactive in the following year when a new "revolutionary" calendar would be adopted.

The next day, on a petition from duc du Orléans, Danton proposed that to prevent their removal by popular violence, the entire administrative corps be stricken—municipal and judicial. Danton accentuated the matter: "Those who have made it their profession to act as judges of men are like priests; both of them have everlastingly deceived the people. Justice ought to be dispensed in accordance with the simple laws of reason."

Paine, rising and speaking through another deputy since his French was not sufficient for purposes of formal discourse, proposed postponing a decree to allow a more thorough discussion. The royal apparatus, the King's hirelings, he said, must be removed along with the King—but with only partial reforms the judiciary would not have the coherence it required to make it effective; persons might be changed, but not the law; and finally, justice could not be administered by men who did not know the law. (8)

While Danton welcomed Paine's views, the convention went on to decree that the administrative bodies be recast by popular elections, eliminating the limitations on eligibility fixed by the Constitution of 1791, viz., a municipal officer need not be a proprietor, a judge need not be a lawyer.

Stepping back to his chair, Paine could not yet have been cognizant of the portentous factional divisions that were about open, driving France toward the abyss, but whose shadow lay even now athwart the promise of the new convention.

The world-changing events Paine saw it his privilege to participate in were augured on the outcome of the *Battle of Valmy,* which had precluded the invasion of France led by the Duke of Brunswick. Brunswick's plan had been to move his army westward between the two defending armies—the French Armée du Nord commanded by General Charles Dumouriez, replacing Rochambeau, and the Armée du Centre commanded by General Francois Kellermann, replacing Lafayette—protecting his flanks with two Austrian corps as he advanced. The invading coalition, comprised of Prussians, Austrians, Hessians, and French Émigrés (who had been congregating at Coblenz and supplied with horses through the agency of British services), armies totaling 84,000 men, after conquering the French border fortresses, intended to move onto the fertile plain before Paris. On the eve of battle, they were moving through a terrain consisting of marshy low lands and narrow defiles west of the Argonne. With the French at his back in the east, Brunswick could have broken toward Paris across open country, but chose instead to protect his supply lines and turned to fight.

The village of Valmy lies between hills on its north, west, and south; Dumouriez's forces forming a line east of the village, while Kellermann commanded a line drawn up along a ridge west of the village topped by a large windmill. The Coalition had the superior force in infantry and guns and expected to prevail against undisciplined raw troops, but the French guns were manned by trained and proficient former royal gunners, and in the French infantry where men who would fight that day with élan. Regarded as trivial as a military engagement, the clash on September 20, 1792, is often referred to, not as a battle, but a "cannonade." In terms of losses to both sides it was certainly slight, but it was enough to cause the Duke, undoubtedly a splendid and sagacious soldier, to deem it prudent to break off the fighting. Thus, he lost the opportunity to capture Paris and to restore the Bourbon dynasty.

Coming at the moment of the convocation of the National Convention, the news of victory spurred the decree of the end of monarchy in France, and is therefore, hailed as among the most important military engagements in history. The German poet of genius Johann Wolfgang von Goethe, whose politics tended toward enlightened-royalism, witnessed the battle from the Prussian side as the invited guest of his patron Charles Augustus, Duke of Saxe-Weimer, who commanded a regiment of Prussian cuirassiers. Goethe was riding with a cavalry squadron as the battle, his first, unfolded.

Not surprisingly, his observations on seeing a French battery firing read as the citation of an observer of natural phenomenon: "Balls were falling by dozens...not rebounding, luckily, for they sank into the soft grounds; but mud and dirt bespattered man and horse." Of the shriek of shells, he wrote— "The sound of them is curious enough, as if it were composed of the humming of tops, the gurgling of water, and the whistling of birds." As they bivouacked around campfires later, purportedly asked by some officers what he thought of the battle, Goethe is widely reported to have said: "From this place, and from this day forth, commences a new èra in the world's history; and you can all say that you were present at its birth." (9)

Once again, let 's resort to Blake's revolutionary hymn to re-score what was said earlier. Countless readers have intoned the accented stresses of the lines in *The Tyger*—

> When the stars threw down their spears,
> And water'd heaven with their tears.

David Erdman, in his *Prophet Against Empire,* hears reference to Valmy and the defeat of the 1ˢᵗ Collation and of European Royalty, as, twelve years previously, to Yorktown and the defeat of Cornwallis and the British Crown. America and France were the twin pillars in Blake's vision of a world uprising and transformation, to be followed by the same in Britain. Erdman wrote: "The creator must have smiled at Yorktown and at Valmy, not because his people were warlike, but because they seemed ready to coexist with the Lamb, the wrath of the Tiger having done its work." (10) In Blake royalty is associated with the heavens and with stars, and both of Erdman's associations are apposite.

But it could as cogently be read as the assault of the Tuileries Palace in August where Louis XVI ordered the Swiss Guard back to their barracks. At that moment, literally the King's guards were ordered to lay down their arms before their slaughter, hence too, manifestly there was occasion for tears. But these actualities have long evaded appraisals of Blake's clearly innovatory canticle. In his *Introduction* to the cycle of poems designated *Songs of Experience,* didn't the London bard extol the change come upon the earth:

> Hear the voice of the Bard!
> Who Present, Past, & Future, sees;
> Whose ears have heard
> The Holy Word
> That walk'd among the ancient trees,
>
> Calling the lapsed Soul,
> And weeping in the evening dew;
> That might control
> The starry pole,
> And fallen, fallen light renew!
>
> "O Earth, O Earth return!
> Arise from out the dewy grass;

> Night is worn,
> And the morn
> Rises from the slumberous mass. (11)

In Blake's symbolism a cycle in the history of humanity, which has been in a fallen state, has ended after six thousand years. America and France did not yet, to the bard's presentment, represent freedom attained, but they were preparing the way for a new millennium.

On September 25 Paine addressed a letter to the people of France, published by Nicolas de Bonneville (Paine's writing for the Convention were usually translated into French by Sophie de Condorcet), acknowledging the honor of being bestowed with citizenship and election to the Convention. He wrote, very much apropos Blake's sentiments just cited :

> ...I feel my felicity increased by seeing the barrier broken down that divided patriotism by spots of earth, and limited citizenship to the soil, like vegetation. Had these honors been conferred in an hour of national tranquility, they would have afforded no other means of showing my affection, than to have accepted and enjoyed them; but they come accompanied with circumstances that give me the honorable opportunity of commencing my citizenship in the stormy hour of difficulties. I come not to enjoy repose. Convinced that the cause of France is the cause of all mankind, and that liberty cannot be purchased by a wish. (12)

The National Convention was composed of three broad divisions. To the right of the president now sat the Girondins;

not accurately described as a 'party', they were men who had learned their republican values largely from American events and from the philosophes of the enlightenment. They were revolutionaries, albeit practitioners of the art of politics, including that of nepotism, many of whom found they were comfortable amidst the pomp and frill of Parisian society. These men were lawyers for the most part, but also among them were merchants and industrialists, as there were journalists. On the left, on the upper benches, afterwards called *La Montagne* (the Mountain), sat the bloc whose most active members were from the popular clubs, the Jacobin or Cordeliers clubs, and while they also were predominately lawyers and hence bourgeois, they were impatient with the political shibboleths of the Girondins, and were acutely aware that the revolution France was experiencing was for the benefit of the broad commons of the nation, especially of those they were allied, the so-called sans-culotte. They were willing to make tough political calculations necessary to achieve their goals, and would pursue their agenda with ruthless energy, even violence. They formed the least numerous faction.

Between these increasingly antagonistic groupings, again, was the so-called "Plain", the most numerous entity, and although also not constituting a distinct party, they were the "moderates" professing to keeping "open minds", albeit to be disparaged as "crocking frogs".

At first the *Plain* would support the *Girondins*, but when compelled by fear, later they would support the *Montagne*. These divisions were immediately evident in the conventions discourse, as one after another of those prominent in the factions came under attack. A dispute whether to maintain a bodyguard for the security of the Convention against the threat of popular violence devolved into acquisitions that among them were those who desired dictatorship for themselves or for others. Robespierre in particular was denounced by name. Jean-Paul Marat, too, who had been elected deputy of his Parisian section, was attacked by Danton for his purported excesses. Had not, Danton asked, the refuge Marat sought in cellars "ulcerated his soul?" (13)

At that point, the entire Convention seemed ready to follow the intimation of Danton that Marat be sent "into the wilderness". Even among the Montagnards there was a conviction that his vehemence was prejudicial to their bloc as a whole. Amid cross-argumentation and vociferous accusations, Marat demanded to be heard.

Mounting the tribune amidst hectoring voices, Marat began by reading out the final number of *L'ami du peuple* in which he'd declared that all of his efforts to save the people would be in vain without a new insurrection:

> When I look at the stamp of the majority of the deputies to the National Convention, I despair of the public safety. If in the first eight sittings the complete basis of the Constitution is not laid, expect nothing more from your representatives. You are crushed forever. Fifty years of anarchy await you, and you will not be relieved from it except by a dictator, a true patriot and statesman. O people of talkers, if you only knew how to act!

As if a single tempest, the whole convention now rose; while from the right came shouts from hoarsening voices, "To the guillotine!"

Waiting for the tumult to subside, Marat resumed: "Gentlemen, I have in this Assembly a great number of personal enemies." At this, three-quarters of the deputies leapt to their feet—"All of us! All of us!" Again, waiting for a lull, Marat continued:

> I have in this Assembly a great number of personal enemies. I recall them to modesty. It is not by clamours,

menaces, and outrages that you prove an accused man to be guilty; it is not in shouting down a defender of the people that you show him to be a criminal. I return thanks to the hidden hand that has thrown in the midst of you an idle phantom to frighten timid men, dividing good citizens and making odious the Parisian Deputation. I return thanks to my persecutors for having furnished me with an opportunity of opening my mind fully. They accuse certain members of the Paris Deputation of aspiring to the dictatorship, to the triumvirate, to the tribunate. This absurd accusation is only able to find partisans because I form part of this deputation. Well! gentlemen, I owe it to justice to declare that my colleagues, notably Danton and Robespierre, have constantly repudiated all idea of dictatorship...when I put it before them; I have myself broken many lances with them on this subject. (14)

This speech occurred on September 25, and Marat reported on it in *Journal de la Republique*: "Let friends of the country know...the Guadet-Brissot faction had plotted to cause me to perish by the sword of tyranny or the poniard of brigands. If I fall beneath the stroke of assassins, these friends will hold the clue for tracing the deed to its source." (15)

On October 11, a committee to frame a new constitution was impaneled. The leading lights among the Girondins, Brissot sat on it, as did Vergniaud, along with independents like Sieyès and Condorcet, as it included Danton and Paine. Facilitating Paine's role, four members of the committee spoke English, as he became intimate with Danton, as Brissot, who had first met Paine in America where they found they shared literary interests, as they did a fervor "for negro emancipation", was among his closest confidants. (16) Carlyle noted in his volume, "Deputy Paine and France generally expect all finished in a few months."

But the implementation of this constitution was to be delayed, and subsequently it never saw the light of day. Thomas Clio Rickman, Paine's friend and biographer was to give this assessment, which would have come from his conversations with Paine in the fall of 1793:

> This delay was owing to the jealousy of Condorcet, who had written the preface, part of which some of the members thought should have been in the body of the work. Brissot and the whole party of the Girondites lost ground daily after this; and with them died away all that was national, just and humane: they were, however, highly to blame for their want of energy. (17)

Another commentator on Paine's importance in the deliberations was Paul Desjardins, who wrote in his *Thomas Paine: Father of Republics*: "We do not know exactly what part he took in the labors of the Committee; but it is pretty certain that he had a good deal to do with the project of Condorcet." (18) That project, "suggested doubtless to his friend Condorcet" was consecrated in universal suffrage, the affirmation of religious toleration, the guarantee of liberty of press, promulgation of universal instruction, the abolition of hereditary functions, and the right of citizens to protest and censor the whole system of assemblies, the communes, and finally, those of the republic.

Overlong and overwrought, when presented to the Convention on February 25, 1793, the constitution was still borne. It was 85 pages and had 368 articles, resembling a philosophic tract more than a foundational framework. It met with so much disfavor that others would form a committee to draft alternatives. Sharing his views with Danton during the debate, Paine confided that the nation needed something different, a briefly worded and more fundamental text that would appeal to the other European nations struggling against despotism. The document required must—"speak for other nations who cannot yet speak for themselves. She must put thoughts into their minds, arguments into their mouths, by showing the reason that has induced her to abolish the old system of monarchical government, and to establish the representative." "France is now in a situation to be the orator of Europe," Paine wrote. (19)

September 25, 1792, Paine had published his arraignment against the misconceptions of royalism in Brissot's journal *Le Patriote français*, where he wrote:

> We are astonished at reading that the Egyptians set upon the throne a stone, which they called king. Well! such a monarch was less absurd and less mischievous than those before whom nations prostrate themselves. At least he deceived no one. None supposed that he possessed qualities or a character. They did not call him Father of his people; and yet it would have been scarcely more ridiculous than to give such a title to a blockhead whom the rights of succession crowns at eighteen. A dumb idol is better than one animated. (20)

On the 27th Paine's letter of congratulations for the abolition of monarchy as representative of the department of Pas-de-Calais was read to the Convention. A pithy memorandum, its second paragraph reads, "Amid the joy inspired by this event, one can not forbear some pain at the folly of our ancestors, who have placed us under the necessity of treating seriously the abolition of a phantom." (21)

As it was read in the Convention, at the utterance of the word "fantome," the deputies, it was reported, responded with applause. This expressed the essence of Paine's contention, viz., although the King was in the Temple a prisoner of state, in reality, he was insignificant. With the overthrow of an idol, it is the pedestal that need be dismantled—the office, rather than the officer, was the true talisman.

A little more than a year before, Paine, with a small number of conferees had placarded Paris and nailed their "Republican Manifesto" on the door of the Constituent Assembly; now he was sitting in conference with Abbé Sieyès and other deputies drawing-up a constitution for a state on that model. But the situation in France was crouched in difficulties that had not needed to be dealt with in America, which was largely being taken for a prototype. These were that America had a relatively sparse population except in a few leading cities, and had emerged, as it were, out of virgin forest, albeit from which its original inhabitants had been expelled and dis-spoiled. That it had been separated by an ocean from the monarch it would dethrone, and where its internal enemies, too, the Tories, could be ostracized. The Duke of Brunswick, representative of the brother-monarchs of Louis XVI had indeed retreated across the frontier, but everyone in France now adherent to "republicanism" knew that the nation was burdened with enemies.

The discord in the Convention was revealed most emphatically in regard to the fate of the King, when on November 20, all calculations changed as the Minister of Interior, Jean-Marie Roland, disclosed to the Convention that Louis XVI's secret correspondence had been discovered hidden in an *L'armoire*

de fer (an iron cabinet), concealed behind wainscot in his apartment at the Tuileries. It contained many compromising and revealing letters, involving his dealings with leading French politicians and of his machinations with foreign crowned heads of state. Half of Paris seemed to shout in unison "Treason!" The resulting scandal would completely discredit Louis XVI, as it was from his person sprang the fount of conspiracy, as it made all those suspect who were disposed to deal less harshly with him—supporters of "indulgence" as they were to be referred to.

Preeminent among those exposed for venality and duplicity was Mirabeau. However recently interred, his remains would be removed from the Panthéon, and his bust in the National Convention smashed. The correspondence involved mostly cabinet ministers, but also, generals Lafayette and Dumouriez, and even Santerre were compromised, as were prominent bishops, statesmen, and nobles.

Roland filed the documents with the office of the Convention, but controversy soon raged concerning their provenance. There had been a time lapse between their discovery and disclosure. Hadn't some of the documents been removed to prevent implicating others; hadn't Roland destroyed letters involving his colleague Danton? These disclosures, coming just as the Convention was debating a trial for the King, had nothing but a deleterious effect on the King's prospects. It was now certain Louis XVI was to pass through the ordeal of trial—it was either that, or death at the hands of popular vengeance.

That night Paine sat in his quarters carefully composing a letter to the president of the Convention. Finished before morning, it was translated and ready to be read that same day. The King should be tried, wrote Paine, but such trial should have its basis in justice and policy. If innocent, he must be allowed to prove it; if guilty he must be punished or pardoned by the nation. But individually, the King should be "beneath the notice of the republic." (22) The significance of the trial should be to bring out that there was a conspiracy against "liberty", not only in France, but in all nations of Europe, by "crowned brigands" with Louis XVI a partner in it. His utility at trial should be in ferreting out the entire conspiracy; but he should only be tried in the interest of all Europe. Paine elaborated:

> If, seeing in Louis XVI only a weak and narrow-minded man, badly reared, as all like him, subject, it is said, to intemperance, imprudently re-established by the Constituent Assembly on a throne for which he was unfit, if we hereafter show him some compassion, this compassion should be the effect of national magnanimity, and not a result of the burlesque notion of pretended inviolability. (23)

December 3 the First Deputy for Paris in the Convention, Robespierre, mounted to the tribune to demand that the King be put to death. That resolved in the affirmative, on the proposal of Marat, on the 6th the Convention ruled that each deputy must individually and publicly declare his vote on the death penalty for the King. Thus, the divisions within the National Convention would stand in stark contrast.

The path proposed by Paine now became to work through the Convention to find a majority, who having condemned the King, would be willing to save the man; and in pardoning him, retain him as an imprisoned hostage to guarantee the restraint of his fellow monarchs. (24) But the only object should be to de-crown Louis Capet, as he was now exclusively referenced by this family name.

13.

In tears & iron bound

On December 11, 1792, after Louis Capet entered the chamber of the Convention and had taken his seat, the president, Bertrand Barere, said—"Louis, the French Nation accuses you of having committed a multitude of crimes to establish your tyranny, in destroying her freedom." The charges concerned broken oaths, collusion with foreign aggressors, the conduct of émigrés, military failures, the bloodletting on the Champs de Mars in 1791 and at the Tuileries on August 10 in 1792—a recitation encompassing the entire history of the Revolution, from the calling of the Estates-General to his ultimate dethronement. The deposed monarch exculpated himself on every point; whether deflecting responsibility to his ministers, asserting his privileges under the existing constitution, professing his ignorance or calumny on the part of his accusers, or his immunity from prosecution under the constitution of 1791.

Coinciding with Paine's trial in London begun 18 December; throughout Britain there had been a holocaust of "Paines", (1) he being burnt in effigy at Bridgewater on that day, while magistrates sat at table taking oaths of loyalty to King and the "present constitution" from the populace. Another report recorded—"1792 (Dec.)—this month, Thomas Paine, author of the 'Rights of Man,' &c. &c., was burnt at most towns and considerable villages in Northumberland and Durham." (2) December 12, the *Bury Post*, published near

Thetford, Paine's birthplace, reported:

> The populace in different places have been lately amusing themselves by burning effigies. As the culprit on whom they meant to execute this punishment was Thomas Paine, they were not interrupted by any power civil or military. The ceremony has been at Croydon in Surrey, at Warrington, at Lymington, and at Plymouth. (3)

These pyromanias were all carried out amid acclamations of "God save the King, etc."

Paine's trial for high treason was held in the Court of King's Bench by special jury. His lawyer, Lord Erskine—who lost his position as legal advisor to the Prince of Wales to which he'd been appointed in 1786—knowing, as did Paine's supporters, that he could not gain an acquittal, hoped to obtain "some definitive adjudication on the legal liabilities of writers and printers", and "an affirmation of their constitutional rights". (4) Paine, of course, being called to France, was not present to contest his prosecution, but in a letter to the court stating his position, admitted he was author of "Rights of Man." And as this was the sole point on which his prosecution was based, while reading the letter the prosecutor was enabled parenthetically to remark—"If I succeed in the prosecution he shall never return to this country otherwise than *in vinculis,* for I will outlaw him." (5) This verdict, no doubt, for the jury hearing the case, as for the government, would be a fitting rebuke to the trial of the King soon to be under-way in France, as to the sanguinary events there in September.

The defense of Louis Capet began 26 December, with a notable team of lawyers variously described, since indubitably they were, as "illustrious" and "brilliant". As the basis of the defense they took the constitution of 1791 under which the

King was immune from prosecution. Furthermore, they held the National Convention had been convened to write a new constitution and to form a government, and had no right to stand as judge and jury. Finally, the defense rejected all charges, giving a thorough 'royalist' re-counting of events since 1789, maintaining Louis was "the restorer of French Liberty."

In ending his summation, the lead lawyer, Raymond Deseze, pronounced—"Citizens, I cannot finish...I stop myself before history. Think how it will judge your judgement, and that the judgement of him will be judged by the centuries."

But the fate of Louis Capet had already been decided, and in any event, he had been damned by his own testimony. The verdict arrived at on January 14 and 15 was unanimous for guilty, with 693 deputies voting 'yes', and 49 deputies either absent or abstaining.

At Paine's trial in England, as his prosecutor had promised, when found guilty he was outlawed, and therefore liable, if captured if ever within British jurisdiction again, to be hung. The special jury sitting for the trial, all men of the "respectable class", were then treated to a dinner, and given two guineas for the conviction. Had they voted for acquittal they would have received but one guinea, and no dinner.

In his *The Life of Thomas Paine*, Moncure Conway wrote on the last day of that year there came two "remarkable" British diplomatic communications. The first made reference to the effect of Paine's outlawry on English radicals then in Paris: "Tom Payne's fate and the unanimity of the English has staggered the boldest of them, and they are now dwindling into nothing." A second contained the following: "Tom Payne has proposed banishing the royal family of France, and I have heard is writing his opinion on the subject...." (6)

On January 17, *Le Moniteur* printed Paine's argument for mercy for the deposed monarch, unread in the Convention, and along with it his own lawyer's lengthy speech at his trial in London. Conway wrote: "So on the 19th, when Paine entered the Convention, it was with the prestige not only of one outlawed by Great Britain for advocating the Rights of Man, but of a representative of the best Englishmen and their principles." (7)

When the vote came on the fate of Louis Capet, Paine rose to declare in clear voice and in French, "I vote for the detention of Louis till the end of the war, and after that his perpetual banishment."

Paine's argument was that Louis had abdicated when he fled in June 1791, and that he should never have been brought back. The former assembly, therefore, shared an equal guilt by compelling his return. Against the ex-king's transgressions should be balanced his crucial aid in breaking the shackles of despotism in America:

> Let then those United States be the guard and the asylum of Louis Capet. There, in the future, remote from the miseries and crimes of royalty, he may learn, from the constant presence of public prosperity, that the true system of government consists not in monarchs, but in fair, equal, and honorable representation. In recalling this circumstance, and submitting this proposal, I consider myself a citizen of both countries. I submit it as an American who feels the debt of gratitude he owes to every Frenchman. I submit it as a man, who, albeit an adversary of kings, forgets not that they are subject to human frailties. (8)

Any blood spilled during a revolution, Paine warned, could merge to become a torrent washing away the civility vital to republican liberty: "He that would make his own liberty secure, must guard even his enemy from oppression; for if he violates this duty he establishes a precedent that will reach to himself."

But the so-called Montagnards, the Jacobins, were adamant for the King's death. Paine reminded the Convention of Robespierre's appeal against the death penalty the previous year; "As France has been the first," he said, "of European nations to abolish royalty, let her also be the first to abolish the punishment of death, and find out a milder and more effectual substitute."

Although Paine was beginning to be suspect for his association with the "Brissotins", neither Robespierre nor Marat yet held the animus for him that they had for their many political opponents. Marat had remarked privately to Paine, "It is you, then, who believe in a republic; you have too much sense to believe in such a dream." Meanwhile, wrote Conway, according to Lamartine "Robespierre affected for the cosmopolitan radicalism of Paine the respect of a neophyte for ideas not understood." (9)

But the signs of trepidation and fearfulness were becoming unmistakable, as the majority began to buckle under the assault of the minority. In early January, the Montagnards had aired damaging accusations against three Girondin leaders asserting that they had had treasonable contacts with the court on the eve of battle on 10 August, and they were producing witnesses to back up their allegations.

When the vote was taken on the penalty for Louis there was a slight weighing in favor of death. Beginning at 10 o'clock on the morning of January 16 until 10 o'clock in the night of January 17, each deputy was to vote out loud from the tribune, and each was to give the reasons for their vote, many adding extenuating remarks; a voice vote lasting for thirty-six hours. With that question settled, another arose: Should the sentence be immediate, or should there be a delay? But if there was postponement, would Louis ever be executed? A final vote on this question was slated for the following day.

On 20 January, as Paine's speech on the question was being read for him to the Convention by Jean Henri Bancal, Marat interrupted—"I submit that Thomas Paine is incompetent to vote on this question; being a Quaker his religious principles are opposed to the death-penalty." At that, there was pandemonium among the Montagnards, as they refused to hear more of the speech. Finally, Paine's words could again be heard:

> Very sincerely do I regret the Convention's vote of yesterday for death. I have the advantage of some experience; it is nearly twenty years that I have been engaged in the cause of liberty, having contributed something to it in the revolution in the United States of America. My language has always been that of liberty and humanity, and I know by experience that nothing so exalts a nation as the union of these two principles, under all circumstances. I know that the public mind of France, and particularly that of Paris, has been heated and irritated by the dangers to which they have been exposed; but could we carry our thoughts into the future, when the dangers are ended, and the irritations forgotten, what to-day seems an act of justice may then appear an act of vengeance. (10)

The present convention, said Paine, could not be presumed to last more than six months more. After the constitution was formed, there would be elections and another assembly. It was, therefore, incumbent upon, and the duty, of those here to consider those who shall replace it. By the act of regicide, the enemies of France would be increased, its friends diminished. The finances of the nation would be more strained in the future, than now—"We should not be justifiable for having thus unnecessarily heaped obstacles in the path of our successors. Let us therefore not be precipitate in our decisions."

One of the deputies seated with the Montagne sprang to his feet—"This is not the language of Thomas Paine." Marat then mounted the tribune and directed a few remarks in English at Paine. As he descended from the tribune he addressed the assembly in French, "I denounce the interpreter, and I maintain that such is not the opinion of Thomas Paine. It is a wicked and faithless translation." (11)

Paine stood stoically as a storm broke over the hall, till at last the translation of his speech could proceed:

> Your Executive Committee will nominate an ambassador to Philadelphia; my sincere wish is that he may announce to America that the National Convention of France, out of pure friendship to America, has consented to respite Louis. That people, your only ally, have asked you by my vote to delay the execution.

> Ah, citizens, give not the tyrant of England the triumph of seeing the man perish on a scaffold who helped my dear brothers of America to break his chains. (12)

At this, from the middle of the floor, Marat cried out that Paine had "voted against the punishment of death because he was a Quaker." Paine replied—"I voted against it both morally and politically."

The next day a large number of the sans-culotte supporters of the Jacobins were outside the Convention hall shouting "Justice!" as the vote was taken. A majority of seventy prevailed for the execution of Louis Capet to take place within 24 hours. Robespierre, conceding he himself had brought a bill against the death penalty, decided since it had not succeeded, and that the penalty had been maintained for the poor, why then should it not be appended for a king. The exception in favor of such punishment, should be for the royal criminal. (13) The French historian Jules Michelet writing in the mid-nineteenth century wrote: "The army did not want the death [of the King], and France did not want it; an imperceptible minority wanted it; and yet things had gone so far, the question been placed on a point so hazardous, that saving Louis XVI would have put the Republic at risk." (14)

Such was the arena where the trial and the sentencing to death was enacted. Yet as Carlyle reminds his readers it would be a mistake to "fancy it of a funereal, sorrowful or even grave character." It had taken on the atmosphere of an opera in which the Montagne acted the part of ushers—

> opening and shutting of Galleries for privileged persons, for "D'Orléans Egalité's mistresses," or other high-dizened women of condition, rustling with laces and tricolor. Gallant Deputies pass and repass thitherward, treating them with ices, refreshments and small-talk; the high-dizened heads beck responsive, some have their card and pin, pricking down the Ayes and Noes, as at a game of *Rouge-et-Noir*: Further aloft reigns Mere Duchesse with her unrouged Amazons; she cannot be prevented making long *Habas*, when the vote is not La Mort. In these Galleries there is refection, drinking of wine and brandy 'as in open tavern, *en pleine tabagie*'. (15)

The execution of Louis Capet took place at the *Place de la Revolution* on January 21, 1793, at about 11 AM. He awoke at five on that morning, and after dressing with the aid of his valet, he gave confession to a non-jurant priest. Receiving the priest's blessing, he went to meet Antoine Joseph Santerre for his escort and transport to the execution site.

Proceeded by drummers, and by cavalry with drawn sabers, the carriage traversed streets lined with men-at-arms with colors flying, National Guard and sans-culotte, where all shutters were drawn and all shops closed. No citizens of any kind were allowed along the whole concourse, the entire train moving at a measured and abstemious pace.

When the procession arrived at the Place de la Revolution the square was exclusively occupied by soldiers and National Guard; the scaffold erected in its center, high and conspicuous, directly faced the gate of the garden of the Tuileries, surrounded by soldiers bearing bayonets and sans-culotte with pikes, with the windows of all the contiguous houses opened and filled with on-looking women.

The path to the scaffold made for difficult passage, but the step down from the throne was merely a transitory one. Arriving at the foot of the contrivance, Louis Capet looked up for a moment as if examining the instrument. When stepping forward before being restrained on the plank, he cried out, "My people, I die innocent." His voice stifled as the drums were struck, turning to his executioner, Charles-Henri Sanson, and his assistants, he declared, "Gentlemen, I am innocent of everything of which I am accused. I hope that my blood may cement the good fortune of the French."

The blade falling upon the neck of Louis Capet severed his head from his body. The executioner, raising the head from the basket by the hair, and showing it to the multitude— whereupon a cry arose, with the fluttering of caps, and shimmering of pikes, "Vive la Nation!" "Vive la Republique!"

The entire spectacle had taken twenty-two minutes. The destroyed remains of the monarch were placed in a black coffin; and the entire train now returned to the Temple, horses at the gallop. It was a procedure whose workings would be re-enacted thousands of times in the ensuing two years. If a king could be beheaded, why not an ordinary mortal? Whereat, as if he himself had been present, after the *Introduction* in *Songs of Experience,* the London bard wrote in *Earth's Answer*:

Earth rais'd up her head
From the darkness dread & drear.
Her light fled,
Stony dread!
And her locks cover'd with grey despair. (16)

14.
Thus was the howl thro' Europe

Throughout the whole of Europe monarchists, royalists, and conservatives were horrified and enraged by the execution of Louis XVI, as Danton's voice rang-out: "The kings in alliance try to intimidate us. We hurl at their feet, as a gage of battle, the French King's head." On January 25, 1793, the *London Times*, averred: "The Republican tyrants of France have now carried their bloody purposes to the uttermost diabolical stretch of savage cruelty. They have murdered their King without even the shadow of justice.... The vengeance of Europe will now rapidly fall on them...."

The day after the deed was consummated Great Britain expelled the French ambassador in London, prompting the National Convention less than a week later to declare war upon Britain and its ally Holland. War between France and the Coalition, which included nearly all of Europe's crowned heads, and the counter-revolution of royalists and intriguers within France, would now exasperate the political divisions in the National Convention leading to the rapid ascendency of the Montagnards over Girondins. Led by Jean-Paul Marat and *Les Enragés,* so-called because they were so radical their opponents deemed them mad, their demands became the order of the day in steering the Jacobins to supremacy.

Following the retreat of the Prussians after the astonishing victory at Valmy, French soldiers had marched east into Germany, and into the Swiss Confederation, as into Savoy, and north across the Belgium lowlands to the border of Holland, with another astonishing victory of the French against the Austrians at Jemappes. For the politicians of the Convention these advances began to take on a millenarian aspect, and political figures began forecasting matters and affairs presaging extraordinary consequences for the future. Wasn't it the Revolution's destiny to liberate the peoples of Europe, where the end of monarchy would mean the beginning of a new era of universal brotherhood and peace? Even Poland, Naples, and Spain might be freed from tyranny. Late in November 1792, Brissot had written to the laureled general and war minister Dumouriez, that soon French armies might be marching into Berlin, urging that he forget the old manner of waging battle and concluding alliances, as had been the past practice of ministers. How "can their petty schemes," he wrote—"compare to the uprisings of the whole planet and the momentous revolutions that we are now called upon to lead?" (1)

On February 14, the Convention annexed the Principality of Monaco, followed by the annexation of Belgium on March 1. On February 21, to consolidate French forces the Convention merged the volunteer (les bleus) and the line regiments (les blancs) in the army, and three days later called for a levee of 300,000 men to defend the republic. By March 7 war was declared on Spain. On the 9th the Convention created *envoyes en mission,* dispatching agents across France to organize the war effort, and to quell dissension and the insurgency that would inevitably be occasioned. Yet by the beginning of March the Austrians would counter-attack in Belgium, as had the Prussians in western Germany. Two weeks later there was a calamitous defeat for the French at Neerwinden, and the evacuation of the whole of Belgium by revolutionary republican troops, as too, they were pushed back into Alsace from Germany.

Simultaneous with these reversals came news of a revolt of peasant conscripts in the Vendée, a coastal region in west-central France immediately south of the Loire River, as the royalist rebellion there also gained traction, as similar revolts broke out in the northern coastal region, Brittany, and elsewhere across wide tracts of the French countryside.

In Paris, with the sugar shortage continuing and with prices increasing on staples—when the cost of coffee soared as well, there had been petitions sent to the Convention for a law to set limits on prices. Suddenly, on February 25 and 27 there was a flurry of pillaging by women of food stuffs from stalls and stores in the sans-culotte faubourgs of Paris. Many goods were seized directly, but many items were paid what the participants deemed "fair prices". The accomplices were all poor working-class women, evidently organized, a few observers discerned, into semi-cohesive mobile units and directed by an affiliated leadership of roughly twenty to thirty individuals. A few of the leaders were suspected of being deputies in the National Convention, informally allied with sans-culottes. These became known collectively as *les Enragés* for their advocacy and practice of direct democracy, and for demanding price controls on staple commodities, or the law of *le maximum* as it became known.

On March 10, there was a second action in Paris, as large crowds descended upon several printing establishments issuing royalist and constitutionalist deputy/journalists tracts in the National Convention. The most prominent of those coming into notoriety was Jacques Roux, a juring priest of the

Gravilliers section and an ally of Marat who had first come on the public scene as part of the escort for Louis Capet on his way to the guillotine. He was the man who led the ex-monarch to the blade. Another of *les Enragés* was Jean-Francois Varlet, an employee of the Paris Post Office become a raucous street orator, and one of a handful of radicals calling for a "third insurrection" beyond those represented by the storming of the Bastille and the women's march to Versailles in 1789, and the *Journée* of 20 June and the assault on the Tuileries in 1792—to begin a direct sectional democracy in Paris to contest the 'rule' of the Girondins.

The initial response to *les Enragés* and to the revolt in the Vendée were decrees for the death penalty to anyone advocating radical economic programs, and for all those resisting conscription, on March 18 and 19 respectively, as the Convention sought to right its listing ship. But this could only be achieved as each faction sought to out-bid the other, and would lay the institutional and procedural foundations for the *Terror* in year II of the republic.

On March 10 too, an *Extraordinary Criminal Tribunal* had been created for the trial of political offenses; of people accused of attacking liberty and equality, and the unity and indivisibility of the Republic. In October, it would be renamed the *Revolutionary Tribunal*, also called the "Popular Tribunal", composed initially of five judges, a twelve-man jury, with a public prosecutor, all nominated by the Convention, a format that would spread to 200 additional municipalities. Judgements by the tribunal could only be for acquittal or death, from which there was no appeal, and its judges and juries must vote in public and out loud.

In advocating for the tribunal Danton said, "Let us be terrible to dispense the people from being so." Denouncing the tribunal as a more awful inquisition than that in Spain, Pierre Vergniaud on March 13 cautioned the deputies of the

Convention, uttering his prescient remark, "...thus, citizens, it is permitted to fear that the Revolution, like Saturn, devouring successively all its children, will accomplish in the end only despotism and all calamities which accompany it." (2)

Within a period of weeks all of the components for a *reign of terror* would be realized. The *Tribunal* was followed by the creation of "surveillance committees" to track political dissidents; followed by the representatives *en mission*; then by the *Committee of Public Safety,* headed at first by Danton until he lost favor with the military reversals, but soon to become crucial to daily governance as Robespierre rose into its leadership. Later came the decree ordering the arrest of suspicious foreigners, and then, ominously, on April 1 a decree ending parliamentary immunity.

Keeping a watchful eye on Parisian events throughout March, General Charles Francois Dumouriez, struggling to stabilize his army in Flanders, after being heralded a military hero as victor at Valmy and laureled as the "liberator of the Belgians", began denouncing revolutionary anarchy at the rear. On March 30, the National Convention ordered his recall to Paris, dispatching four commissioners to arrest him. Instead, Dumouriez arrested the commissioners as they arrived, handing them over to the Austrians for imprisonment, as he sought to persuade his army to march on Paris to disperse the Jacobin "anarchists". But he had not arrested all of the deputies *en mission*, as these forestalled any more deleterious effects of the general's actions, so closely allied in a marriage of convenience with the Girondins. As he needed supporters in the National Convention, they required a general to give them legitimacy with the army.

Seeing Dumouriez's dissatisfaction after so recently achieving such dramatic successes, receiving accolades from all quarters among French revolutionists, Thomas Paine wrote a letter to the Convention suggesting that the general might be maintained in his current position if some of its deputies were appointed to "dispassionately" and "coolly" hear him out, to learn grievances, and go to him armed with the power to address these. Having finished the letter, Paine was on his way to Brissot's in order to meet Barrere to propose the adjustment, when he was informed the Convention had passed a decree offering a bounty for the general's head, and making it high treason to propose anything in his favor.

Declared an outlaw by the Convention, Dumouriez went the way of Lafayette, defecting to the enemy. He would however avoid Lafayette's lengthy confinement, only to wander the courts of Europe before settling in Britain during the Napoleonic wars as an adviser to Wellington.

On April 3, the Convention ordered the arrest of one of their own deputies, Philippe Egalité, formerly known as Philippe de Boucher, Duke of Orléans, and cousin of Louis XVI. Among aristocrats he'd been a key supporter of the republic and of the King's execution, and was a member of the Jacobin Club. He had come under suspicion, as his nineteen-year-old son, an officer under Dumouriez, decamped with his commander. As this was happening, following Varlet's call to arms, the delegated sections of Paris met, appointing a committee of six to plan a new uprising. When news of the French defeat at Neerwinden arrived, followed by that of Dumouriez's attempt to turn his troops on Paris so to place what he called "the sane portion of the Assembly" in complete charge, and at last, report of his defection, Marat issued a circular dated April 5, 1793, read in all the popular clubs:

> To arms! To arms! The hour has come when the defenders of the country must either conquer or bury themselves beneath the ashes of the Republic.... Our enemies have now put the finishing stroke to their perfidies, and to consummate them, Dumouriez and his

accomplices are about to march upon Paris.... But, brothers and friends, your greatest dangers are in the midst of you. It is in the Senate that parricidal hands would tear out your vitals! Yes, the counter-revolution is in the Government, in the National Convention! (3)

On April 10 Robespierre delivered a vitriolic speech against the Girondins, and against Vergniaud in particular because he'd been a close ally of Dumouriez. The Girondin deputies retorted that Philippe Egalité, the father of the duc de Chartres (later to become Louis Philippe, "King of the French", 1830-1848) who had escaped with General Dumouriez, was a member of the Montagnards, while Danton himself was accused of complicity with the general. Hadn't even his Secretary, Fabre d'Eglantine, once proposed the restoration of the monarchy?

With charges and counter-charges traded, the Girondins called for a Committee of Enquiry to investigate the circumstances of Dumouriez' treason, as Danton brazenly answered back, to the applause of the Montagnards, that Brissot, Gersonne and Guadet, the leaders of the Girondins, had been the general's closest supporters.

The Committee of Public Safety now ordered the seizure of Interior Minister Roland's papers, mindful of his wife, Madame Roland's castigation of Danton and the Montagnards, as Camille Desmoulins produced a pamphlet titled *L'histoire des Brissontins*, calling on the Convention to "vomit the Girondins from its belly". With neither faction backing down, Danton offered a palliative, aware that he himself was in danger of sliding under the same accusations the Montagnards were leveling. "Let bygones be bygones," he had proposed privately to the leaders newly singled out in Desmoulins polemic. To which Guadet retorted, "Let it be war, and let one side perish!" (4) "You want war, then, Guadet, do you?" thundered Danton. "Then you shall have death."

On 25 February, an article had appeared in Marat's *Journal* concerning the famine conditions raging in sans-culotte and poor sections of Paris:

> In every country where the rights of the people is not an empty phrase, ostentatiously recorded on paper, the sacking of a few shops, at the doors of which 'forestallers' were hanged, would soon put a stop to those malversations which are driving five millions of men to despair, and causing thousands to perish of want! (5)

That advice, seemingly, had been acted upon that afternoon and evening in some sections of Paris, i.e. unlawful action had been taken against "forestallers", those buying the available supply of bread and selling it at exorbitant prices. With the riots recurring, several deputies rose in the Convention to denounce the anarchic scenes; finally, one of them said, "I come to denounce one of the instigators of these troubles—it is Marat." (6)

On 12 April Marat came under furious attack by the Girondins. To support the charges against him, Marat's circular was read in full, when he rose to declare simply "It is true". With the entire Jacobin bench ranged in his support, the Girondins demanded a decree of accusation against Marat. Mounting the tribune, Marat exclaimed:

> What is the use of this vain talk? They seek to throw dust in your eyes by an imaginary conspiracy, in order to hush up a conspiracy which is only too real. There is no longer any doubt about it. Dumouriez himself has set the seal to it…. But wishing to give…unequivocal proofs to my loyalty, I have demanded a decree which shall put a price

on the head of the younger Egalité .... I will renew my proposition and we will see on which side are the supporters of Orléans. (7)

Danton rose in support of the proposition; but after rancorous debate the Girondins succeeding in carrying their demand against Marat. With the sitting raised and the deputies dispersing, fifty Montagnard deputies and sympathizers made a cordon around Marat as he made for the door, where an officer of the guard waited with the decree in hand. In the rush, however, those bringing this joust against the "Friend of the People" had neglected to have it properly signed. With his supporters packing the hall, Marat refused arrest, and following the crowd, exited the Convention.

The next day an address prepared by Marat was read in the Convention in which he described the decree of accusation as nothing less than "the first step in an organized conspiracy to effect the political extinction of the Jacobins and the Mountain." (8) If they succeeded in their ruse—

> ...soon they will come to Robespierre and Danton and all patriot deputies who have given proof of energy.... Before belonging to the Convention, I belong to the country. I am now going to protect myself against their attempts, continuing to support the cause of liberty by my writings, until the eyes of the nation are opened to their criminal projects. Only a little patience, and they will fall beneath the weight of public execration.

During this bitter debate, Danton, "his lips curled in that expression of contempt which was peculiar to him," rose to exclaim:

> Citizens of the Mountain. You are the true friends of the welfare of the people. Your judgement has been clearer

than mine . . . I was wrong. I am now convinced that no truce is possible between the Mountain, the patriots who wanted the King's death, and these cowards who slandered us throughout France in the hope of saving him . . . No more terms with them! I have returned to the fortress of Reason. I will have it armed with the artillery of Truth in order to blow these enemies to dust! (9)

Marat's address, on the demand of Danton, was laid on the table as the entire Montagne bench stepped down to sign it. Finally, a roll call of names was ordered. With the Girondins still exercising sufficient influence over the deputies of the Plain, the decree was secured by a majority of twenty-eight votes.

Dropping the question of Marat's manifesto which had been the pretext of the attack against him, the counts of accusation were based on two articles in *Journal de la Republique*—the first dated January 5, when proceeding the trial of the King, Marat had proposed the National Convention be dissolved; and the second, the article dated 25 February with the suggestion of action against "forestallers." A third charge, that Marat advocated a dictatorship, was now appended.

On April 15, the newly elected mayor of Paris, Jean Nicolas Pache, having been removed as head of the Ministry of War, formerly an ally of Roland but now a recruit to the Montagnards, appeared before the Convention with a deputation to present an address of protest by thirty-five of the forty-eight sections. They did not want a dissolution of the National Convention, Rousselin, the presenter asserted; they wanted the expulsion of the twenty-two leading Girondin deputies in the Convention as slanders of Paris, as accomplices of the traitor Dumouriez, as enemies of the clubs!

The Convention returned the petition to the Mayor,

pronouncing it "calumnious".

Marat's summons arrived on the 22nd, as he sent notice on his new sheet, as his *Journal* was suspended—"People, tomorrow your incorruptible defender will present himself before the Revolutionary Tribunal." The following evening, accompanied by "numerous colleagues" and by a colonel of the National Guard, Marat was constituted a prisoner. (10)

In London, it can be supposed, the bard and engraver as ever was bent over his work table absorbed in his task, his graver wielded by work-soiled hands. Blake would sustain more than passing interest in affairs across the Channel, as in the far-off West Indies, as across the Irish sea, and all the flash points of conflict in the British Empire. His attentions are undoubtedly reflected in a letter written by fellow engraver George Cumberland, a political radical and member of the *Society for Constitutional Information*, who was conversant with Blake for over a decade—"No news, save that *Great Britain* is hanging the Irish, hunting the Maroons, feeding the Vendée, and establishing the human flesh trade." (11)

Cumberland's testament, and the specificity of these artisans at work, are an often-unseen or neglected feature for scholarship, as likely unobserved are the distinctive circumstances constituting this very modern tableau. Its known sometime during this period Blake had etched in copper, but did not print, an inscription under the title *Divine Image*:

> The Human Dress, is forged Iron
> The Human Form, a fiery Forge.
> The Human Face, a Furnace seal'd
> The Human Heart, its hungry Gorge. (12)

15.

Thorns were my only delight

With the Paine-Condorcet Constitution framed prior the trial of the King, and its hearing postponed during his prosecution, in spring 1793 that debate was to be stifled by war and the economic emergency, as every possible obstruction was placed in the way of its adoption. Marat and the leaders of the Commune and the political clubs were determined there would be no new government, and they had seen to the creation of instruments absorbing all legislative, judicial and executive functions of a purely arbitrary structure within the Convention, as they did those of the ministries. In all of this, the Girondins had acquiesced, even actively participating in their design.

The constitution under consideration had omitted all mention of a deity, and "here," wrote Moncure Conway, "was the immemorial and infallible recipe for discord, of which Robespierre made the most, and he took the "Supreme Being" under his protection." Conway adding—"[t]hat (Condorcet remarked) in preparing a Constitution for France they had not consulted Numa's nymph or the pigeon of Mahomet; they had found human reason sufficient." Whereas Robespierre as he rose to the pinnacle of power would proceed to invent a supreme being and his cult and was hailed by the divineness

Catharine Théot, the reincarnate "Word of God." Robespierre like-wise raising 'virtue' as his paramount principle, had taken morality under his protection, insisting that the Paine-Condorcet Constitution gave "liberty even to illicit traffic." (1)

Having determined his attitude vis-à-vis these matters, concurrent with the proceedings leading to Marat's trial Paine sent a letter to Thomas Jefferson, the American Secretary of State, dated "April 20th, 2nd year of the Republic":

> Had this revolution been conducted consistently with its principles, there was once a good prospect of extending liberty through the greatest part of Europe; but I now relinquish that hope.... As the prospect of a general freedom is now much shortened, I begin to contemplate returning home. I shall await the event of the proposed Constitution, and then take my final leave of Europe. (2)

Concluding he could no longer reside "among such sanguinary men", and exhausted and put upon by meetings and visitors, after the execution of the King and the weeks of ensuing strife, Paine had removed from his lodgings at White's Hotel in central Paris, to the village of Saint-Denis a few miles to the north of the city. Known as the birthplace of Gothic architecture for the basilica built in the 12th century as the burial place of the French King, with its pointed arches, flying buttresses, and ribbed vaulting; here Paine would reside until the end of the year, among whose residents were a young Englishmen, Dr. William Johnson, and his friend William Choppin, among others. The two youths had followed, as devotes of Thomas Paine, from London where they'd met, and then followed him to the outer reaches of Paris.

With many in the Convention now contemplating Marat's assertion that there were traitors in that body, Paine had written a short notice for *Le Moniteur* reporting on Marat's remarks to him disparaging of republican democracy, at a time when Marat, like most other revolutionaries, had been a constitutional monarchist. He and Marat only met once, with Paine finding him pompous, with his hair tied back and wearing a red bandana, stalking about dressed as a sans-culotte, pistols tucked into his belt. In Paine's view, he seemed hopelessly distressed.

Shortly thereafter, Johnson, himself distraught over the course of the Revolution, and seeing a sanguinary future for himself and his companions, had attempted suicide. Knife in hand, standing on the stairs of their lodgings, he had stabbed himself twice in the chest. As a third thrust was averted, he fell into Choppin's arms as he had rushed to his aid. Handing him a parting missive; near death he'd handed Paine (who may have averted the third thrust), his now blood-spattered watch. Fortunately, with their quick action, a local doctor was summoned and he was able to maintain the would-be-suicide's life pulse.

Marat's trial began on 24 April, the hall of the tribunal filling with his supporters, and with other observers. Marat introduced himself with these words: "Citizens, it is not a criminal whom you see before you, it is the apostle and martyr of liberty; it is only a group of factious persons and intriguers who have obtained this decree of accusation against me." (3)

The presiding judge called upon the accused to state his name, profession, and residence. "My name is Jean-Paul Marat, aged forty-nine years, a doctor in medicine, residing in Paris, Rue de Cordeliers, No. 36."

The decrees of accusation were cited, i.e. of Marat's having provoked in his paper murder and massacre, shown contempt for and advocating the dissolution of the Convention, and for advocating the establishment of a power destructive of liberty. Passages published by Marat in his journals in support of the allegations were read by the public prosecutor, which upon interrogation, the defendant avowed.

In a stratagem to draw out those deputies practicing the interdicted journalism still sitting in the Convention, specifically Brissot, the first individual cited by the prosecution was the young Englishman of wealth named William Johnson; who it was alleged, had heard remarks said to emanate from Marat menacing to Thomas Paine. To wit: "The French are mad to let foreigners to live among them. They should cut off their ears, let them bleed for a few days, then cut off their heads." (4)

Johnson, it was also alleged, afterward heard an article of Marat's read in translation reprinted in Brissot's journal *Le Patriote francais*, advocating the killing of all Englishmen in France. That journal then ran a notice on the 16th detailing his situation:

A sad incident has occurred to apprise the anarchists of the mournful fruits of their frightful teaching. An Englishman, whose name I reserve, had abjured his country because of his detestation of kings; he came to France hoping to find there liberty; he saw only its mask on the hideous visage of anarchy. Heart-broken by this spectacle, he determined on self-destruction.

Before dying, he wrote the following words, which we have read, as written by his own trembling hand, on a paper which is in possession of a distinguished for-eigner:—"I had come to France to enjoy liberty, but Marat has assassinated it. Anarchy is even more cruel than despotism. I am unable to endure this grievous sight, of the triumph of imbecility and inhumanity over talent and virtue." (5)

The first witness called was the Englishman, Choppin, the friend of Johnson. On the invitation of the judge, Marat asked him if he had seen Brissot and others of the Girondins at Paine's residence. He replied he had not.

The judge now sent a letter to the president of the Convention requesting a summons be issued that Brissot appear. With this in abeyance, the acting editor of Brissot's journal was summoned before the tribunal. He arriving, when put under examination about who had sent the letter that was the basis of the article in *Le Patriote francais*, declared it had been sent by Paine to Brissot. Marat interjecting—who had furnished Brissot with the article since the Convention had already promulgated a decree interdicting journalism to deputies? The editor testifying that the note had been handed him by Brissot who'd obtained the original from Thomas Paine.

Did the witness possess the note allegedly given Brissot by Thomas Paine? The witness replied—probably the printer had it. It will be noted, Marat, was under the same interdiction, he circumventing the decree by maintaining that *L'ami du peuple*, as it was then constituted, was not journalistic, but was comprised of opinion pieces. The decree had not been intended to forbid deputies from expressing their opinions.

Subpoenas were immediately issued against the printer, and also for the youth named Johnson; for contrary to the articles report, his status was very much among the living. The next witness called was Thomas Paine himself who had been sitting as an observer of the trial.

Paine objected to being called, protesting that he saw no relevance of Brissot's paper to the allegations against Marat; but then proceeded to answer the following:

President: Did you give a copy of the note to Brissot?

Paine: I showed him the original.

President: Did you send it to him as it is printed?

Paine: Brissot could only have written this note after what I read him, and told him. I would observe to the tribunal that Johnson gave himself two blows with the knife after he had understood that Marat would denounce him.

Marat: Not because I would denounce the youth who stabbed himself, but because I wish to denounce Thomas Paine.

Paine: (continuing) Johnson had for some time suffered mental anguish. As for Marat, I never spoke to him but once. In the lobby of the Convention he said to me that the English people are free and happy; I relied, they groan under a double despotism. (6)

The printer now arrived, and being disposed said he'd been ill for some time and knew nothing about the matter. He had however brought with him several slips of copy, which on the demand of Marat, were handed to the usher.

As the Englishman, Johnson, arrived he too was disposed, but nothing further was obtained from his testimony, he concluding, "The friendship I had for Thomas Paine led me to want to kill myself."

Without waiting for the arrival of Brissot, the president called upon the prisoner for his defense. (7)

Marat: Citizens, if the Girondin and Brissotin faction, and the other satellites of despotism—if, I say, this horde of criminals, who do not cease to persecute 'patriots,' had not accused me of being a man of blood, an inciter of crime, I should never have been permitted myself to express such opinions as those contained in the numbers of my journal that have been cited.... My most earnest solicitude has always been that the Convention should receive the confidence of the people. To wish to dissolve it as I am accused of doing is farthest from my thoughts.

Giving a brief recital of his services in the cause of liberty, beginning with *Chains of Slavery*, he passed on to give a scathing expose of the reign of the Girondins, especially as regarded actions and statements against the principle leaders of the Montagne, and of the Commune and the Parisian sections. But the bringers of the accusations, said Marat, had been compelled by popular pressure to alter the original basis of their indictment relating to his solicitude for the atrocities in the previous September, with two new charges having nothing to do with it. Did they not thereby exhibit the animus actuating them? He then moved to his concluding statement.

Marat: Full of confidence in the judgment, equity, and good citizenship of the tribunal, I myself desire the most rigid examination of this affair.... I claim nevertheless a consecutive reading of the denounced numbers, for it is not from isolated and excised passages that one can judge the meaning of an author, it is only by reading what precedes and what follows that we can estimate his intentions rightly... If, after such a perusal, there remain any doubts, I am here to dispose of them.

He would, finally, accept the judgment of the jury on the incriminated numbers.

The public prosecutor recapitulated the facts enclosed in the decree of accusation; after which the president offered a summation, stating the question pertinent to the jury's verdict.

> President: Is it proved that there are in the writings... passages provoking to, pillage, and the dissolution of the national representation? And further, is it true that Marat...has published them with counterrevolutionary intent?

After sitting through the seven-hour trial the jury took only a cursory moment to acquit, stating in the judgment—"...we cannot impute criminal intentions to the intrepid defender of the rights of the people. It is difficult for an ardent patriot to keep back his just indignation when he sees his country betrayed on all sides."

The presiding judge ordered the accused set at liberty and that the judgement be officially published. Turing to the court, Marat declared: "Citizens, jurors, and judges, who compose the Revolutionary Tribunal, the fate of the traitors to their country is in your hands; protect the innocent, punish the guilty, and the country will be saved." (8)

Applause and cheering erupted in the court among Marat's supporter's, quickly spreading down the staircase and into the corridor, out into the street. As Marat emerged, he was embraced and hoisted from his feet, to be borne aloft now seated in a chair the distance between the Palais de Justice and the Convention Hall. Bouquets and garlands offered to *the hero* by women were soon strewn along the path of the procession, the triumphal scene attracting in its wake a host of admirers. Although he could scarcely have been accustomed to such display, and perhaps temperamentally inclined to resist it, an oak leaf garland had been placed on his head.

Repeatedly halted to receive the congratulations of the heads of sections, as the entrance to the Convention was reached, to rising accolades the doors were pushed open and Marat was carried in by national guards.

Making way to the president's chair, with the powerful intercession of the voice of Danton, the homage-payers were permitted to file past. A sapper from the engineer corps took it upon himself to proclaim: "Citizen President, we return to you our brave Marat. We know well how to confound all his enemies. I have already defended him at Lyons, and I shall defend him here, and he who would take the head of Marat must first take the head of a sapper." (9)

'The peoples friend' ascended the tribune to cries of "Long live the Republic!", "Long live the Mountain!", "Long live Marat!" Marat proclaiming:

> Legislators, the proof of good citizenship and of joy which resound throughout this building are a homage rendered to the national representation, to a colleague in whose person the sacred rights of a deputy have been violated. I have been perfidiously inculpated; a solemn judgment has assured the triumph of my innocence; I bring you back a pure heart, and I shall continue to defend the 'rights of Man,' of the citizen and of the people, with all the energy nature has given to me. (10)

As pikes quivered and Phrygian caps soared, another acclamation was accorded this embodiment, momentarily, of the Revolution. After the National Guard carried Marat to his place on the benches, individual by group, the multitude slowly began to dwindle. "From end to end of France," his biographer Ernest Bax has written, Marat's name "was a household word to be loved or feared." (11)

Thomas Paine and Jean-Paul Marat were comprised of two entirely dissimilar mental constituencies; one it seems would destroy the other. Are they William Blake's Lamb and Tyger? "Did he who made the Lamb make thee?" To be sure, Marat's eyes, were said to resemble "a tiger cat."

Songs of Experience included therein a poem titled *The Human Abstract*. Two of its stanzas follow, defying a more facile appraisal of the tree growing "in the Human brain":

> Soon spreads the dismal shade
> Of Mystery over his head;
> And the Catterpiller and Fly
> Feed on the Mystery.
>
> And it bears the fruit of Deceit,
> Ruddy and sweet to eat;
> And the Raven his nest has made
> In its thickest shade. (12)

16.
The furious terrors flew around

The Girondins had been obliged to accede to the formation of the tribunal and to the creation of the committees, but on May 18 when they hit back by decreeing an *Extraordinary Commission of Twelve* tasked with investigating members of the Paris Commune, accused of promoting anarchy, of seeking to enrich themselves, and with attempting to undermine the National Convention—they were clambering on to the last plank of their political existence.

The Commission of Twelve were Girondin deputies all. After a cursory investigation, arrests of *les Enragés* and their allies were ordered. The most vexatious of these was the radical journalist and deputy *procureur* (executive) of the Commune, Jacques Hébert, popular with the sans-culotte for the observations of the *Pere Duchesne* character in his paper of the same name, who spoke a in rough scatological slang appealing to that papers' readers, widely distributed in the army. Another of those arrested was Jean Varlet, and another was the president of the Cité section of Paris, a man named Dobsen.

The next day, Jacobins demanded the detained be released as about 400 sans-culottes forced their way into the Convention to press the issue. Demanding the abolition of the Commission of Twelve, in retort the presiding officer of the

Convention, Maximin Isnard, a wealthy perfumer and owner of a soap factory, expressed his vitriol for those calling for a new insurrection:

> ...if they should take the shape of even an attempt to coerce the national representation, I tell you, in the name of the whole of France, that Paris will be annihilated. Yes, France will take such vengeance on the guilty city, that it will soon be necessary to inquire on which bank of the Seine the capital had once stood. (1)

These words were regrettably close to those broadcast in the *Brunswick Manifesto,* and the Montagne erupted with a scorn all their own. The following day, the arrested *Enragés* were released, as Robespierre, speaking at the Jacobin Club, called on the people to revolt and the Jacobins declared themselves in a state of insurrection.

Maximilien Robespierre, now president of the Jacobin Club, is described as a small, thin, dogmatic man. Age thirty-two, his eyes were gray with a greenish glint, as his complexion too, many of his contemporaries observed, had a greenish pall, which was often lent emphases when he wore a green jacket, giving him, as Carlyle made much of, a "sea-green" attendance. Short-sighted, he often shifted his tinted spectacles and squinted at his audiences and interlocutors. His face pock-marked, with prominent cheekbones and long thin lips, was surmounted by a large bony forehead; his hair, thick and always carefully curled, brushed and powered. To compensate for his height, he wore high-heeled shoes stepping briskly through the streets; his attire as impeccable, many have remarked, as that of a royal tailor. When amused, which wasn't often, he had a hollow dry laugh; not noted either for his way with women, his food neither interested him, partaking lightly of bread and milk for his breakfast. In the evenings for dinner his fare was also sparing, his wine diluted with water. A friend who'd observed him at parties said he attended to his plate like a cat lapping vinegar.

He is not noted to have taken a hand in any of the *journées* that had propelled the Revolution thus far, and Robespierre's Girondin opponents accused him of having hidden in a cellar while the Tuileries was assaulted on 10 August, and when the King was executed, that he had remained in his sparsely furnished room behind closed shutters. Even Marat remarked, "Robespierre avoids any group where there is unrest. He grows pale at the sight of a sabre." Yet he was a man who handled others with Machiavellian skill. A rival said of him— "in dividing men and sowing differences between them, of enticing others to test the ground for him and then abandoning them or supporting them as prudence or ambition dictated"—Robespierre was almost without peer.

The concluding chapter in the strife roiling between *Montagne* and *Girondins* was now to take place in the Royal Theatre in the Tuileries, as the sittings after May 10 were no longer held in the old riding academy, but in the same house the comedies of Moliere had played a century before for the restitution and delight of the court. In the center of the ensuing calamity, with its admixture of tragedy and farce, was that loose affiliation whose appeal resided with the sans-culottes and the sections of the Paris Commune, who were the most effective ally of the Jacobins in the increasingly intransigent struggle deplored by Paine in the National Convention—*les Enragés*.

On May 4, in a calculated shift of strategy, the Jacobins succeeded in passing a decree fixing the prices of wheat and flour, something the Girondins had adamantly opposed. Arguing against it, a deputy of the Gironde said—"These words, 'hoarders' and 'monopolies', are only the dangerous visions of foolish persons and ignorant women." Words given standing in spring 1793 by the spokespersons for *les Enragés,* like Jacques Roux who argued that "goods necessary to all should be delivered at a price accessible to all." This formulation was included in the so-called *Manifesto of the Enragés*, a speech Roux delivered to the Convention on June 25 at the height of his influence, where he declared his credo: "I am ready to give the last drop of my blood to a Revolution that has already altered the fate of the human race by making men equal among themselves as they are all for all eternity before God."

During this castigation of the Convention, the former priest asked:

> Why have you not climbed from the third to the ninth floor of the houses of this revolutionary city? You would have been moved by the tears and sighs of an immense population without food and clothing, brought to such distress and misery by speculation and hoarding, because the laws have been cruel to the poor, because they have been made only by the rich and for the rich.... You must not be afraid of the hatred of the rich—in other words, of the wicked. You must not be afraid to sacrifice political principle for the salvation of the people, which is the supreme law.

The following citations from a letter dated "May 6th, 2nd year of the Republic," addressed to "Citoyen" Danton from Thomas Paine is credited by Moncure Conway to the discovery Hippolyte Taine; Taine remarking, he was surprised to read such cogent thoughts, given the time in which they were written:

I am exceedingly disturbed at the distractions, jealousies, discontents and uneasiness that reign among us, and which, if they continue, will bring ruin and disgrace on the Republic. When I left America in the year 1787, it was my intention to return the year following, but the French Revolution, and the prospect it afforded of extending the principles of liberty and fraternity through the greater part of Europe, have induced me to prolong my stay upwards of six years. I now despair of seeing the great object of European liberty accomplished, and my despair arises not from the combined foreign powers, not from the intrigues of aristocracy and priest craft, but from the tumultuous misconduct with which the internal affairs of the present revolution is conducted. (2)

Paine continued:

As soon as the constitution is established I shall return to America; and be the future prosperity of France ever so great, I shall enjoy no other part of it than the happiness of knowing it. In the meantime I am destressed to see matters so badly conducted, and so little attention paid to moral principles. It is these things that injure the character of the Revolution and discourage the progress of liberty all over the world.

Paine had experienced the untoward effect of "price fixing", or as it was called in France the *Law of the Maximum*, during his American period, and included treatment of it in his letter to Danton:

[I]f this measure is to be attempted it ought to be done by the Municipality. The Convention has nothing to do with regulations of this kind; neither can they be carried into practice. The people of Paris may say they will not give more than a certain price for provisions, but as they cannot compel the country people to bring provisions to market the consequence will be directly contrary to their expectations, and they will find dearness and famine instead of plenty and cheapness. They may force the price down upon the stock in hand, but after that the market will be empty.

The Law of the Maximum or General Maximum first decreed and partially implemented May 4, 1793, would be extended on September 29 of that year, setting uniform price ceilings on grain, flour, meat, oil, onions, soap, firewood, leather, and paper; regulating the sale of these items at one-third over the maximum prices set in 1790. Merchants had to display a full list of maximum rates in a prominent and easily accessible location, and were subject to inspection by police and local people, as those who reported violations were protected by law. The law became a symbol of the *reign of Terror*, and would ultimately ruin the grain trade, create artificial famine, and concomitantly contribute to the growth of contraband trade.

Everyone from Danton to Marat, to Paine, to Brissot, knew that the underlying problem had much to do with the assignats and with excessive printing of that currency. With no rise in wages and with the accompanying speculation, the effect was to make everything seem dear. With prices rising, and as grain ceased circulating due to a dearth of transport because of war requisitions, the outcome was adulteration of supplies, in the case of flour either with chalk or with pulverized bone fragments.

Commenting finally on the most fractious element, as it played out at the end of the month, Paine confided to Danton:

For my own part I shall hold it a matter of doubt, until better evidence arises than is known at present, whether

Dumouriez has been a traitor from policy or resentment. There was certainly a time when he acted well, but it is not every man whose mind is strong enough to bear up against ingratitude, and I think he experienced a great deal of this before he revolted. Calumny becomes harmless and defeats itself when it attempts to act upon too large a scale. Thus the denunciations of the Sections [of Paris] against the twenty-two deputies falls to the ground.

The departments that elected them are better judges of their moral and political characters than those who have denounced them. This denunciation will injure Paris in the opinion of the departments because it has the appearance of dictating to them what sort of deputies they shall elect. Most of the acquaintances that I have in the convention are among those on the list, and I know there are not better patriots than what they are.

I have written to Marat of the same date as this but not on the same subject.

The letter to Marat referenced has never been discovered.

It was at this time too that Théroigne de Mericourt had thrown down "her last effective die in the cause of liberty." (3) A circular she had printed and distributed around Paris addressing the forty-eight sections under her name, began:

Citizens! Hear me! I am not going to utter fine phrases; I am going to tell you the pure and simple truth. Where do we stand? All the conflicting passions which have been aroused to carry us away...let us stop, and reflect or we are lost. The moment has arrived when it is to the interest of all to reunite, to sacrifice our hates and our passions for the public welfare. (4)

Evidently suffering mental anguish for her complicity in the murder of the royalist journalist Suleau, and distraught and revolted by the violence being propagated by the Jacobins and their supporters, she was proposing women be organized into detachments to promote peace and act as propagandists for liberty. She wrote in her circular:

> ...I propose that in each section there shall be chosen six of the most virtuous citoyennes, the gravest for their age, to conciliate and reunite the citizens, to remind them of the dangers by which the country is threatened. They shall wear a wide sash, on which will be inscribed the words 'Friendship and Fraternity.' Every time there is a general assembly of the section, they shall gather for the purpose of calling to order every citizen who stands aside and who does not respect the liberty of opinions, which is so necessary in forming a good public spirit.

On the 15th of that month, Théroigne was seen passing along the terrace of the Feuillants, as she walked boldly toward the Convention. Encountering the women there who had formed the *Club de Citoyones Revolutionaries*, and who had posted themselves in the previous days at the doors to intercept and turn away all those who were not Jacobins and supported the Montagnards, as Théroigne approached, shouted "Down with Brissot and the Brissotins."

Seizing her, in the ensuing struggle the unfortunate Amazon was stripped nude to the waist and whipped, then beaten about the head with stones. As she was being dragged toward the basin for drowning, the guard arrived. On May 17,

Les Courrier des Departements reported, the guard had "saved the victim from the fury of these indecent maniacs. Marat, who was passing, took the beaten one under his protection." On the 16th, *La Revolution de Paris* reported:

> For the last few days a number of women have been policing the Tuileries gardens and the corridors of the National Convention. They have taken it upon themselves to examine all the cockades and stop the people whom they suspect of wavering. It was they who...took the whip to Théroigne, calling her Brissotine.

Marat's intervention was later recorded in the "Memoirs" of Paul Barras. Marat had taken her by the hand, Barras wrote, and leading her away from her assailants, he said: "Citizens, are you bent on attempting the life of a woman? Are you going to sully yourselves with such a crime? The law alone has the right to strike. Show your contempt for this courtesan and reserve your dignity, citizens." (5)

"The poor Demoiselle's head and nervous-system," Carlyle wrote, "none the soundest, is so tattered and fluttered that it will never recover; but flutter worse and worse, till it crack; and within year and day we hear her in madhouse and strait-waistcoat, which proves permanent!" (6) There were some eight thousand women in the organization calling themselves *Dames de la Fraternite*, "with serpent hair, all out of curl'" he wrote, "who have changed the distaff for the dagger."

A few days before this wanton attack, Thomas Paine had again been at a trial before the Revolutionary Tribunal. This time for one of the generals of Dumouriez's army of the North, Francisco de Miranda. He was a Venezuelan from a prominent family in Caracas, and another of those children of the Enlightenment. He had pursued studies at the Royal and Pontifical University in classical literature and history. Moving thence to Spain, he participated in the first of his military campaigns in Morocco, and by the last years of the American War for Independence was commanding Spanish troops trying to expand that nations hold on territories in Florida and Louisiana, attacking the British at Baton Rouge and at Natchez. In 1780, he participated in the Siege of Fort Pensacola, and in the following year contributed to the French success at Chesapeake Bay by assisting the French admiral Count de Grasse in raising funds and supplies. Running afoul of Spanish authorities and subject to the Inquisition after the failure of a scheme to drive the British from Jamaica, by 1782 Miranda was in exile in the United States where he passed through Charleston, Philadelphia, New York and Boston, meeting and befriending the patriot luminaries, Hamilton, Jefferson, Samuel Adams, generals Washington and Knox, as well as Thomas Paine.

By 1793 Miranda was a general in Dumouriez's Army of the North invading the Austrian Netherlands to great success, and then on to Holland, a campaign that also met success as Dumouriez captured a succession of coastal forts and Miranda began a siege of Maastricht at the southern extremity of the Netherlands. But with the Austrian counter-attack, Dumouriez was compelled to retreat into Belgium and Miranda was forced to break off his siege, resulting in the disaster at Neerwinden.

As Dumouriez's fortune foundered he pinned the blame for his debacle on Miranda and he was promptly arrested, but successfully defended himself with the aid of the "Brissotins" on the floor of the Convention. With the Jacobins able to reverse this decision, Miranda was re-arrested and imprisoned and put on trial May 12, 1793.

Paine and Miranda had met ten years before in America and again in London just as *Rights of Man* was being published. During the past year, he together with Paine and others had been discussing plans to spread the Revolution to South America, and the French National Convention was preparing to commission him to lead such an expedition. Paine was called to appear at his trial as a character-witness. Said he, through his translator:

> It is impossible for one man to know another man's heart as he knows his own, but from all that I know of General Miranda I cannot believe that he wanted to betray the confidence which the republic has placed in him, especially because the destiny of the French Revolution was intimately linked with the favoured object of his heart, the deliverance of Spanish America—an object for which he has been pursued and persecuted by the Spanish Court during the greatest part of his life. (7)

On 28 May, the initiatory steps toward a new insurrection were taken when the Cité section called the other Parisian sections to a meeting at the Eveche (the Bishop's Palace), at which both Varlet and Dobsen, now freed, were present. The next day the delegates representing thirty-three of the sections formed an insurrectionary committee with nine members, as, the following day, many of the departments gave their indorsement to the undertaking.

Sitting on the Insurrectionary Committee, besides Varlet and Dobsen, was Rousselin, a journalist and editor, and Hassenfratz, who held an important post at the war office, together with five men who were virtually unknown today, chosen presumably, as Taine remarked, because they were ready to act as string-puppets to these leaders. There was a printer and a painter, a toy-maker and an usher, and a ribbon-maker, along with a déclassé aristocrat named Duroure. One of the chief organizers behind the movement, which included Fournier l'Amercain and the others from the cast of the storming of the Tuileries, as everyone knew, was Marat.

The tocsin sounding from the belfry of the Hôtel de Ville in the early morning on the 31st was rung by Marat, who took it upon himself because the ringing of bells or the firing of alarm-guns had been decreed a capital offense by the Convention. The uprising was to proceed by the tired method of the 10th of August.

At six o'clock in the morning, led by Dobsen, the delegates of thirty-three sections presented themselves at the Hôtel de Ville where the municipality was retired to an adjoining room; but this time, it was immediately reinstated in its functions. The Insurrectionary Committee, convening in the municipal building, dictated the measures the Commune was to take. Francois Hanriot, a Jacobin leader and a former clerk and a brandy seller, described as "a coarse and irascible man who never opened his lips without bawling", was appointed commander-in-chief of the National Guard of Paris, while it was announced that sans-culottes under arms would receive 40 sous a day. With the Parisian authorities co-operating, the Insurrectionary Committee's membership grew to twenty-one.

As noon approached, the alarm-gun was fired and Hanriot ordered the seizure of the boat basin, the arsenal, the Palais Royale, the Pont Neuf, and that the city barriers be closed, as prominent "suspects" were arrested. As May 31 was a Friday and workers who would fill the battalions from the faubourgs were at work, it was not till the afternoon that the *journée* began to take shape. In the Convention, the Girondin deputies protested the closing of the city gates, and remonstrated against the firing of the alarm gun.

At five o'clock, at the bar of the Convention, petitioners

presented the "people's demands"—the foremost of these was for the arrest of the twenty-two Girondins deputes, and for the suppression and arrest of the Commission of Twelve, and that all be brought before the Revolutionary Tribunal. Also included: the price of bread should be fixed at 3 sous per pound; nobles in senior ranks in the army should be dismissed, and that armories should be created for arming the sans-culottes. Finally, the right to vote should provisionally be reserved for sans-culottes; and a fund set apart for the relatives of those fighting against royalist invaders, and to secure relief for the aged, the infirm.

Ascending to the tribune, Robespierre supported the suppression of the Commission of Twelve and their arrest, as also, of the Girondin deputies. When Vergniaud called on him to conclude, Robespierre turned toward him and said:

> Yes, I will conclude, but it will be against you! Against you, who, after the revolution 10 August, wanted to send those responsible for it to the scaffold; against you, who have never ceased to incite the destruction of Paris; against you, who wanted to save the tyrant; against you, who conspired with Dumouriez.... (9)

Marat, believing that no measures could be carried in the Convention as it was constituted, shuttled throughout the afternoon between the Committee of General Security, having its influence in the police and the justice ministry, and the Committee of Public Safety and the Hôtel de Ville. Relating his activities when his *Publiciste* resumed publication on June 4, he wrote:

> On my return, I discovered a great crowd in the Rue Saint Nicaire; I am recognized and followed by the crowd. From all sides, I hear demanded the arrest of traitor-deputies and intriguers. From all sides shouts of 'Marat,

save us!' Arrived at the Carrousel. I observe multitudes of citizens in arms. The crowd increases, always repeating the same cry. (10)

Returning to the Royal Theatre, Marat found that Robespierre's demand for the indictment of the Girondin deputies together with members of the commission was "being backed by the acclamations of the public galleries and the sectionaries at the bar." (11) Mounting the tribune, not "to clinch its victory," but so as to appear magnanimous by seeking the exclusion of three names from the indictment, Marat said:

> As to the really guilty, it is not on account of their action with regard to the tyrant that they merited punishment; this would be to attempt to suppress liberty of opinion, without which there can be no public liberty at all. Their real guilt lies in their long series of machinations and slanders against the Parisians, and their complicity with Dumouriez, together with the protection they have always accorded to traitors. (12)

He then read the names of the deputies who were to be impeached.

By the end of its setting, without bringing accusations against the 22 Girondin deputies, the Convention had suppressed the Commission of Twelve, stipulating a report be made on its proceedings within three days. Also approved was the resolution of the Commune that workmen under arms would be paid forty sous per day, as it was decided that the galleries should be opened, without requiring tickets for admission.

During the night Paris continued under arms, patrols and sentinels remaining in the streets, with the bridges and the sections under guard. With all other issues in abeyance, the whole of Saturday, June 1, was occupied with negotiations between the Committee of Public Safety and the Insurrectionary Commune. In these negotiations, an expediency was finally hit upon; there should be a voluntary and reciprocal resignation of the leaders of the political factions. But Robespierre and the Montagne would not countenance it.

With the crucial issue at a stand-off, Dobsen, and even Pierre Chaumette, one of the most radical of *les Enragés* in the Commune, were accused by Varlet of vacillation, while Robespierre declared the *journée* of 31 May had not been enough. The Commune demanded a "supplement" be prepared to the previous day's action. Hanriot was now ordered to "surround the Convention with an armed force sufficient to command respect, in order that the chiefs of the faction may be arrested during the day, in case the Convention refuse to accede to the request of the citizens of Paris." (13)

At daybreak, the tocsin sounded and the *générale* beat as vast crowds carried from various tributary streams coming from the faubourgs began congregating. Before eight o'clock in the morning Hanriot's troops were in position in front of the Tuileries in the Place du Carrousel, and were deployed around the palace. Marat, appearing at this time, walked up and down the ranks—"exhorting them to be induced neither by threats nor promises to lay down their arms until the momentous crisis had...passed." (14)

In the Royal Theatre, the sitting of the Convention was opened with the demand by a "statesmen" for the annulment of the Insurrectionary Commune and the outlawing of its members. No sooner had the speaker finished than the petitioners of the sections, again, demanded the arrest of the deputies, the previous speaker included. The petitioner's address ended: "The people are tired of having their happiness postponed; they leave it but a moment in your hands, save it, or we declare the people will save it themselves." (15) But instead of considering the petition, the Convention passed to the order of the day, causing the deputation of the sections to withdraw and a large portion of the gallery with it. Shouts coming from outside, "To arms! To arms!", showed the seriousness, as it did the urgency of the moment.

The spokesman for the Committee of Public Safety, Barrere, now made his report. Based on the negotiations of the previous day, the committee recommended that the accused members voluntarily accept suspension. With some accepting, and others rebuffing the suggestion, Marat announced his willingness to suspend himself, provided the decree of accusation was passed, and the modification of the names he'd proposed was adhered to. At that moment, a "Dantonist" deputy who'd been absent—"returned in a state of violent agitation, declaring the Convention was virtually a prisoner in its own house." (16)

As outrage redounded on the "right" and on the Plain, it was decided that the President, Hérault de Séchelles, re-placing, Isnard (the position changed hands every twelve days at this time), should conduct a procession of the deputies out of the sitting to attest for themselves whether they were free or not. This proposal was adopted. Marat outlined the scene in his *Publiciste*:

> He descends from his seat, nearly all the members following him, forces open the bronze doors, while the guard makes way. Instead of at once returning and demonstrating thereby the falsity of the clamours, he conducts the Convention in procession round the terraces and gardens. I had remained at my post in the company of about thirty other 'Montagnards.' The galleries, impatient at not seeing the Assembly return, began to murmur loudly.... (17)

De Séchelles (who was wearing his hat while the remainder of the deputies were bare-headed), approaching Hanriot with his cannonries at the ready (with his plumed staff standing behind him), demanded, "Make way for the National Convention." "Not an inch of way does Hanriot make," Carlyle remarked. (18) Hanriot responding—"I receive no order, till the Sovereign, yours and mine, have been obeyed." Hanriot then ordered his cannonries ready, and fuses were lit.

Taine takes up the scene: "Forced back on this side, the unhappy Convention turns to the left, passes through the archway, follows the broad avenue through the garden, and advances to the Pont-Tournant to find an outlet." (19) But the bridge was raised, and everywhere they saw only an impenetrable forest of pikes and bayonets. At this impasse, says Taine, up comes Marat carried on his short legs "barking" at the deputies. Marat completes this leaf-through, "I exhort it to return to its post; it returns, and reassumes its functions."

Once back in the Royal Theatre the paralytic Couthon, whom Carlyle remarked possessed "a singular power of face," was carried to the tribune in his wheelchair: "Citizens, all members of the Convention must now be satisfied of their freedom.... You are now aware that there is no restraint on your deliberation." (20)

The decree of accusation against the twenty-two Girondin deputies, against the Commission of Twelve, against the Minsters—were summarily passed. The implicated were placed under arrest, and ordered to remain in their houses "under safeguard of the French people," each with two gendarmes as guard. But already the Insurrectional Committee had ordered the arrest of Madame Roland and imprisoned her in the Abbaye; her husband had fled, says Carlyle, "no man knows whither." "The comedy," said Taine, "is at an end. Even in Moliere there is none like it." (21)

On June 3, Marat offered his summation at the Jacobin Club:

> We have given great impetus to the Revolution, it is for the Convention now to confirm the bases of the public happiness. Nothing is easier; you only must make up your minds definitively. We wish that all the citizens spoken of as sans-culottes may enjoy happiness and comfort. We wish that this useful class should be helped by the rich in proportion to their capacities. We do not wish to attack property. But what is the most sacred property? It is that of existence. We wish this property respected.... Acknowledge that we are the great number, and if you do not help us to turn the wheel, we shall drive you out of the Republic, we shall take possession of your property, and divide it among the sans-culottes. (22)

All counted, 80 thousand National Guard together with the men and women of the Parisian sans-culotte were said to have packed the squares and gardens around the Tuileries. They remained, bearing pikes and rifles and muskets with bayonets, and with every other conceivable weapon, an impassable and disciplined formation throughout the day, with provision-carts at their call, with liquor and wine for those who wanted refrehment, all men at arms under pay. Because of their solid phalanx, the 'intransigency' of Girondin faction was shattered.

Thomas Paine had not been in his seat in the Convention on 2 June, having been warned to stay away by Danton, Moncure Conway surmises, although he does not authenticate it, leaving that to after coming biographers. It's now said, during the events on Sunday, report had reached Saint-Denis early in the morning. Paine rose, and dressing, hurried to the Tuileries hoping to add his influence to the Convention's preservation. As he arrived at the Convention was meeting *en camera*, with the building surrounded by National Guard troops, and armed sans-culottes from the Parisian faubourgs. Despite his credentials, he had not been allowed to enter the building, Hanriot telling Paine he'd have better use for the paper he was offering in curling his hair. Inside, he was told, the galleries were clamoring for the resignation or arrest of twenty-two Girondins leaders, some of whom had already buckled under the pressure and consented to their own suspensions.

Standing nearby was Danton. He advised Paine that he should not risk going inside, where chances were, he'd end up on the list of "enemies of the revolution." Hadn't Vergniaud been right in likening the French Revolution to Saturn devouring his own children, Paine replied. To which Danton curtly quipped, "Revolutions cannot be made with rosewater." (23) And who among them could not sense the air of foreboding and trepidation hoovering perilously? And who cannot hear the fearsome passage in the interrogatory of William Blake in his ballad "Fayette"?

> O, who would smile on the wintry seas,
> & Pity the stormy roar?
> Or who will exchange his new born child
> For the dog at the wintry door? (24)

17.

But now the caves
of Hell I view

The Jacobin coup d'état brought in its wake rebellion in Lyons and in Marseille, and these in addition to that already underway in the Vendée, while more than half the departmental directories protested against the purge of 2 June. But after pleas for unity and warnings were issued from the Convention, the threat of this broad opposition abated, with thirteen departments continuing their defiant stance, and six passing over into armed rebellion against the Convention's authority. Revolt spread from Lyon and Marseille, to Toulon and Bordeaux; and as royalist's gained control of the rebellion in Toulon, by late August its port would be opened to occupation by the British Royal Navy.

Some of the purged Girondin deputies submitted quietly to house arrest in Paris, while others fled to organize a movement in the provinces against the capital. Among those escaping, Brissot was one of the first to be captured on the way to Caen, where Barbaroux, Buzot, and Pétion were trying to stir up resistance, capping their movement by organizing a "Federation of United Departments". Traveling with false papers, Brissot was caught and taken back to Paris on June 10. Roland escaped to his home region, Rouen, where he was in hiding; while many of the deputies too sought refuge in their home departments, most to the Gironde, and its main municipality, Bordeaux, where anti-Jacobin sentiment flourished.

Jacobins stigmatized this opposition as 'federalism', implying the purged deputies did not believe in a unified republic. In their propaganda, Jacobins dwelt upon Girondin forbearance in the trial of Louis XVI, saying that even if their opponents voted for death they'd proposed that the penalty be brought before the French people in a plebiscite, thus revealing their true intention of providing an escape for the condemned monarch and inaugurate a civil war. That they'd been supporters of the "traitor" Dumouriez, and were, like the general, treasonous; that they'd once been supporters of a constitutional monarchy, and were therefore outright "royalists" concealing it under a 'popular' guise. In short, they were counter-revolutionaries all, and their fate should be political extermination!

These deputies, in fact, had substantively all been 'republican,' but since they were the dominant faction in the convention at the time of France's military reversals against the Coalition, and with conditions in Paris and in other population centers nearing famine, they failed to respond to the demands of *les Enragés* and the sans-culottes, as the Jacobins had.

On June 10, the Montagne succeeded in gaining control of the Committee of Public Safety, which had remained inactive during the coup d'etat. By June 13 the purged politicians still in the capital were interned in one or another of Paris's prisons in conformity with a decree of the Convention dated December 16, 1792: "The National Convention decrees, that whoever shall propose or attempt to destroy the unity of the French Republic, or to detach its integral parts in order to unite them to a foreign territory, shall be punished with death." (1) A new Jacobin Constitution, which had been charged to a committee led principally by Louis Saint-Just and

Robespierre, both to be elevated to the Committee of Public Safety on July 27, was first presented to the Convention on June 10. Approved on June 24, the document represented a significant divergence for the Revolution, promising radical democratization and redistribution of wealth. But this constitution would be suspended with the decree of a Revolutionary Government on October 10 and was never implemented. The still born Girondin Constitution had raised the ire of Jacobins principally because it had stipulated the abolition of communal municipalities in favor of cantonal councils of administration. The Montagnards were decidedly opposed to this in that it would destroy the unity of Paris and the Commune, as it demanded that each town of more than 50,000 inhabitants be divided into several municipalities.

The rapid substitution of constitutions, came with a flurry of decrees intended to solidify and extend the power of the Convention. The first of these was to be a taxation in the form of a forced loan from the rich to subvent the cost of the war; then a decree fixing the maximum for the prices of commodities; followed by a decree for the restoration of communal lands, under attack for nearly two centuries; and then the decree of July 17, abolishing *en toto* the feudal laws, many of which had been untouched even with the abolition of feudalism in 1789. That decree read: "All dues formerly seigniorial, feudal rights, both fixed and casual, even those reserved by the decree of August 25 last, are suppressed without indemnity." That is, all rents and obligations of feudal origin were irrevocably abolished.

That a Jacobin dictatorship came into being has been ascribed to the Commune and to the Parisian sans-culottes, with *les Enragés* being the spearhead of the movement. But after attaining power, Robespierre and the Montagne turned against those who wished for "the Revolution in deeds, after it had been accomplished in thought", and in turn quashed them. (2) Jacques Roux's speech to the Convention on June 25—less than four weeks after the *journée* of May 31-June 2— was received with angry howls and hoots. Even Hébert allied with the Montagnards against him, and the next day he and Robespierre would go to the Cordeliers Club to demand *les Enragés* be excluded. Roux had been a critic of the Jacobin constitution, saying it offered no solution to the social and economic needs of the poor. Said Jacques Roux: "[T]he people, suffered more under the Republic than under monarchy." This earned him the enmity of Robespierre who never failed to describe Roux as a "base priest" and a "scoundrel" who "endeavoured to excite baneful disturbances to injure the Republic." (3) Roux would die in prison the following January, of a self-inflicted knife wound.

With the suppression of the 'left' opposition, the 'right' resistance would also wane, except where already indicated. In Caen, an epicenter of this resistance, when its leaders attempted to marshal a campaign against Paris, only a few dozen volunteers were found at the ready. In Normandy and Brittany only five to six hundred men enlisted. Despite the material weakness of the Jacobin authority, across vast swathes of contestable territory the Girondins opposition expired for want of popular support.

The day after the fateful 'step forward' for the Revolution of 2 June, Marat addressed a letter to the Convention, saying—"I hereby renounce the exercise of my function as deputy, until judgement has been passed on the accused representatives." (4) Those tempestuous days had had a marked effect on Marat's health too, as he was seen to withdraw from his journalistic endeavor. In the weeks between his acquittal at trial in April and the days in which he'd been all activity in late May and early June, Marat's illness worsened, and that final effort would prostrate him. The skin disease from which he suffered was complicated by serious symptoms appearing in his left lung, and by nervous exhaustion verging on brain fever that left him convalescing in a medicinal bath, and spending much of the month in bed. In these days, his journal was mainly composed of letters, to which he added his reflections, having his correspondence and reports on the sittings of the Convention brought to his bedside. He continued to maintain contact in writing with his colleagues, but complained "of the lack of attention his communications...received." (5) Marat wrote, "...I have addressed several letters to the Convention, in which I proposed useful measures on important subjects. They have not been read. Yesterday again the letter that I sent to the President had the same fate." (6)

Marat felt his only recourse was to reclaim those functions from which he'd abjured, appearing in the Convention on June 22. But that was to be for one day only, and he returned to his convalescence and to his journal to which he now devoted all his waning vigor and attention.

Hearing that Girondin volunteers in the departments were combining for a march on Paris, he wrote: "Let them come; they will find Thuriot, Lindet, Saint-Just, all the brave Montagnards; they will see Danton, Robespierre, Panis.... Perhaps they will come to see the Dictator Marat. They will behold a poor devil in his bed, who would give all the dignities of the earth for a few days health...." (7) In the last article from his hand, Marat reviewed the character and the composition of the Committee of Public Safety whose members he considered lax, devoting too little time to their duties. He wrote:

They are ignorant of almost everything that is done there.... Among their number, is one, moreover, whom the Mountain very impudently nominated, and whom I regard as the most dangerous enemy of the country. It is Barrere.... As regards myself, I am convinced that he swims between two streams, to see which one will gain the ascendant.... I challenge him to furnish proof to the contrary when...I denounce him as a Royalist. (8)

Several deputations were sent to inquire about Marat's condition; members of the Jacobin Club visiting on July 12, reported to its members:

We have been to see our brother Marat; he is very thankful for the interest you take in him; we found him in his bath, a table with an inkstand and some journals by his side, occupying himself ceaselessly with public affairs.... He complains of the forgetfulness on the part of the Convention in neglecting to read several measures of public safety he has addressed to it. (9)

A similar group sent by the Cordeliers Club came the following day urging that Marat devote his entire time to hastening his recovery. Marat's colleague and friend, the neo-classical painter Jacques Louis David, had also been by on the 12th. David was an active Jacobin and republican revolutionary, a deputy of the Convention representing Paris and member of the Committee of Public Security. He was also importantly a member of the art commission, busying himself, among his other duties, with revolutionary propaganda. His visit that day would allow him to observe the details he would use in his famous painting, *The Death of Marat*: the green rug drawn over a board across the tub to serve as a desk, the papers, the pen, the wooden crate holding Marat's inkstand, the towel soaked with vinegar wrapped around Marat's temples to lessen his fever. No doubt his artist's eye, if not his Jacobin proclivities, discerned in Marat working in his bath a model of 'virtue', whose famous rendering of the martyr, the poet Baudelaire would write in 1846, "...contains something both poignant and tender; a soul is flying in the cold air of this room, on these cold walls, around this cold funerary tub." (10)

The morning of 13 July at a small hotel in the Rue de Vieux Oldestein a 24-year-old woman from Caen left her room, and after buying a journal, was seen strolling through the Palais Royal. Passing a cutler's shop, she went in for a moment, asking to see some well-made knives. Shown one with an ebony handle in a leather case, she decided it would suit her purpose and purchased it for forty sous. Returning to her room, she would venture out again at 11:30, hailing a hackney coach. Arriving at No. 36 Rue de Cordeliers, she knocked at the door of the domicile and office of the journalist and deputy of the National Convention, Jean-Paul Marat. The door opening, she was informed Marat was ill and he could at present receive no one. Returning to her hotel she composed the following note, sent by messenger to the address of "the Peoples Friend":

> Citizen, I come from Caen; your love for your country makes me suppose you will like to know the unhappy events in that part of the Republic. I shall present myself at your house about seven o'clock; have the goodness to receive me and to accord me a moments interview. I shall put you in a position to render a great service to the country. (11)

The woman's name was Marianne Charlotte de Corday d'Armont, or as she is known Charlotte Corday, of *petite noblesse* family in line of descent from the dramatist Corneille. She had been sent to a convent for her education in her teens, and by the early years of the Revolution lived with an aunt in one of the old patrician houses in Caen. There, in addition to busying herself with chores, and showing affections to one or another suitor, she became a reader of the literature of the day, but seems to have been mostly impressed by Plutarch's *Lives* and other classics, with depictions of ancient persons of the sort with which David's art was dedicated, before his strikingly modern painting of Marat done in the manner of Caravaggio's *The Entombment of Christ*. Corday was also reading the revolutionary papers in the district of the variety that were Girondin in tendency. Conceiving a hatred for the Jacobins, and for the leading figures, Danton, Robespierre, and Marat, when the Girondin deputies arrived she made, through Buzot, their introduction, particularly of the vigorous and handsome and dandified Barbaroux. He and Pétion had formed a committee sitting at the Hôtel de Ville at Caen, and were enlisting citizens to serve in an army to depose the Montagnards in Paris. Here she found men who shared her invective and began to conceive a plot, as the historian Alphonse de Lamartine, the poet and politician of the second republic (made famous in 1820 for his masterpiece *Les Meditations Poetiques*), would later phrase it, in *Histoire des Girondins* (1847), with herself as "the Angel of Assassination."

Ostensibly seeking Barbaroux's help to secure the pension of the Lady Superior of a local convent which she had lost at the time of the general suppression of ecclesiastical pensions, Corday obtained a letter of introduction to his colleague who had remained in the Convention named Duperret. Bidding adieu to the Girondin deputies—Pétion, who enjoyed women's charms, termed her the "beautiful aristocrat who [is] going to see the Republicans." To this she replied, with a slight intimation of her purpose, "You judge me to-day without knowing me, Citizen Pétion; the day will come when you will know who I am." (12) When Corday called at Marat's apartment once more demanding admittance, he was feeling better, but again, she was denied admittance. With the sound of quarreling reaching Marat, he inquired what was the matter? Hearing that the woman from Caen was at the door, he bid she be permitted access for an interview.

There were five people besides Marat in the apartment that evening, four of them women: Simonne Evard, Marat's common-law wife, and her sister Catherine, the cook Jeannette Marechel, and the concierge of the house, Madame Pain; while the only other man was the compositor of the journal, Laurent Bas. That previous evening, Charlotte Corday was occupied with drawing up a manifesto justifying the act she was about to commit, in which she sought to reassure her family, "...be not uneasy, no one knows of my project."

Marat's apartment, situated on the first floor, was comprised of five rooms, the first being the anteroom and was lighted by a window. After entering and turning toward the interior door, there were three rooms; on the left was a room with a window looking out on a court, on the right a bedroom with a window with a view of the street, and in between was the bathroom. The fifth room was a salon entered from the anteroom on the left, with a window looking out on the street as well.

When she entered the bathroom, Marat bid she take the chair beside his bath.

"What is happening then at Caen?" he asked. "Eighteen deputies in sympathy with the department are supreme there," she answered.

"What are their names?"

On hearing names well-known to him, Marat began compiling a list and when he'd finished, remarked, "It will not be long before they are guillotined." At that, Corday rose, and drawing the knife concealed in her corset, thrust it forcefully into Marat's upper chest, piercing his lung and severing an artery. Falling back, with his last breath Marat uttered a cry for Simonne. "A moi! Chere amie! A moi!"

On hearing his cries, Simonne rushed into the room, exclaiming in horror, "O my God! He is assassinated." Throwing Corday to the floor, she had been followed into the bath by the others. As Charlotte Corday rose, she was felled by Laurent Bas with the chair she had been sitting on moments before. Again, Corday rose to escape but this time was stopped by an anxious crowd that had pushed into Marat's apartment on hearing cries from the Street. Corday's wrists were bound. She carried a letter concealed in her bodice that now became visible, written in the event she had not gained admittance:

> I wrote you this morning, Marat, have you received my letter? I could not believe you had as they refused me admittance; I trust that to-morrow you will accord me an interview. I repeat that I came from Caen. I have secrets to reveal to you of the utmost importance to the safety of the republic. Besides all this, I am persecuted for the cause of liberty. I am unhappy; this itself is sufficient to give me a claim on your protection. (13)

This last phrase, said biographer Ernest Bax, "might serve as an epitaph for the "People's friend."

At this junction in a narrative of this kind is it apropos to cast a glance forward, before looking again to the travail behind? True, historicism does not willingly suffer this expectancy; but in reality, the individual can only attain and possess the universal, as Hegel disclosed, by living with death, i.e., by "tarrying with the negative", which necessarily accompanies each of us into the future. From a natural point of view, the human is this living with expiation. Our desire does not desire a thing, as William Blake had shown, it desires for desire itself.

Thus, it is with civilization, the universality attained can be said to be erected on a scaffold and in a compost of corpses. (14) Which, as regards the heads rolling down from the guillotine during the *terror*, had no greater significance than did cabbages cleaved in twain. This was the judgement of Hegel in his famous *The Phenomenology of Mind* finished in 1806 just as Napoleon was crushing the Prussian army near Jena where he lived. It was only when the dead enter the symbolic realm that they become signified; ancient peoples unquestionably knew this, as does Freudian psychoanalysis. As an historian, Taine knew this too, and little else.

Taine wrote:

> Let us enter the cabinet of Roland, Minister of the Interior, a fortnight after the opening of the Convention, and suppose him contemplating, some evening, a foreshortened picture of the state of the country administered by him.... Madame Roland, I imagine, works with her husband, and the couple, sitting together alone under the lamp, ponder over the ferocious brute which they have set free in the provinces the same as in Paris. (15)

And what of the leaders, or of those at least who were selected as the penultimate representatives of the revolutionary type? Of Danton, of Marat, of Robespierre? Let's hear again from Taine:

> Even with the determination to remain decapitator-in-chief, Danton could never be a perfect representative of

the Revolution. It is an armed but philosophical robbery; its creed included robbery and assassination, but only as a knife in its sheath; the showy, polished sheath is for public display, and not the sharp and bloody blade. Danton, like Marat, lets the blade be too plainly visible. At the mere sight of Marat, filthy and slovenly, with his livid, frog-like face, with his round, gleaming and fixed eyeballs, and his bold maniacal stare and steady monotonous rage, common-sense rebels; no-one selects a homicidal maniac as a guide. At the mere sight of Danton, with his porter's vocabulary, his voice like an alarm bell of insurrection, his cyclopean features and air of an exterminator, humanity takes alarm; one does not surrender oneself to a political butcher without repugnance. The Revolution demands another interpreter, like itself captivatingly fitted out, and Robespierre fits the bill with his irreproachable attire, well- powdered hair, carefully brushed coat, strict habits, dogmatic tone, and formal studied manner of speaking. No mind, in its mediocrity and incompetence, so well harmonizes with the spirit of the epoch. The reverse of the statesman, he soars in empty space, amongst abstractions, always mounted on a principle and incapable of dismounting so as to see things practically. "That bastard there," exclaimed Danton, "is not even able to boil an egg." (16)

Four days after slaying Marat, Charlotte Corday was to mount the scaffold, her head cleaved from her body by the knifes-edge of the guillotine.

At her trial before the Revolutionary Tribunal, Fouquier-Tinville, the Attorney-General, the cousin of Camille Desmoulins, had been there with his indictments, as had witnesses such as the cutler who had sold Corday the knife. To the astonishment of everyone, she said—"All this is needless. It was I that killed Marat. I killed one man to save a hundred thousand; a villain to save innocents, a savage wild beast to give repose to my country. I was a Republican before the Revolution; I never wanted energy." (17)

18.

The deep of winter came

The events of 31 May-June 2 had been the ruin of Paine's expectancy of seeing liberty flourish on the European continent, "and his visions of the Commonwealth of Man." (1) Throughout the subsequent weeks, he was relegated to setting in his room alone, overwhelmed by the agony of being shorn from his dearest friends; he afterwards telling Clio Rickman, "borne down by public and private affliction," he sought oblivion in brandy. Brissot, Vergniaud, Lanthenas, and other leaders identified as Girondins, had been among his closest intellectual coadjutors in the Convention—now he was staring into the approaching abyss of their murder. His excessive drinking, which detractors have elevated to his prime trait, was apportioned primarily to this time, when on July 13' the shock of "Charlotte Corday's poignard cut a rift in the dark cloud;" and briefly he held hope that his friends might be salvaged. (2)

Paine himself described these months in a letter to a woman who appears to have sought his help as a deputy of the National Convention in a matter involving her husband, the English banker Sir Robert Smyth, who would also suffer long imprisonment during the *reign of Terror*. Lady Smyth wrote Paine just as he was released from the Luxembourg, addressing him from a "little corner of the world", while he corresponded with her from "the castle in the air". Now preserved in volume 3 of Paine's writings collected by Conway in an essay titled *Forgetfulness*, he tells of his environs and of his frame of mind:

> ...I used to find some relief by walking alone in the garden, after dark, and cursing with hearty good-will the authors of the terrible system that had turned the character of the Revolution I had been proud to defend. I went but little to the Convention, and then only to make my appearance; because I found it impossible to join in their tremendous decrees, and useless and dangerous to oppose them. My having voted and spoken extensively, more so than any other member, against the execution of the king, had already fixed a mark upon me; neither dared any of my associates in the Convention to translate and speak in French for me anything I might have dared to have written.... Pen and ink were then of no use to me; no good could be done by writing, and no printer dared to print; and whatever I might have written, for my private amusement, as anecdotes of the times, would be examined, and tortured into any meaning that the rage of party might fix upon it. And as to the softer subjects, my heart was in distress at the fate of my friends, and my harp hung upon the weeping willows. (3)

Paine's residence was an old mansion farmhouse, enclosed by a wall and gateway from the street, its yards stocked with fowls, rabbits and pigs, with a garden of more than an acre replete with fruit trees—orange, apricot, and greengage plum. Paine's apartment consisted of three rooms, with a sitting room looking out on the garden through a glass door. Here he kept company with his young English friends, Johnson and Choppin, mentioned in the trial of Marat, and some half-dozen others, in an arrangement of cooperative housekeeping, with the chief meals taken outside at a restaurant. In the evenings, among those appearing were Nicolas Bonneville, formerly a leader through his newspapers in propagandizing egalitarian ideas and now an opponent of the Jacobins, together with his family; Joel Barlow, the American diplomat and poet; Mary Wollstonecraft and her consort, the American businessman Captain Imlay; and the family of Brissot. English refugees of the Sedition Act were welcomed, and Paine's friend Clio Rickman was a guest. Rickman describes one of those dinners on a night he records Mary Wollstonecraft was present for some lively conversation:

> For above four hours [Paine] kept everyone in astonishment and admiration of his memory, his keen observation of men and manners, of Franklin, Washington, and even of his Majesty, of whom he told several curious facts of humour and benevolence. His remarks on genius and taste can never be forgotten by those present.

In the second volume of his Paine biography Conway excerpts from the journal kept by one of the visitors of the time, Daniel Constable:

> The little happy circle who lived with him will ever remember those days of delight: with these select friends he would talk of his boyish days, played at chess, whist, piquet, or cribbage, and enliven the moments by many interesting anecdotes...and then retire to his boudoir, where he was up to his knees in letters and papers of various descriptions.

Paine's main preoccupations however were hardly frivolous, he presiding over a "little cosmopolitan Cabinet", as if a premier in deliberation. The Girondins were still alive, as were many swept into the same fate as they, and there was work to be done in saving them. Papers were produced to be sent along to one or another of the revolutionary committees. The first headed "Observations on the situation of the Powers joined against France", where it was noted:

> It appears at first sight that the coalition against France is not of the nature of those which form themselves by treaty. It has been the work of circumstances. It is a heterogeneous mass, the parts of which dash against each other, and often neutralize themselves. They have but one single point of reunion, the re-establishment of the monarchical government of France. (4)

But would England fight to re-establish the Bourbons, against which it had contested since the beginning of its existence? And supposing a resulting alliance between powers occupying both sides of the channel through which the shipping of the northern countries of Europe need pass—could these tolerate it? And would Prussia consent to the reestablishment of an alliance between France and Austria; or Austria between France and Prussia; or Spain allow France and its fleet to ally with England? Weren't all these cases presented with the restoration of the Bourbons, Paine asked? (5) Weren't all the powers leagued against France fighting for an object injurious to themselves? (6)

Paine drove in his point: "In short, every circumstance is pregnant with some natural effects, upon which intentions and opinions have no influence; and the political error lies in misjudging what the effect will be." Austria regarded any 'duet' between France and Prussia with a jealous eye, as in turn, did Prussia between France and Austria. England had wasted vast treasure to prevent a Bourbon compact with Spain; while Russia was averse to a hand extended between France and Turkey, as Turkey became anxious at displays of sympathy between France and Russia. Paine summed up this European multi-lateral minuet: "Sometimes the quadruple alliance alarmed some of the powers, and at other times a contrary system alarmed others, and in all those cases the charge was always made against the intrigues of the Bourbons."

It now began to appear as certain that Paine's fate was to be determined between Pitt on one side, and Robespierre on the other. Pitt because Paine could not leave France for America, which would have been his plan but for the danger of being seized at sea and returned to England for hanging; and Robespierre in obvious expectation of a looming death-sentence from his very hand. British cruisers were then seizing American ships engaged to carry cargo to France, and French cruisers were ordered to embargo American vessels in port without reloading lest they should be captured at sea by their enemy. There were ninety-two American vessels idled at Bordeaux.

Gouverneur Morris had been the American minister to France since 1792, a New York native and a man of wealth whose proclivities extended toward aristocracy, and in the present situation, his sympathies were with England. This impounding of American vessels was a violation of treaty obligations, and Morris wrote to Secretary of State Jefferson in consultation. The captains of the vessels however, with these communications being a protracted affair, had more urgent requirements. Angry with Morris's seeming "indifference to their relief", and unable to move him, they applied to Paine. (7) This was a humiliation for Morris, and that it came through Paine, it was doubly so, since he already held him in enmity; and more so in that this was damaging to his overall purpose, that of transferring alliance from France to Britain.

Paine wrote to Barrere, chief of the Committee of Public Safety, regarding the disposition of Morris in French matters, remarking—"I shall return to America on one of the vessels which will start from Bordeaux in the month of October." He continued:

The American Captains left Paris yesterday. I advised them, on leaving, to demand a convoy of the Convention, in case they heard it said that the English had begun reprisals against the Americans, if only to conduct as far as the Bay of Biscay, at the expense of the American government.... If events force the American captains to demand a convoy, it will be to me that they will write...and not to Morris, against whom they have grave reasons of complaint. (8)

France had made demands for Morris's recall; yet, with arrival of such notice in abeyance, commissioners might be sent, or perhaps Paine himself represent the situation before Congress on his return to Philadelphia. The French minister to America, Edmond-Charles-Edouard Genet, had already been recalled for diplomatic intercessions known as the "Genet Affair". Genet had negotiated with Kentucky, admitted to the American Union June 1, 1792, over the expulsion of Spain from the Mississippi, and had commissioned privateers to conduct a campaign from United States ports against British commerce; one of these armed and dispatched under his authorization was the prize ship *Little Sarah*, refitted as *La Petite Democrate*. Earlier too, on his appointment, Genet had not been announced to Morris, but through the introduction of Thomas Paine. Morris wrote President Washington, December 28, 1792—"Perhaps the Ministry think it is a trait of republicanism to omit those forms which were anciently used to express good will."

On the day Paine wrote his letter to Barrere, September 5, 1793, the chief of the Committee of Public Safety reported in the Convention, "Let us make terror the order of the day!" The previous day some two thousand sans-culotte demonstrators had been in front of the Hôtel de Ville, shouting "Bread, bread!", Jacques Roux among them. But the instigator of the protest had been Hébert, the deputy procureur of the Commune, who persuaded the crowd to gather the next day in front of the Convention, when it would be stormed with Hébert at their head. The demands of the protesters—which they succeeded in getting passed by sheer intimidation of the deputies—included a forced loan upon the rich, expansion of the revolutionary tribunal and broadening of the law of suspects, and the creation of an *Armée Révolutionnaire* of 6,000 foot soldiers and 1,200 gunners to enforce the laws fixing prices.

But Hébert was to be outplayed by Robespierre later that day, who was determined he remain atop the crest of the advancing sans-culotte wave, when he led a deputation from the Jacobin Club, together with delegations from the forty-eight sections, who came before the Convention also demanding a revolutionary army to commandeer food supplies, which had been the Hébertist demand, and the dismissal of all nobles from public service. But Robespierre's ultimate demand had been—*qu'on place la Terreur a l'order du jour* (put terror on the order of the day).

Robespierre had been elected to the Committee of Public Safety July 27, as noted, which was becoming the functioning agency of government as it had supervision of foreign affairs and of appointments. Genet's recall presumably portended he was headed for execution, but for the fact that he found an asylum with New York's Governor Clinton, and in the affections of his daughter. At this time Paine was not aware Robespierre held animus for him, but a jotting found in "the Incorruptible's" notebook, and presented in Conway's volume, reads—"Demand that Thomas Payne be decreed of accusation for the interests of America as much as of France." Commenting on this sentence in a letter in 1802, Paine wrote: "There must have been a coalition in sentiment, if not in fact, between terrorists of America and the terrorists of France, and

Robespierre must have known it, or he could not have had the idea of putting America into the bill of accusation against me." "Terrorists of America", was an unambiguous reference to the so-called Federalists who, as a sign of their animus would succeed in passing the infamous *Alien and Sedition Acts* in Congress, authorized by President John Adams in 1798. This stroke would be carried against the supporters of the French Revolution in America, notably Jefferson's Democratic-Republicans; the Act prohibiting public opposition to the government, with fines and imprisonment levied against those who "write, print, utter, or publish...any false, scandalous and malicious writing."

On October 3 when the accusations against the Girondins were read, Paine was included, to wit: "...[T]he Englishman Thomas Paine, called by the faction to the honor of representing the French nation, dishonored himself by supporting the opinion of Brissot, and by promising us in his fable the dissatisfaction of the United States our natural allies, which he did not blush to depict for us full of veneration and gratitude for the tyrant of France." (9) But a deputy must be formally accused before he could be tried by Revolutionary Tribunal; a subterfuge need be found in order to imprison Thomas Paine.

Among Paine's close intellectual coadjutors prior to the calamity was the Enlightenment *philosophe* and mathematician Nicolas de Condorcet who'd been prominent in the revolutionary changes in France since their inception, as Paine was also an intimate of his wife Sophie, and with the couple's young daughter. Condorcet had been elected, at age twenty-one, in February 1769, to the *Academie Royale des Sciences*; a member of the nobility and, therefore, of the second estate, he'd also been a proponent of the abolition of feudalism, and a formulator, along with Lafayette of the *Declaration of the Rights of Man and the Citizen.*

Like Paine, Condorcet was a relentless anti-cleric and an advocate of the cause of liberty, of equality and the rights of man, and was among a handful of men, whether pamphleteer, or representative, or advanced thinker, to advocate women's rights, authoring in 1790 "For the Admission to the Rights of Citizenship of Women." Condorcet wrote:

> The rights of men stem exclusively from the fact that they are sentient beings capable of acquiring moral ideas and of reasoning upon them. Since women have the same qualities, they necessarily also have the same rights. Either no member of the human race has any true rights, or else they all have the same ones; and anyone who votes against the rights of another, whatever his religion, colour or sex, automatically forfeits his own.

Condorcet took the same position in regard of the rights of Africans in the French colonies, joining Brissot in the *Society of the Friends of the Blacks*, and advocating the abolition of the slave-trade. He had also been appointed, as was discussed, to the committee drafting the first republican constitution in the National Convention, and although both Paine and Condorcet are often loosely associated with the Girondin faction, they likewise deplored its factionalism, as they did that of the Jacobins, and were hewers of their own independent action.

Both objected to the Conventions assumption of judicial functions, as they had to the infliction of the death penalty in the trial of Louis XVI. While both saw the necessity of the trial, Paine proposed banishment for the king, as Condorcet favored the galleys, and neither favored a plebiscite on his fate before the French people. Both also saw a reprieve as an opportunity to use the King's person as bargaining leverage, and a way of staving off, as did Brissot, a massive royalist rebellion.

The arrest of the twenty-two Girondin "statesmen" brought with it Condorcet's condemnation, as he publicly offered a critique of the Jacobin constitution to replace the one he'd been counseling, published anonymously but later identified as his authorship, titled "Advice to the French on the New Constitution". Also disparaging the violent conduct of the Montagne and the Commune and their sans-culottes allies— for these sins against the new power, Condorcet was declared a traitor and outlawed on July 18 by the Convention. Threatened with arrest and imprisonment, he had immediately gone into hiding.

No one could possibly have known, not Robespierre nor Saint-Just or any other Jacobin, what all the radical economic and political changes they were introducing at the behest of the sans-culotte and the Commune portended, but September 5, 1793, is accepted as the starting of the terror. The next day the Committee of Public Safety had been enlarged to accept two new members, both of them *Hébertistes*. In this way, Robespierre had co-opted the left-wing of the revolution within the revolutionary government. By September 29 the Convention would pass the *maximum general* covering prices and wages, and immediately afterward made it clear they had no intention to enact the new constitution, announcing on October 10 the government of France would be revolutionary until the attainment of peace.

Saint-Just explained the rational: "In the circumstances in which the Republic finds itself, it would become the guarantee of attacks on liberty, because it would lack the force necessary to suppress them." In December, in the continuing effort to provide justification for the new state of affairs, Robespierre would pronounce—"We must organize the despotism of liberty to crush the despotism of kings." (10)

On October 3, Marquis de Condorcet was sentenced in absentia to be guillotined. Of one-hundred and eighty deputies in the Convention comprising the Girondins, one-hundred and forty perished, or were in prison, or fled under sentence of death. 14 October Marie Antoinette's trial before Revolutionary Tribunal took place, where she was accused of orchestrating orgies at Versailles, of indulging in profligate spending ruinous to the French people, of planning massacre, and finally of engaging in incest with her son. This last drew an indignant response from the disposed queen, who refused to answer the charge, appealing to all the mothers then present in the room. On October 16, she was convicted of high treason and condemned to the guillotine.

Wearing a plain white dress, her proud hair shorn, with her hands tightly pinioned at her back and restrained with a leash, she was conveyed to her execution in an open tumbril. Reaching the scaffold, she maintained her composure, when mounting it she accidently stumbled against the executioner's shoe. "Pardon me sir, I did not do it on purpose, she said." Then quietly she submitted to her expiation.

The trial of the twenty-two accused deputies before the Revolutionary Tribunal, with Pierre Chaumette and Jacques Hébert acting as prosecutors on its behalf, took place 24 October, where each of the inculpated was aware that his appearance before that body was but the anteroom for the guillotine. Of the quickening pace of accusation and execution in the late summer and fall, Carlyle later wrote:

> Daily the great Guillotine has its due. Like a black Spectre, daily at eventide, glides the Death-tumbril through the variegated throng of things.... The Guillotine, we

find, gets always a quicker motion, as other things are quickening. The Guillotine, by its speed of going, will give index of the general velocity of the Republic. The clanking of its huge axe, rising and following there.... (11)

The condemned Girondin deputies were delivered to the scaffold on the morning of 31 October. Valaze, one of the older deputies, had stabbed himself in the chest before leaving the court, and it was decreed his corpse should suffer decapitation by guillotine with the others. Vergniaud having been supplied with poison, seeing it was not enough to go around, rather than abandon his friends, before reaching the scaffold threw it away. Carlyle, again, on how they died:

All Paris is out; such a crowd as no man had seen. The death-carts, Valaze's cold corpse stretched among the yet living twenty-one, roll along. Bareheaded, hands bound, in their shirt sleeves, coat flung loosely round the neck; so fare the eloquent of France; bemurmured, beshouted. To the shouts of Vive la Republique, some of them keep answering with counter shouts of Vive la Republique. Others, as Brissot, sit sunk in silence. At the foot of the scaffold they again strike up, with appropriate variations, the hymn of the Marseilles. Such an act of music; conceive it well! The yet living chant there, the chorus so rapidly wearing weak! Sanson's axe is rapid; one head per minute, or a little less. The Fauchet chorus is wearing weak; the chorus is worn out; farewell, forevermore, ye Girondins, Te-Deum has become silent; Valaze's dead head is lopped; the sickle of the guillotine has reaped the Girondins all away. (12)

When discovered in hiding in Saint-Emilion near Bordeaux, Charles Jean Marie Barbaroux attempted to kill himself by pistol shot; failing this, he was taken to Bordeaux and subjected to the guillotine. Francois Buzot seeking sanctuary in Saint-Emilion was proscribed by the Convention, it decreeing—"that the house occupied by Buzot be demolished, and never to be rebuilt on this plot. [Instead] a column shall be raised, on which there shall be written: 'Here was the sanctuary of the villain Buzot who, while a representative of the people, conspired of the overthrow of the French Republic." Together with Jerome Pétion, the former mayor of Paris and deputy of the Convention, they were suicides in the forests near Bordeaux; their remains discovered a month afterwards half-devoured by wild dogs.

November 3, Olympe de Gouges turned out upon the scaffold, one of one hundred and sixty-six women to mount the grim machine, and thus, to become "no more", after she was arrested for a poster that went the rounds on the walls of Paris, titled "The Three Urns, or the Salvation of the fatherland, by an Aerial traveler." The three urns being a reflection on the political struggle roiling France the past four years: whether a unitary republic, a federalist government, or a constitutional monarchy, that she demanded be decided by plebiscite. In farewell to her son, she wrote: "I shall die, my son, victim of my idolatry of my country and its people. Their enemies, beyond the specious mask of republicanism, remorselessly led me to the scaffold . . . Farewell my son, when you receive this letter I shall be no more."

Philippe Egalité—a title bestowed on Louis Philippe d'Orléans by the Commune—mounted the scaffold November 7. Impeccably attired and elaborately powered and made-up, still the wealthiest man in France, he remarked "this seems a bit of a joke".

Madame Roland following the next day; she had remarked upon her conviction before the Tribunal—"You judge me worthy to share the fate of the great men whom you have assassinated. I shall endeavor to carry to the scaffold the courage they displayed." (13)

Revert now to 9 August 1793 . . . as Taine had written, "...by order of the Convention, the delegates meet in the Tuileries garden, where divided into as many groups as there are departments, they study the programme drawn up by David, in order to familiarize themselves with the parts they are to play in the festival the following day. What an odd festival and how it expresses the spirit of the time! It is a sort of opera played in the streets by the public authorities...." (14)

So, to the 10th, year two of the Republic. Thanks again to the painter David, there is "a Scenic Phantasmagory unexampled," wrote Carlyle, "whereof History, so occupied with Real Phantasmagories, will say but little." Called the *Fête de la Reunion et l' indivisbilite*, it began on the ruins of the Bastille where a gigantic plaster-of-Paris Statue of Nature had been erected in the form of a woman from whose breasts shoot founts of water. President Hérault de Séchelles, still alive and very handsome, lifts an iron chalice and fills it and drinks from it, proclaiming solemnly, "Nous sommes tous ses enfants." Then the sacred waters are passed on to the Departmental Deputies who also imbibe, intoning solemnities against a background of wind-instruments with trumpet blasts, punctuated by the firing of artillery. This had been the festival's first act.

The second act had seen the officials and deputies promenading down the boulevards, each holding or bound within an indivisible tri-color ribbon. Walking in informal order, symbolizing their complete equality and unity, and surrounded by sans-culottes carrying pikes and the implements of their many trades, such as hammers—all are following behind a kind of chariot with "ancient Baucis and Philemon seated on it", drawn by children. Along with this welter moves the newly imprinted Jacobin constitution in a suitable cedar case, or ark or casket, as it were, to be sited later in an honored placed near the president's chair in the National Convention.

The revue then passes through triumphal arches, the throng coming to the seated heroines of the Women's March on Versailles of October 1789. Each woman is decorated with oak-leaf adornment and tricolor, whom Herault eloquently addresses, honoring them, but also admonishing them to be good mothers. They all rise in unison and join the march.

Now the Place de la Revolution is gained, and in its center, a figure shrouded with canvas and prepared with pulley and rope as it awaits unveiling. It is a Statue of Liberty (still modeled in clay but in expectancy one day of metal), standing where the bronze figure of Louis the 14th once stood. In this portion of the pageant, three thousand birds are let loose, each with the tag fastened to its neck, "we are free, imitate us."

The whole concourse now passes on toward the river and the Champ-de-Mars, where another mammoth statue rests. This time it was Hercules as *le Peuple Francois*, leaning on a club that touches the ground, symbol of un-conquerable might. Beside him is a many-headed dragon—the dragon de mar, which was slain. Hercules, in David's design, represented the amalgamation of social and of natural man *a la* Jean-Jacques Rousseau; the dragon, those "outside nature", those who perpetuate the practices of the *ancien regime* with their masks and disguises.

Now return to the moment at hand in this narrative, not much more than two months into what was then still called the future. The scene is *Marie-Jeanne* conveyed to the scaffold dressed in white. She is going to her death as she desired—a citizen of the Republic and no subject of monarchy! As she approaches the scaffold, her mind welling with involuntary thoughts; is it creditable she asks for a pen that she might jot them down, as was reputed?

In *Memoires de Madame Roland* written during her confinement and published in 1795, she had put down: "I know not any longer how to guide my pen amidst the horrors that devour my country: I cannot live above the ruins; I choose rather to bury myself under them. Nature, open thy bosom!" (15)

In this moment, she stands opposite the recently unveiled Statue of Liberty, before the guillotine with its waiting blade, an everlasting black specter.... Carlyle wrote of her—"Like a white Grecian statue, serenely complete, she shines in that black wreck of things...." (16)

She who cried, "O Liberty, what crimes are committed in thy name."

One week after hearing of the death of his wife, her husband, Jean-Marie Roland, is discovered seated against a tree with a cane-sword thrust into his heart—a suicide. A note attached to his outer garment, reads: "From the moment when I learned that they had murdered my wife, I would no longer remain in a world with enemies."

Finally, when the Republic had re-conquered its lost cities, the Convention decreed—"The name of Toulon shall be abolished...." "The name of Lyon shall be stricken off the list of towns belonging to the Republic...." (17)

19.
With hoarse note
curse the sons of joy

On 20 Brumaire (24 October) Year II on the new Revolutionary calendar adopted retroactively (1793), introduced ostensibly to make France worthy of the Enlightenment, another pageant travelled from the Circus of the Palais Royal toward the Cathedral Notre Dame, which hereafter was to be renamed the "Temple of Reason." Organized by the ultra-revolutionaries Pierre Chaumette and Jacques Hébert, the pageant included a Goddess of Reason portrayed by an opera singer borne on palanquin shoulder high, with red woolen cap, holding in her hand the pike of the Jupiter-*Peuple*. "[A] woman fair to look at," wrote Carlyle, "when well rouged." (1)

Designated the *Festival of Reason*, it marked the commencement of a de-Christianization campaign in which churches all over France were stripped of their sacerdotal objects, as altars were dismantled, while articles of value made of gold and silver were sent to the treasury, and bells to arms foundries to be cast into cannon, excepting those needed to sound the tocsin. Subsumed under the banner "Liberte, Egalité, fraternite," a so-called *Cult of Reason* was to replace the Catholic Church.

It was, in any event, to be a short-lived movement that became the defining feature of the Hébertist faction, among the most vociferous advocates of the *Terror*, as it had too, many sans-culotte adherents. Drawn up yet again by Jacques-Louis David; for the fete, the alter at Notre Dame had been dismantled and a dais of Liberty raised in its place—a papier-mache and painted linen mountain, with a faux Greco-Roman temple erected at its summit beneath the gothic vault. It bore the inscription "To Philosophy," and was decorated with the busts of the philosophes significant to the Enlightenment. As a body, the deputies of the National Convention did not attend the affair, Robespierre calling it a "ridiculous" farce; but many hundreds of deputies and officials of the Commune were participants. The Bishop of Autum, Talleyrand, officiating at the devotional ceremony, where Anacharsis Clootz pronounced the opening words, declaring the Republic would acknowledge but "one God only, Le Peuple."

The occasion too was one marked by gratuitous vandalism; altar pieces and stained-glass windows were broken, statues smashed, devotional manuals and hymnals burned. "Church and counter-revolution are one and the same", Chaumette had pronounced.

Impersonated by another opera singer, clad in white Roman garments, and again wearing a Phrygian bonnet and holding a pike, the demure figure of Liberty was seated on a bank midway up the mountain. Graciously bowing in the direction of a flame of reason, she was attended by girls also dressed in white Roman tunics with tricolor sashes, with flowers, garlands and greenery draped and strung about, while it was reported "the *Hymn to Liberty*, words by Chenier, music by Gossec", was sung.

Withal, the procession to and from the Cathedral was said to have had a "licentious" air, as, through every portal, people came and went, and men and women danced the meandering lively dance of peasant origin, the Carmagnole. Some celebrants, imbibing brandy from chalices, as these emptied, stopped at dram-shops to have them refilled. Wending its way afterwards to the Convention, the Saturnalia thronging the boulevards, was seen (again from Carlyle)—"masked like mummers in fantastic sacerdotal vestments; bearing on hand-barrows their heaped plunder."

It was during these autumnal days Thomas Paine began work on what is regarded as the last of his trilogy, after *Common Sense* and *Rights of Man*, titled *The Age of Reason*; taking up the labor of centuries as the emblem of his treatise, just at the moment that "reason" appeared to be reaching its nadir. Written on the supposition that a "revolution in the system of government would be followed by a revolution in the system of religion", Moncure Conway called it his "testimony under the guillotine": (2) "This was the task which he had from year to year adjoured to his maturest powers, and to it he dedicates what brief remnant of life may await him. That completed, it will be time to die with his comrades, awakened by his pen to a dawn now red with their blood." (3)

Paine, however, found his situation conducive in bringing his mind to the unguent promptings and concentration requisite the task: The time of writing the first part occupying him steadily till December 28, 1793, when he would lay down his pen six hours before his arrest, and the manuscript had been safely given into the hands of Joel Barlow—or as he wrote in the dedication, under the protection of "my fellow-citizens of the United States."

Paine wrote in the introduction to his anti-theological tract:

The circumstance that has now taken place in France of the total abolition of the whole national order of priesthood, and of everything appertaining to compulsive systems of religion, and compulsive articles of faith, has not only precipitated my intentions, but rendered a work of this kind exceedingly necessary, lest in the general wreck of superstition, of false systems of government, and false theology, we lose sight of morality, of humanity, and of the theology that is true. As several of my colleagues and others of my fellow citizens of France have given me the example of making their voluntary and individual profession of faith, I also will make mine; and I do this with all that sincerity and frankness with which the mind of man communicates with itself.

I believe in one God and no more, and I hope for happiness beyond this life. I believe in the equality of man; and I believe that religious duties consist in doing justice, loving mercy, and endeavoring to make our fellow creatures happy.

The foregoing was written as he sat down to address his own time, and his country—Britain, France, and America, to all of which he belonged—his lamp burning, or in the daylight hours, as the case may be, bent over his manuscript, opening his mind, inscribing his bequest.

During his years in France Paine had become more persuaded than ever of the enervating and reactionary role played by the clergy in political affairs—particularly in the alliance between higher clergy and the aristocracy and monarchy. To contribute to breaking this relationship, he was determined to expose the false character of the source of the priesthood's authority—scriptural revelation. Organized religion was "set up to terrify and enslave mankind, and monopolize power and profit", wrote Paine. But above all, he saw it was necessary, in order to preserve republican principles, to destroy the power of the priesthood. His aim, further, became both to rescue Deism from the atheism he perceived manifesting among the Jacobins, and republicanism itself from their despotism, which required for it to succeed, a milieu of civic tolerance. As such, scriptural texts are scrutinized in light of the Newtonian principles of science and the Lockean philosophy of government; Paine's theological treatise essentially being an application of the power of reason to the religious systems propounded by the Jewish, the Christian, and as he calls it, the Turkish, or the faith of Mahomet, and to their texts, particularly the *Old* and the *New* testaments.

The ideas Paine expressed did not originate exclusively with him—in France Diderot and Voltaire had already articulated the same—but he put them into cogent form outside of the salon and the artfully wrought treatise, making them accessible to the quotidian individual. These were the laymen, the artisans, and small shop keepers, the newly literate laborers and tradesmen, self-emancipating women, and bohemians, those beginning a burgeoning intellectual life with the proliferation of the printing press and accessibility to writers and their books, and periodicals. So, for a third time, as with his earlier treatises, these eagerly responded to Paine's *The Age of Reason,* issued, yet again, at a nominal price.

That fall, Paine had arranged for his young English friends, Johnson and Choppin, to leave France by way of Switzerland. They left at four one morning for Basel, only two days before a guard came to the residence to place them under arrest in accord with the law against foreigners. Earlier too Paine had been obliged to make an intercession on their behalf. Learning they were detained at a guardhouse in the neighborhood, he wrote and signed a certificate for their release in his capacity as deputy of the Convention. Paine related the incident in *Forgetfulness*:

> Just as I had finished it a man came into my room dressed in the Parisian uniform of a captain, and spoke to me in good English, and with good address. He told me that two young men, Englishmen, were arrested and detained in the guard house, and that the section, (meaning those who represented and acted for the section), had sent him to ask if I knew them, in which case they would be liberated.

That matter settled, the officer and his interlocutor fell into mutual conversation about the Revolution, touching upon the "Rights of Man" which he had read in English. In parting, Paine related, he "offered me in a polite and civil manner, his services." Given the times, this was utterly incongruous, as the officer was none other than Charles-Henri Sanson, the public executioner who would perform 2,918 executions in a forty-year career before retiring in 1795, including the execution of Louis XVI. He lived in the same section and on the same street as Paine.

Sanson, who might be said to have treated his charges with a modicum of decency, notwithstanding the obvious inconvenience to them, was a swift and efficient executioner who owned the guillotine he operated, maintaining it at his own expense. To complete the tableau of this singular tradesmen, in his spare time he was also a devoted and conscientious player of both the cello and the violin, as well as being a grower of medicinal herbs in his garden. Later when meeting Napoleon Bonaparte, he was asked if he could sleep at night? Sanson replied with laconic tongue, "If emperors, kings, and dictators can sleep well, why shouldn't an executioner?"

On Christmas night, as he sat finishing Part I of *The Age of Reason*, Paine was informed he'd been denounced in the Convention and expelled. That past June, as the Montagne grasped for power, Robespierre had demanded a more stringent law against foreigners, and one was speedily decreed ordering their confinement, excepting two deputies of the Convention, Thomas Paine and Anacharsis Clootz; although the measure was intended as a warning even to these. Paine was protected, however only as an American citizen, the French republic's only ally. But that fall when Morris sorted out relations with the new Foreign Minister, Deforgues, dealing with the interference by the French minister in America, Genet, and with the matter of the American sea captains and their impounded vessels, he deliberately prepared the way for accusation to be brought against Paine. In a confidential letter to Washington, Morris reported:

> I have insinuated the advantages which might result from an early declaration on the part of the new minister that as France has announced the determination not to meddle with the interior affairs of other nations, I told the minister that I had observed an overruling influence in their affairs which seemed to come from the other side of the channel.... This declaration produced the effect I intended. (4)

This intimation by Morris was an unmistakable reference to Thomas Paine. On the night of December 27, the Committee of General Surety and Surveillance sent the following document to the National Convention: "The Committee resolves, that the persons named Thomas Paine and Anachrsis Clootz, formerly Deputies to the National Convention, be arrested and imprisoned, as a measure of General Surety; that an examination be made of their papers...." (5)

Anacharsis Clootz, a Prussian national and nobleman, was, like Paine, a proponent of a more embracive and internationalist understanding of the French Revolution's potential. First in Paris in 1776 when he took part in the compilation of Diderot's *Encylopedie*, assembled from 7,000 articles on every conceivable subject, with 30,000 illustrations and diagrams. After travels through Europe in 1789 he returned, when he became an enthusiast for revolution and a 'democrat', dropping the title Baron, for the title "citoyen de l'humanite". Rather incongruously he would follow the Hébertist leadership to the scaffold March 24, 1794, losing his head before what was said to be the largest crowd for a public execution ever assembled in Paris. (6)

Another figure crucial in the Revolution, among "the sons of joy", was the Marquis de Condorcet, hereafter to be referred to without noble title. For his safe keeping, the individual approached was the widow of the sculptor Louis-Francois Vernet, Madame Vernet, relative of that great family of painters. She owned a house on Rue Servandoni in Paris, a small street leading down to the Luxembourg Gardens, who sometimes let lodgings to students. Asked by his friends whether she was willing to shelter a proscribed man, she enquired, "Is he a good man?" Assured such was the case, she replied—"Then let him come at once. You can tell me his name later. Don't waste even a moment. While we are speaking, he may be arrested."

After going into hiding, Condorcet was urged by his wife, through surreptitious contact with his protector and hostess, as well as by several friends, that he now devote himself to a work already begun, rather than, as might be expected, one of a polemical nature or a justification of his actions. In any event, securing his own vindication is what he had first given his attention to, where he had begun: "As I do not know if I shall survive the present crisis, I think I owe my wife, my daughter, my friends, who might be the victims of slanders against my memory, a simple statement of my principles and my conduct during the revolution." (7)

He was now to give his time wholly to writing what is considered his greatest work, he merely styling it a "prospectus" for the larger work he'd intended. It bears the title *Esquisse*, meaning a drawing without shading and unfinished, and translated into English in full is *Sketch for a Historical Picture of the Progress of the Human Mind*. Condorcet's aim was to point the way toward an optimal future which he believed would allow for the continual improvement in the human condition, believing, it would be humanities store if only we could decide to make it a reality. It is this work for which he is best known, and it was by far, not excepting Paine's reflections, the most comprehensive and reasoned meditation achieved by anyone in the revolutionary period in France.

Condorcet's *history* consists of nine "epochs" of the past, starting from humanity's primordial constitution in hunter-gather hordes forming the first basis for social cohesion, up to the present, the epoch of revolution in America and almost contemporaneously by the even more fundamental revolution in France, demonstrating how reason was formed through this advance, manifest in the development of cognition and in the sciences. The idea of perfectibility, or in the mundane expression, of progress, is that the human mind is open to an indeterminate historical imminence, as Condorcet's *Sketch* ends with a tenth epoch, the future.

He wrote: "...is it not requisite to study, in the history of the human mind, what obstacles remain to be feared, and by what means those obstacles are to be surmounted?" (8) The human mind had no fixed limits to its advancement in knowledge, and human society is capable of indefinite perfectibility—in virtue, and indeed, in the prolongation of bodily life. In Condorcet's view, there were three tendencies contributing to this historical movement: The first was the gradual ablation of inequality between nations, a second was in the erosion of inequality between classes, and a third was in a tendency for improvement in the all-around well-being of the individual. Progress would come about not in absolute terms, but as greater equality in rights and in freedom were attained. Condorcet's *Sketch* became a veritable hymn to improvement in the modern world, as he wrote at its commencement:

> ...that the progress of this perfectibility, henceforth above the controul of every power that would impede it, has no other limit than the duration of the globe upon which nature has placed us. The course of this progress may doubtless be more or less rapid, but it can never be retrograde; at least while the earth retains its situation in the system of the universe, and the laws of this system shall neither effect upon the globe a general overthrow, or introduce such changes as would no longer permit the human race to preserve and exercise therein the same faculties, and find the same resources. (9)

William Blake, who must be reckoned part of this movement discerning the emancipatory potential still in the year 1794, printed his illuminated book titled *Europe, A Prophecy* that year on the back of the plates he used for *America* (as he sometimes also bound the two together), and in the same year also produced *Songs of Experience*. Since the appearance of *America* the previous year, and as economic dislocation swept through England with the declaration of war between Britain and France, and as the disasters of war would overwhelm its armies and the allies throughout the following year, Blake, as had Paine, had been hopeful of seeing the triumph of revolution and the establishment of republics across Europe.

For Blake *prophecy* in his sense was not a vision of the future, but as he wrote later in *Milton* (1804-1808), the prophet's responsibility was—

> To open the eternal worlds, to open the immortal eyes
> Of man inwards into the worlds of thought: into eternity,
> Ever expanding in the bosom of God, the human
>   imagination. (10)

A universal uprising, in Blake's expectation, had been ignited with the American Revolution, followed by that in France, and a British revolution would follow in its course. In *America*, Blake had written...

> ...had America been lost, o'erwhelmed by the Atlantic,
> And Earth had lost another portion of the infinite,
> But all rush together in the night in wrath and raging fire.

America and *Europe* together are among Blake's most political poems, as well as containing some of his most lyrical and rhapsodic verses, while the printed plates of *Europe* depict some of Blake's most striking images. Images that had acquired a central importance and that take up entire pages of the book, that are barely illustrative of the text. The historical passages in *Europe* concern the suffering of the population of London, and of the politics of William Pitt, King George III's prime minister, and of the attempt of the "Angels of Albion" to shut the minds of "the youth of England" to ready them for the terrors of the impending Armageddon. A reckoning that had begun, Blake was aware, with the edict against "divers wicked and seditious writings" promulgated against Paine's *Rights of Man.*

On May 24, 1792, as Pitt began Britain's military preparations, the London *Chronicle* had assured its public that "the little encampment on Bagshot Heath" was formed for the study of new Prussian military maneuvers being introduced to the British army, "and not from the most distant idea of any armament being at this time requisite on the part of Great Britain." (11) The preparation for these evolutions had involved regiment after regiment of the youth of England marching through London to their country-side encampment; something no doubt observed first hand by the bard.

On March 30, the display at Bagshot Heath had been previewed by king and princes, as London's "idlers" also were on hand; as before each mock battle was conducted, chaplains prayed at the head of each corps. But the marching and counter-marching so wearied the young soldiers with their seventy-pound-sacks, that many began to wear a hostile glare as their outward countenance. On August 2, the London *Times* correspondent wrote: "We never beheld troops suffer more; it may be a *Camp of Pleasure* to lookers on, but it is a very different affair to the poor soldiers." (12)

Late that summer, just as Pitt began erecting barracks to house troops near the industrial towns, to stifle Paine's growing influence with "Sheffield cutlers" Secretary of War Dundas sent his deputy adjutant-general on tour to ascertain the disposition of troops in event of an emergency. Reporting he—"found that the seditious doctrines of Paine and the factious people who are endeavouring to disturb the peace of the country had extended to a degree very much beyond my conception;" he also related 2,500 "of the lowest mechanics" were enrolled in the *Society for Constitutional Information* in Sheffield. (13)

Then, in France came the assault on the Tuileries Palace and the incarceration of the King and his family, where the British ambassador gave warning he would quit Paris "the moment a debate is brought on for deposing the King." In the following year, Blake would have been readying his plates for *Europe* for printing, whose verse also had something informing the poet's revolutionary prophecy. Reporting on incidents of the growing unrest, E.P. Thompson writes: "The crimping-houses used for military recruiting in Holborn, the City, Clerkenwell and Shoreditch were mobbed and destroyed in three days of rioting in August 1794." (14) In his verse Blake essayed this strife:

> The youth of England, hid in gloom, curse the pain'd
>   heavens compell'd
> Into the deadly night to see the form of Albion's Angel.
> Their parents brought them forth & aged ignorance
>   preaches canting,
> On a vast rock, perceiv'd by those senses that are closed
>   from thought—
> Bleak, dark, abrupt it stands, and over shadows London
>   city. (15)

This is an evident restatement of the poet's "mind-forg'd manacles", while there also follows another political reference, although obscure today. One of the first victims of Pitt's anti-Jacobin campaign was not Thomas Paine but the Lord High Chancellor and Keeper of the Seal and Guardian of the King's Conscience, Chancellor Thurlow. He had offended Pitt by opposing his funding bill in Parliament, calling Pitt "a mere reptile of a minister", and Pitt had promptly asked the King for his dismissal, and Thurlow was compelled to relinquish the

Great Seal. Blake wrote of the struggle in which one of "the smitten Angels of Albion" was dispensed with because alarm for the constitution in the King's mind was the greater concern. Thurlow straightaway was sacked as the King tugged off his official insignia on June 15, 1793, and he was seen rushing off, sans his judicial gown and wig, in humiliation and anger through St. James Park. (16)

> Above the rest was heard from Westminster, louder and
>   louder;
> The Guardian of the secret codes forsook his ancient
>   mansion,
> Driven out by the flames of Orc; his furr'd robes and false
>   locks
> Adhered and grew one with his flesh and nerves, and
>   veins shot thro' them,
> With dismal torment sick, hanging upon the wind he fled
> Grovelling, along Great George Street, thro' the Park
>   gate....

The political cartoonist and caricaturist James Gillray, Blake's exact contemporary and with whom he'd studied at the Royal Academy, published, on December 30, 1792, a print to the specific occasion of an Edmond Burke speech before parliament in favor of the Alien Bill, a measure designed to ferment suspicion that foreign agents were abroad in Britain. At the climax of this speech Burke unsheathed a dagger; as he flung it to the floor, pointing to it he said, "This is what you are to gain with an alliance with France." Gillray's editorial was titled "The Dagger Scene; or, the Plot Discover'd", as Burke is caricatured as a vigilant watchman defending Crown and Cross against "atheistical revolutionists". Mocking Burke's histrionics—the thrown dagger, the gesturing hand, his startled auditors—Gillray's print suggests the real plot of the speech was in diverting the public.

Gillray was also to issue a caricature of Paine, 2 January 1793, titled "Fashion before Ease;—or,—a good Constitution sacrificed for a Fantastck form". It shows Paine with both hands grasping onto the laces of the corset of a damsel depicting Britannia, as a measuring tape inscribed "Rights of Man" and a pair of scissors protrude from his pocket. Paine wears the bonnet rouge with cockade, his accustomed pig-tail, his face splotched and reddened from the abuses of alcohol; he has one foot placed securely on the back-side of a demure Britannia, as she glances in consternation over her shoulder, clutching with both hands to a large old oak. Against the oak leans the emblazoned shield of Britannia, a fallen spear on the ground across which has also dropped a severed sprig from the tree, indicating a struggle. Behind the Paine figure, at the corner of a cottage, just under the roof is a plaque which reads, "Thomas Pain, Stay Maker from Thetford. Paris Modes, by express."

The first plate of Blake's *Europe*, titled *Preludium,* which might easily have been part of a portfolio of late 18th century prints, and certainly belongs to the same world as Gillray's cartoons, as David Erdman maintains, shows a bandit or highwayman with a concealed dagger at his back, awaiting the approach of an unwitting wayfarer "on his peaceful pilgrimage, or more specifically, the Patriot on his progress to Paradise." (18) Erdman apprises the face of Blake's assassin as being the same as Gillray's Burke, making his entire design "a prophetic transformation" of the Gillray satire. The connection drawn is persuasive, and is buttressed with further examples, the inference being that among his other aims, Blake intended his "continental prophecies", as they are called, to be indissociably tied to satire of royalty, and of priest-craft.

Blake concludes with a fiery incantation meant to embrace the events that had exploded into the crisis of the epoch: the dialectic of *contraries* that was now at work in the revolt of Energy against the restraining order of kings and priests. He wrote:

> And in the vineyard of red France appear'd the light of
>   his [Orc's] fury,
> The Sun glow'd fiery red!
> The furious terrors flew around
> On golden chariots, raging with red wheels, dropping
>   with blood!
> The Lions lash their wrathful tails!
> The Tigers couch upon the prey and suck the ruddy
>   tide....

In the textual part of *Europe*, awakened from her dream of eighteen-hundred years, "Enitharmon groans & cries in anguish and dismay" to find the years have fled "as if they had not been." And as it is the contrary of restraint and tyranny, of the "thou shalt not", arise the passionate flames of Orc, the revolt and energy that would break their bonds. As Blake gives intimation to a coming phase that is to restore human society to harmony, his vision is not completed by mere revolution:

> Then Los arose: his head he rear'd in snaky thunders clad;
> And with a cry that shook all nature to the utmost pole,
> Call'd all his sons to the strife of blood.

In his plates for *Europe,* Blake was now applying color directly, to be transferred promptly onto the paper, with additional pigmentation and detail to follow. The front piece, as he independently produced it, later was called "The Ancient of Days", is the depiction of a vision Blake said he'd seen hovering at the top landing of his staircase in the Lambeth cottage some time before. It was the figure he called Urizen (a pun on 'your reason,' and derived also from horizon); a bearded, naked and aged man, but depicted here still with the vigor of youth, his white hairs and beard bent horizontally to a raging wind. He crouches within a suspended orb representing the sun darkened by the nether world, as the abyss whirls about him. He is holding the large bright bronze dividers of a compass, as he extends a reaching muscular left arm into the void below, powerfully guiding it in his grasping hand—the moment of reduction from the infinite to the finite.

In Blake's developing mythopoetic vision, Urizen represents an authority figure, a god or a king, whose rule is by tyranny. He represents, too, the tyrannous cycle of ageing, of rising and setting suns, of the rounds of the seasons, and of the priests who insert themselves between fallen humanity and the sky. *Enitharmon*, the female embodiment of fallen nature and history, is the emanation of *Los*; as she has given birth to *Orc* (from the Latin "Orcus" for Hell), the spirit of revolt. Los is associated with the perception of a time that has begun to be industrial—a blacksmith pounding on an anvil with his hammer, a name suggestive of "loss." This arrangement became Blake's alternative testament, as he said in *The Marriage of Heaven and Hell*: "I have also The Bible of Hell: which the world shall have whether they will or no."

Again, *Europe* is a text to which Blake has affixed his name in a defiant gesture on the title page; a work, insistently developing an alternative mythic structure that should be seen as being quite child-like in disposition and character.

Wholly attentive to her guests' needs, Mme. Vernet saw to it that his eminence had no distractions from the assigned task of writing his masterwork, one undertaken without the aid of any reference, and relying totally on an evidently prodigious memory. Their relation-ship was entirely filial, Condorcet accepting the elderly woman as his own mother—he was then fifty—and she establishing a system of surveillance, together with the other lodgers, to guard his safety at every hour.

By the middle of March 1794, the last lines of his disquisition were on paper. Concerned for the viability of his sanctuary, and that his presence might pose a threat to his hostess, on the 1st of April Condorcet appeared in the drawing room, and as he sat down remarked that he'd forgotten his snuffbox in his room. So as not to trouble him, Madame Vernet said she would retrieve it. Condorcet took that as the opportunity to slip out into the street and into the Luxembourg Gardens.

Seeking safe-harbor with a friend, the journalist Jean-Baptiste Suard; he would regretfully be turned away, Suard saying there was another boarder in the house whom he thought surely would betray him. With the nominal disguise of a carpenter's jacket, a woolen cap, and a scarf, Condorcet began walking into the countryside for an undisclosed destination. Becoming disoriented, he was to struggle for three days and nights through thickets and the stone-quarries around the village of Clamart. Chaffed and famished, with torn garments and blistered feet, Condorcet walked into a country tavern.

Settling at table, he called for an omelet. "How many eggs in your omelet?" "A dozen," he replied. This omelet is called *trop imposante,* to which no peasant or workman could aspire.

"What is your trade?" "A carpenter."

On being scrutinized, Condorcet was told carpenters didn't have hands like his. Asked for his papers, he had none. His name was Pierre Simon, he said. On his person only a copy of Horace's *Epistles* was found. He was seized and bound.

On the return to Paris, confined to a temporary lodging in Bourg-la-Reine prison, on the second morning of his imprisonment, he was found lifeless on the flagstones of the prison floor. From apoplexy or from poison? no one has been able to ascertain. It is widely believed that a friend, the physiologist Pierre Jean Georges Cabanis, gave Condorcet a dram of poison fitted into his ring, possibly a mixture of Datura Stramonium and opium, which he meted out for himself in his cell.

"The Notabilities of France disappear one after one," wrote Carlyle, "like lights in a theatre, which you are snuffing out." (19) A dauntless and intrepid adventurer in humanities stream, Condorcet ended his magnificent hymn to human perfectibility with his pledge to after years; asking what is there—

> ...to consul the philosopher lamenting the errors, the flagrant acts of injustice, the crimes with which the earth is still polluted? It is the contemplation of this prospect that rewards him for all his efforts as a part of the eternal chain of the destiny of mankind; and in this persuasion he finds the true delight of virtue, the pleasure of having performed a durable service, which no vicissitude will ever destroy in a fatal operation calculated to restore the reign of prejudice and slavery. This sentiment is the asylum into which he retires, and to which the memory of his persecutors cannot follow him.... (20)

As further testament of his assiduous ethicality, Condorcet left a short essay titled "Advice from an Outlaw to his Daughter." This daughter, nick-named Eliza, then five years old, would devote a life-time to her father's legacy. *Whither his body went?* no one knows.

On his arrest, Thomas Paine was taken to the Luxembourg, the former palace where all of the important political prisoners were held—the French nobility, men as well as women, and the English. Danton and Camille Desmoulins were there in turn.

Approaching Paine and a few others in the courtyard Danton said to Paine—"That which you did for the happiness and liberty of your country, I tried in vain to do for mine. I have been less fortunate, but not less innocent. They will send me to the scaffold; very well, my friends, I shall go gaily." (21)

In a letter to his beloved wife, from the Luxembourg Desmoulins wrote: "[I]t is marvelous that I have walked for five years along the precipices of the Revolution without falling over them, and that I rest my head calmly upon the pillow of my writings.... I have dreamed of a Republic such as all the world would have adored. I could never have believed that men could be so ferocious and so unjust." (22)

As he approached the guillotine that would end his life, Danton requested of Sanson that he hold his severed head before the crowd. "It is worth seeing," he remarked. (23)

Paine's reminiscence written to Lady Smyth has this:

> I was one of the nine members that composed the first Committee of Constitution. Six of them have been destroyed.... Herault Séchelles...was my suppliant as a member of the Committee of Constitution.... He was imprisoned in Luxembourg with me, was taken to the tribunal and guillotined, and I, his principal, left. There were two foreigners in the Convention, Anacharsis Clootz and myself. We were both put out of the Convention by the same vote, arrested by the same order, and carried to prison together the same night. He was taken to the guillotine, and I was left.... One hundred and sixty-eight persons were taken out of the Luxembourg in one night, and a hundred and sixty of them

guillotined next day, of which I knew I was to be one; and the manner I escaped that fate is curious, and has all the appearance of accident. (24)

Three others were lodged together in the room with Paine, all Belgian nationals. Lying prostrate with fever, and in reduced condition, the door was left open by his jailer during the day to let in air and visitors. The inside of the door was against the outer wall facing outwards, and as the turnkey came around marking the pertinent doors with chalk and the number of persons to be taken out for execution the next morning, inadvertently he left his mark on the inside of the door. As night came, the door was again closed, and as he returned, no mark was as yet visible. "The destroying angel" had passed him by.

Paine comments that many days of his imprisonment are blank in his memory. At last, as he regained consciousness he learned of the fall of Robespierre.

"Ah, France!" lamented Paine to Lady Smyth—"thou hast ruined the character of a Revolution virtuously begun and destroyed those who produced it."

20.
The furious wind still rends around

Before midnight, December 19, 1793, in the port of Toulon and along its waterfront there began a stunning display of military pyrotechnics. Continuing into the early morning hours, eight French ships of the line and three frigates were ablaze, as the naval arsenal burned and several powder hulks caught fire in the harbor and blew up. With the sky a deep admixture of flame, smoke, and cinder, the shock of detonations reverberated for miles around, while, in silent procession, British and Spanish squadrons floated out of sight on the horizon. As many as twelve thousand Royalist refugees were being carried away with them, as the forces of the French revolutionary government readied to retake Toulon.

Near dawn when they entered the city gates, the republican troops were led among others by two deputies of the National Convention *en mission,* Paul Barras and Stanislas Fréron. They were met by the naval troops of Toulon who had served under the invaders—Englishmen, Spaniards, Sardinians, Piedmontese, Neapolitans, and French royalists—as a band played revolutionary hymns and buildings and streets were sparingly decorated with the tricolors. With delegations hoping to convince their liberators of their loyalty to the Republic, wearing the revolutionary cockade and holding out laurel wreaths, two hundred marines were hastily lined against a wall to be summarily shot. The next day Fréron wrote his colleagues: "The national vengeance is deployed; we shoot them in force. Already all the naval officers are exterminated. The Republic has avenged herself in a manner dignified of her." (1)

Up till then Stanislas Fréron had been accounted for in some of the principal events in the Revolution, among them the storming of the Bastille and the *journée* of 10 August, 1792. His closest associates were Desmoulins, Robespierre, and Marat, as he too longed to share in their success and fame. A member of the Cordeliers Club, he began bringing out his own paper, *Orateur du peuple,* in May 1790, printed every two days and consisting of eight pages entirely penned by him, as he wrote as many as half the articles published in Desmoulins' journal. Emulating the polemical style of Marat, whom he came to idolize, he considered himself, as did his journalist colleagues, "a missionary of liberty". His actions in Toulon were to somewhat tarnish that reputation.

With looting, rape, and mass shootings occurring over several days, finally legality took hold in the form of a revolutionary tribunal and the guillotine. Thereafter, two hundred heads were lopped off each day for weeks, and would reach such a pitch that on one day in the span of twenty minutes, nineteen heads were tallied as they became disembodied.

One of the observers of these scenes was the twenty-four-year-old Napoleone Buonaparte (as he then spelled his name), captain of the artillery. He had written his younger brother Lucien six months earlier:

> Among so many conflicting ideas and so many different perspectives, the honest man is confused and distressed and the skeptic becomes wicked.... Since one must take sides, one might as well choose the side that is victorious,

the side which devastates, loots, and burns. Considering the alternative, it is better to eat than to be eaten. (2)

Buonaparte was not witness to the initial massacre, having a bayonet wound to his leg tended after the battle. He would be laureled for his crucial command of artillery in the siege, and would soon depart for Italy, with the rank of brigadier general conferred under the auguries of Augustin Robespierre, the handsome younger brother of Maximilien, where he marshaled a French army stranded on the side of a mountain.

The killings in Toulon are estimated to range from seven to eight hundred, with six thousand executions by guillotine. Meanwhile, Fréron was referring to Toulon as "Ville plate" instead of *Port-de-la Montagne* as the Convention suggested, and announced that as many as twelve thousand masons would be summoned from across Southern France so that Toulon "would be razed in 15 days". (3) The National Convention would order that the houses of the wealthy in the interior of the city be demolished, and only those structures servicing the army and navy be saved.

Living a celibate's life as a lodger since relocating to Paris, Maximilien Robespierre occupied simple rooms in the house of a master carpenter named Duplay. Living solely on his salary as deputy of the National Convention, he refused to take a carriage, walking everywhere in his rounds. Fastidious about his dress, as was noted, he was immaculately groomed as he'd risen to power when placed on the Committee of Public Safety, quickly becoming one of its most powerful members. But even then, this was only due to alliance with other effectual representatives such as his younger protégé Louis Antoine

Saint-Just. He would supervise Robespierre's consolidation of power, organizing the arrest and prosecution of many of the well-known figures of the Revolution after the Law of Suspects was decreed 17 September 1793. That law authorized the creation of revolutionary tribunals to try persons suspected of treason against the Republic, and to punish those convicted with death.

Saint-Just came into prominence as he was the first to demand the death penalty for Louis XVI, as Chaumette had also been its vociferous advocate. With the subsequent rise to power of the radical Jacobins, Saint-Just's oratory in the Convention evinced a predilection for the Roman Republic of the classical age. He was puritanical, as was Robespierre, as he was perhaps as some commentators have remarked, stuck in adolescent posturing. Camille Desmoulins wrote of Saint-Just, "He carries his head like a sacred host." (4)

War had provided cover for the Jacobin moratorium on constitutional democracy, with supreme power passing to the sitting Convention, and the Committee of Public Safety setting atop its administrative pyramid. That committee owed its appearance to the first successes of the allied monarchical regimes, led by Austria and Prussia, as the threat these posed to the Republic inspired the decree that the nation was in danger, which led to mass conscription or *levee en masse,* and to the creation of the *Terror.*

By 1793 France was being confronted along all of its frontiers by hostile armies—the alliance of the *1st Coalition* as it is known to historiography. The French armies that were fielded to oppose them became known for the regions of their operation—the armies of the North, of the Ardennes, of the Rhine, of the Coasts of La Rochelle, of the Moselle, of the Alps, of Italy, and of the Pyrenees. These mass conscripted armies were largely due to the organizational ability, as to his capacity to enforce discipline, of the famed mathematician and physicist Lazare Carnot, elected to the Committee of Public Safety 14 August 1793, who took charge of the military situation as one of the Ministers of War. He would be the first strategic planner to implement war in its modern mode.

Two days after Carnot's ascension the *levée en masse* for 300,000 able-bodied men between age 18 and 25 was decreed, published on 23 August as drafted by Barere in consultation with Carnot:

> From this moment until such time as its enemies shall have been driven from the soil of the republic, all Frenchmen are in permanent requisition for the service of the armies. The young men shall fight; the married men shall forge arms and transport provisions; the women shall make tents and clothes and shall serve in the hospitals; the children shall turn old lint into linen; the old men shall betake themselves to the public square in order to arouse the courage of the warriors and preach hatred of kings and the unity of the Republic. (5)

Every citizen a soldier, every soldier a citizen! was the gist of the decree; a deployment of man-power far in excess of what the monarchical states could muster.

With the earlier decree of 24 February, by mid-year, the French army numbered 645,000 men, and would rise to 1,500,000 by September 1794, with 3/4 million of these effectively deployed in fighting forces. At the same time, much of the civilian population was mobilized for employment in armaments production and in other war industries, as well as in supplying food and provisions to the front. National buildings were converted into barracks, public places into armament workshops, while the decree ordered the soil of cellars "shall be washed in lye to extract saltpeter therefrom." The decree further stipulated—"it is authorized to constitute all establishments, manufactories, workshops, and factories deemed necessary for the execution of such works, as well as the requisition for such purpose, throughout the entire extent of the Republic, the artists and workmen who may contribute to their success."

This mobilization was the largest Europe had seen, as it called for an entirely new concept—that of a nation at war. Nearly all subsequent commentary agrees that it was by the extraordinary resort to the *terror* and *the levee en masse* that the Jacobins were able to gain and hold on to power during a time of unprecedented internecine political turmoil within, and the assault of the armies of the 1st Coalition without, as they created a citizen army with reliance on the sans-culotte. But this success was to come at tremendous cost to the nation, to constitutional and representative governance, as to the 'rights of the citizen'.

The overweening influence wielded by Robespierre would reach a peak as the Revolutionary armies began to prevail against their enemies by the end of 1793, only to culminate in his precipitous fall less than two months after he was elected president of the National Convention, June 4, 1794. Robespierre's election was quickly followed by the *Law of 22 Prairial* (June 10, 1794), reorganizing the Revolutionary Tribunal, which deprived the accused of counsel, and removed the need for witnesses to substantiate accusations. In effect, the tribunal became a committee of condemnation, while executions, already unprecedented under the year-long Jacobin reign, dramatically increased. Between June 12 and July 28 nearly 1,300 people were sent to the guillotine in Paris, or at a rate of 28 beheadings per day, many of these officers, as even generals who had lost their commands for the loss of crucial battles or for poor performance, were forced under the blade. With the *terror* as a whole claiming an estimated 55,000 lives nation-wide, Paris, where the practice was particularly egregious, lopped-off upwards to 17,000 heads by the guillotine. (6)

A few days before the law increasing the pace of executions, Robespierre and Jacques-Louis David had put on an elaborate masquerade in the Champ de Mars called the *Festival of the Supreme Being* in which Robespierre led the procession and gave an oration where he dwelt upon his concept of the Supreme Being, espousing the cherished principles of his "republic of virtue" stemming largely from his reading Jean-Jacques Rousseau: "Is it not He whose immortal hand, engraving on the heart of man the code of justice and equality, has written there the death sentence of tyrants? Is it not He who, from the beginning of time, decreed for all ages and for all peoples' liberty, good faith, and justice?"

Robespierre and David's elaborate pageant was contrived to offset the damage done by the de-Christianization campaign and the Cult of Reason promoted by the now guillotined Hébert and his supporters. Seen ascending and descending the promenade of the mountain constructed with timber, plaster-of-Paris and papier-mâché, with boulders and rocks strewn in profusion, shrubs and flowers, all illuminated with mirrors and lamps—at the summit of which was a platform with a Doric column atop which, again, stood the statue of Hercules. Carlyle reported, Robespierre was wearing, "a sky-blue coat, made for the occasion; white silk waistcoat broidered with silver, black silk breeches, white stockings, shoe-buckles of gold;" (7) his detractors remarking, he almost looked as if he thought himself a new Moses. Danton's ally, Jacques-Alexis Thuriot, not impressed by the histrionics, muttered, although apparently audibly—"Look at the bugger! It's not enough for him to be in charge, he has to be God."

In the second of two speeches marking the occasion, as the Parisian public watched from below, the "Incorruptible" intoned:

The monster which the genius of kings vomited over France has gone back into nothingness. May all the crimes and all the misfortunes of the world disappear with it! Armed in turn with the daggers of fanaticism and the poisons of atheism, kings have always conspired to assassinate humanity. If they are able no longer to disfigure Divinity by superstition, to associate it with their crimes, they try to banish it from the earth, so that they may reign there alone with crime. O People, fear no more their sacrilegious plots!

As Robespierre gained new office, and just as the army, too, secured important victories against the royalist coalition, mutterings began to be heard that Robespierre was grasping for dictatorial power. Exhausted, doubtless from his untiring devotion to work, Robespierre had become weary, and for a month after his signature festival was unseen in the Convention, he, appearing when he felt it suitable at the Jacobin Club. In this situation, the compulsion of fear under the grip of the Montagne began to loosen, as the public, too, began to turn its back on the spectacle of perdition. By the time Robespierre reappeared on 9 Thermidor (July 27, 1794) to deliver a two-hour address to the Convention in which he railed against enemies and conspiracies within powerful committees, his voice had ceased to carry weight with many deputies, and his opponents were determined to undo him. Many of the most cynical "terrorists" were in fear for their own lives, and the representatives of the Plain were now becoming indifferent to Robespierre's appeal. Pierre Toussaint Durand de Maillane wrote, "Every tyrant who threatens but does not strike, is himself struck." (8)

On 9 Thermidor, Robespierre spoke of "rogues" who had found a harbor for their traitorous conspiracies in the Convention. But the next day when challenged to name them, he refused. When he was interrupted, his voice cracked as he became hoarse. A deputy shouted: "Danton's blood is suffocating you." When at-last able to resume, Robespierre said "And so it's Danton you want to avenge. Cowards! Why didn't you defend him?"

As the blade poised to put an end to Robespierre at age thirty-six fell, he let out a shriek as the bandage that held his shattered jaw (from a wound, whether self-inflicted or the shot of another directed at him), was wrenched away in order to expose his neck. It was the cry of an ensnared beast that was heard throughout the square, and would be an enduring memory for those hearing it. Twenty-one of his colleagues would perish with him, including Saint-Just, who accepted his fate stolidly, and the younger Robespierre who jumped out of a window at the Hôtel de Ville in a bid to escape, where they had all sought refuge during the night, and had broken both legs. Also going with them was the paralytic Couthon, who had been stabbed and thrown down a flight of stairs, and the commander of the Parisian National Guard, Hanriot, who also jumped from a window, he landing in a passing manure and straw wagon. When finally arrested he was handled so roughly one of his eyes was dislodged from its socket.

Two days before Saint-Just was executed, a woman of the revolution, Théroigne de Mericourt, now incarcerated in an asylum in the Faubourg Marceau, wrote him asking his help in obtaining her release:

> I should be charmed to see you for a moment. If you cannot come to me, if your time does not permit it, could I not be accompanied on the way to see you? I have a thousand things to say to you. It is necessary to establish the union; it is necessary for me to develop my plans, to continue to write as I have written. I have great things to say.... (9)

Her addressee, however, never saw the letter.

In 1807, she was to be sent to La Salpêtrière Hospital where she lived until her death in 1817. Intermittently lucid, she was continually repeating the words and slogans of the Revolution; complaining of burning sensations, she remained mostly naked in her cell, often dousing her body and bedding with cold water, crawling on all fours, and eating straw and excrement and feathers. One clinician diagnosed Théroigne was a victim of "excesses".

The day after Robespierre's demise eighty-two representatives of the Commune mounted the scaffold. August 1 the Convention abolished the law of 22 Prairial and decreed the arrest of the Revolutionary Tribunals notorious prosecutor, Antoine Fourquier-Tinville, who, like Robespierre, had become known for his ruthless and efficient devotion to the Revolution made emblematic by the blade of the guillotine, earning a reputation as one of its most sinister figures. The power in the Convention of the Montagnards had been shattered, as a so-called Thermidorian Convention was ushered in.

As executions were temporarily suspended on the 10th the Convention decreed that all the cases of imprisoned persons be reviewed, as many inmates were released from prisons. On the 24th the number of surveillance committees was reduced to one per district, and their members were ordered to rotate every month, as one-quarter of the members of the Committee of Public Safety were mandated to retire each month, and would not immediately be eligible for reelection. The concentrated powers of the Committees of Public Safety and General Security were abolished, and their responsibilities dispersed among sixteen other committees.

To ensure that certain of the Montagnards would never hold positions in these committees again, on 28 August seven of their deputies were denounced in the Convention. On

September 18, the Convention renounced Robespierre's "constitutional church" and "cult of the Supreme Being".

As the curtain is drawn between acts of that extraordinary prodigy christened *The French Revolution*, let's hear again from the London bard, who, among his notable attributes, had a flare for the theatrical. This, from his *Motto* of the *Songs of Innocence and the Songs of Experience:*

> The Good are attracted by Men's perceptions,
> And think not for themselves;
> Till Experience teaches them to catch
> And to cage the Fairies & Elves.
>
> And then the Knave begins to snarl
> And the Hypocrite to howl;
> And all his good Friends shew their private ends,
> And the Eagle is known from the Owl. (10)

21.

Fill'd with immortal demons of futurity

After Robespierre's downfall, Paine remained incarcerated for three months, even as the surviving Girondin deputies were freed, indicating he had enemies still on the Committee of Public Safety: that the interdiction against Englishmen was still in effect, and there had been no intercession by the United States government on his behalf. Finally, on 18 Brumaire (month of fog, November 3) in the third year of the Republic (1794), the order was published that—"The Committee of General Surety orders that the citizen Thomas Paine be set at liberty, and the seals taken from his papers, on sight of these presents." (1)

Entirely prostrate when taken from the Luxembourg, Paine would convalesce for over a year at the home of the new American Minister to France, James Monroe, responsible finally, for obtaining his release, replacing Morris who moved on to Britain as minister to the Court of St. James. Suffering from an abscess in his side and in critical condition, with those in care of him in expectation of his approaching demise, gradually he recovered what little strength he could gather, and began finishing part two of *The Age of Reason,* already begun during his confinement.

The fall of Robespierre had been received with broad approval among the French public, and the men of 9 Thermidor were under pressure to make full restitution for the perceived injustices and hardships wrought by the *terror*. Eradication of the Jacobin Club became the primary goal of the Thermidorian Convention, along with the destruction of the influence of their sans-culottes supporters. Stanislas Fréron became a fervent spokesman for this reaction, directing an offensive in the National Convention and in his journal against the remainder of the Montagne. (2)

The abolition of the Revolutionary Tribunal and the arrest of its chief prosecutor was the first decisive indication of the change. "All of Paris," Fréron told the Convention, "demands from you the justly deserved punishment of Fourquier-Tinville. I demand that he goes to expiate in Hell the blood he has spilt." (3) His trial lasted 41 days; guillotined May 7, 1795, together with 15 former functionaries of the Revolutionary Tribunal. This episode in the Revolution's history is now called the *White Terror*.

Despite the measures enacted by the anti-Robespierre reaction, and of a press typified by Fréron's *Orateur de peuple* resuming publication 25 Fructidor (month of fruit, or September 11), actual supremacy over the sans-culottes and the Jacobin Club could only be gained in the streets. (4) For that Fréron served as liaison and prompter for an amorphous assortment of disaffected youth spontaneously emerging with the slackening of the restraints of the *terror*. Christened *Muscadins* for their musk perfume, or *Jeunesse dorée* (glided youth), they exhibited themselves as dandies, a species of "cloth animal," Carlyle called them.

With long square-cut coat tails and wearing over-sized

elaborately tied cravats, with a crape knotted around their left arm for the victims of the terror; they wore their breeches tight, with large diaphanously colored lapels, often with black collars symbolizing mourning for Louis XVI. Their heads embellished with "long flowing hair-queues", their weapons of choice were bludgeons loaded with lead they dubbed "constitutions", often twisted wood serving as walking sticks. Coming largely from bourgeois families, and from the families of petit officials and shopkeepers, some had just been released from prison, others were absentee conscripts or army deserters, and in political sentiment often may nominally be republican, or more likely constitutional monarchists, if not out-right royalists. There were two to three thousands of them in Paris, and Fréron saw in them an instrument to realize Thermidorian goals. (5)

Their prime rendezvouses were in the cafés (or coffee houses), where they could discuss the latest news coming out from the reactionary press. Fréron's polemics especially had appeal to them, as he, like-wise took interest in them, praising and encouraging their activities. This symbiosis grew, and as he sought to enhance their effectiveness, they sought to protect their vigilante activities and gain influence within the Convention. Fréron began recruitment, particularly in the Lepelletier section of Paris, a royalist enclave, where the Café des Chartes became the groups designated headquarters. As effective communications were established, meetings became more frequent, with training and drilling provided to turn undisciplined street-brawlers into coordinated combatants.

On September 10, the Jacobin Club was denounced in the Convention as a "nest of brigands"; they were attempting to establish themselves as a rival government in Paris, and were planning an insurrection, it was alleged. In his journal of October 7, Fréron challenged the Jacobin Club:

"Audacious rivals of the National Convention, renounce

your criminal intentions and purify yourselves." (6) As he continued to assert the Jacobins and the sans-culottes were preparing to attack the Convention, Fréron encouraged the *Muscadins* to intensify the campaign against them.

By early October the last of the original members of the Committee of Public Safety had been rotated and replaced by Thermidorians. On 13 Brumaire (Nov. 4) Billaud-Varenne, who had been among the most ruthless promoters of the *terror* made a speech in the Jacobin Club in which he said: "The lion is not dead when it sleeps, and on its awakening, it exterminates all its enemies. The trench is open; the patriots will stir themselves and urge the people to awaken." (7)

Billaud-Varenne's speech occurred in the middle of the important trial of Jean-Baptiste Carrier for his notorious use of the *terror* in Nantes when he was representative *en mission*. His actions were just the kind that Jacobins wanted to retort on Paris, Fréron warned his followers. The allusion to sleeping lions only confirmed it, and this brought the issue of the closure of the Jacobin Club to the fore.

On November 6, a decree was proposed in the Convention that deputies should be forbidden membership in the popular societies during their term of office. Three days later, in the evening, two to three hundred *Muscadins* besieged the Jacobin Club, breaking windows and trying to force the doors, as Jacobins fought back. After several hours, the Committee of General Security sent a force to end the fracas. The next day, with the Jacobins an object of derision, the Convention debated the matter. On the 11th, again in the evening, several thousand *Jeunesse dorée* rallied at the Palais Egalité. Toward 10 in the night Fréron appeared and gave the call to action: "Let us go and surprise the wild beast in its den...Good young men...let us be on our way." (8)

This time the Jacobin hall was easily breached, its members beaten with canes and clubs, as the galleries too were attacked; the women present flogged, and all were driven into the street. The next day the Convention voted to close the hall and the Committee of General Security ordered the police commissioner to confiscate the keys and place a padlock on the main entrance. In issue no. 29 of *Orateur du peuple*, Fréron wrote: "It is a truly touching spectacle to see the joy of the people since the extinction of the Jacobins...Many French citizens have put lights in their windows...some want an official celebration...Amiable French gaiety is finally reborn under the most happy auspices." (9)

On December 8, the surviving seventy-three Girondin deputies were readmitted to the Convention, as the criminalization of émigrés had been lifted, while military action against royalist insurrection continued in Britany and the Vendée. On December 16, Jean-Baptiste Carrier was executed for atrocities known as the "drownings of Nantes", where a large number of priests and nuns, women and children, had been placed on board vessels that were then sunk in the Loire, where it was also asserted male and female youths had been tied together naked, before drowning, called euphemistically "Republican marriages". But Carrier was in fact only one of many representatives who could have been charged with crimes, and anyone reading his correspondence on his activities to the Convention can only find positive evidence for actions carried out at its behest, seemingly for the most assiduously republican and national motives. Carrier's trial took place before the Convention, where he said to his fellow representatives: "Everything here is guilty, including the bell."

Meanwhile in the war the French armies had captured Amsterdam and with it the Dutch fleet, which had become immobilized in ice, as the left bank of the Rhine had been annexed. Finally, the Law of the General Maximum (controls on prices and wages) was abolished December 24, 1794.

Now held to be one of the most notorious and bellicose figures instrumental behind the *terror*, after his assassination Jean-Paul Marat's funerary service had been organized *en grande* by Jacques-Louis David, with the entire National Convention attending, along with thousands of *citoyens e citoyennes*. The body had been interred in the Panthéon, with a eulogy delivered by the Marquis de Sade as delegate of the Section Piques, no doubt with appropriate decorum and solemnity. Marat's heart had been embalmed and kept in an urn at the Cordeliers Club, evidently to fortify the speeches given by its members there; while the port city Le Havre-de-Grace was changed to Le Havre-Marat. By February, 1795, his remains were unceremoniously yanked out of the Panthéon, and his bust and sculptures destroyed all over France, all four thousand of them. February 4 of that year *Le Moniture* reported, "his busts had been knocked off their pedestals in several theatres and that some children had carried one of these busts about the streets...(before) dumping it in the rue Montmartre sewer, to shouts of "Marat, voila ton Panthéon."

The winter of '74-'75 was exceptionally harsh, where the Seine froze over and many of the poor saw their daily ration of bread fall as low as two ounces per person, and where the inflation of *assignats* became rampant. This only led to the printing of more currency, which in turn saw it drop to 10% the value it initially held when issued in 1790; and would fall even lower, so that traders and merchants refused to accept them. The result was that the sans-culottes of Paris were far worse off than they had ever been at any other time. Nicolas Raualt, a Parisian bookseller, wrote his brother a letter dated 24 Germinal year III of the Republic: "Public affairs are a thousand times worse in Paris than with you.... We are lost here in an immense chasm. We have become a hydra with 650,000 heads with as many empty stomachs that have been hungry now for a long time, and it is impossible, not necessarily to satisfy the hunger, but to half feed it."

After the revocation of price controls the debacle came swiftly, as the government was without resources and it became almost incapable of administration. With hunger and poverty pervasive, the rich and the bourgeoisie, with property and with the means to circumvent the economic calamity, were again putting their wealth on display, which had forever been their wont. With finery and ostentatious consumption burgeoning in Paris's restaurants and theatres, an outcry was heard in the streets against the policies of the Thermidorian government. Journalists and agitators began asserting that a major factor in the demise of the Jacobin regime had been their failure to implement the Constitution of 1793, and it was that constitution, they maintained, that now pointed the way out of the current impasse.

One of the journals raising the chorus of "hunger" and "Constitution" was *Tribun du peuple* (Tribune of the People), put out by Francois Babeuf, a journalist retaining the name "Gracchus" after the martyred second century B.C. Roman peoples' tribunes Tiberius and Gaius Gracchus, and who is now known as the first communist revolutionary. Babeuf was perhaps saved from obscurity by the economic conditions prevailing in winter and spring of 1795, believing, as the *Manifesto of Equals* would proclaim when published in the next year, that—"[t]he French Revolution was nothing but a precursor of another revolution, one that will be bigger, more solemn, and which will be the last"—an appraisal that would have resonance throughout the succeeding two centuries.

Babeuf had written in his journal on 9 Pluviose (month of rain, 20 Jan.-18 Feb.), that an insurrection "pacifiquement, even more than May 31" [1793], was desirable. "Now we will shock certain men not expecting this conclusion: the word 'insurrection' no longer signifies torrents of blood and heaps of corpses. We have experienced that insurrections can rest on other bases." (10)

Shortly afterward Babeuf was arrested, and his newspaper "solemnly burnt" by the *Jeunesse Doree* in the Theatre des Bergeres. He would be imprisoned till October of that year in Arras, where he was able to bring the formulation of his political program to completion, as there was a very great number of political revolutionaries incarcerated at that time, making for a rich tutorial milieu. It was with 13 Vendemiaire (month of vintage, 22 Sept.-21 Oct.) when Bonaparte gave a royalist insurrection a "whiff of grape shot", that Babeuf would conclude the Thermidorian Convention could be brought down by an armed conspiracy with support among the sans-culottes. The term Babeuf used for the social order he desired was "bonheur commun" (common happiness); the word *communism* only coming into usage in subsequent decades.

Throughout the winter, in the streets of Paris there were repeated demonstrations by desperate hungry women, which became a flood, joined too by squalid hungry men, shouting "Bread, bread and the Constitution of 93" as spring came. "Paris has risen, once again, like the Ocean-tide", Carlyle wrote. On 12 Germinal (April 1) as this ocean-tide swept into the Convention Hall—"Bread and Constitution" was its desperate cry.

The demonstrators had easily swept aside the *Jeunesse dorée* who tried to block their path, and the gendarmes, but unarmed they were no match for the National Guard. Their leaders, it was evident, had been unable to marshal the sections, as had been so necessary to the success of previous *journées*. This time *les miserable* were assuaged by the remaining deputies of the Montagne, as they were coaxed into marching past the bar and exiting the chamber. But Paris was in tumult as a result, as the Panthéon and Cité sections declared themselves in permanent session. That night by order of the Convention, the city was placed under martial law, as disquiet continued in Faubourg Quinze-Vingts.

In consequence of "12 Germinal", as this *journée* is known, the Convention immediately voted the deportation of three ex-members of the Committee of Public Safety to Guyana, including Billaud-Varenne, and ordered the arrest of eight prominent Montagnards, as the leaders of the demonstrations were also arrested. In the following week, there was to be a wholesale disarming of sans-culottes who played a role in the *terror*, with an estimated 1600 effected in Paris, and which was extended to the Provinces.

On 14 Germinal the Convention had appointed a seven-person commission to "prepare" the 1793 Constitution for ratification, but such preparation implied a thorough re-writing of that document, while eliminating its most radical provision, universal male suffrage.

In the subsequent weeks, insurrection was again gestating in the viscera of Paris, one deputy in the Convention, Rovere, reporting in that body on the presentiments he'd heard. Then on 30 Floreal (May 19, 1795) an anonymous manifesto was distributed throughout the faubourgs and in central Paris, under the title *Insurrection of the People to Obtain Bread and Reconquer Its Rights*. This was the signal for the movement to begin, as it provided agitators with a clear-cut objective expressed in a single word: bread. (11)

For its political goals, the plan was for putting into practice the '93 constitution, and for the election of a legislative assembly, and the freeing of imprisoned "patriots", viz. Jacobins and sans-culottes. I-4 *Prairial* was to be the last of the sans-culotte centered uprisings and may be considered a precursor of the popular revolts to follow in the nineteenth century, making their debut in Paris in June 1832, whose distinctive feature would be a proletariat engaged in raw combat with the bourgeois state. Carlyle, as he concluded his account of *Prairial* had written—"Sans-Culottism. . . was it the frightfulest thing ever born of time?" It was one of them he concluded, and "it still lives, and is not dead but changed." (12)

The sheer doggedness of this 'plebian' uprising was of *woman born*: (13) because it was she who saw her suckling's drawing blood at her breast, and not milk. As it was women who came into the streets in the early morning hours, assembling in front of bakeries in Popincourt, Gravillers, and the Droits de'l Homme sections. As it was women who rang the tocsin in the Faubourg Saint-Antoine and in the Jardin des Plantes, and women who went into the workshops of Faubourg du Nord calling the men out. Finally, the commencement of the revolt was marked by waves of women streaming through the alleys and intersections, and along the boulevards toward the Convention, calling everyone to insurrection. One ringleader cried—"We must support the faubourgs, who are going to come down. All these rascals will have to fart." (14)

As they issued out of Faubourgh Saint-Antoine, women began forcing other women from their houses; and they were driving them from the shops where they worked or hoped to obtain their meager ration of bread—beseeching they refuse their rations. And they were stopping passing coaches—"You will March!" was their demand. Men joining the march were urged to chalk the slogan "bread and the Constitution of 1793" on their hats, as women had affixed the same to their bonnets, or on their blouses. One police observer later wrote—"Bread is the foundation of their insurrection physically speaking, but the Constitution is the soul." (15)

Around ten o'clock a troop of about four hundred women set out for the Convention, drum beating double time, led by a "coal woman" dressed as a man and wearing a three-cornered hat adorned with a red and blue plume, with an unsheathed saber in hand. By the end of the morning, with the growing welter of women, along with miscellaneous men, the Tuileries was mobbed on the fares in front of the Convention. As they insisted they be granted entrance, those women already sitting in the galleries rushed down to join them, and they were able to wrench the bronze doors of the Convention hall open.

National Guard with bayonets and gendarmes with sabers now pushed in to drive the women back, as the galleries were cleared by gendarmes and by *Jeunesse dorée,* who flayed women with postilion's whips. The deputies in the Tuileries theatre now declared the "leaders of demonstrations" to be "outlaws" and called on "all good citizens" to defend the national representatives. (16)

With their bid to enter the hall barred, and with several women receiving cuts or superficial wounds, rumor was soon overstating the issue, and indignation grew in the faubourgs. "Run, run, go to the Convention, women are being killed there," became the cry. By the early afternoon armed men were assembling in the Faubourg Saint-Antoine ready to descend on the Convention, as there was general tumult in Saint Marceau, in the quarter of the Temple, in the Rues Saint-Denis and Saint-Martin, and especially in the Cité. The leading bourgeois journal, *Le Moniteur,* published a notice that suggests its reporter had just opened his pocket-watch: "At three thirty-three a large crowd of women and men armed with guns, pikes, and sabers entered the Convention." One historian recorded this enduring impression of that scene: "The convention presented the appearance of a battery or strong hold disputed by contending armies. Bayonets crossed and flashed, and a volley of musketry poured into it, luckily had no effect, except to shatter the walls and windows." (17)

Deputies were chased from their seats, *Le Moniteur*'s article continued, in order that the demonstrators could have them for themselves, while deputies took refuge on the upper benches. (18) For a time, there was pandemonium, as deputies were shouted down, as some of the sans-culottes endeavored to give speeches, and there was a general din and rolling of drums. The president of the convention, Boissy d'Anglas, sitting in his chair elevated above the Convention floor, bayonets and pikes glimmering menacingly around his head, put his hat on to signify the session was suspended; he, however, continuing in his chair. One of the deputies, Jean-Bertrand Féraud, a young man with a stentorian voice with carefully powered and quaffed hair, attempted to clear the hazard from before the President's chair. A woman who'd earlier received a superficial wound, recounted: "We had entered the Convention to demand bread, and these scoundrels said that we were riffraff. I noticed the deputy Féraud and grabbed him by the neck. Several of us got together and dragged him out of the hall by his hair and then cut off his head." (19)

As Féraud was engaging in his harangue he had been grazed in the shoulder by a pistol shot, fired, it was believed, by a woman. As he fell to the floor, another hit him on the head with her clog, as a knife in the hand of a man sufficed to remove his head. This murder, evidently un-premeditated, and in the circumstance, might be considered almost accidental, some have supposed the unfortunate Féraud had been mistaken for Fréron. (20)

At that point in his career, Deputy Féraud, who earlier had

been a protégé of both Danton and Robespierre, but had protested the exclusion of the Girondins, was charged with ensuring that supplies of grain and food reached Paris. He managed to escape the proscription of his colleagues because he'd been a representative *en mission* to the Army of the Pyrenees. Joining the Thermidorian reaction, he led troops, together with Paul Barras, in rounding up Robespierre and his confreres at the Hôtel de Ville the night before their execution. The sight of Féraud's head on the end of a pike, re-introduced in the Convention a short while later, and garishly paraded around the chamber, is well-known for being depicted in a painting by Alexander-Evariste Fragonard circa 1831, which shows Boissy d'Anglas occupying the president's chair as he impassively salutes Féraud's grizzled head held aloft amid the general riot and pandemonium of the sans-culottes.

About nine that evening D'Anglas quit the chair, whether in horror or from fatigue, when Vernier took his place, commanding silence. Finally, the document that had heralded the deluge was read to the deputies, "The Insurrection of the People..." which enumerated eleven demands and the political means of achieving them:

> The people, considering that we are being inhumanly starved to death by the government...have made the following determination: ...Today, without delay, the citizens of Paris, both men and women, will proceed en masse to the National Convention to demand: 1, Bread; 2, The abolition of the "revolutionary government", of which every faction, each in turn, has taken advantage to ruin, starve, and subjugate the people; 3, [T]he immediate proclamation and establishment of the Democratic Constitution of 1793; 4, The removal of the current government. . .and the arrest [of its] members, Etc. (21)

Breaking ranks with the Convention, the Montagnard deputies remaining in the Convention were able to pass legislation releasing "patriots" arrested after Germinal, restore sectional assemblies, establish an extraordinary food council, and sanction searches of houses of suspected hoarders, while implementing a special committee to realize the Constitution of 1793. But the several hours that passed in rancorous chatter and speechifying, not to mention the macabre display of Féraud's head, had given the Thermidorian deputies ample time to send representatives to call upon supporters in sections belonging to the "party of order"—with Butte Moulins, Museum, and Lepeletier in the forefront.

Around midnight, as those occupying the Convention began to disperse, the supporters of the Thermidorian Convention, together with National Guard and gendarmes, entering on the right of the chamber and leaving the doors on the left open, were able to force the sans-culottes from the faubourgs out of the Convention hall and out of the Tuileries environs.

The Thermidorian deputies immediately nullified all the motions passed by the Montagnards, burned the minutes and arrested the deputies. Adolphe Thiers, without irony, for indeed such an attitude was not yet conceivable, offered these lessons for the insurrection of *1 Prairial* in his ten-volume history of *The French Revolution*:

> All that the insurrectional committee had been able to do was to set the populace upon the convention; but... obscure leaders, such as are left at the fag-end of a party, having at their disposal neither the commune, or the staff of the sections, or a commandant of the armed force, or deputies, had not been able to direct the insurrection with the prudence and the vigor which would have insured its success. (22)

As reprisals were called for, particularly against those Montagnards "who had rendered themselves conspicuous by extraordinary missions in the departments", i.e. by instituting and overseeing the *terror*, one of the leading Thermidorian deputies declared:

> Let us have no more half measures. The object of this day's movement was to re-establish the Jacobins, and particularly the commune: we must destroy what remains of them...This is only the prelude to the measures which the committee will submit to you. Vengeance, citizens, men, vengeance against the murderers...Let us take every advantage of the unskillfulness of these who fancy themselves the equals of those who overthrew the throne, and strive to compete with them.... (23)

It was decreed that on the following Quintidi (Sunday) 4 Prairial (May 24), the sections would assemble and disarm "the agents of the tyranny which preceded the 9th Thermidor". It was also decided, until further order, women would not be admitted as spectators into the tribunal councils. Then at three in the morning when all was quiet in the streets of Paris, the Convention adjourned till ten o'clock, 2 Prairial. (24)

But the defeat of the *journée* only provided impetus for a mightier demonstration as a call to arms sounded in the Quinze-Vingts section an hour before the Convention's recess. And as morning fairly began, the tocsin was renewed in Fidelite and Droits de L'Homme where "illegal" assemblies were convened, with Arcis, Gravillers, and Popincourt, following suit. The Faubourg Saint-Antoine was again to be the primary driver of the machinery of insurrection, as the sans-culottes sprang to arms and were marching on the Tuileries by ten o'clock that morning. An insurrectionary committee had proclaimed itself in "permanent insurrection", establishing its headquarters in the accustomed place, in the house of the brewer Santerre.

One of three insurgent columns issuing from Saint-Antoine was led by a West Indian wheelwright and captain of the gunners of Popincourt, Guillaume Delorme by name. As these marched on the Convention, without the concourse of people seen on the previous day, they were supported by sections of the center, all told a force under arms estimated to be in the range of 20,000 experienced and drilled men. (25) Converging on the Place du Carrousel by eleven o'clock, their arrival at the Tuileries was almost simultaneous with that of men from the Lepelletier, Butte-des-Moulins, and of the other sections, as the troops of "loyalists" and "patriots" had comingled on the tramp down the boulevards.

Deploying on opposite sides, so as to defend or to assail the Convention, they presented a vast pageant; together with the National Guard and the gendarmes present, with the *Jeunesse dorée* and the cavalry of the sections under General DuBois, the "party of order" formed a troop upwards of 40,000 men. As both sides fell into their arrangements, in an propitious nod to their prospects, the canonries of the "loyal" sections—mechanics and revolutionists all—changed sides joining the insurgents of the Popincourt, Montreuil, and the Quinze-Vingts sections. Guns were now loaded and trained on the Convention, as shouts "To arms!" were heard. Delorme, captain of the gunners lit a fuse, and at that moment, "whether victory would remain with the defenders of the national representative" was uncertain. (26)

With the sounds outside filtering into the Convention, members rose to speak, deputy Legendre exclaiming: "Representatives! Be calm, and remain at your post. Nature has decreed that we must all die; whether a little sooner or a little later is of no consequence. Good citizens are ready to defend you. Meanwhile the most becoming motion is to keep silence." (27)

Outside, with combatants deployed and ready, voices broke across the standoff, prompting answering voices on the opposing side. Wasn't it grievous for citizens to slaughter one another? At least they ought to explain themselves and try to understand one another. As the ranks on both sides wavered, members of the committee's present introduced themselves endeavoring to encourage reconciliation. In a short time, it was agreed a deputation should be sent to the bar of the Convention to urge they send out twelve members to join the fraternization.

The Convention however was reluctant to give its assent. Still, it might prevent the effusion of blood! Soon twelve deputies were out talking among to the sans-culottes led sections, with men on both sides engaging the other. With this co-mingling, Thiers noted:

> The uncultivated man of a lower class is always sensible of the amicable demonstrations of the man who is placed above him by dress, language, and manners. The soldiers of the three adverse battalions were affected, and declared that they would neither spill the blood of their fellow citizens, or be deficient in the respect due to the national convention. (28)

The leaders of the sans-culottes, however, insisted that their petition be heard; whereupon General DuBois and the twelve representatives consented to introduce a deputation from the battalions at the bar. The spokesman of this group began: "We are commissioned to demand at your hands the Constitution of 1793, and the release of the patriots." The galleries shouted, "Down with the Jacobins!"

As silence was imposed, the speaker continued: The citizens of the faubourgs were ready to retire, but they would rather die than yield with their concerns unresolved. The president replied that the Convention had just passed three decrees relative to articles of consumption, and these were read. Then the president added that they would examine the proposals of the petitioners, but that all should defer to their judgement on them. He invited the petitioners "to the honours of the sitting."

Outside, the antagonists continued intermingling, sans-culotte with bourgeois; as the former realized they were opposed by twice their number. Sensing the deficit, without desisting from their demands, nor from their arms, they began to return to the faubourgs. All participants had shown, remarked historian Eyre Evans Crowe, writing about the time of Carlyle, "a forbearance and a fear of shedding blood, certainly credible to them." But he also noted that this acquiescence by the sans-culottes was a sign of their growing apathy, and that they had at last become weary of disorder. (29)

On the morning of 3 Prairial, the Convention consolidated the army troops in the vicinity of Paris dispersed protecting grain shipments, authorizing them to resort to force to assure "public tranquility". It also decreed, six months imprisonment for anyone beating a drum without an order, and the death penalty to anyone beating the *générale* without authorization by "a representative of the people." A military commission was formed for the trial and execution of any prisoner taken on 1st Prairial, and the decree of accusation was converted to a decree of arrest for all the Montagnards implicated in the uprising, and extended to the Germinal rising. The citizens of the "loyal" sections called to defend of the Convention were to remain under arms, and were to welcome the youths called *Muscadins.*

The first person to be tried and condemned was the decapitator of Féraud, who the commission directed should be executed that very day. That afternoon as the culprit was conveyed to the scaffold, an armed contingent from the Faubourg Saint-Antoine seized the prospective executant, dispersing the gendarmerie and spiriting him to safety. With preparations begun to fortify the faubourg to withstand siege, barricades were thrown-up as the populace remained under arms.

Now the Convention began its arrangements, appointing General Menou commander of a force consisting of three to four thousand troops of the line, 20,000 men or more of the armed sections, and several thousand *Jeunesse dorée.* Their advance came on 4 Priarial, as Menou cut the faubourgs communications with the adjoining sections, occupying five major outlets. The sprightly attired *Muscadins,* emboldened to lead the way, marched down the principal approach, the Rue Saint-Antoine, and were able to advance until the enemy's barricades loomed in their front. Suddenly discovering they were surrounded on all sides, as women appeared at every window ready to hurl stones down on them, their elaborate motif became one of self-mockery. But the husbands and brothers, fathers and sons of the women had no intention of trashing the dandified youths, and they were allowed to retreat; their bravado chastened as some were grabbed by their oversized lapels, and given a drubbing.

With these preliminaries concluded, Menou readied his cannon to bombard the sans-culottes in their re-doubt, first calling for a deputation to hear his demands. All arms must be surrendered he said, together with the murderer of Féraud. In the event of refusal, they would be declared in a state of rebellion and all the means at his disposal would be brought to bear against them.

With capitulation determined; a search was begun for the offender, and the cannon surrendered, as Menou was able to return to the Convention to report they no longer had anything to fear from insurgent sans-culottes. The military commission immediately commenced the trial of prisoners. Thiers clinched the matter this way:

> It condemned to death some gendarmes who had sided with the rebels, some mechanics and shopkeepers, members of the revolutionary committees, and taken *flagrante delicto* on the 1st Prairial. In all the sections the disarming of the patriots and the apprehension of the most notorious individuals commenced; and as one day was not sufficient for this operation, the sections were to continue their sittings till they had concluded.

The number of sans-culottes disarmed and arrested is thought to be considerably greater than the 10,000 reported May 28 in the *Gazette Française*, as in several sections former members of revolutionary committees and soldiers of the armée revolutionaire were arrested or disarmed irrespective of their involvement in either Germinal or Prairial.

The Commission sat for ten weeks, trying 132 persons, acquitting the bulk of these, while nineteen were condemned to death, including six Montagnard deputies. These deputies of the Montagne, considering Liberty undone, tried to terminate their existence by summarily stabling themselves, each with a single knife they took up in turn; the knife passing from one to another—memorialized in a painting by Charles Ronot titled *Les derniers Montagnards* (1882).

The first, fearing he'd failed to make the mortal thrust,

stabbing himself several times—in his breast, in his throat, in his face. The next made a clean blow, expiring as he fell; and from his hand to those remaining, whose wounds were not fatal: to be conveyed, bleeding and stained with their own blood, to the scaffold. The first maintaining his composure, with dignified bearing; the second, mortified at his failure, calling out, "Enjoy, enjoy your triumph, messieurs royalists!"; a fourth, as the fatal blade was drawn-up, declaring "that none could die more devoted to his country, and more anxious for her prosperity and liberty."

Again, hear it from Thiers:

All hearts revolted on learning the particulars of this execution and it caused the Therimdoreans merited disgrace. Thus, in that long succession of conflicting ideas, all had their victims, the very ideas of clemency, humanity, reconciliation, had their holocausts; for in revolutions no one idea can remain guiltless of human blood. (30)

22.
The Beast & the Whore
rule without controls

Few in France knew more about the Revolution in all its phases than Thomas Paine, or had more intimate acquaintance with its principal actors. He was witness as well to the terror wielded by both factions, Jacobinian and Therimdorian, as he knew too first-hand the perilous influences that poisoned people's minds, as undoubtedly, he was unique among all those who'd been deputies in the Convention in that he had nothing in his past performance to cause him embarrassment or the fear of enemies.

That spring as he convalesced in the home and with the family of James Monroe, among the sounds reaching Paine's ear would have been those of the demonstrations with the chant "Bread and the Constitution of ninety-three!" The constitution that those thronging in the streets were calling for, was, to Paine's presentiment, really not the Robespierrean corruption "given out...as an opiate to keep the country asleep", but the one over which he and Condorcet had labored and finally sacrificed. (1) As the summer approached, through a Committee of Eleven led by Boissy d' Anglas, the Convention was deliberating on a new constitution, with the Abbé Sieyès making the prime behind the scenes contribution. In Paine's view, there was now likely to be some element of monarchy in it.

As he was restored to his seat in the Convention together with the Girondin deputies, he prepared a "Dissertation on First Principles of Government", a condensed statement of the principles underlying the constitution supplanted by the Jacobins. Paine wrote:

> Had a Constitution been established two years ago, as ought to have been done, the violences that have since desolated France and injured the character of the revolution, would, in my opinion, have been prevented. The nation would have had a bond of opinion, and every individual would have known the line of conduct he was to follow. But, instead of this a revolutionary government, a thing without either principle or authority, was substituted in its place; virtue or crime depended upon accident, and that which was patriotism one day, became treason the next. (2)

In this testimony, floating like a banner over the entire misadventure known as the *Great Terror*, he included this:

> An avidity to punish is always dangerous to liberty. It leads men to stretch, to misinterpret and to misapply even the best laws. He that would make his own liberty secure, must guard even his enemy from oppression; for if he violates this duty he establishes a precedent that will reach himself.

The new constitution under consideration was to have a bicameral legislature, with a Council of Five Hundred and a Council of Ancients with two hundred and fifty seats. To assure a separation of powers the Ancients could not initiate laws, but had the power of veto over those proposed by the Council of Five Hundred. A total of thirty thousand qualified voters was required to constitute an electoral assembly in each of the French cantons, who would then choose representatives to elect the members of both houses. Each of the members selected would have a term of three years, with one-third being renewed each year.

Francois Antoine de Boissy d'Anglas, leading the Committee of Eleven, a moderate sitting with the Plain, but who supported Robespierre during the early stage of his ascension, serving on the Committee of Public Safety, and during the Directory became associated with royalism, informed the Convention:

> We propose to you to compose an executive power of five members, renewed with one new member each year, called the Directory. This executive will have a force concentrated enough that it will be swift and firm, but divided enough to make it impossible for any member to even consider becoming a tyrant. (3)

A single chief would be dangerous, he stressed, and each member would preside in rotation for a three-month term, during which each would have "the signature and seal of the head of state." Directory members had to be at least forty years old, and the candidates would be chosen by secret ballot in the Council of Five Hundred, whereupon five members were to be selected by secret ballot in the Council of Ancients. One director chosen by lot was to be replaced each year; ministers from the Departments were to aid the directors, but would not form a cabinet nor be delegated powers of government. Neither directors nor ministers could have a seat in either house, and neither had a voice in legislation or taxation.

The municipality of Paris, which had dominated events through the phases of the Revolution, was abolished, as the political clubs had been, and the city was placed under direct authority of the national government. Paris became a new department, the Department of the Seine, and was divided into twelve *arrondissments*, each governed by its own committee.

The constitution of Year III began, as had the earlier versions, with the *Declaration of the Rights of Man and of the Citizen*, declaring that "the Rights of Man in society are liberty, equality, security, and property." It prohibited armed assemblies and public meetings of political societies, as it stipulated only individuals or public authorities could tender petitions. In order to vote, citizens need meet property and residency standards, as well as educational requirements such as literacy. In towns of over six thousand, a voter had to own or rent property with a revenue equal to the standard income of at least one hundred fifty to two hundred days of work, and have resided in his residence for at least a year. This effectively disenfranchised most of the French population, particularly those who'd made gains during the previous era. Thus, the constitution was an instrument codifying the defeat of both the Jacobins and the Commune by the Thermidorian reaction, and of their paramount ally, the sans-culottes. The constitution was debated 4 July thru 17 August, and formerly adopted on 22 August 1795.

On July 7 Paine appeared for the last time in the Convention to give his address. Ascending to the tribune "with feeble step" and with white hair, to stand with his translator as the speech was read, that address, said to be intensely received, began:

> Citizens, The effects of a malignant fever, with which I was affected during a rigorous confinement in Luxembourg, have thus long prevented me from attending at my post in the bosom of the Convention; and the magnitude of the subject under discussion, and no other consideration on earth, could induce me now to repair to

my station. A recurrence to the vicissitudes I have experienced, and the critical situation in which I have been placed in consequence of the French Revolution, will throw upon what I now propose to submit to the Convention the most unequivocal proof of my integrity, and the rectitude of those principles which have uniformly influenced my conduct. In England I was proscribed for having vindicated the French Revolution, and I have suffered a rigorous imprisonment in France, for having pursued a similar line of conduct. During the reign of terrorism I was a prisoner for eight long months, and remained so above three months after the era of the Thermidor. I ought, however, to state, that I was not persecuted by the *people*, either of England or France. The proceedings in both countries were the effects of the existing despotism in their respective governments. But, even if my persecution had originated in the people at large, my principles and conduct would have still remained the same. Principles which are influenced and subject to the control of tyranny have not their foundation in my heart. (4)

In regard to much that was included in the proposed constitution (there were 377 articles contrasted with 124 in constitution of 1793), Paine took exception to some of its restrictions, such as the radical narrowing of voter qualifications, although he deferred to the sagacity of its basic structure:

> If you subvert the basis of the Revolution, if you dispense with principles and substitute expedients, you will extinguish that enthusiasm which has hitherto been the life and soul of the revolution; and you will substitute in its place nothing but cold indifference and self-interest, which will again degenerate into intrigue, cunning, and effeminacy.

This was the last time he was to appear in person in the political arena. Shortly after this there was a report on Paine's condition in a letter of James Monroe to a relative, Judge Joseph Jones of Fredericksburg, Virginia, dated September 15, 1795. Concerning travel plans to see the Judge's son and his tutor at Saint Germaine, where they intended to stay several months in the autumn, Monroe remarks they'd been obliged to cancel—

> ...on account of the ill-health of Mr. Paine, who has lived in my house for about ten months past. He was upon my arrival confined in the Luxembourg, and released on my application; after which, being ill, he has remained with me. For some time the prospect of his recovery was good; his malady being an abscess in his side, the consequence of a severe fever in the Luxembourg. Latterly his symptoms have become worse, and the prospect is that he will not be able to hold out more than a month or two at the furthest. I shall certainly pay the utmost attention to this gentleman, as he is one of those whose merits in our Revolution were most distinguished. (5)

William Blake's avowal of support for the French Revolution and for the American Revolution before it, and for all others, is often underestimated, or at any rate does not appear in the foreground in much of the analysis of the work of this singular artisan—poet and artist. That he had had the temerity, often remarked upon, during a period to appear in public in London wearing the French Revolutionary headwear, symbol first of Liberty and then of radical republicanism, showed his identification and solidarity not only with France but with London's laboring and artisan class. Appearing in May 1790, introduced by a Girondin "statesman", by the time the sans-culottes invaded the Tuileries Palace in June 1792, and Louis XVI had been compelled to wear the *bonnet rouge*, it was fully in vogue.

To Blake the blindness of brute force corresponded to a divine form of excess; what was always at hazard for him was that which was "too great for the eye of man", the "portions of eternity." In 1800, writing of his associates and of those who were his antecedents, as well as some of the events of his time, Blake gave the following account—"When Flaxman [the sculptor] was taken to Italy, Fuseli [the painter] was given to me for a season ... Milton lov'd me in childhood and shew'd me his face ... Shakespeare in riper years gave me his hand...."

Blake continues his precis:

Paracelsus & Behmen appear'd to me, terrors appear'd in
the Heavens above
And in Hell beneath, & a mighty & awful change threated
the Earth.
The American War began. All its dark horrors passed
before my face.
Across the Atlantic to France. Then the French Revolution
commenc'd in thick clouds,
And my Angels have told me that seeing such visions I
could not subsist on the Earth.... (6)

Clearly Blake's feeling of solidarity was not confined to the Revolution's earliest phases nor shunning its darker episodes, but continued into 1794, even as it became evident that the revolution, in its most embracive and most radical social character, was headed for reversal and defeat. *The Tyger,* published by Blake in 1794, lucidly expresses his reaction to the *terror,* even as more facile commentary overlooks this, assured and misled by Blake's illustration of the quadruped in that text—looking somewhat like a stuffed child's toy rather than a sanguinary beast. But just as the Revolution's prospects darkened Blake had etched into the marginal space of plate 2 of *America* he was then preparing for printing, beneath the figure of Orc (the spirit of rebellion and freedom) budding from furrows of earth, the following quatrain:

> The stern Bard ceas'd, ashamed of his own song; enraged
>   he swung
> His harp aloft sounding, then dash'd its shinning frame
>   against
> A ruin'd pillar in glittering fragments; silent he turn'd
>   away,
> And wander'd down the vales of Kent in sick & drear
>   lamenting.

Erdman maintains, as Blake had advertised *America* as early as October 1793, the "ruin'd pillar" on which the bard shatters his harp, suggests it may have been the vote of Parliament in January 1793 for war with the French Republic—a shock felt by all English Jacobins. Blake masked this added script in his printings in those years, it appearing, scholars maintain, only in two printings in subsequent decades. In the final plate of *Europe* depicting a ruined pillar in the midst of a raging fire, a bard (or Los) is seen rescuing a woman, whom he carries on his shoulder, and a child from the flames. (7) The culmination of all his hopes for Revolution?

In 1795, in the period reached in this narrative, as a kind of summation and as a natural progression from brushing color on copper plates and printing it, Blake was to paint a series of twelve images two of which remain among his most well-known, that were arranged in pairs as "contraries," as was his penchant. In these, Newton is coupled with Nebuchadnezzar.

The painter's method, which Blake called "tempura," was to take a millboard and draw his design upon it in ink, then paint it in roughly and quickly with pigments mixed with glue. Before the paint had dried, he would print it on a wet paper, completing the image afterward in watercolors and ink. A contemporary described the technique: "This plan he had recourse to, because he could vary slightly each impression; and each having a sort of accidental look, he could branch out so as to make each one different. The accidental look they had was very enticing." He could as he wished re-print an image by applying new paint.

With *Newton* and *Nebuchadnezzar* Blake depicts a "fallen" material world, where each figure is symmetrically set within the flat plane of the composition, symbolic of the repressed imagination and of man enslaved by his senses, conditions antithetical to Blake's vision. Blake's print of Nebuchadnezzar, Gilchrist wrote, shows the—"...mad king crawling like a hunted beast into a den among the rocks; his tangled golden beard sweeping the ground, his nails like vultures' talons, and his eyes full of sullen terror." The hair on the body of the figure is bestial, with reptilian or "toad-like ... spottings on the skin...." (8)

In the *Book of Daniel,* the great King of Babylon was deemed an enemy of the god of the Israelites for destroying the temple in Jerusalem, and as his captive, the prophet Daniel interprets a dream of the king which foretells of his downfall unless he accepts the Israelites god, when he is "driven away from men, and did eat grass like an ox." This madness lasts for seven years, when the King's lucidity is restored as he gives praise to the deity. For Blake, a contemporary parallel in creating the image was Britain's George III. After losing "his" American colonies the sovereign had been called the "mad King"; afflicted by mania, he would speak continuously for hours at a time, so that he foamed at the mouth and became hoarse, sometimes convulsing. Witnesses spoke of the king's "incessant loquacity"; where he frequently repeated himself, and his sentences could have as many as four hundred words with eight verbs, as his vocabulary became more complex. The affliction, first coming upon him in an incapacitating way in 1788, perplexed his doctors, as rumors spread about his condition. A regency was long considered by William Pitt and the King's ministers to stand in on royal functions, and that finally became the recourse late in George III's long reign.

Again, Blake's graphic depiction of the sovereign's condition with *Nebuchadnezzar* bears the contours of the contemporaneous scene, in the war of Pitt's government against the French republic. Deciding it could take advantage of France's preoccupation with war on its frontiers by seizing Saint-Domingue, and re-instituting slavery there, the Royal Navy landed on the island in September 1793. But, with furious resistance from the blacks, Britain only succeeded militarily in establishing several tenuous coastal enclaves. These enclaves too were devastated by yellow fever or the "black vomit", and subjugating the colony became impossible. By the following year, 12,000 Englishmen had been expended in the West Indies, as Pitt would commit far more manpower and treasure to the Caribbean than he did to Europe in the years 1793-1798, an ordeal paralleling the tribulations of Nebuchadnezzar in the prophetic imagination of Blake, the painter.

Realizing France's hold on the island would be strengthened by freeing the blacks, slavery was abolished by the National Convention in February 1794. The Convention's decree reads: "The National Convention declares the abolition of Negro slavery in all the colonies; in consequence it decrees that all men, without distinction of color, residing in the colonies are French citizens and will enjoy all the rights assured by the constitution."

Then on 21 June 1795, assisting French Royalists in a landing called the Quiberon Expedition, France was invaded on its Brittaney coast in an effort to support the Vendée revolt; the Royal Navy committing 60 troop transports protected by two squadrons of warship. Carrying two divisions of French émigrés, about 3,500 men, these landed together with three regiments of British foot soldiers, bringing with them supplies and the accouterments for an army of 40,000. This incursion was repulsed July 21, a defeat that helped to consolidate the French Republic.

In November 1795 Pitt would be ready to try again in Saint-Domingue, and 218 ships carrying 30,000 men were landed in what the prime minister called the "great push"; the largest expedition Britain had ever launched. Despite the risks involved, conquering the colony was seen as crucial to strengthening Britain's negotiating stance vis-à-vis the French Republic when the time came to make peace. Again, a formidable adversary and yellow fever made the project daunting, but Pitt citing "honor" in keeping his pledge to the French planters to see to their restitution, would only abandon the endeavor in August 1798, having forfeited 4 million pounds and almost 100,000 men. During this time to the ordinary soldier and sailor, service was considered a virtual "death sentence", and there were riots in Dublin and Cork as conscripts learned they were being sent to Saint-Domingue. While these events were to fall on either side of Blake's execution of the painting of the travails of the Babylonian King, *The Songs of Experience* begins, as already quoted:

> Hear the voice of the Bard!
> Who Present, Past, & Future, sees....

The meaning of prophecy in Blake, again, did not imply foretelling the future; rather the tyranny of Urizen, particularly for one with his eye on eternity, was foreshadowed by preparations in the past and continuing into the present, as the connecting links of the chain of slavery. Or as the "Fairy" sang at the opening of Blake's *Europe* of the five windows that lighted "Cavern'd Man":

>...thro' one can look
>And see small portions of the eternal world that ever
>   groweth;
>Thro' one himself pass out what time he please....

Blake's *Newton* shows the natural philosopher sitting nude on a large rock enveloped in the surrounding darkness, with a highly muscled, youthful body. Hunched over an unfurled scroll, he has a white tunic draped over his left shoulder, while, with his left hand he guides a compass, his right hand and outstretched arm are pinning down the opened scroll, plotting the arch as it is drawn—a diagram outlining and calculating the abstract ratios of the world.

The gaze of Newton is completely proscribed, but it is also one of favorless privilege. The rock he sits on is encrusted with lichen and algae and other organisms, giving it a multi-hued texture that the mathematician is entirely oblivious to. Unconcerned and unaware of the fabulous environs, he's charting a universe at the bottom of the sea, as his stony bench, in Blake's satire, has the appearance of a bidet.

In Blake's opinion, the Newtonian mathematical vision of the world was dead and inert, "Petrifying all the Human Imagination into rock & sand"; whereas Blake saw that "every particle of dust breaths forth its joy." Newton's was "vegetative" "single" vision, as opposed to the "four-fold" vision disclosed to the Imaginative eye in each of us. "For everything that lives is Holy!" became the bard's refrain.

The "songs" with which William Blake communicated his message were entirely of his own unique creation; but since moving to Lambeth, and as he began his series of Prophetic

Illuminated Books, he'd kept his extraordinary creativity and genius advancing as if borne on the crest of a surge for liberation with continental breadth. His output had been extraordinary, including *The Marriage of Heaven and Hell, Visions of the Daughters of Albion, America* and *Europe,* the *Songs of Experience,* and *the Songs of Los* and the *First Book of Urizen,* where Africa and Asia too are invoked. Blake's embracement of revolt, of revolution in the world had been quite nearly unprecedented. Now that period was at an end, and he began printing up his entire production on folio-sized paper.

In its cultural life, Paris had seen dramatic changes after 9 Thermidor, where dance halls were being reserved and almost overnight the city sprang to life with gaiety and celebration. At first, appropriately these were designated "victim's balls", but eager to make up for lost time, everyone, albeit excepting the poor, began indulging in pleasure-seeking of diverse sorts. Luxurious brothels and gaming rooms, elegant cafés and restaurants, all began to bustle with their zealous clientele. The brother's De Goncourt, Edmond and Jules, wrote from the retrospective view of mid-nineteenth century in their *Histoire de la société française pendant le directoire,* that never had Paris seen so many public dance halls:

> She dances since thermidor, she dances as she sung before; she dances to revenge herself, she dances to forget; between her bloody past and her dark future she dances. Scarcely saved from the guillotine, so as to believe it no longer, and the leg outstretching, the ear to the tune, the hand on the shoulder of the first comer,

France still bleeding, and quite ruined, hops and trips and capers about, in an immense and maddening saraband.

With all of 'society' scurrying to balls under blazing chandeliers, Parisian interiors came to life. Everywhere were violins and dancing-masters, as wine flowed till four in the morning, in an intoxication of melody and lights, and of shimmering gauze—a complete abandonment to a voluptuousness of the senses. "One dances in thin shoes; one dances in rough sabots; one dances to the snuffling of bag-pipes; one dances to the suave notes of the flute...," the De Goncourt's wrote.

The style of dress for women changed too, to an antique Grecian style. And everywhere Mademoiselles were displaying more bosom; wearing short-waisted gowns, with long tight sleeves, or else with short sleeves with bared arms, or wearing long kid gloves—their skirts trailing, trimmed with gimp laid in Greek patterns, white stockings barely showing under their dresses.

Women, as did men, were donning felt hats; hers trimmed with flame-colored ribbons, or else Mademoiselle wears a turban turned up with blue feathers. "What confusion, and what fickleness!" noted the De Goncourt's. "Of all this," wrote Moncure Conway, "we may be sure, the invalid hears many a beguiling story from Madame Monroe."

One of the initiators of this fashion was Theresa Taillen, known as Madame Tallien, famous for her salon, who often wore gossamer gowns without underwear, and with either pink or blond wigs. Seeing her at the Paris Opera on one occasion, Talleyrand commented—"One could not be more sumptuously unclothed." She, the friend of Josephine de Beauharnais, wife of Alexandre vicomte de Beauharnais guillotined in June 1794, and afterwards mistress of Paul

François Barras; he the cousin of the Marquis de Sade, she to become the "incomparable Josephine", enchantress and future wife of Napoleon Bonaparte.

On 22 August 1795 when the constitution was formerly adopted, the Convention proposed that in the first election two hundred and fifty new deputies would be elected while five hundred from the old convention would remain in their seats until the next election. In other words, the expiring legislative body was to hold a two-thirds majority in the new bodies; this, so as to ensure that those who had abolished the feudal system, and those who had overturned the throne, and who had severed the head of the Bourbon dynasty, would retain power during the transition to the directorial constitution. This selection was to take place in the primary assemblies. After taking their votes on the constitution and the decrees, these should meet again to make that choice; in addition, the armies of France were to be given an interest, and would assemble on the field of battle to vote on the constitution.

The enemies of the Convention, particularly royalists expecting to gain by the vote, were mortified by the 2/3's decree, as many of the more ambitious among the bourgeoisie were perplexed as they saw the places they might occupy in the new government dwindle. Agitation began on the question in the Parisian sections by representatives of both classes: The men who had spread scaffolds across France, they said, were determined on keeping power, and might at any moment renew their crimes; only if the new legislature could be freed from these terrorists, would France's future prosperity be assured. Soon entire sections were in commotion.

The head of the royalist agency, Lemaitre, in pamphlets

and with speeches saw to it that dissatisfaction among his peers was universal, and that the imaginations of those susceptible to dissuasion, when the clamoring became pervasive, were in turmoil. (9) The plan to be pursued was therefore to accept the constitution, but reject the decrees. The insurgency insisted the assemblies should then declare themselves permanent and the Convention expired; then they would be free to choose whomsoever they desired, and vowed only to disband after a freely chosen legislature was installed. Thiers offers further details:

> The agents of Lemaitre acquainted the environs of Paris with this plan; they wrote to Normandy, where there was great intriguing in favor of the constitution of 1791, to Brittany, to the Gironde, and to every quarter with which they had correspondences. One of their letters was seized and made public from the tribune. The convention saw without alarm the preparations making against her, and awaited with calmness the decision of the primary assemblies of all France.... (10)

In order that it be prepared for the possibility of renewed conflict, however, the Convention ordered troops advanced for its defense to a camp outside Paris. Royalist sections, led by men from Le Pelletier, took this as the opportunity to address petitions to the representatives: asking, had the Parisians done anything that could account for this recent military move? "Make yourself worthy of our choice, and do not control it," they added with a touch of presumption. The Convention replying, it awaited the manifestation of the national will, which it would submit to as soon as it was known, as it would compel everyone else "to submit themselves to the same authority." (11)

Acting on the model now well established in French

revolutionary practice, the Le Pelletier sectional leaders underwrote themselves as the center of insurrection, broadcasting that trope that the powers of the constituent body cease when the sovereign people were present, proposing the forty-eight sections each nominate a commissioner to express the sentiments of its citizens upon the constitution and the decrees. But the assemblies had been prohibited by the Thermidorian Convention from communicating or from sending commissioners to address one another. The Convention, therefore, invalidated the resolution, declaring it would consider its execution an attempt upon the public safety.

The voter turn-out on the Constitution was slight, showing a general malaise among the French populace. Of five million eligible voters, 1,057,390 voted approval, with 49,978 opposed. The vote for the 2/3's proposal was 205,498 in favor, with 108,754 opposed. The constitution of Year III of the Republic was officially proclaimed on the 1st Vendemiaire (23 September), the Convention further declaring that the primary assemblies, not yet named, should finish nominating before 10 Vendemiaire, with the electoral assemblies meeting on the 20th and concluding their work on the 29th. The new legislative bodies were scheduled to meet on 15 Brumaire (November 6). Thiers continuing:

> ...[T]he intriguing royalists and the ambitious thrust themselves into the sections, talked of public benefit and honour, said that there was no safety in being governed any longer by conventionalists, that they should always be exposed to terrorism; that, besides, it was disgraceful to give in, and to suffer themselves to be trampled upon ...Groups of young men paraded the streets, shouting, *Down with the two thirds!* When the soldiers of the convention attempted to disperse them, and to prevent them from uttering seditious cries, they replied with a

volley of musketry. There were different riots, and
considerable firing even in the middle of the Palais Royal.
(12)

Meanwhile, to ripen their plans, Lemaitre and his
colleagues had brought to Paris and kept in hiding several
Chouan chiefs from the Vendée, a word derived from Jean
Chouan (the nickname of the leader of the royalist uprising
known for his imitation of an owl's cry, the rallying signal of
insurgents), as well as a number of noble émigrés who
awaited an auspicious moment to appear. The problem
remained how to set up a central executive committee for the
insurrection. The solution came when the Le Pelletier section
offered a resolution: the electors nominated by the primary
assemblies should meet immediately, rather than wait till 20
Vendemiaire. This was communicated to the other sections,
several approving, and a meeting was fixed for the 11th at the
Odeon Theatre.

On that day, a small number of electors met in the theatre
under the protection of the National Guard, now purged of the
lower classes, as a growing throng of sectionals filled the
auditorium and the boxes, and the Place de L'Odeon became
thick, both with the committed and with curiosity seekers. All
of this was reported to the Convention; and although in that
day's session busy observing funerary solemnities for the
expunged faction now known as the "Girondins", they issued
a decree calling for the dispersal of the convening electors
meeting for purposes extraneous to their electoral functions.
The Convention further decreeing that persons drawn to such
meeting, on withdrawing, need have no apprehension of
prosecution. Then a body of police were dispatched, escorted
by dragoons, to communicate the decrees.

As it was dark when they arrived, the officers walked out
onto the stage carrying torches to illuminate the dimly lit

theatre. With the decrees read, the entire house began exiting onto the Place de L'Odeon, where the police were surrounded, their torches wrested from their hands and extinguished, and the multitude forced the dragoons to withdraw. The throng now regained their seats in the theatre and on the stage, where felicitations were exchanged for the bravado displayed in face of the Convention's decrees, as all swore an oath to defend themselves against tyranny. Withal, each was seemingly appreciative of the advantage that had just been gained.

As the night wore on, the crowd occupying the theatre thinned, as did those thronging outside. With the theatre empty and quiet, General Menou advanced with a column of troops with two cannons in tow as directed by the committees earlier in the day. The report of an army advancing on a vacant theatre just turned out by men swearing heated vows, caused a sensation as it spread through Paris the following morning: it was incontrovertible proof of the viability of the insurrection!

The previous night, as the meeting at the Odeon had been ongoing, gatherings of "patriots" from the faubourgs, sans-culottes, and Jacobins, some of whom had just been released from prison, descended on the committees pleading that they be armed to defend the republic. These were joined by a great number of officers then in Paris who'd been struck from the lists of the army. In the morning, their petitions were taken up by the representatives, who consented that the "patriots" might be let loose on the royalists, but that they would be imprisoned again should that become necessary, as command was given to unattached officers.

This news began rapidly circulating through Paris, as it became fodder for agitators who also spread throughout Paris. The "terrorists" were being re-armed, they said; property and persons were no longer safe; the sections must resort to arms to defend themselves!

The sections of Le Pelletier, Butte-des-Moulins, Contrat-Social, Théâtre-français, and nearly half-a-dozen others beat the *générale* and declared themselves in rebellion against the Convention, bidding citizens and National Guard to join their battalions to maintain the public safety. Le Pelletire became the center for this intrigue, as that sections sittings became permanent. Responding in kind, the Convention made its sittings permanent; and the earlier decree disarming the "patriots" was enjoined, while they issued a proclamation justifying the act and endeavored to give confidence in the men restored to arms. Menou and his troops and cannons were again ordered out, this time to surround and to disarm the Le Pelletier section. But Menou was not facing his "natural enemy" as in *Prairial*; "it was the flower of the capital," he was being directed against—"it was the youth of the best families, it was in short the class that dictates public opinion, that he had to fire upon with grapeshot, if it would persist in its imprudent course." (13) The general was, therefore, very solicitous in his deployment and in allowing "the sections whatever they liked during the whole day of the 12th."

At last, late in the evening, after secretly parleying with some of the leaders of the rebellion, and after refusing command of the "patriot battalions", Menou advanced upon Le Pelletier. But instead of tactically deploying, he packed his infantry, together with artillery and cavalry, in a street without room for maneuver in front of the convent of the Filles-Saint-Thomas, the hall of the section's meetings. There he found its members, armed and ranged in line behind their president, with every outlet cutoff and surrounded by sectionalists, who also filled every window in every house. When summoned to surrender their arms, these 'gentlemen' steadfastly refused. Observing Menou's predicament, the president replied warmly that he must now either retire or fight. Promising to withdraw on condition the rebels promptly dispersed, the result was a foregone conclusion as some of Menou's own troops began to file off.

Thiers resumes his narration:

> Menou, on his part, went away with his troops, and suddenly withdrew his columns, who had great difficulty to pass through the crowds that choked the neighboring wards. While he had the weakness to retreat before the firmness of the section of Lepelletier, the latter had returned to the place of its meetings, and, proud of its resistance, was still further confirmed in its rebellion. A report instantly gained ground that the decrees were not executed, that the insurrection remained victorious, that the troops were returning without asserting the supremacy of the convention. (14)

Witnesses to all of this hastened to the Convention to speak from the tribune: "We are betrayed! We are betrayed! Call general Menou to the bar!" There were demands that Menou immediately be arrested and tried; but that, all realized, would do nothing to relieve the present predicament of the Convention. The appointment of a new chief was considered, deputy Paul Barras, a former military officer, being suggested. He had been, as noted, one of the representatives *en mission* to Toulon, who along with Fréron had been credited with its liberation, as he was associated with the timely intervention on 9 Thermidor that put an end to Robespierre and his clique. Now appointed general of the army of the interior, Barras had in his circle of acquaintance, through Madame Tallien, a young Corsican he knew was an effective commander, whom he'd first met at Toulon. The young man was then in Paris without employment, involved as Barras knew in pleasurable pursuits, as he was also engaged in the cultivation of his intellect through intensive reading. Barras thought of him on the night of the 12th, and learning he was occupying a box at a performance at the Feydeau Theatre, sent for him.

Napoleon himself remarked at St. Helena in his *Memoirs*, that he had been alerted by a friend of the overwhelming response of the royalists and the bourgeoisie of the Le Pelletier section, and of Menou's difficulties, and had hastened to the Convention where he was sitting in the galleries to witness their historic response. His appointment as Barras' second was submitted to the Convention that same night, which approved immediately. Once summoned, the youth, who was twenty-six, with wain features and scraggy shoulder-length hair, with a flair for the dramatic, was said to have taken half an hour to consider.

Barras would parley 13 Vendemiaire into a dominate position when the five-member Directory was formed in the subsequent weeks, and is inextricably linked with the rise of his protégé. He is supposed to have confided the military arrangements to Bonaparte, "who immediately took them all upon himself, and set about giving orders with extreme activity." (15) In his *Memoirs*, Barras maintains his was the critical agency on that night and the following day, and the Corsican was merely his aide-des-camp, on foot most of the time, charged with protecting government buildings on the right bank in front of the Tuileries.

That Barras had his part to play in the performance is certain, but it was later to be viewed above all as the curtain-raiser on a world-historic career. Barras did at least supply the accruements; Napoleon, wearing threadbare clothing, was authorized by Barras only days afterward to draw upon the government commissary for his uniform and sword, selecting from the best materials and weapons. Barras would also bequeath his own mistress, Josephine, six years older than Napoleon, with two teenage children. From Martinique, she bade Barras not disclose to her suitor her true financial status—that of indebtedness, whereas he thought her wealthy—as Barras penned a portrait of her as a soulless courtesan: "Her libertinism sprang merely from the mind, while the heart played no part in the pleasures of her body; in a word, never loving except from motives of interest, the lewd Creole never lost sight of business." (16)

Paul Barras, of course, was notorious for his own amorality; enjoying the life of a voluptuary, he had enriched himself during the Revolution, and was a thorough discredit to the Directory he would lead. A knave he was, it's been remarked, but what redeemed him, was "that he was a very great knave." (17)

The sectionalists, who saw the renewal of the government and retirement of the old as a point of honor, had as their object to bring together the greatest possible number of combatants, and to make the republic subservient to the cause of royalty. (18) They would draw six times greater numbers than the Convention, which mustered only 5000 men for its defense. But bourgeois and royalist Paris was engaged as protagonist in a drama little suited its inclinations or pursuits, against an opponent who understood their weakness.

For the Convention, the moment of truth had arrived. For government troops and the "patriots" to do more than defend the Convention was out of the question, and the very men who hurled their wrath against the Tuileries on 10 August, were drawn-up now in front of that chateau; 1400 men styling themselves the *Sacred Battalion of the Patriots of 1789*. Bonaparte had witnessed their assault in 1792, and knew if artillery had been used against them they would have had no chance of besting the Swiss Guard. In a brief interview with General Menou, detained in a room in the Tuileries, it was learned that forty heavy cannons were in a camp outside Paris. Hearing this, Napoleon's eyes darted among the officers of his entourage, his glance resting on Joachim Murat, commander of the 21st Regiment of Chasseurs. Ordering him to go immediately with horses and retrieve the guns, he adding— "Use the sword if necessary, but bring them! You will answer to me. Go!"

As soon as Murat returned, Bonaparte distributed the artillery at all the points where the Convention was exposed. On the Pont Neuf, Pont Royal, and in the Rues Cul de Sac, Dauphine, L'Echelle, Rohan, and Saint-Nicise, and at the Vendome. Murat's cavalry and a part of the infantry were now stationed in reserve at the Carrousel and in the garden of the Tuileries. Provisions were ordered brought in to the Tuileries, and a depot of ammunition and a hospital staffed by the wives and daughters of the representatives were temporarily established in its ancillary rooms. An avenue of retreat was secured in the event of defeat, while chests of arms were conveyed to the Faubourg Saint-Antoine, and to the Quinze-Vingts section disarmed in *Prairial*. All this had been completed by early morning on the 13th with orders the republican troops should calmly await the attack, but by no means provoke it.

Meanwhile, in the Le Pelletier section a central committee had been formed under the presidency of the newspaper editor Richer-Seiry, and a military committee instituted. The committees of government by the Convention had been outlawed, and an ad hoc tribunal established for trying those challenging the sovereignty of the sections. Several generals who had been active in the Vendée civil war on both sides, now dissatisfied with affairs, stepped out of hiding to lead the insurrection, as did a number of noblemen and a young émigré named Lafond, who would be among those most active in the fighting on that day. The commander-in-chief of the military committee was a man named Danican, a former associate of Hoche, the last republican commander in the Vendée, not himself a military man, but a club orator. With fight resolved upon, a plan of insurrection was presented. Thiers disclosed it as follows:

> The sections of the faubourg Saint-Germain, under the command of count de Maulevrier, were to start from the Odeon, for the purpose of attacking the Tuileries by the bridges; the sections of the right bank were to make the attack by the Rue Saint-Honore, and by all the cross streets communicating between the Rue Saint-Honore to the Tuileries. A detachment under the command of young Lafond was to secure the Pont Neuf, so as to put the two divisions of the sectionist army in communication with each other. The young men who had served in the armies, and were most capable of standing fire, were placed at the head of the columns. Out of forty thousand men of the national guard, twenty or twenty-seven thousand at most were present under arms. There was a much safer maneuver than that of presenting themselves in deep columns to the fire of the batteries; this was to barricade the streets, and thus to confine the assembly and its troops to the Tuileries, to occupy the houses in the immediate neighborhoods, and from them keep up a destructive fire, to kill one by one the defenders of the convention, and thus soon reduce them by famine and musket balls. (19)

Early that morning the sectionalist intercepted the arms shipment intended for the Quinze-Vingts section, as the provisions intended for the Tuileries were also intercepted. A detachment of the Le Pelletier section captured and invested the treasury building, as another slipped into the Hôtel de Hoailles, within musket range of the Tuileries. Lafond, at the head of several companies prepared an attack on Pont Neuf, as the Pont Royal too came under attack, as several battalions marched down Rue Dauphine. With the sectionalists closing in on the Tuileries, Danican sent out a flag of truce to propose terms.

His messenger was conducted in blindfold before the committees. The offer, delivered in bellicose terms, was nevertheless for peace, with the conditions that the "patriot" battalions be disarmed and that the decrees be rescinded. Such the committees would not consent to, but without answering, it was resolved to appoint twenty-four deputies to go out to fraternize with the men of the sections.

Receiving no answer, Danican gave the order to attack.

Bonaparte now directed eight hundred muskets and sufficient ammunition be brought into one of the rooms used by the Convention to arm the deputies themselves, to serve as a corps in reserve. The president, Legendre, addressed the Convention: "Let us receive death with the audacity that belongs to the friends of Liberty!" As was the practice, as the battle raged outside, the deputies maintained a vigil in absolute silence.

Napoleon, who characteristically placed himself near the front in battle, toward the end of the morning, had his horse shot out from under him during a moment of hand-to-hand combat where cannon could not intervene. After hours of intense fighting, by half-past four in the afternoon, with the sectional battalions covering the entire length of the Rue Saint-Honore, they had gained the steps of the church of Saint-Roch constituting an elevated position commanding the Rue Cul de Sac and Dauphine, and by it the Convention and the Committees, with an advantageous position for firing upon its gunners. Again, let's hear it from Thiers:

Bonaparte, who was capable of appreciating the advantage of the first blow, immediately directed his artillery to advance, and ordered a first discharge. The sectionists replied by a sharp fire of musketry; but Bonaparte, showering down grape-shot upon them, obliged them to fall back upon the steps of Saint-Roch; he then immediately debouched in the Rue Saint-Honore, and let loose upon the church itself a band of patriots who were fighting at his side with the greatest valour, and who had cruel wrongs to revenge. The sectionists, after a stout defence, were dislodged. Bonaparte, then turning his guns right and left, made them sweep the whole length of the Rue Saint-Honore. The assailants instantly fled on all sides, and retired in the greatest disorder. Bonaparte then committed to an officer the duty of keeping up the firing and making the defeat certain; he next went up to the Carrousel, and hastened to the other posts. Everywhere he witnessed these unfortunate sectionists, imprudently exposed in deep columns to the effect of the artillery, take to flight. (20)

Still, the insurgents were resolved upon attack, conceiving a general charge upon the bridges. Six to eight thousand men were directed toward Pont Neuf near which Lafond's troops were posted, falling in with thousands coming from Rue Dauphine under command of count de Maulevrier. These began advancing in close columns along the Quai Voltaire toward Pont Neuf and Pont Royal. Bonaparte lost no time in breaking up these columns, placing batteries on the quay of the Tuileries parallel with the Quai Voltaire, and began to enfilade the insurgents, combining with a shower of grape coming in from the cannons on the bridge.

Again, Lafond rallied his men to take the bridge. Driven back by the fire, he endeavored once more to bring them up, but these fled, dispersed by well-aimed artillery fire.

This was 13 Vendemiaire on the Revolutionary Calendar (the month of vintage, or 5 October 1795). It was only a year later that Napoleon Bonaparte first conceived his flight of high ambition, after his victory at Lodi against the Austrians, May 10, 1796, which was to become a central element in the Napoleonic legend. Napoleon declared at St. Helena—"From that moment, I foresaw what I might be. Already I felt the earth flee from beneath me, as if I were being carried into the sky."

When he returned to Paris in December 1797, he was given a triumphal reception, and was elected a member of the Mathematical Section of the National Institute (replacing the French Academy), although his studies didn't go beyond trigonometry. Gathering in solemn ceremony in the court of the restored Luxembourg Palace where an altar to the fatherland, replete with captured enemy flags, had been erected, in his welcoming speech foreign minister Talleyrand said—"Ah! Far from fearing what some would call his ambition, I feel that the time will come perhaps when we must tear him away from his studious retreat."

In the imagination of the European public there now stood a slender, eagle-faced young Corsican, supplanting that of the *bestial blood bespattered* sans-culottes as defender of the Republic; or as Ralph Waldo Emerson was to remark decades later, surveying the scene—these began "to look on Napoleon as flesh of his flesh and the creature of *his* party."

Bonaparte had given the royalist opponents of the republic a "whiff of grape shot", wrote Thomas Carlyle, which has since become the stock trope for historians of the era. But, "[i]t is false," he chronicles Napoleon saying, "that we first fired with blank charge; it had been a waste of life to do that." Carlyle adding this bit of poetry:

Most false: the firing was with sharp and sharpest shot: to all men it was plain that here was no sport; the rabbets and plinths of Saint-Roch Church show splintered by it to this hour...and the thing we specifically call French Revolution is blown into space by it, and become a thing that was! (21)

And more, the "...sacred right of Insurrection was blown away...." (22)

23.
Now the times are return'd upon thee

His life ebbing from him, Thomas Paine would muster all he could of his will as he completed the second part of *The Age of Reason; Being an Investigation of True and Fabulous Theology.* Its two parts composed in successive years, the first part published in France January 1794, with the second in October 1795, also in France, and finally a third part written after his return to America and published in 1807. Apportionments, Moncure Conway reiterated, that "are interesting as memorials of the circumstances under which they were written and published." (1)

The enduring effect of Paine's tract was to be felt not in France, for whom it was intended, but in Britain, and in turn in America as it redounded to the detriment of the author's legacy and reputation. It is a work arguing the philosophical position of Deism, as earlier suggested, while it broad-lit the corruption of the state sanctioned Christian churches, as the author rejected the supernatural and miracles and held that the Bible was not divinely inspired but instead an ordinary work of literature. Inscribing on his banner as a militant, "My own mind is my own church"; he pronounced for a religion which was authentic in its sense of right, of justice, of love and mercy. As again, he deployed his ideas in an engaging if "impertinent" style, appealing and accessible to the newly literate of the 'lower classes'.

As Part 2 far exceeded the circulation of Part 1, it spawned a veritable fount of unfavorable replies, and Thomas Williams, its publisher in England, was prosecuted. Most of these replies were from clergy advocating a literal reading of the Bible, while they mounted ad hominem attacks against Paine. But Paine's deism was even too radical for Joseph Priestley and for Johnson's *Analytical Review,* and peradventure for their Unitarianism, as both were far from being embracive of it. One minister opined, that—"the mischief arising from the spreading of such a pernicious publication was infinitely greater than any that could spring from limited suffrage and septennial parliaments." (2)

With Britain at war with revolutionary France, and with the concomitant drain on its treasury, London, not unlike Paris, was a city with widespread privation and poverty as the price of wheat soared after severe weather the previous winter. On October 26, 1795, reformers of the *London Corresponding Society* held a protest rally in Copenhagen Fields, Islington, with over one hundred thousand attending. John Thelwall, the radical orator and political reformer, was one of the main speakers, where he advanced a proposition that was prohibited since national organizations were illegal, as he called for "the whole nation" (to combine] "in one grand political association, or Corresponding Society, from the Orkneys to the Thames, from the Cliffs of Dover to Land's End." (3)

With platforms set up for three speakers, these still could only be heard by a fraction of those assembled, as remonstration was voiced against the King and Parliament: "...in the midst of apparent plenty, are we thus compelled to starve? Why, when we incessantly toil and labour, must we pine in misery and want? . . . *Parliamentary Corruption.* . . like a foaming whirlpool, swallows the fruit of all our labours." (4) At the rally, resolutions were passed and members of the Corresponding Society delegated to go to the principal towns and cities throughout the kingdom to bring their demands before a broader public: that the parliament and the government begin instituting reforms to bring universal male suffrage and end the war. As it was suggested too, that they again make their protest felt by assembling in three days time when the king would open the houses of parliament.

On that date, the 29th, with protestors thronging Whitehall, as the King's carriage approached, it was inundated between St. James Palace and the Carlton House by crowds and separated from the guard. "Down with Pitt!", "No war!", "No King!", "Peace", were among the cries heard. As a man selling the "Rights of Man" was arrested, he was freed by the crowd and "chaired" in defiance through the cheering throng. Then, with constables straining to secure the gates at Horseguards, after the King's carriage passed through, protestors stampeded in behind it. As the royal carriage drew onto Great George Street, one of its windows was penetrated by a projectile leaving a smooth round hole. Without injury to the King, the carriage reached the entrance to the House of Lords, and as he emerged it was purported the King stuttered he'd been shot at.

No one had heard a gun discharge. Was it perhaps a stone or a marble fired from an air gun? On-lookers supposed it may have come from an upstairs window on nearby Margaret Street. Was it an attempt on the life of the sovereign, as the government and its supporters and its press asserted in subsequent days?

At 3 PM when the King left Parliament, his procession was

met with "silent indifference" by the still massed crowds outside. As jeering began again, about thirty men surged toward the King's carriage as the guard battled to hold them off. There was a fuselage of stone throwing, splintering part of the coach's frame. As St. James Palace was reached, a large rock shattered another of the coach's windows, sprinkling the King's garments with shards. As he was ushered into the royal residence, his conveyance was seized and all but demolished.

A dozen or so men were pulled from the crowds by constables and arrested for the supposed part they played in the fracas. Sometime later, determined to join his family in Buckingham Palace, George III left by a rear door in a smaller coach. Spotted by the swarm still persisting, the King was again jeered and booed, and the coach subjected to projectiles. With people chanting "Bread, Bread! Peace, Peace!", the coach was halted, where determined men tried to separate the wheels from the axils. With a civil servant brandishing a pistol to prevent anyone from opening the latch of the door, a guard arrived to escort the King to safety in nearby Buck House.

In the minds of government ministers, prosecutors and establishment on-lookers—the throng on the streets and their deportment were a grim re-enactment of all that had been previewed in France during the past six years. With food prices rising and growing hardship nearing starvation for the more destitute, as with dissatisfaction with Pitt's war against France, the "insidious influences" represented by the London Corresponding Society and the Constitutional reform societies, it was apparent need be curtailed. Two Acts of Parliament were quickly drawn up and enacted, receiving royal assent on November 18. Known as the *Seditious Meetings Act* and the *Treasonable Practices Act*, these were popularly dubbed the "two acts," or the "gagging acts".

The first restricted public meetings at any place or room without prior permission from a magistrate to no more than

fifty persons, and any establishment where seditious, treasonous, or blasphemous speech was uttered would be declared a
house in disorder and punished. The second made it
treasonous to "imagine, invent, devise or intend death or
destruction...of the person of...the King." As Parliament had
also suspended habeas corpus—to the list of offences liable to
capital punishment was added that of disregarding the order
of any magistrate.

During the debate in Parliament on the acts, in response
the *London Corresponding Society* called an emergency
demonstration for November 12 where upwards to 200,000
men, women and children, gathered. This was to be followed
in December by another great demonstration in Marylebone
Fields, that included a threat from one of numerous speakers
that Pitt be brought to "publick execution." Said Pitt when he
heard of it, "My head would be off in six months, were I to
resign." (5)

But as Pitt's status with the public fell, his powers of
suppression only increased. While he'd already effectively
been deploying spies on a broadened scale for several years, in
the wake of the governmental clampdown, the reform
movement would face a dispersal outlasting a generation. (6)

This sequestering of protest and dissent in fact had already
effectively begun with the sedition trial and outlawing of
Thomas Paine. But before Paine's trial had even gotten
underway in December 1792, John Frost, the secretary of the
London Corresponding Society, and the man who'd accompanied him to Dover, was arrested for uttering seditious
remarks in a tavern where he was overheard by one of Pitt's
spies, allegedly saying "Equality, and No King." Visiting France
briefly after Paine's departure, he too was outlawed, but
returned to challenge the judgement. He was convicted and
imprisoned for six months at Newgate.

Then late in 1793, the publisher Daniel Isaac Eaton was

arrested for publishing a speech by the radical lecturer John Thelwall, who'd told an anecdote about a tyrannical gamecock named "King Chanticleer" who was beheaded for his despotism. After a trial ruinous to his interests, Eaton was acquitted. But Pitt had obtained his objective as the prosecution put Eaton out of business.

At that time, Thelwall based his lectures on the *Enquiry Concerning Political Justice* by William Godwin, a book published in 1793 and which was gaining wide readership despite its cost. Arguing, as did Condorcet, for perfectibility in human enlightenment, Godwin saw that it was the constraints of political institutions—the monopoly of property, of marriage and of monarchy—that need be abolished. Godwin's book was widely reprinted in extract in journals, coming into the hands of readers the likes of William Wordsworth, Samuel Coleridge, and a bit later of Percy Shelly, and others. For Godwin, however, political revolution was out of the question, "the task which, for the present should occupy the first rank of man is enquiry, communication, discussion", he wrote.

In this period, with the *London Corresponding Society* and the *Society for Constitutional Information* enjoying increasing influence and membership, several societies had jointly convened a meeting in Edinburgh to deliberate on the best way to call for "a great Body of the People" to carry through with their reform initiatives, following Paine's precept that a "national convention" be summoned. Viewing the meeting as seditious, the government tried three of its leaders, and each was sentenced to fourteen years of service in Botany Bay.

Then in summer 1794, as a plan was circulated to convene the proscribed meeting, the government arrested six members of the *Society for Constitutional Information* and thirteen members of the *London Corresponding Society*, including its secretary Thomas Hardy. Among the other arrestees were John Horne Tooke, John Thelwall, Thomas Holcroft, and

Unitarian minister Jeremiah Joyce. The arrests had taken in thirty individuals in all. The government charged each with "treasonous practices" in trying to get up—"a pretended general convention of the people, in contempt and defiance of the authority of parliament and on principles subversive of the existing laws and constitution, and directly tending to the introduction of that system of anarchy and confusion which has fatally prevailed in France."

After a nine-day trial Hardy was acquitted; as John Horne Tooke, too, won acquittal; and Thelwall's discharge soon followed. Afterwards the remaining cases were dismissed. Hardy's attorney, Thomas Erskine again defending, asserting the revolution advocated by the reform societies was a revolution of ideas as embodied in the Enlightenment, and that no violence in any form had been advocated. There had been no plan to overthrow the government by insurrection as in France; the prosecution's case had been based on "strains of wit" founded on the testimony of spies.

But loyalists now only believed the discharged were guilty, as Secretary of War William Windham referred to the discharged as "acquitted felon[s]", while William Pitt charged they were "morally guilty". Not a government victory, the trials nonetheless had the desired effect as many radicals now withdrew from active politics, and some of their societies disbanded.

On February 22 1795—President George Washington's sixty-third birthday—for allowing him to languish in prison without the American government's intercession, Thomas Paine had penned "a letter of sorrowful and bitter reproach" to his comrade-in-arms in six years of war. (7) After the original of this epistle had been entrusted for delivery with the new French counsel to America about to depart, a copy was shown to James Monroe, and Monroe dissuaded Paine from allowing it to proceed, and it was retrieved. That letter began:

As it is always painful to reproach those one would wish to respect, it is not without some difficulty that I have taken the resolution to write to you. The danger to which I have been exposed cannot have been unknown to you, and the guarded silence you have observed upon that circumstance, is what I ought not to have expected from you, either as a friend or as a President of the United States.

You know enough of my character to be assured that I could not have deserved imprisonment in France, and, without knowing anything more than this, you had sufficient ground to have taken an interest in my safety. Every motive arising from recollection ought to have suggested to you the consistency of such a measure. But I cannot find that you have so much as directed any enquiry to be made whether I was in prison or at liberty, dead or alive.... As everything I have been doing in Europe was connected with my wishes for the prosperity of America, I ought to be more surprised at this conduct on the part of her government. It leaves me but one mode of explanation, which is that everything is not as it ought to be amongst you, and that the presence of a man who might disapprove, and who had credit enough with the country to be heard and believed, was not wished for. This was the operating motive of the despotic faction that imprisoned me in France (though the pretence was that I was a foreigner); and those that have been silent towards me in America, appear to me to have acted from the same motive. It is impossible for me to discover any other. (8)

This was the bitterest of condemnations, as, as has been discussed, it had been revealed to Paine that there clearly was collusion between Robespierre and Gouverneur Morris when he was minister to France that had allowed him to be imprisoned as an Englishman. With Morris moving on to the Court of St. James and the successful negotiation of the *Jay Treaty* between the United States and Great Britain, it was evident that any publicity given to the support of England's "outlaw", Thomas Paine, from the American side in that negotiation, would have given offense to the British government. Concluded in November 1794 and ratified by the Senate June 1795, the Jay Treaty—officially known as the "Treaty of Amity Commerce and Navigation between His Britannic Majesty; and the United States of America"—took effect in February 1796 when ratified by the British Parliament.

Those alluded to in Paine's letter as "silent towards me in America" have been designated the *Federalists*, of whom John Jay, along with Alexander Hamilton, were then the leading exponents. Together with James Madison, they had written a total of eighty-five opinion articles under the pseudonym *Publius,* published in New York and now referred to as *The Federalist Papers.* Outlining their position during the framing of the new constitution in 1787 to supersede the *Articles of Confederation*, they favored a strong centralized national government, and were intent on insuring the new compact would have a firm financial foundation, consolidating the dominant role in that government, therefore, of large property holders, of bankers and financiers, and of manufacturers and merchants and of shipping interests. "Are those men", Paine later wrote, *"federalized* to support the liberties of their country or to overturn them? To add to its fair fame or riot on its spoils? The name contains no defined answer." (9)

By his second term, Washington deferred to this

"Federalist faction", led by his Secretary of the Treasury Hamilton, along with his vice-president John Adams. These had been pilloried as secret monarchists and enemies of Republican values by their opponents, the anti-federalists or the Jeffersonian republicans, who sought to maintain a diplomatic alliance with the French Republic, and the political dominance of the citizen farmer and planter in an agrarian economy. Jay directed American foreign policy in the 1780's as Secretary of Foreign Affairs in the government under the *Articles of Confederation*, and then as the first Secretary of State on an interim basis with the ratification of the *United States Constitution*.

Under that constitution and during the first presidency of George Washington, Jay had been appointed Chief Justice of the Supreme Court, and in 1794 was in London as America's special envoy, proceeding largely under the instruction of Alexander Hamilton, to resolve outstanding issues—that of the British forts still maintained in the Northwest, among others, and the seizure of American shipping, carrying goods from France's West Indian colonies and the impressment of American sailors to fight in the Royal Navy against France. Jay's treaty negotiation's neglected settlement of the latter, even conceding that Britain could seize U.S. goods bound for France if they were paid for, and could confiscate without payment French goods on American ships.

As a result of Britain's war with France, between 1793 and 1812, the Royal Navy was to grow from 135 ships to 589, and personnel expand from 36,000 seamen to 114,000. The overwhelming majority of these seamen were obtained by the 'press gang', where men of the 'lower classes' were seized, often in taverns or at roadside. During this period, the Royal Navy became extremely aggressive, both in halting and searching merchant ships, while even searching American port cities. Britain did not recognize 'naturalized' American citizenship during this time, treating anyone born a British subject as still British. As a result, 15,000 men claiming American citizenship were impressed during the Napoleonic Wars, along with seizures of naval and military supplies.

But for those promoting the treaty, avoiding war with Britain was the paramount objective, as concomitantly they sought to establish increasing American trade with Britain and its West Indian colonies; while, in fact, it's opponents charged, it "disgracefully surrendered the right and freedom of the American flag."

For the American's little outside commercial agreements had been achieved, as even the relinquishment of the forts had already been stipulated in the Treaty of Paris in 1783. With Britain at war with France, the treaty implied a shift away from America's only ally, France, in favor of the former enemy against which it had waged the war for its existence. Thus, the Jay Treaty was a repudiation of the foreign policy views of the Jeffersonian republicans, the opposition party in the government, as it redounded to the debility of France "without whose assistance", Paine was to write, "Mr. Washington would have cut a poor figure in the American war." (10)

In February Paine had refrained from sending his epistle in compliance with Monroe's counsel, but having completed his theological testament he could no longer brook further acquiescence, one must suppose, it weighing hourly on his perishing thoughts. He had not taken any part in the disputes arising in the framing and ratification of the new constitution, but as in France, he deplored factionalism and parties as a determent to a republic, as he saw that a unitary presidency could only be representative of a faction or party, as it too, had much the form and appearance of a military government, and hence potentially could become a despotic one; as the length of term, too, and manner of election specified for senators was conducive of aristocracy.

These issues bore on his perception of American developments—from the Jay Treaty to the conduct of Washington in the office of president, to the rising factionalism—and on September 20, 1795, he again wrote to Washington:

> Sir,—I had written you a letter...but at the request of Mr. Monroe, I withdrew it, and the letter is still with me. I was the more easily prevailed upon to do this, as it was then my intention to have returned to America the latter end of the present year; but the illness I now suffer prevents me. In case I had come, I should have applied to you for such parts of your official letters (and your private ones, if you had chosen to give them) as contained any instructions or directions to Mr. Monroe, to Mr. Morris, or to any other person, respecting me; for after you were informed of my imprisonment in France it was incumbent on you to make some enquiry into the cause, as you might well conclude that I had not the opportunity of informing you of it. I cannot understand your silence upon this subject upon any other ground, than as connivance at my imprisonment.... (11)

Shortly after this, James Madison wrote to Jefferson, with whom, notwithstanding he was the chief framer of the new constitution and a contributor to the Federalist Papers, he became an important ally in the government. The letter is dated 10 January 1796:

> I have a letter from Thomas Paine...and [it] contains some keen observations on the administration of the government. It appears that the neglect to claim him as an American citizen when confined by Robespierre, or even to interfere in any way whatever in his favor, has filled him with an indelible rancor against the President, to whom it appears he has written on the subject. His

letter to me is in the style of a dying one, and we hear
that he is since dead of the abscess in his side, brought
on by his imprisonment. His letter desires that he may
be remembered to you. (12)

But as his malady was surgically removed, and as he
slowly recovered his strength, Paine found that a year had
passed since his first letter had been withdrawn, and another
six months since his following letter. This, on a matter about
which Washington surely had more than peripheral awareness.
They had, in fact, formerly been mutually supportive and
solicitous in their conduct toward one another, as evidenced
in their correspondence as variously cited in this narrative.
During the war for the existence of the American Republic,
they had often sat in counsel as comrade-in-arms; as between
them, Conway tells readers, was shared "little oyster suppers"
in Paine's room as they talked over the events of the day and
his projected publications in the *Crisis* series, so important to
the morale of the officers and troops of the Continental Army.
But the long-awaited accounting never came.

Paine now began composing a pamphlet that would bear the
title *Letter to George Washington,* dated July 30, 1796, on
completion. It would be published in Philadelphia later that
year by Benjamin Franklin Bache, the grandson of Benjamin
Franklin, and editor of *The Aurora and General Advertiser,*
commonly known as the *Aurora.*

Under the mentorship of his famous grandfather, when
Bache was seven, and Franklin departed for London and then
Paris on his nine-year diplomatic mission, he accompanied the
elder man who saw to it he received an education imbibing the

principals of the age of *Enlightenment*. At twenty, Franklin Bache inherited the two-story print shop from his grandfather a few blocks from Independence Hall, using the presses and printing fonts Benjamin Franklin had used when he began publishing his *Pennsylvania Gazette*. Bache's *Aurora* appeared six days a week and became a platform for the anti-federalists; his editorial mission, to champion the rights of the citizens of the republic, rather than those who governed the republic.

Bache perceived that with the rule of the Federalist party the government had departed from the ideals of the American Revolution of 1776, and that the republic he envisioned was periled by the policies of Hamilton. 29 January 1795 an editorial in the *Aurora* had stated:

> The American Constitution is said to resemble the fabled constitution of Great Britain; it must, then, have monarchy, aristocracy, and democracy blended with it. Each of these three forms of government is said to contain imperfections;—how then can it be expected that a composition of imperfection can constitute perfection?

To Bache and to other critics, the Jay Treaty represented the crossing of the Rubicon, and he published its entire text in the *Aurora*, thereby raising considerable ire among the Federalists for the unauthorized printing. September 8, 1795, the paper stated that in approving the treaty the Senate and the President "gives weight" to the "pretensions" of the "merchants and traders" by "recognizing them as a privileged class." In sum, the creation of a public debt tied to the British commercial banking system would only restrict American independence while it benefited a few wealthy creditors.

In his "Letter to George Washington", along with publishing his previous two letters, Paine presented his analysis of the Jay Treaty and the current state of the government, together with the story of his imprisonment and death sentence, the misconduct of Morris, along with remarks depreciative of Washington's character, and of Washington's military and political achievements as against his mistakes and failures.

"By the advantage of a good exterior", Paine wrote, "he attracts respect, which habitual silence tends to preserve...." Of the paucity of benefit from his military campaigns as seen against the contributions of other generals, Paine caustically remarked—"No wonder we see so much pusillanimity in the President, when we see so little enterprise in the General!" America, with the Jay Treaty, was realigning with a despotic against a republican state. Paine wrote: "Could I have known to what degree of corruption and perfidy the administrative part of the Government had descended, I could have been at no loss to have understood the reservedness of Mr. Washington toward me, during my imprisonment in the Luxembourg, there are cases in which silence is a loud language." (13)

Profoundly admixed with his own suffering, Paine's condemnation of Washington, was also then, thoroughly political, issuing from his perception at having been abandoned by the government of the country he helped to establish. It is clear in retrospect that Washington's silence, not alone based on his customary reticence of comment, was a calculated decision to ignore the plight of a former 'patriot' in the national struggle, on whom they now looked upon as hopelessly mired in a badly misfiring 'democracy' in the lower case. Washington had been a beacon in the war for Independence, but neither he nor Hamilton, nor Jay, nor Morris, nor John Adams, and many others were political radicals and republicans in the sense that Paine was. And as his *Age of Reason* would begin to circulate and be read, in the view of his immediate posterity, his was a reputation what was to be drastically downgraded. Washington would die in December 1799 at age 67, and an epigram of Paine's composition, which he never published, was found among his papers, titled "Advice to the statuary who is to execute the statue of Washington."

> Take from the mine the coldest, hardest stone,
> It needs no fashioning: it is Washington.
> But if you chisel, let the stroke be rude,
> And on his heart engrave—Ingratitude. (14)

Many historians regard 13 Vendemiaire as the final act of the French Revolution, as intimated by Carlyle, notwithstanding those who regard the Directory and the accession of Napoleon as its continuation. But let's hear from the vaunted leader of the first "communist" uprising, Gracchus Babeuf, who peradventure gave a foretaste as regards the future. Dictating a letter to the members of the Directory two days after his *Conspiracy of Equals* was preempted with the arrest of the "Secret Directory" fixed for 22 Floreal, anno IV (11 May 1796) of which he was chief, he wrote:

> Citizens and Directors,—would you regard it as beneath you to treat with me as between power and power? You have already seen the vast confidence of which I am the centre! You have seen that my party may well balance yours! You have seen its vast ramifications! I am more than convinced that the outlook has made you tremble! (15)

The *coup de main* with which Babeuf planned to depose the just installed Directory and inaugurate a new epoch in human society based on common property, cannot be appreciated unless viewed integrally with the Thermidorian Reaction. All of the conspirators were from among those *Prairial* or "patriot prisoners" given amnesty on the 4th Brumaire, called *les Eqaux* (the Equals or the Friends of Equality), headed by Babeuf and among whose leaders were Philippe Buonarroti, Felix Lepelletier, and Silvain Marechal, together with a rump grouping of Montagnards styling themselves *Patriots of 1789*, among whom were included a number of former deputies of the National Convention excluded from the new legislative bodies. Buonarroti wrote:

> The incarceration of almost all the friends of liberty, and their frequent translations from one prison to another, procured them the advantage of a better mutual acquaintance, and a closer friendly connection. The prisons of Paris, and particularly those of Plessis and Quartre-Nations, were at that time the foci of a great revolutionary fermentation. (16)

The conspirators were all admirers of Robespierre and the egalitarian principles of government the Jacobins purportedly sought to establish, and wanted to reverse what they perceived as the disaster of 9 Thermidor, albeit ostensibly without resort to terror. These held their initiatory meetings in a refectory of the nuns of St. Genevieve, with the joint object of restoring the constitution of 1793 and with it the reign of political and social equality. Near the end of his life, Buonarroti wrote a tome published in 1828 titled *Gracchus Babeuf's Conspiracy of Equals* in which he related that when the refractory was not available, the society held its meetings—

> ...in a vast vault of the same edifice (probably a crypt), where the dim paleness of the torch-light, the hollow

echoes of their voices, and the constrained position of the persons present, either standing or seated on the ground, impressed on them the greatness and the perils of their enterprise, as well as of the courage and prudence it required. The proximity of this place to the Panthéon caused the new society to be called by the name of this temple. (17)

This "Society of the Panthéon" was soon drawing as many as two thousand members to clandestine nocturnal meetings, whose two factions, the "patriots" and the "equals" rejected the model of the Jacobin and the Cordeliers clubs that flourished in the earlier revolutionary period. Buonarroti elucidated on their structure:

> ...their prudence went beyond even the shackles forged by the new Constitution against the right of assembly. To have a body of rules—a president, secretaries, minutes, a form of admission—this, they taught, was to copy too closely the Jacobin model, and to expose their flanks to a new persecution. They came at length to a mutual understanding, and the society had a code of laws, which, admitting neither registers, nor minutes, nor any other condition of admission, than the presentation by two members, rendered all order next to impossible.... An orator, and a vice-orator, held the places of president and secretary; and to meet the necessary expenses of the institution, there were no other funds than the spontaneous contributions of the members. (18)

The society was known to the police, and to the Directory, but Barras suffered them to continue their activities as a counterbalance to the Royalists, and in any case, with the assiduous publication of their views they were becoming formidable through having many members well-placed among the "patriots". But an insurrection such as Babeuf proposed would have no chance of success unless it gained a military component, and by spring 1796, on Buonarroti's authority, the conspiracy had 17,000 adherents, composed of most of the military members of the old sections, disbanded members of the Army of the Interior, revolutionists of the Departments come to join in the Parisian movement, the grenadiers of the legislative body, almost the whole of the legion of police, and the corps consigned at the Invalides, in addition to counting on the popular masses of Saint-Marceau and Saint-Antoine. All told, they were a force to be reckoned with.

For the direction of the insurrection there were three committees, and on 11 Germinal a "Secret Directory of Public Safety" was instituted whose object was to reestablish popular sovereignty. A Montagnard committee and the Military Committee adopted and published a manifesto to be distributed throughout Paris calling for a general rising, headed "Act of Insurrection". Buonarroti wrote: "It became an admitted principle in the committee, that the laws of liberty and equality could never receive a useful and durable application without a radical reform of the property system...." (19) On April 11, 1796, with the Conspiracy of Equals in preparation, Paris had been placarded with posters calling for the restitution of the constitution of '93 under the heading *Analyse de la Doctrine de Bafoeuf.* This had begun with the sentence—"Nature has given to every man the right to the enjoyment of an equal share in all property."

After listing grievances in justification, a breakdown of twenty objectives of the insurrection ensued. Following are two of these from the manifesto:

2. The object of the insurrection is the re-establishment of the Constitution of 1793, the liberty, equality, and well-being of all.

3. This day, this very hour, citizens and citizenesses will march from all points in their order, without waiting for the movement of neighboring quarters, which they will cause to march with them. They will rally to the sound of the tocsin and trumpets, under the conduct of patriots to whom the Insurrectionary Committee shall have confided banners bearing the inscription—"THE CONSTITUTION OF 1793; EQUALITY, LIBERTY, AND COMMON WELFARE," other banners will bear the words: "When the Government violates the rights of the People, insurrection is for the People, and each portion of the People, the most sacred of rights and the most indispensable of duties. (20)

For resolving and setting the details of the *journée,* an overall meeting of committees was called on the evening of 19 Floreal (May 8). The insurgency was to assemble according to arrondissment, subdivided by sections, with each arrondissment having its chief, and each section its sub-chief. "Generals" distinguished by the tri-color cockade and under orders of the Secret Directory would lead the columns. During the daylight of Floreal 22, the divisions were to march upon the legislative bodies, the executive directory, and the Etat Major of the Army of the Interior. The national treasury was to be seized, the post-office, the houses of ministers, and any public or private buildings containing provisions or ammunition of war.

The objective, finally, was to subordinate and break all existing authority, and any act recognizing the legitimacy of the government was punishable by immediate death. (21) Praising the originators of the September Massacres as "deserving well of their country," the insurrectionists sought, then, to emulate 2-3 September 1792.

Charles Germain, one of the co-conspirators, visited

Barras on 30 Germinal, anno IV (19 April 1796), and reported his interview, and on the language used by Barras, in a letter to Babeuf. After expounding on the dangers to the country from Royalists, Barras asked his visitor what the patriots thought. "We know," he said, "they are preparing a movement. Good men, their zeal has blinded them; they are going to get themselves *prairialised*, whereas, in order to save the country, we have got to *vendemiarise*." (22)

Precluding the "first communist insurrection", on May 10 Babeuf, along with many of his associates, were arrested by the order of Lazare Carnot. These were tried beginning 20 February 1797, at the newly created high court at Vendome. Babeuf and his disciple Darthe were found guilty 27 May, and guillotined the next day; Buonarroti and others were deported, as some were acquitted. A few, including Baptiste Drouet, the former postmaster of Saint-Menehould who had arrested Louis XVI on the occasion of his "flight to Varennes", then a member of the Council of Five Hundred, escaped prosecution with the connivance of the Directory.

When the verdict was announced condemning Babeuf and Darthe, both men tried to kill themselves by thrusting improvised blades into their hearts. Whether the instruments were inadequate, or their thrusts were blocked by gendarmes, they failed in the attempt. Both were conveyed in blood to the scaffold, where, even their most vehement political opponents admitted, they mounted the scaffold "with a splendid courage."

Thomas Paine, following, as ever, the vicissitudes of the French scene, had composed his last great pamphlet in winter 1795-96 titled *Agrarian Justice*. Written as a proposal to the

Directory and the Legislature as they were considering bills for agrarian reform, it laid unpublished for a year until Paine read a sermon by the Bishop of Llandaff, Dr. Richard Watson, titled *The Wisdom and goodness of God in having made both rich and poor;* he countering in the preface to his rejoinder, the creator did not make rich and poor, "he made only male and female, and gave them the earth for their inheritance."

The defect in suffrage in the late constitution was the origin of Babeuf's conspiracy, Paine would write; and in his prefatory inscription to *Agrarian Justice* he left no doubt that Babeuf's plot to 'seize the kingdom of heaven' by violence, and his own pamphlet were no coincidence. As he had unequivocally expressed it when he addressed the expiring Convention in July 1796:

> If there be faults in the Constitution, it were better to expunge them now; than to abide the event of their mischievous tendency; for certain it is, that the plan of the Constitution which has been presented to you is not consistent with the grand object of the Revolution, nor congenial to the sentiments of the individuals who accomplished it.

> To deprive half the people of their rights as citizens, is an easy matter in theory or on paper: but it is a most dangerous experiment, and rarely practical in the execution. (23)

On this point, Paine elaborated:

> As we have not at one instant renounced all our errors, we cannot at one stroke acquire knowledge of all our rights. France has had the honour of adding to the word *Liberty* that of *Equality;* and this word signifies essentially a principal that admits of no gradation in the things

to which it applies. But equality is often misunderstood, often misapplied, and often violated. (24)

In early May of 1797, Paine had gone to Le Havre (the designation Le Harve-Marat having been dropped) intending to sail with the Monroe's for America, leaving his pamphlet in the hands of his translator. But rightly suspecting there was a plan by a British cruiser to capture him at sea, as it had been well known he was in port waiting embarkation, he returned to Paris. Now publishing his pamphlet, he contended that before private ownership of land there was the principle that "the earth, in its natural uncultivated state...was the common property" of the entirety of humanity. The practice and concept of ownership only arose with the advent of civilization and the development of agriculture, as opposed to the hunter-gather and shepherd societies that proceeded it. Subsequently, it had become impossible to distinguish what were merely improvements to land, such as diverse methods of cultivation and facilities for storing the surplus, from the land itself. The basis for the deplorable division into rich and poor was private ownership, something non-existent in humanity's previous organization. Hence "justice" demanded a plan to abolish the systematic bases of inequality. In *Agrarian Justice* Paine wrote:

It is not charity but a right, not bounty but justice, that I am pleading for. The present state of civilization is as odious as it is unjust. It is absolutely the opposite of what it should be, and it is necessary that a revolution should be made in it. The contrast of affluence and wretched-ness continually meeting and offending the eye, is like dead and living bodies chained together. I care not how affluent some may be, provided that none be miserable in consequence of it. (25)

Proposing a 10% inheritance tax centered on land, the fund accruing therefrom would constitute a form of equality consistent with liberty of ownership. Offering a method of amelioration between that of confiscating wealth proposed by Babeuf's "Equals", and the English Poor Laws which stigmatized the poor and subjected them to harsh workhouse and penal conditions, Paine proposed universal entitlements dispensed without condition. These were to take the form of old age pensions, aid to the blind and those with disability, and as a compensation to all in society on reaching adulthood for loss of their original "natural" inheritance. The community was owed a "ground-rent" from the proprietors of the land who should continue in that state, and in this way, all classes of persons would benefit.

These egalitarian ideals had been espoused too by Nicolas Bonneville, one of Paine's chief confidants and collaborators during his sojourn in France, with whom, and his family, he lived starting in 1797. Bonneville had been a founding member in October 1790 of the *Society of the Friends of the Truth*, known as *Cercel Social*, as discussed earlier, a grouping that included as members Condorcet and Paine, along with both Gracchus Babeuf and Sylvan Marechal, Babeuf's co-conspirator, an essayist and political theorist among those presaging "communism" as a political entity. Begun as a "clearing-house" for correspondence between and among forward-thinking scholars from across Europe, the Cercel Social solicited comment upon political affairs to be published in its journal *Bouche de Fer* (The Iron Mouth), and thus became the first revolutionary confederacy to identify itself as a cosmopolitan organization.

Bonneville published *L'Esprit des Religions* in 1791, the year of the founding of the *Republican Society*, where, seeking to resolve the issue of social happiness, he prescribed a universal religion led by philosophers and scholars, instead of a priestly hierarchy. Bonneville encapsulated his goal in the journal as—"The union of all people and all individuals who inhabit the earth into a single family of brothers who rally to pursue for one another the general good."

These ideals—as promoted by Bonneville, Paine, Condorcet, and Babeuf in France, and by Godwin in England—contributed to the formation of Utopian Socialism, expounded in subsequent decades notably by Charles Fourier and Saint-Simon in France and Robert Owen in England and America, among others. Karl Marx, who can be seen to have been inspired to emulate the French revolutionary experience as representing the Revolution par excellence, was to cite the *Cercel Social* in *The Holy Family* (1845) as having "commenced the [modern] revolutionary movement." (26) That movement, in a paramount way, had seen to the triumph of the "interests" of the bourgeoisie; *interests* "so powerful," Marx wrote, "that it was victorious over the pen of Marat, the guillotine of the Terror and the sword of Napoleon as well as the crucifix and the blue blood of the Bourbons." Marx's view that the French Revolution, particularly in its radical Jacobin phase, was the prototype for modern revolution, persisted in his historical and theoretical writing until the defeat of revolution continent-wide in 1848-49,and then subsequently in 1852 with the coup-d'etat of Louis Bonaparte, or the "little Napoleon." Marx would sum up the new phase reached in "the class-struggle" with this famous flourish in *The 18th Brumaire of Louis Bonaparte*:

> The social revolution of the nineteenth century cannot draw its poetry from the past, but only from the future. It cannot begin with itself before it has stripped off all superstition in regard to the past. Earlier revolutions required recollections of past world history in order to drug themselves concerning their own content. In order

to arrive at its own content, the revolution of the nineteenth century must let the dead bury their dead. There the phrase went beyond the content; here the content goes beyond the phrase.

In his youth, in his *Young Hegelian* period after obtaining his doctorate degree from the University of Bonn, having studied there and in Berlin, as Marx began projecting his subsequent career as a revolutionary, as his first great book he started working on a study of the French National Convention, but let it fall before more pressing labors. That envisioned monumental work would eventually become, two full decades later, *Das Kapital.*

Revolutionaries ever since were never to lose sight of this filiation with the French experience; feelings and judgements that by 1917 with the Revolution in Russian, would become retrospective, with the latter taking over from the former the role which had been assigned it, giving to its historiography the facility of masking reality, and so to out-live it.

To a great degree, with the ratification of the Jay Treaty, Washington would forfeit the esteem he had been held in in France for being the 'originator of Liberty' in the modern world. But as he decided he should retire rather than seek another term, among those merits of his service in the cause of the American republic for which he would be revered, appended to the fact that he had taken no pay as commander-in-chief during its war for independence, only asking reimbursement for his expenses—although there would be controversy over the merit of some of those expenses—was added that he retired while deferring claim to all title. As

Paine's *Letter to George Washington* was published in Philadelphia, he had already announced that retirement. Referring to himself in the third person, on January 8, 1797, Washington wrote to David Stuart:

> Although he is soon to become a private citizen, his opinions are to be knocked down, and his character reduced as low as they are capable of sinking it, even by resorting to absolute false-hoods. As an evidence, whereof, and the plan they are pursuing, I send you a letter of Mr. Paine to me, printed in this city, and disseminated with great industry.... Enclosed you will receive also a production of Peter Porcupine, alias William Cobbett. (27)

Cobbett was a young Englishman, arriving in America with his family in autumn 1792, disembarking in Wilmington, Delaware. Just previous to this emigration he had been in Paris, having fled to France to avoid imprisonment for bringing charges against officers in the British army, in which he served, whom he accused of corruption, denouncing their harsh treatment of enlisted men. But his sensibility was soon revolted, too, at what he saw in France, and afterwards he manifest an intense antipathy for the revolutionary leaders, including Paine. Now intending to remain in America, on November 2, 1792, he'd written Secretary of State Thomas Jefferson: "Ambitious to become the citizen of a free state I have left my native country, England, for America. I bring with me youth, a small family, a few useful literary talents, and that is all."

Supporting himself and family by teaching English to French émigrés, he soon relocated to Philadelphia, where he began his career as a journalist with a pamphlet titled *Observations on the Emigration of Joseph Priestley*, who was being acclaimed by his new countryman after his emigration in 1794, but who Cobbett denounced as a "traitor". For the next six years, he wrote copiously under the pen-name Peter Porcupine, often adopting a tone of "asperity", and had taken up Paine's "Letter to Washington" in his monthly *Porcupine's Political Censor* for December 1796. Straight off Cobbett extended Paine his sharpest quill: "Your *"private affairs,"* were long ago public. Everyone knew, and every honest heart rejoiced, that you had found a Bastille in the purlieus of your palace of freedom; that your filthy carcass was wasting in chains, instead of wallowing in the plunder you had promoted."

Another of those taking issue with Paine, and with his *The Age of Reason* the Second Part, as already stated, was Bishop Richard Watson, Doctor of Divinity, whose *An Apology for the Bible in a Series of Letters Addressed to Thomas Paine,* published in 1796 at the instigation of William Pitt's Tory government, was the most well-known of the failed refutations following that work. He too evinced a desire to see his adversary decedent, or at any rate at the commencement of his ten missives he wrote:

> I begin with your preface. You therein state—that you long had an intention of publishing your thoughts upon religion, but you had originally reserved it to a later period in life.—I hope there is no want of charity in saying, that it would have been fortunate for the Christian world, had your life been terminated before you had fulfilled your intention. (28)

Watson's sanction came into the hands of William Blake, who assuredly had been following on his friend's misadventures in France, and who in any event was obviously an attentive reader of Paine, from *Common Sense* to *Rights of Man*, and then *The Age of Reason*, as he too was aware of his imprisonment and brush with death. Annotating Watson's *Apology*, Blake responded furiously to his openly arrogant *ad hominem* attack, calling Watson "a state trickster": "Presumptuous Murderer dost thou O Priest wish thy brother's death when God has preserved."

Blake, of course, was a defender of the Bible, not as a work of historical fact, but as an authentic expression of the human imagination. "I know of no other Christianity", Blake had said, "and no other gospel than the liberty both of body and mind to exercise the divine arts of imagination." Thus, his ground was diametrical to that of Watson, and he could support Paine although they differed in attitude vis-à-vis deism and the worldly manifestations of the divine presence, which to the bard was eminently human in the figure of Jesus. On the back of the title page Blake has written an assertion, presumptively after carefully reading the whole book, that implies what a really effective defense of the Bible might lead to, which Watson had in no wise attained: "To defend the Bible in this year 1798 would cost a man his life." On the same page Blake supplies the reason thereof: "The Beast and the Whore rule without controls." And further, this follows:

> It is an easy matter for a Bishop to triumph over Paine's attack, but is not so easy for one who loves the Bible.... Mr. Paine has not extinguish'd, & cannot extinguish, Moral Rectitude; he has extinguish'd Superstition, which took the Place of Moral Rectitude. What has Moral Rectitude to do with Opinions concerning historical fact?

Finally, on the last page of Watson's *Apology for the Bible* Blake had written: "I have read this book with attention & find that the Bishop has only hurt Paine's heel while Paine has broken his head. The Bishop has not answer'd one of Paine's grand objections." (29) Neither does Blake nor Paine's arguments have to do with mere intellections, but is thoroughly bound up with the specificity of their time, and the very year Blake has explicitly named, as attention will show.

By 1795 as the great epoch of revolution was straining toward its dénouement, Blake was publishing the last of his Lambeth books that were later designated his "minor prophesies", closing out an extraordinary period of creativity, while having achieved a wondrous corpus with the production of his Illuminated Books.

In London, as averred to, it was a year of famine and of exasperated social tensions. A contemporary of Blake, and an engraver, wrote—"the engraving of Pictures is at present a dull business. The war occasions a scarcity of cash, people in general find it difficult to obtain the necessary comforts of life, and have not a surplus of money for elegancies." (30) Sometime in 1794-95, however, Blake had secured a commission to produce engraved illustrations for Edward Young's *The Complaint: or, Night Thoughts on Life, Death, & Immortality* first published by that poet between 1742 and 1745, and the commission was initially projected to be the biggest of his career, as he would make 500 large preliminary watercolors and over 40 engravings. Intended as a four-volume collection in "Atlas-sized quarto", despite Blake's prodigious labor, the bookseller, Richard Edwards, before completion, reduced it to one volume, hence also reducing Blake's expected commission. But out of this was to emerge one of Blake's most formidable efforts, structured as had been Young's *Night Thoughts,* over "nine nights". Using the proofs and the paper left over from his curtailed commission, and extending it over 2,000 lines by 1797, but never completed—although Blake would continue to work on it till 1807—it has been called "the greatest abortive masterpiece of English Literature." (31)

At inception titled *Vala*, which had reference to the succession of veils separating man from woman, or humankind from nature, the nine nights of the poem are one long night ending in the final judgement day and the rending of the veils. For his master-work Blake finally settled on the title, *The Four Zoas*.

The name Zoa was adapted by him from the Greek, which he began studying—from Zoon, meaning a living creature. The four Zoas were invented as a diagrammatic of the human psyche after the fall of pre-Adamic mankind; each Zoas being for the poet a constituent of psychic experience and having the active character of thinking, desiring, and suffering; as each forms alliances, competes and struggles with the others. Blake had previously invented the patriarchal Urizen representing the rational, Luvah the emotions, Urthona, creative imagination, and a fourth, Tharmas, as passivity, existing for the most part in the shadows, but in principle uniting them all. As each Zoa also had a feminine counterpart; in order, Ahania, Vala, Enitharmon, and Enion.

The image for this quartet and their female emanations, Blake derived from the *Book of Revelation* where Saint John on Patmos sees four such creatures bearing a vision of God in the air, which to Blake became the divine form of the human. Blake now designated universal humanity as "Albion the ancient man", who has fallen from eternity into a nightmarish sleep we call history, wherein the constituent Zoas' have been torn and must struggle for supremacy. Only when they succeed in cooperatively interacting will wholeness be restored to human civilization.

Each of Blake's designs for Young's *Night Thoughts* were executed within a red border on the margins, on the inside in which was affixed each letter-printed page of the text. Blake's illustrations have a simplicity, but pearl-like quality about them, as they have all been derived from single lines of text.

Blake related: as he was sitting in his study reading the poem, he came to a line where the poet askes "who can paint an angel?" By his account, musing on the question, he closed the book as he asked aloud, "Aye! Who can paint an angel?" Whereupon a voice replied, "Michael Angelo could." Looking about the room, he saw no one, but saw a greater light than usual.

"And how do you know?" Blake asked in his querulous cockney.

"I *know*, for I sat to him: I am the arch-angel Gabriel."

"Oho! You are, are you? I must have better assurances than that of a wandering voice; you may be an evil spirit— there are such in the land."

"You shall have good assurance. Can an evil spirit do this?"

As he looked whence the voice emanated, Blake related, he saw a great shining shape with bright wings: "As I looked, the shape dilated more and more: he waved his hands, the roof of my study opened; he ascended into heaven; he stood in the sun, and beckoning to me, moved the universe. An angel of evil could not have *done that*—it was the arch-angel Gabriel." (32)

The purport of this citation is to suggest that the legacy of William Blake lies not only in his extraordinary art and poetry, but in his visions, without which they would not exist— illuminating as they do the threshold of his flight into the imagination, opening to him first in his perambulations as a boy, extending through his apprentice years, and into the maturity of his Lambeth creations in the wake of revolution in America and in France, and then the fully visionary work of his later years with the long poems *Milton* and *Jerusalem*. Eidetic imaginings that can now only be corroborated through their substrate in his art—but that were, alike existent.

A half-dozen years later Blake was to render *Ezekiel's Vision of the Whirlwind*, which expresses his conception of

The Four Zoas. Ezelkiel's vision in the Bible, reads in part—
...out of the midst therefore came the likeness of four
living creatures. And this was their appearance: they had
the likeness of a man, and every one had four faces, and
every one had four wings.... As for the likeness of their
faces, they four had the face of a man, and the face of a
lion, on the right side; and they four had the face of an
ox on the left side; they four also had the face of an
eagle...and their wings were stretched upward; two
wings of every one were joined one to another.... Their
appearance and their work was as it were a wheel in the
middle of a wheel. When they went, they went upon their
four sides....

This "four-fold vision" became a paradigm for Blake's
prophetic art; the work he was *called* to create, even if all the
world "should set their faces against it." "I have Orders," he
wrote, "to set my face like a flint, against their faces, & my
forehead against their foreheads." (33)

Who was William Blake, or perhaps what was he? Mystic
or a mad man? It is clear, as he himself said of the eye, that
the age will be seen *through*, not with the poet and his art.
Anyone spending time with any of his productions must
therefore be cognizant of the myriad influences that were
brought to bear on his intuition in the creation of his vision:
those that were his contemporaries that influenced him, as
well as the great figures that were his antecedents; as also,
perforce, the historical context of their making. With the
writing of *The Four Zoas*, the scholar Northrup Frye
remarked, Blake was writing what he was brought into to the
world to create. (34)

Among those well-known contemporary influences on
Blake's art, and vice-versa, was the painter Henry Fuseli (1741-
1825), many of whose works exhibit a "super-natural" subject-
material such as his noted *The Nightmare* (1781), a haunting

evocation of erotic obsession and infatuation; who indeed said of Blake, he was "damn good to steal from." Another of Blake's contemporaries was the artists Joseph Farington, who recorded a conversation he had with Fuseli regarding Blake in his diary about this time:

> Fuseli called on me last night & and sat till 12 o'Clock. He mentioned Blake, the Engraver, whose genius & invention have been much spoken of. Fuseli has known him several years, and thinks He has a great deal of invention, but that "fancy is the end, and not a means in his designs." He does not employ it to give novelty and decoration to regular conceptions; but the whole of his aim is to produce singular shapes & odd combinations. He is abt 38 or 40 years of age, and married a maid servant, who has imbibed something of his singularity. They live together without a servant at a very small expence.... Fuseli says, Blake has something of madness abt him. (35)

And what then of that advent burning in human fires in the years 1776 and 1789?—a fiery dawn to be heralded by the burgeoning literati to be christened as *Romantic*? Before the end of the decade Wordsworth would abandon the French Revolution and London in despair for the "open fields", as he yielded up the moral question, abandoning his effort to discern where political justice and moral duty lay. Southey turned away even more severely, as Coleridge, turning a phrase, declared he was shattering his "squeaking baby-trumpet of sedition" to cultivate his own garden. (36)

Blake did not turn away, but discovered he'd "greatly miscalculated", wrote David Erdman, learning that the mere fall of a Pitt or of a Napoleon would not constitute real change for the English or the French people; as "[e]ach stage in the transformation of Bonaparte from artilleryman of the

Republic to lawgiving Emperor seems to have delivered a direct shock to the symbolic consistency and frail narrative frame of Blake's epic." (37) Frye was to pronounce the "Four Zoas" "in its unfinished state" was "a major cultural disaster." (38)

Not at all blithely, Blake himself assessed the completion of that fateful decade, and of all its hopes:

> What is the price of Experience? Do men buy it for a
> song?
> Or wisdom for a dance in the street? No, it is bought with
> the price
> Of all that a man hath, his house, his wife, his children.
> Wisdom is sold in the desolate market where none come
> to buy
> And in the wither'd field where the farmer plows for
> bread in vain. (39)

In 1800, after being sued for slander by Dr. Benjamin Rush (for his advocacy of "bleeding" during a yellow fever epidemic), ending his tenure personifying that querulous creature so beloved by Benjamin Franklin, Cobbett returned to England, where he enjoyed an importance as a journalist and as a commentator contra the industrialism beginning to ravage the countryside and Albion's communities alike. By then he'd completely changed his view of "the Infamous Tom Paine"; a conversion occasioned he says after reading Paine's *Decline and Fall of the English System of Finance*, which predicted the suspension of gold payments that followed the year after the pamphlet's publication in 1796. Richard Carlile in his *Life of Paine* (1819) was to write: "Mr. Cobbett has made this little pamphlet a text-book for most of his elaborate treatises on our finances... On the authority of a late *Register* of Mr. Cobbett's I learn that the profits arising from the sale of this pamphlet were devoted [by Paine] to the relief of the prisoners in Newgate for debt." (40)

Paine, writes Conway, also gained great favor with the French government for the pamphlet, and it appeared throughout Europe in translation into French, German, Polish, and Russian. There Paine compared the disasters wrought in America and in France by the issuance of paper money—Continental bills and assignats. In contrast, the English funding system, begun in 1697 at the end of the war of the Grand Alliance against the French King, Louis XIV, had the capacity to endure five to six times longer, perhaps even twenty times longer, wrote Paine. Yet "at the end of that time it would arrive at the same common grave, the Potter's Field of paper money."

The proportion of twenty to one, Paine had remarked, "is the difference between a capital and the interest at five per cent." In England, the accumulation of paper money was proportional to the interest accrued on every new loan. Thus, the progress of dissolution would be slower than if the capital were emitted and put into circulation immediately. Twenty years in the English system equaled one year in the American and French systems; the difference being funding on interest and the issuance of the whole capital without funding. The inability of procuring loans would not break the system, rather it was the facility with which loans could be procured that would hasten the event.

Paine wrote finally: "When I said that the funding system had entered the last twenty years of its existence, I certainly did not mean that it would continue twenty years, and then expire as a lease would do. I meant to describe that age of decrepitude in which death is every day expected, and life cannot continue long." (41)

Having been among his most violent assailants, in after years Cobbett became eloquent in his praises of Thomas Paine, acknowledging: "Old age having laid his hand upon this truly great man, this truly philosophical politician, at his expiring flambeau I lighted my taper." (42)

finis

Postscript

William Blake

Dying at age 70 in London on August 12, 1827, a neglected and beshrouded poetic genius; William Blake's hand produced and hand-painted *Songs of Innocence and Songs of Experience* sold fewer than twenty copies in the years since he'd issued them, while his prophetic books had vanished almost without leaving a trace. Only one of his poems, "The Tyger" had been anthologized.

Thomas Paine

Dying at age 72 in Greenwich Village on the morning of June 8, 1809, in a small rented room on Reason Street (later re-named Grove), a narrow, twisted alley; Thomas Paine's funeral cortege included only six persons following the 25 miles up to his farm in New Rochelle: Madame Bonneville and her two sons in a carriage, a Quaker named Willett Hicks on horseback (one of the ascendants to the "Hicksite" Quakers), and on foot, two now unknown black men—testament to Paine's long adhesion to the principle of universal liberty, to include the lineage of those men, women, and their children enslaved from Africa.

Refused internment in the Quaker burial ground in New Rochelle, the body was put to rest on Paine's own farm under a walnut tree. Curiously Cobbett would return to New Rochelle, and to Paine's burial site, a decade after Paine's death, unearthing his bones. These were transported back to his native England, with the intention they would one day lie in a crypt above which would rise a suitable monument to commemorate Paine's grand behest in the cause of liberty. This, Cobbett never realized, and *whither his bones went, no one knows.*

Jean-Paul Marat

Deceased at age 50 by the thrust of a poniard July 13, 1793, Jean-Paul Marat is a figure still possessing fascination, darkly drawn on pages scripted in ink and blood. As his bust was elevated to one of the prime pedestals on display in the French Revolutionary Panthéon—it was only to be drawn down again as he was discredited and his likeness smashed.

Bibliographical Essay

In books lies the soul of the whole Past Time; the articulate audible voice of the Past, when the body and material substance of it has altogether vanished like a dream.

Thomas Carlyle, "The Hero as Man of Letters" (1840)

The Life of William Blake, "Pictor Ignotus" is crucially the standard reference on William Blake, by the writer and art critic Alexander Gilchrist (1828-1861). Born the year after Blake's death, Gilchrist died at age 33 of scarlet fever he contracted from one of his children. The book was finished by his wife Anne, who had been his amanuensis, and published in two volumes in 1863, with Dante Gabriel Rossetti (1828-1882), the English poet and painter, responsible for the entirety of the 2nd volume—a complication of Blake's poetry and prose writings, together with his plates and art works.

Rossetti, who owned a collection of Blake's manuscripts wrote his friend the poet William Allingham, November 1, 1860: "A man (one Gilchrist, who lives next to Carlyle) wrote me the other day saying he was writing a life of Blake, and wanted to see my manuscript by that genius...I have told him he can see it here if he will give me a day's notice." One of the items given credence was a notebook mostly in pencil that had been worked for thirty years by Blake. It had been that of his younger brother, Robert, who died in February 1787, and first filled out by 1793, when the bard, reaching the last page, turned it over and worked from back to front. Containing the early drafts of "London" "The Tyger" and "The Chimney

Sweeper", besides drafts of other poems, it includes prose fragments, and sketches and emblem designs, filling 58 leaves, used by this author as a kind of template to the reading of Blake's output in the first half of the decade in the 1790's. Rossetti had come into possession of the notebook in 1847, purchasing it for 10 shillings from William Palmer, brother of Samuel Palmer, Blake's student and one of the "Ancients", a group of young artists devoted to the older William Blake. Samuel Palmer had been presented with the notebook in 1827, the year of Blake's death, by his widow, Catherine.

Broadly conversant with the life and writings of Thomas Paine, I have held him in esteem for my entire adult life, with antecedents still in my childhood. I have referenced here largely from the three volumes of writings (1894) complied and brought before the public by Moncure Daniel Conway (1832-1907), and with his two-volume study of *The Life of Thomas Paine* (1892), which has been my principal support.

All subsequent modern writing on Paine originates with Conway's treatment of this greatest of the pamphleteers and *patriot* of both America and France and Britain, Conway rendering a vivid portrait of one of the most extraordinary apostles of Liberty in the 18th century. A biography which brings forth Franklin, Jefferson, and Washington, Lafayette, Blake, and Burke, Mary Wollstonecraft, Joseph Johnson, Danton and Condorcet, as well as Marat and Robespierre, Gouverneur Morris and many others.

Another of the authors sourced is Ernest Belford Bax (1854-1926), who as a sixteen-year-old in Victorian England had his interest in radical politics piqued in 1871 by the Franco-Prussian War and by its sequel, the revolutionary Parisian commune. Becoming a barrister and campaigner for "men's rights", while living in Berlin he became as well an ardent of German philosophy epitomized by Kant and Hegel. Becoming an advocate of working-class emancipation through

Socialism, among his historical writings relevant to this text are *Jean-Paul Marat: The People's Friend* (1879) and *The Last Episode of the French Revolution: Being a History of Gracchus Babeuf and the Conspiracy of the Equals* (1911). Bax's view of history has the strong impress of Hegel, as also of Marx and his friend and collaborator Engels, whom he knew, although Bax diverged from these on their "materialist conception of history," holding it was not sufficient.

In contrast to Carlyle's characterizations of Marat as an "obscene spectrum", a "dogleech", and whom other writers have designated a "monster", and as the "personification of murder", etc., Bax draws a dispassionate portrait divesting Marat in the pages of his book "of this grotesque suit of malevolence" to show a man "possessed of a moral earnestness and steadfastness of purpose rarely met with...."

Peter Ackroyd's *Blake: A Biography* has been thoroughly searched by this writer; as were David Erdman's *Blake, Prophet Against Empire*, and Northrop Frye's *Fearful Symmetry*; as also Leo Damrosch's *Eternity's Sunrise*. Subsequent to these readings, I found and read Bronowsik's *William Blake*. As to Blake's poetry, I have used for my primary reference, books that have been in my personal library nearly fifty years, *The Portable Blake* selected and arranged by Alfred Kazin; and a facsimile of *The Marriage of Heaven and Hell,* produced by Blake in 1789-90, with an introduction and commentary by Geoffrey Keynes. I have, as well, utilized the resources made available online by the *Blake Society*, as by the Tate Museum and others, for Blake's prints, watercolors and paintings, and reproductions of his Illuminated Books, as well as fortuitously viewing an exhibition of Blake's prints and paintings at the Tate in January 1973. Chapter titles have been obtained from Blake's *Europe* and *America, The Marriage of Heaven and Hell,* as well as elsewhere in his writing, as they could be ascribed to events and circumstances of which they may be descriptive.

Among other Paine biographies cited in the text, I 've referenced John Keane's *Tom Paine, A Political Biography* (1995). Thomas Paine presents unprecedented problems to our retrospective understanding of a citizen of the 18th century, and books of too recent a publication to have been consulted for corroboration by this author, have since been read: Carine Lounissi's *Thomas Paine and the French Revolution* (2018); J.C.D. Clark's *Thomas Paine: Britain, America, and France in the Age of Enlightenment and Revolution* (2018); and Vikki J.Vickers's *Thomas Paine and the American Revolution* (2006). While I am reminded that historiography is a collaborative enterprise that allows the accruing of its stock over generations, none of these, I found, compel me to make amendment to an already accomplished research.

Substantiating the chronology of this narrative, and the actual physiognomy of the French Revolution, are well-known studies by Albert Mathiez (1874-1932), Georges Lefebvre (1874-1959), and Albert Soboul (1914-1982), all read by this author over the course of decades; as also, more recently, George Rude's (1910-1993) *The Crowd in the French Revolution*, Peter Kropotkin's (1842-1921) *The Great French Revolution,* and Daniel Guerin's *(1904-1988) Class Struggle in the First French Republic, Bourgeois and Bas Nus--1793-1795;* and lastly Francois Furet's (1927-1997) *Interpreting the French Revolution.* A reading supplemented by *The Days of the French Revolution* (1980), Christopher Hibbert, and *The French Revolution, from Enlightenment to Tyranny (*2016*)*, Ian Davidson.

As also, fresh readings of Eric J. Hobsbawm's *The Age of Revolution 1789-1848*, and Edward P. Thompson's *The Making of the English Working Class* were undertaken; as T.S. Ashton's *The Industrial Revolution 1760-1830*, and C.L.R. James' *Black Jacobins* were thoroughly scrutinized.

Deployed as a kind-of intra-textual foil in much of the narrative are three well-known, but today, undoubtedly, unread writers on the French Revolution. Starting with *The French Revolution* completed in 1837 by Thomas Carlyle (1795-1881); a well-documented study written from sources available in London at the time, rendered with memorable character sketches, in writing that is passionate, immediate, and persuasive—the work of a great polemicist.

A second is the *History of the French Revolution* by Adolphe Thiers (1797-1877), born at the time of the rule of the Directorate, and written during the Restoration when the tri-color flag and the singing of the Marseillaise were forbidden. The first two volumes were published in 1823 as Thiers became well-known both in the literary and journalistic milieus in France, and the last two in 1827, by which time he saw the path to a long political career. Acclaimed in France as it won him a seat in the *Académie Française* in 1834, Thiers history was soon translated into English. Thiers went on to become a Deputy, twice a Prime Minister, and was the first president of the 3rd Republic; as he was head of the French government when the Paris Commune was suppressed in blood in 1871.

Appreciative of the principles and accomplishment of the leaders of the 1789 Revolution, Lafayette and Mirabeau, he depreciated the subsequent insurrections bringing to the fore the leaders of '93 and '94, Danton, Desmoulins, and Marat, and the terror overseen by Saint-Just and Robespierre, while equally Thiers condemned the monarchy and aristocracy. For his favorable persuasion on Napoleon, Carlyle maintained Thiers' treatment was as "far as possible from meriting its high reputation", although he conceded it "will tell you much if you know nothing."

A third is Hippolyte Taine (1828-1893), that extraordinary scriber and proponent of sociological positivism and practitioner of historicist criticism. Taine's monumental analysis

The Origins of Contemporary France is now credited with providing the frame-work for French "right-wing" historio-graphy. The first volume "The Old Regime" published in 1876, with three volumes on the Revolution published between 1875-85. Taine shares Edmund Burke's hostile overview of the French events, published in 1790; but his idiosyncratic and complex assessments are filled with forebodings of horror and ruin as Taine summons the shades of a darkening tableau intriguing to this reader—a retrospective glance at the inevitability of catastrophe.

This author has also had the pleasure of re-reading Charles Dickens' (1812-1870) *Barnaby Rudge* (1841) and *A Tale of Two Cities* (1859), while perusing a number of the *Memoirs* of the time—Madame Roland, Joseph Priestley, Paul Barras, Louis-Stanislas Fréron, et. al. It is in narrations such as these—in the desire of an individual to have their story recounted—that the possibility of that category called *history* is born; along with that fabulous historicizing characteristic of Dickens.

My brief, finally, remains an offering to an on-going historiography, as a kind of panegyric to what can be regarded as the core of those insurrectionary arts originating in the last quarter of the 18th century, intellectual and of arms, and having recurring life in subsequent years, that have since also passed before us. No one in France on the eve of the outbreak of the Revolution could know anything about its result, but it has tracked a course, and behold the changes come over the world—matters that can be apprehended only in the re-telling, and not as abstractions.

What then of that puzzle posed by the triangulation of these three—William Blake, Thomas Paine, and Jean-Paul Marat? Either neglected in the broad treatment of the era, or depreciated and downplayed in their consequence. It is my view that a text as it is structured forms a kind of mask, that an author holds up so as to see things that are no longer present to our sight, and thus it becomes a device to see what is missing, but that remains with us as it is seen through this concealment.

The impetus for this scripting, at last, has been the Peter Weiss play *The Persecution and Assassination of Jean-Paul Marat* etc., as staged and presented in a film directed by Peter Brook in the 1960's. I saw it as an 18-year-old student, and still retain many fresh impressions from it and of that era.

Meanwhile, valuations are always shifting, always changing—always approaching the point of disarray in a world of fluctuating perceptions, wherein vision and facticity intermingle. Nevertheless, as in this instance, these events are esteemed a watershed, now actually unfolding in the intricate but unfinished present.

As it would also appear, they are at the point of expiring.

Endnotes

The employment of endnotes in the text has been sparing, and is meant to suggest some of the sources, but by no means all. Where no citations are provided, there are always multiple texts being consulted, and these I've synthesized for my own purposes. The responsibility in all cases, is entirely my own.

Chapter 1 - Songs of Innocence

1. *The Portable Blake*, Edited by Alfred Kazin, Penguin Anthology, 1977, 90.
2. Ackroyd, P, *Blake A Biography*, Ballantine, 1996. An exemplary port of entry into Blake's world.
3. Ibid., 42.
4. Frye, N., *Fearful Symmetries*, A Study of William Blake, introduction.
5. Quoted from Gilchrist in Ackroyd, *Blake*, 55.

Chapter 2 - King Mob

1. British History on-line, chapter LII, Newgate; *Old and New London*: vol. 2, originally published by Cassell, Petter & Galpin, London, 1878.
2. Ibid.
3. Gilchrist, A., *The Life of William Blake*, John Lane, The Bodley Head, 1907, Harvard University/Google, 35-36.
4. Ibid.
5. Erdman, D. *Blake, Prophet Against Empire*, 55.

6. *The Portable Blake*, 112.

7. On-line, Vague 33 HM King Mob, Tom Vague, *London Psychogeography*, 2010.

8. Ibid.

9. *The Portable Blake*, 311; cited by David Erdman in *Blake, Prophet Against Empire*, 7.

10. *The Portable Blake*, 314.

Chapter 3 - For Empire is no more

1. Keane, J., Tom Paine, A Political Life, 2.

2. Conway, M., *The Life of Thomas Paine*, vol. 1, G.P. Putman's Sons, New York, 1893, Thomas Paine National Historical Association 39.

3. Ibid. 41.

4. Ibid., 67.

5. Ibid., 56.

6. Ibid.

7. Ibid., 62.

8. Quoted in Keane. J., *Tom Paine*, 173.

9. Ibid., 174.

10. Ibid., 175.

11. Robert Morris, "To the Public," *Pennsylvania Packet*, Jan. 9, 1779.

12. Thomas Paine to the US Congress, Philadelphia, Jan. 8, 1779.

13. Sparks, J., *The Life of Gouverneur Morris, with Selections from his Correspondence and Miscellaneous Papers*, vol. 1 (Boston, 1832, 199-202).

14. Conway, 168.

15. Ellis, Joseph J., *The Cause - The American Revolution and its Discontents, 1773-1783*, Liveright, New York, 2021, 178.

16. Conway, 168.

17. *The Portable Blake*, introduction by Alfred Kazin, 5.
18. Quoted in Bentley, G.E. (Jr.), *The Stranger from Paradise*: New Haven, Yale University Press, 2003.
19. Erdman, D., *Blake, Prophet Against Empire*, 22.
20. *The Portable Blake*, 304.

Chapter 4 - Albion's Mills

1. Ackroyd, 100-102.
2. *The Portable Blake*, 79-80.
3. The author is indebted to many sources, among them vol. 1 of Marx's *Capital*, London, 1867, but more-so here to T.S. Ashton's perspective on *The Industrial Revolution: 1760-1830*, Oxford University Press, 1997.
4. Southey, R., *Letters from England, 1802-3*, "Excursion to Greenwich." The on-line Books Page.

Chapter 5 - Awake the thunders of the deep!

1. *The Papers of Thomas Jefferson*, vol. 15, Boyd, J., ed. Princeton University Press, 1958.
2. Ibid.
3. Alger, J.G., *Englishmen n the French Revolution*, chapter II.
4. Quoted in *Jean-Paul Marat*, part 1, Bax, E. Belford, London, 1900, 96. Marxist Internet Archive.
5. Ibid. Chapter 5, "Marat as Revolutionary Pamphleteer and Journalist."
6. Ibid., 71.
7. Ibid., 227.
8. *The Portable Blake*, 137-8.

Chapter 6 - Without Contraries is no progression

1. Gilchrist, A., *The Life of William Blake*, 95.
2. Ibid., 92.
3. Frye, N., *Fearful Symmetry, A Study of William Blake*, 92.
4. *The Portable Blake*, 294-5.
5. *The Life of Thomas Paine*, vol. 1, 294-5. Conway, M.
6. Ibid., 252.
7. Keane, J., *Tom Paine, A Political Life*, 268-69.
8. quoted in Ackroyd, *Blake, A Biography*, 158.
9. Conway, 274.
10. Ibid., 266.
11. Ibid., 273.
12. Keanne, 205.
13. Carlyle, T., *The French Revolution, A History*, 264.
14. Conway, 266.
15. Blake, *The Marriage of Heaven and Hell*, plates 6-7, A Memorable Fancy.
16. Ibid., plate 4, The Voice of the Devil.
17. Ibid., plate 14.
18. Damrosch, L., *Eternity's Sunrise: The Imaginative World of William Blake*, Yale,2015, 31.
19. Gilchrist, 90.
20. *The Portable Blake*, 441.
21. Gilchrist, 80.
22. *The Marriage of Heaven and Hell*, plates 17-20, A Memorable Fancy.
23. *The Portable Blake*, 558-63.
24. Vickers, Vikki J., *"My Pen and My Soul Have Ever Gone Together: Thomas Paine and the American Revolution*, Routledge, 2006, 31.
25. Ibid., 37.
26. Gilchrist, 90.
27. Ackroyd, 193.

28. *The Marriage of Heaven and Hell*, plates 25-27.

29. Conway, vol. 1, footnote 1, 276.

30. Ibid., 284.

31. *Selected Writings of Thomas Paine, The Rights of Man.*

32. Conway, 214.

33. Damrosch, L., *Eternity's Sunrise, The Imaginative World of William Blake*, Yale, 2015, 231.

34. Ackroyd, P, *Blake, A Biography* 157-8.

35. Conway., 301.

365. Ibid.

Chapter 7 - A Mighty Spirit Leap'd

1. James, C.L.R., *The Black Jacobins*, Vintage, 1989, 61.

2. DuBois, L., *The Avengers of the New World: The Story of the Haitian Revolution*, Belknap Press, 21.

3. James, 50.

4. DuBois, L., 40-43.

5. James, 85-86.

6. Conway, M. *The Life of Thomas Paine*, vol. 1, 312.

7. *The Portable Blake*, 137-9.

8. Conway, 306.

8. Ibid., 307.

10. Conway, *The Writings of Thomas Paine*, vol. 3, see editor's introduction.

11. Conway, vol. 1, 308.

12. Clapham, J., *The Abbé Sieyès, An Essay in the Politics of the French Revolution*, 131-33.

13. Conway, vol. 1., 311.

14. Ibid.

15. Priestley, J., *An Appeal to the Public on the Subject of the Riots in Birmingham*, printed by J. Thompson, on-line Google Books.

16. Conway, 310, footnote 1.

17. Ibid., 323.

18. James, 87.

19. Ibid., 88.

20. Ibid., 90-94.

21. *The Portable Blake*, 300-313.

22. Erdman, D., *Blake, Prophet Against Empire*, 291.

Chapter 8 - Thus, her voice arose

1. Dobson, Austin, *Four French Women*, London, 1890, 54.

2. Moore, L., Brooks, J., Wigginton, C., *Transatlantic Feminisms in the Age of Revolutions*, Oxford University Press, 2012, 245).

3. Anderson, F.M., ed., *The Constitution and Other Selected Documents of the History of France, 1789-1907*, Russel and Russel, 1908; Levy, Applewhite, and Johnson, eds., *Women in Revolutionary Paris, 1789-1795*, University of Illinois Press, 1980, 87-96.

4. Abbott, J., *Madame Roland*, Hathitrust Accessibility, on-line, 114.

5. Ibid., 112-3.

6. Price, R., Price, S., editors, *Stedman's Surinam: Life in an Eighteenth-Century Slave Society*, John Hopkins University Press, 1992, 47.

7. *The Portable Blake*, 288-9.

8. Conway, 316.

9. Ibid., 320-321; 291.

10. Ibid., 322.

11. Ibid., 320.

12. Ibid., 322.

13. Thompson, E.P., *The Making of the English Working Class*, Vintage Books, New York, 108.

Chapter 9 - Deluge o'er the earth-born man

1. Dickens, C., *A Tale of Two Cities*, Knopf, 2006, 388.
2. Hamel, F., *A Woman of the Revolution, Théroigne de Mericourt*, Brentano's, New York, 1911, 322.
3. Hobsbawm, E., *The Age of Revolution, Europe 1789-1848*, A Mentor Book, 83.
4. *The Portable Blake*, 127.
5. *The Portable Blake*, 107.
6. Hobsbawm, 89.
7. Lefebvre, G., *The French Revolution from its Origins to 1793*, Routledge, London and New York, 2001, 223. Void Network.
8. Conway, 340.
9. Ibid., 342.
10. Alpaugh, M., *The Making of the Parisian Political Demonstration: A Case Study of 20 June 1792*, Journal of the Western Society for French History, vol. 34, 2006.
11. *The Portable Blake*, 106.

Chapter 10 - When the stars through down their spears

1. Thiers, A., *The History of the French Revolution*, Carey and Hart, Philadelphia, 1843, 110.
2. Taine, THÉROIGNE ., *The Origins of Contemporary France; The French Revolution*, vol. 2, 612; Project Gutenberg EBook.
3. Ibid., 603.
4. Quoted in *The French Revolution*, Davidson, I., Pegasus Books, 2018, 97.
5. Thiers, 118.
6. 129. McPhee, P., *The French Revolution 1789-1799*, Oxford University Press, 2002, 97.
7. Taine, THÉROIGNE ., vol. 2, The Jacobin Conquest, 1878, trans. Durand, J., Indianapolis: Liberty Fund, 2002.

8. Thiers, 125.

9. Jaures, J., *Socialist History of the French Revolution*, The Insurrection of August 10, 1792, Pluto Press, 2015.

10. Hamel, F., *A Woman of the Revolution, Theroigen de Mericourt*, Brentano's, 1911, 76.

11. Ibid., 316-18.

12. Ibid., 319.

13. Kropotkin, P., *The Great French Revolution 1789-1793*, chapter 33, The Tenth of August: Its Immediate Consequences, 1909. The Anarchist Library.

14. Taine, 622.

15. Ackroyd, 143-47.

16. Ibid.

17. Erdman, D., *The Illuminated Blake*, Dover Publication, Inc., New York, 84.

18. Taine, vol. 3, 298.

19. Thiers, 131.

20. Hazan, E., *A People's History of the French Revolution*: The Assembly and the Insurrectional Commune, Chapter 7, Verso, 2017.

21. Thiers, 133.

22. Bax, Chapter 8, Marat ad Advisor to the First Paris Commune and Deputy of the National Convention, part 1, 200).

Chapter 11 - What the hand, dare seize the fire?

1. Marxist Internet Archives, *Prospectus for Journal de la republique francaise*, August 1792.

2. Bax, part 1, Chapter VIII.

3. Quoted in Mathiez, *The French Revolution*, (2012), 223.

4. Hazan, Chapter 7.

5. Davidson, I, *The French Revolution-From Enlightenment to Tyranny*, Pegasus Books, New York, 2016, 111.

6. Taine, 650.

7. Hazan, Chapter 7.

8. Ibid.

9. Ibid.

10. Quoted in Hibbert, C., The Days of the French Revolution, William Morrow, 1980, 174.

11. Carlyle, T. *The French Revolution, A History*, The Modern Library Classics, New York, 2002, 541.

12. Taine, 680.

13. Hardy, B.C., *The Princesse De Lambelle, A Biography*, Archibald Constable and Company LTD, London, 1908, 287.

14. *The Portable Blake*, 108.

15. Damrosch, L., *Eternity' Sunrise*, 81.

16. Ibid., 84.

Chapter 12 - Divide the heavens of Europe

1. Conway, *The Life of Thomas Paine*, vol. 1, 350.

2. Ackroyd, P., *Blake, A Biography*, 41-42.

3. Gilchrist, 97.

4. Conway, ed., *The Writings of Thomas Paine*, vol. III, G.P. Putman's Sons, New York and London, Online Library of Liberty1791-1804. Letter dated September 15, 1792.

5. Conway, vol. 1, 349.

6. Conway, *Writings*, vol. 3.

7. Conway, *The Life*, vol, 1 354.

8. Ibid., 355.

9. Doyle, *The Oxford History of the French Revolution*, Oxford University Press, 193.

10. Erdman, D., *Blake: Prophet Against Empire*, 196.

11. *The Portable Blake*, 99.

12. Thomas Paine National Historical Association, *Address to the People of France*, with introduction by Philip Foner, on-line.

13. Bax, part 1, 220.

14. Ibid., 221-2.

15. Ibid., 229-30.

16. Conway, vol. 1, 357.

17. Rickman, T., in *Life and Writings of Thomas Paine, containing a biography by Thomas Clio Rickman and appreciations by Leslie Stephen, Lord Erskin, Paul Desjardins, Robert G. Ingersoll, Elbert Hubbard and Marilla M. Ricker*, Vincent Parke and Co., New York, 1908, 42.

18. Ibid., Desjardins, P. *Thomas Paine: Father of Republics*, 246.

19. Keane, J., *Tom Paine: A Political Life*, 357.

20. Conway, vol. 1, 357-8.

21. Ibid., 359.

22. Ibid., 363.

23. Ibid.

24. Ibid., 365.

Chapter 13 - In tears & iron bound

1. Conway, vol. 1, 370.

2. Ibid.

3. Ibid., 371.

4. Ibid., 372.

5. Ibid., 374.

6. Ibid., 376.

7. Conway, *The Life of Thomas Paine*, vol. 2, Chapter I, "Kill the King, But Not the Man".

8. Ibid.

9. Ibid.

10. Ibid.

11. Ibid.

12. Ibid.

13. Ibid.

14. Davidson, I., *The French Revolution*, Michelet quoted on 141.
15. Carlyle, T., *The French Revolution: A History*, 592.
16. *The Portable Blake*, "Earth's Answer", 100.

Chapter 14 - Thus was the howl thro' Europe

1. Tackell, T., *The Crisis of March 1793 and the Origins of the Terror*, 109.
2. Horan, J., *Emergency Measures and Contingency in the French Revolution, 1792-94*, doctoral thesis on-line Central Florida University, 26-7.
3. Bax, *Jean-Paul Marat*, part 1, 249.
4. Hibbert, C., *The Days of the French Revolution*, William Morrow, New York, 2002, 195-6.
5. Bax, 251.
6. Ibid., 257.
7. Ibid., 259.
8. Hibbert, 196.
9. Bax, 260.
10. Ibid., 263.
11. Quoted in Thompson, E.P. *The Making of the English Working Class*, 163-4.
12. *The Portable Blake*, 120.

Chapter 15 - Thorns were my only delight

1. Conway, *The Life of Thomas Paine*, vol. 2, chapter III, Revolution vs. Constitution.
2. Ibid.
3. Bax, part 1, 263.
4. *Life and Writings of Thomas Paine*, Paul Desjardins, 225.
5. Conway, vol. 2, Chapter III, Revolution vs. Constitution.

6. Ibid.

7. Bax, part 1, 266.

8. Ibid., 267-9.

9. Ibid., 270.

10. Ibid., 270-1.

11. Ibid., 271.

12. *The Portable Blake*, 113.

Chapter 16 - The furious terrors flew around

1. Bax, 276.

2. Conway, vol. 2, Chapter III, Revolution vs. Constitution.

3. Hamel, F., *A Woman of the Revolution, Théroigne de Mericourt*, 334.

4. Mathiez, S., *The French Revolution*, Alfred Knopf, New York, 1929, 324.

5. Ibid., 329-33.

6. Carlyle, 634.

7. Keane, J, *Tom Paine: A Political Life*, 379.

8. Bax, part 1, 280.

9. Ibid.

10. Ibid., 281.

11. Ibid.

12. Ibid.

13. Mathiez, 324.

14. Bax, 281-2.

15. Ibid., 284.

16. Ibid., 283.

17. Ibid., 283-4.

18. Carlyle, T., *The French Revolution*, 694.

19. Taine, *The French Revolution*, vol. 2, 827.

20. Carlyle, 828.

21. Taine, 828.

22. Kropokin, P., *The Great French Revolution*, 1789-1793, chapter 46, "The Insurrection of May 31 and June 2".

23. Keane, J., 380-1.

24. *The Portable Blake*, 137-9.

Chapter 17 - But now the caves of Hell I view

1. *The Private Memoirs of Madame Roland*. A.C. McClurg & Co., 1901. Google, University of Michigan.

2. Kropotkin, Chapter 60.

3. Ibid.

4. Bax, part 1, 288.

5. Ibid., 289.

6. Ibid.

7. Ibid., 292.

8. Ibid., 293.

9. Ibid., 301.

10. Baudelaire, C., *Art in Paris 1845-1862, Salons and Other Exhibitions*, "The Museum of Classics of the Bazar-Nouvelle," Oxford, 1965, 34-45.

11. Bax, 300.

12. Ibid., 302.

13. Ibid., 307.

14. Althusser, L., *The Spectre of Hegel*, "On Content in the Thought of G. F. Hegel", Verso, London and New York, 1997, 94.

15. Taine, vol. 2, 708-9.

16. Taine, vol. 3, "The Men in Power, Chapter 1, Psychology of the Jacobin Leaders, III Robespierre".

17. Carlyle, 648-49.

Chapter 18 - The deep of winter came

1. Conway, *The Life of Thomas Paine*, vol. 2, chapter III, "Revolution vs. Constitution".

2. Ibid.

3. Ibid., chapter IV, "A Garden in the Faubourg St. Denis".

4. Ibid.

5. Ibid.

6. Ibid., Paine's unpublished address to the "Citizens of Europe".

7. Conway, vol. 2, Chapter V, "A Conspiracy".

8. Ibid.

9. Quoted in Davidson, I., *The French Revolution*, 188.

10. Quoted in Hibbert, C., *The Days of the French Revolution*, 224.

11. Carlyle, 667.

12. Ibid., 672-673.

13. *The Private Memoires of Madame Roland*, 365.

14. Taine., Book V, 857.

15. Quoted in Godineau, D., *The Women of Paris and Their French Revolution*, University of California Press, 1988.

16. Carlyle.

17. Taine, vol. 3, chapter 1, "Jacobin Government, IX Destruction of Rebel.

Chapter 19 - With hoarse note curse the sons of joy

1. Carlyle, "Carmagnole Complete," 695.

2. Conway, vol. 2, chapter VI, "A Testimony Under the Guillotine".

3. Ibid., Chapter V.

4. Ibid.

5. Ibid., Chapter VI.

6. Arago, F., *Condorcet*, Wikisource la bibliotheque libre, 207.

7. *Sketch for a Historical Picture of the Progress of the Human Mind*, 23. Online Library of Liberty.

8. Ibid., 11-12.

9. Ibid.

10. Damrosch, L., *Eternity's Sunrise*, 163.
11. Erdman, D., *Blake, Prophet Against Empire*, 215.
12. Ibid., 247-248.
13. Thompson, E.P., *The Making of the English Working Class*, 102-103.
14. Ibid., 81.
15. *The Portable Blake*, "Europe", 315-327.
16. Erdman, 214.
17. Ibid., 219.
18. Ibid.
19. Carlyle, 726.
20. *Sketch*, 293.
21. Conway, vol. 2, Chapter VIII, "Sick and in Prison".
22. Claretie, J., *Camille Desmoulins and his Wife: Passages from the History of the Dantonists*, London, Smith, Elder & co., 1876, 303.
23. Conway, Ibid.
24. ibid.

Chapter 20 - The furious wind still rends around

1. Green, K., *The Rise and Fall of a Revolutionary: The Political Career of Louis-Marie Stanislas Fréron, Representative on Mission and Conventionel 1754-1802*, PhD. Dissertation, on-line, 89.
2. Herold, C., *The Age of Napoleon*, American Heritage Publishing Co., Inc., New York, 18-20.
3. Green, 92.
4. Scurr, R., *Fatal Purity: Robespierre and the French Revolution*, New York, 1989, 221.
5. Stewart, J., *French Military, A Documentary Survey of the French Revolution,* New York Macmillan, 1951, 472-474.
6. Many sources offer these details, but for a quick grasp of them see Hibbert's *The Days of the French Revolution*, "The Days of the Terror."

7. Carlyle, T., *The French Revolution*, Chapter IV, Mumbo-Jumbo, 728.
8. Hardman, J., *French Revolution Documents 1792-95*, vol. 2, Barnes & Noble Books, 1973, 253.
9. Hamel, *A Woman of the Revolution*, 346.
10. *The Portable Blake*, "Motto to the Songs of Innocence & of Experience", 136.

Chapter 21 - Fill'd with immortal demons of futurity

1. Conway, *The Life of Thomas Paine*, vol. 2, Chapter VIII, Sick and in Prison, 1794.
2. Green, Chapter 6, "Fréron and the Thermidorian Reaction".
3. Ibid., 125.
4. Ibid., 130.
5. Ibid., 131.
6. Ibid., 131, footnote 28.
7. Ibid., 139.
8. Ibid., 142.
9. Ibid., 143.
10. Alpaugh, M., *Non-Violence and the French Revolution, Political Demonstrations in Paris, 1787-1795*, 162.
11. Rude, G., *The Crowd in the French Revolution*, Clarendon Press, 1959, "Germinal-Prairial", 142-159.
12. Carlyle, T., *The French Revolution*, vol. 4, 311.
13. Godineau, D., *The Women of Paris and Their French Revolution*, University of California Press, 1998, Chapter 15 "Bread and the Constitution", 332.
14. Ibid., 338.
15. Breaugh, M., *The Plebeian Experience: A Discontinuous History of Political Freedom*, Columbia University Press, 2013, 139.
16. Godineau, 336.

17. Crowe, E., *The History of France*, vol. 2, 105. Eyre Evans Crowe, English journalist and historian, 1799-1868.
18. Sydenham, M., *Leonard Bourdon: The Career of a Revolutionary, 1754-1807*, WLU Press, 1999, 275.
19. Breaugh, 138.
20. Thiers, 556.
21. Ibid., 557.
22. Thiers, 558.
23. Ibid.
24. Ibid.
25. Ibid.
26. Ibid., 559.
27. Rude, G., *The Crowd in the French Revolution*, Oxford University Press, 1959, "Germinal-Prairial".
28. Ibid., 561.
29. Crowe, vol. 2, 106.
30. Thiers, 559.

Chapter 22 - The Beast & the Whore rule without controls

1. Conway, *The Life of Thomas Paine*, vol. 2, Chapter IX, "A Restoration, 1795".
2. Ibid.
3. Quoted in Wikipedia, French Directory, "The Purpose of the new Constitution".
4. Conway, vol. 2, Chapter IX, "A Restoration, 1795".
5. Conway, vol. 2, Chapter X, "The Silence of Washington".
6. Letter to John Flaxman, in *The Portable Blake*, 186-7.
7. Erdman, *Blake-Prophet Against Empire*, 286 and note 11, Appendix, 514.
8. Gilchrist, 408-9.
9. Thiers, 583.
10. Ibid.

11. Ibid., 584.
12. Ibid., 585.
13. Ibid., 587.
14. Ibid.
15. Ibid., 588.
16. Richardson, *A Dictionary of Napoleon and His Times*, London: Cassell & Co., 1920, 31.
17. Ibid.
18. Thiers, 583.
19. Ibid., 588-9.
20. Ibid., 589.
21. Carlyle, vol. 2, 320.
22. Ibid., 316.

Chapter 23 - And now the time returns again

1. Conway, vol. 2, Chapter XI, "The Age of Reason".
2. Claeys, G., *Thomas Paine: Social and political thought*, Boston: Unwin Hyman, 1989, 185.
3. Quoted in *The Making of the English Working Class*, 144.
4. Ibid.
5. Ibid.
6. Thompson, E.P. *The Making of the English Working Class*, "Planting the Liberty Tree," chap. 5.
7. Conway, vol. 2, chapter XI "The Age of Reason".
8. *Letter to George Washington*, July 30th 1796, on-line, Thomas Paine National Historical Association.
9. *The Writings of Thomas Paine*, Conway, vol.3, To the Citizens of the United States, Letter II, 385.
10. *Letter to George Washington*.
11. Conway, vol. 2, "The Silence of Washington".
12. Ibid.
13. *Letter to George Washington*.

14. Conway, vol. 2, "The Silence of Washington".
15. Bax, E., *Gracchus Babeuf*, 1911, Marxist Internet archive, Chapter VI, "The Catastrophe".
16. Buonarroti, P., *Gracchus Babeuf's Conspiracy of Equals*, 40. Marxist.org/History of the French Revolution.
17. Ibid., 62.
18. Ibid., 63.
19. Ibid., 70.
20. Bax, *Gracchus Babeuf*, Chapter 6, "The Projected Insurrection and its Plans".
21. Ibid., 167.
22. Ibid.
23. *The Writings of Thomas Paine*, vol. 3, Moncure Conway, 279.
24. Ibid., 324.
25 Ibid., 337.
26. Marx and Engels, *The Holy Family, or Critique of Critical Critique*, Foreign Languages Publishing House, 1956, Moscow, 161.
27. Conway, vol. 2, Chapter X, "The Silence of Washington".
28. Watson, R., *An Apology for the Bible in a Series of Letters Addressed to Thomas Paine*, 4. The online Books Page. *Blake Complete Writings*, Keynes, G., ed., 383.
29. Ibid.
30. Ackroyd, P., *Blake, A Biography*, 204.
31. Frye, N., *Fearful Symmetry*, 269.
32. Quoted in Ackroyd, 195; from *Blake Records*, ed. Bentley Jr., G.E., Oxford, 1969, 183.
33. *Complete Writings*, ed., Keynes, g., Oxford University Press, 825.
34. Frye, N., *Fearful Symmetry*, 269.
35. Ackroyd, 196' Bentley, 51-52.
36. Erdman, D., *Prophet Against Empire*, 293.
37. Ibid., 294.

38. Frye, 269.

39. Blake, THÉROIGNE ., *Vala, or the Four Zoas*, Second Night, lines 397-401.

40. *The Writings of Thomas Paine*, vol. 3, Moncure Conway, "Decline and Fall of the English Financial System", footnote 1, 286.

41. Ibid.

42. Conway, *The Life of Thomas Paine*, vol. 2, Appendix A, "The Cobbett Papers".

Index

An INDEX, like a dial, is meant as an indicator to draw attention to a figure; an event or an institution.

A glance by the reader will reveal lapses in my reference to the codex. Most obviously this is in regard to the chronicle of Louis XVI and Marie-Antoinette; as per George III. Their enumeration is something I felt a need to resist; their fate being settled in the body of the book. As perforce with two of the principal figures in this narrative, Blake and Paine, where their writings have been referenced, whereas Marat is treated in the congenital manner. Also treated are various historians, all vital in the evolving historiography of The French Revolution.

By utilizing these, I've sought to open out the text, making the material into a rhizome, and thereby sinking into it as a spiraling eddy.

Acknowledgement

It's a little odd for a writer situated as I am to look around for those who might be saluted in the creation and the stewarding of a book. The myriad sources and persons that come to mind out of the years, suggest a collaborative undertaking. That has all along been my greatest aspiration.

But this book and the work undertaken in the writing and research are singular—it has entirely been my own responsibility.

I can acknowledge with gratitude persons at Atmosphere Press, who having read the manuscript, responded with interest and with alacrity. Providing an engaging platform for an author, they have made this book truly a concerted endeavor, fulfilling my expectations.

Many voices and faces are welling-up, now effaced by gathering night. It is to these, I extend a parting hand....

About Atmosphere Press

Atmosphere Press is an independent, full-service publisher for excellent books in all genres and for all audiences. Learn more about what we do at atmospherepress.com.

We encourage you to check out some of Atmosphere's latest releases, which are available at Amazon.com and via order from your local bookstore:

The Swing: A Muse's Memoir About Keeping the Artist Alive, by Susan Dennis

Possibilities with Parkinson's: A Fresh Look, by Dr. C

Gaining Altitude - Retirement and Beyond, by Rebecca Milliken

Out and Back: Essays on a Family in Motion, by Elizabeth Templeman

Just Be Honest, by Cindy Yates

You Crazy Vegan: Coming Out as a Vegan Intuitive, by Jessica Ang

Detour: Lose Your Way, Find Your Path, by S. Mariah Rose

To B&B or Not to B&B: Deromanticizing the Dream, by Sue Marko

Convergence: The Interconnection of Extraordinary Experiences, by Barbara Mango and Lynn Miller

Sacred Fool, by Nathan Dean Talamantez

My Place in the Spiral, by Rebecca Beardsall

My Eight Dads, by Mark Kirby

Dinner's Ready! Recipes for Working Moms, by Rebecca Cailor

Vespers' Lament: Essays Culture Critique, Future Suffering, and Christian Salvation, by Brian Howard Luce

Without Her: Memoir of a Family, by Patsy Creedy

About the Author

William S. King is an independent scholar living in Ocala, Florida. His previous book, TO RAISE UP A NATION - John Brown, Frederick Douglass and the Making of a Free Country, was selected by CHOICE as the outstanding academic title in its category in 2013; writing, "Well written and thoroughly researched, this book deserves a place as one of the great 'big' histories of the Civil War....Essential." TILL THE DARK ANGEL COMES - Abolitionism and the Road to the Second American Revolution, was a subsequent book.

For more information go to <u>ironcladsnout.com</u>.

Made in the USA
Columbia, SC
24 March 2022

57954746R00293